# Cold Mountain Poems

This book unveils the legendary life and the mystic poems of the iconic Chinese Tang poet Han-shan (known by his pen name "Cold Mountain") and investigates the dissemination and reception of the Cold Mountain Poems (CMPs) attributed to him.

Han-shan and the CMPs are amongst the most legendary literary landscapes and cultural memories in the history of world scholarly exchange. The maniac poet recluse hidden in the Cold Mountains, the delicate poetic realms of Confucianism, Buddhism, Zen and Taoism contained in the Cold Mountain Poems, and the incredible pervasiveness of its text travel and canon construction worldwide, as well as the profound impact of CMPs on comparative literature, world literature and Chinese studies, provide the perfect lens to learn about Chinese language, literature, culture and society. This book is thus intended to investigate CMPs in a coherent global context. Considering the vertical studies of the Chinese literature polysystem, it highlights the horizontal influence of CMPs, literarily or non-literarily. Furthermore, it addresses the making and developing of the Han-shan phenomenon and its implications for translation studies, travel writing, canon construction and literary historiography.

This book is for scholars, researchers and students in literary history and East Asian Studies focusing on Chinese literature and culture and those interested in the history of poetry in general.

**Anjiang Hu** is a full professor of Sichuan International Studies University as well as a distinguished professor of the "Ba-yu Scholars Program" in Chongqing, China. He is the Secretary General of the Foreign Language Interface Studies Committee of the China Association for Comparative Studies of English and Chinese, the Secretary General of Chongqing Translators Society, a council member of the Translators Association of China, and a committee member of the World Interpreter and Translator Training Association. He is also a member of the Research Centre for Country-Specific Translation Competence, Beijing Foreign Studies University. He serves as the deputy editor of *Teaching and Researching Translation and* a member of the editorial board of *Foreign Language and Literature* and *English Studies*. His research interests include translation history, comparative literature and literary translation studies. His recent publications are on embodied-cognitive translatology, tradaptation/transcreation, cultural identity and the role of translators in literary translation.

# Cold Mountain Poems
Text Travel and Canon Construction

**Anjiang Hu**

LONDON AND NEW YORK

Funded by Social Science Planning Project (Special project for Chongqing Talents) of Chongqing Federation of Social Science: English Translations of Cold Mountain Poems (2022YC055).

First published 2024
by Routledge
4 Park Square, Milton Park, Abingdon, Oxon OX14 4RN

and by Routledge
605 Third Avenue, New York, NY 10158

*Routledge is an imprint of the Taylor & Francis Group, an informa business*

© 2024 Anjiang Hu

Translated by Anjiang Hu, Hongyan Peng, and Bingxue Jia

The right of Anjiang Hu to be identified as author of this work has been asserted in accordance with sections 77 and 78 of the Copyright, Designs and Patents Act 1988.

All rights reserved. No part of this book may be reprinted or reproduced or utilised in any form or by any electronic, mechanical, or other means, now known or hereafter invented, including photocopying and recording, or in any information storage or retrieval system, without permission in writing from the publishers.

*Trademark notice*: Product or corporate names may be trademarks or registered trademarks, and are used only for identification and explanation without intent to infringe.

English Version by permission of Tsinghua University Press.

*British Library Cataloguing-in-Publication Data*
A catalogue record for this book is available from the British Library

*Library of Congress Cataloging-in-Publication Data*
Names: Hu, Anjiang, author.
Title: Cold Mountain poems: text travel and canon construction / Anjiang Hu.
Other titles: Hanshan shi. English
Description: Abingdon, Oxon; New York, NY: Routledge, 2024. | Includes bibliographical references and index.
Identifiers: LCCN 2023007370 (print) | LCCN 2023007371 (ebook) | ISBN 9781032542065 (hardcover) | ISBN 9781032542195 (paperback) | ISBN 9781003415749 (ebook)
Subjects: LCSH: Hanshan, active 627–649—Criticism and interpretation. | Chinese poetry—Translating. | Intertextuality.
Classification: LCC PL2677.H3 Z66513 2024 (print) | LCC PL2677.H3 (ebook) | DDC 895.11/3—dc23/eng/20230424
LC record available at https://lccn.loc.gov/2023007370
LC ebook record available at https://lccn.loc.gov/2023007371

ISBN: 978-1-032-54206-5 (hbk)
ISBN: 978-1-032-54219-5 (pbk)
ISBN: 978-1-003-41574-9 (ebk)

DOI: 10.4324/9781003415749

Typeset in Times New Roman
by Apex CoVantage, LLC

# Contents

*List of Tables* vi

   Introduction 1

1 Travel Writing and Translation Studies 8

2 Text Travel and Canon Construction 34

3 Cultural Norms of the Departure and Intralingual Travel of the CMPs 54

4 Cultural Polysystem of Arrivals and Interlingual Travel of the CMPs 113

5 Canon Construction of the CMPs in the Cultural Polysystem of Arrivals: A Case Study on Gary Snyder's Translation of the CMPs 178

6 Return Journey of the CMPs and Their Canon Reconstruction in Chinese Literature 208

7 Concluding Remarks 264

*Afterword* 272
*References* 275
*Index* 288

# Tables

| | | |
|---|---|---|
| 4.1 | Doctoral Dissertations and Postdoctoral Research Reports on the CMPs in Korea | 131 |
| 4.2 | Master's Dissertations on the CMPs in Korea | 131 |
| 6.1 | Doctoral Dissertations on Han-shan Studies in China | 231 |
| 6.2 | Master's Dissertations on Han-shan Studies in China | 232 |

# Introduction

Literary studies have traditionally tended to emphasize the relationship between literature, history and the current situation. Therefore, after researchers lock down their academic topic, target readers will most likely question the historical identity of their research objects and endeavor to contextualize them historically or contemporarily. On the issue of Han-shan (literally, Cold Mountain) and his Cold Mountain Poems (CMPs), however, people may end up at a loss even if they spend a lot of effort. Who on earth is Han-shan? As Edward Schafer (1913–1991), a well-known American sinologist and professor at the University of California, Berkeley, wrote in the appendix of the highly influential anthology *Sunflower Splendor: Three Thousand Years of Chinese Poetry*, which was published in 1975:

> Han-shan means "cold mountain." It is the name of a place, but also the name of a person. Little is known for certain about the man who made that mountain his place of refuge, while Han-shan is the symbol of his spiritual aspirations and his own pseudonym. Possibly he lived in the early T'ang period. Probably he was a farmer who left his family from time to time to embark on obscure pilgrimages to Buddhist shrines or into the wilderness. In his poems, he sometimes rants about the vanity of power, glory, wealth, and female beauty—all mere filth to him. But he could also write tenderly of misty peaks and bird song, and the spiritual satisfactions of quiet and isolation. Centuries after his death, he became a Ch'an myth, especially in Japan. In these later times, he was frequently represented in art as a freak in tattered garments, grinning imbecilely, a happy social reject. It is hard to relate this popular image to the contents of the poems attributed to him.[1]

This was all people knew about Han-shan for thousands of years. Interestingly, Han-shan's reputation in the history of art and religion is, however, far greater than his influence in the world of literature. Especially in the grand narrative system of Chinese literary history, Han-shan and his poems have never truly drawn the attention of Chinese elite intellectuals. Even in the clamor of the post-canonical era, his poems have always been wandering on the edge of the repertoire of the Chinese literary canon.

It is intriguing that since the 1950s and 1960s, the Western world has accorded Han-shan and his poems with lofty literary courtesy. The craze of "Han-shan fever" has swept across the European and American continents. From the west coast of the United States to the countries along the Atlantic Ocean, from the Mediterranean basin to the Scandinavian peninsula, the footprints of Han-shan and his poems are almost everywhere in all the important places of overseas Sinology studies. Whether average literary readers, or the professional intellectual elite, all started to shift attention to and chase after this mysterious traveler without exception.

## 0.1 A Maniac Poet Hermit as a Literary "Outcast"

The pedigree of Han-shan's life experience is now inaccessible in its details. The relevant references that have been handed down are so mixed with legends and myths that it is difficult for researchers to distinguish their authenticity. According to anecdotal records, he called himself Han-shan because he lived for many years in seclusion in the Hanyan area of Tiantai, Zhejiang Province. As a matter of fact, whether there is such a person as Han-shan is still questioned by the academic field. Hence, let's quote the relevant accounts in *Biographies of Eminent Monks in the Song Dynasty Volume 19* (《宋高僧传·卷十九》), written by Zan-ning (919–1001), a renowned Buddhist historian, in order to retrace this uncanny case in the history of Chinese literature.

> Han-shan is a character who is often described as poor and crazy, but his true nature remains unknown. He resided alone in a place called Cold Mountain, which is located seventy Li to the west of Tiantai County in Taizhou City. He would occasionally visit Kuo Ching Temple. Shi-de, who was in charge of the dining hall, resided at the temple. He occasionally saved leftovers in a bamboo tube for Han-shan. Han-shan would come and carry it away. Sometimes, Han-shan would stroll along the veranda, shouting and making noise, or cursing at the sky. The temple monks eventually grew impatient with him and chased him away with a stick. Typically, Han-shan would pause, clap his hands, and laugh heartily for a spell before continuing on his way. He looked like a tramp. His body and visage were worn and aged, his hat was made of birch bark, his clothing was ragged and worn, and his shoes were made of wood. Yet every word he uttered had a meaning consistent with the subtle principles of things, if you thought about it carefully. Everything he said carried a sense of Tao, profound and mysterious secrets. Once an official Lü Qiuyin went to Kuo Ching temple to visit Han-shan, and the abbot named Dao Qiao told him something about Han-shan. He said, "Han-shan is quite a crazy character. He lives on cold mountain and prefers to recite poems. What he says is always strange and odd so that no one knows whether he is good or evil. Nevertheless, he is on good terms with monk Shi-de. They always chat with each other, but we don't know clearly what they are talking about." Lü Qiuyin paid homage to Han-shan and Shi-de, which made monk Dao Qiao quite astonished and puzzled. He asked, "Why should you such a dignitary pay homage to such

a crazy man?" Then, Han-shan and Shi De went out of the temple, laughing loud, arm in arm, and never came back. Lü Qiuyin thus went to cold mountain to visit him again and offered some clothes and medication to him. However, when Han-shan saw them, he uttered, "You bad guys! Go away! Go away!" He then wedged himself into the crack of the rock and said, "All you guys, do your best and rely on your own efforts!" The crack soon closed after he finished his words, and Han-shan was never seen by people afterward. Lü Qiuyin then asked Dao Qiao for help to search for Han-shan's belongings. They found many poems written on leaves and walls with a total number of over 300. Lü Qiuyin then compiled these poems into a collection for people to recite, and later *Han-shan's Poems with Annotations* by Ben-ji, a Zen Buddhist, came into being. Having no knowledge about Han-shan's ancestry, people could only call him Han-shan-zi. There is a line in his poems, "What's beyond the yard? / White clouds clinging to vague rocks." Therefore, the rock standing near the cold mountain got the name of "vague rock".[2]

It is impossible to ascertain to what extent the previously mentioned written records present the historical truth. The legendary color revealed here, however, is indeed surprising. Some Western scholars have ridiculed this style of storytelling as a fanciful tale heard by a busybody from a superstitious Chinese peasant. Some, however, based on the names of people and places, official titles, and stylistic styles listed in the literature, believe that the legendary figure lived in an era when "scholars from all walks of life were keen on writing, reciting and appreciating poems."[3] In reality, later generations of literary books and anthologies used to call him a poet of the Tang Dynasty, although it has been difficult to reach a consensus about his living period.

Leaving aside the previous odd accounts, the reader at least can read a lifelike hermit image between the lines. What's more interesting is that a poor man with an "old and beat" face in "ragged and worn out" clothes has such an unusual "outrageous" self-confidence in his poetic talent and poetic craft:

> When stupid people read my poems,
> they don't understand and sneer.
> when average people read my poems,
> they reflect and say they're deep.
> when gifted people read my poems,
> they react with full-face grins.
> the moment Yang Hsiu saw young woman
> one look and he knew mystery.[4]

It is conceivable that Chinese literary orthodoxy and literary historians tend to look down upon such a poor madman with "unusual speech" hidden among the masses and his poems. Unlike Tao Yuanming (365?–427), a poet from the Six Dynasties (222–589) who was similarly rejected at first but later became very popular and relentlessly portrayed the scenery and sought companionship in the fictional world of his poetry and in the notables of his predecessors, Han-shan not only talks frankly and bluntly about the literary value of his poems, but also expresses publicly in his poems his expectation for future soul mates and his absolute confidence that his poems will eventually "plague the world":

> People laugh about my poems
> my poems are elegant enough
> they don't need Cheng Hsuan's comments
> much less Mao Heng's explanations
> I don't mind few understand me
> those who know one's voice are rare
> if we had no *fa* or *sol*
> my disease would surely spread
> one day I'll meet someone with eyes
> then my poems will plague the world.[5]

Presumably, he is keenly aware that his lower literary origin and the vulgar epithets inscribed in the "village cottage in the woods" cannot be accepted by the world he lives in; the poet accordingly has a little less literary anxiety that surpasses the previous poets, but has a rare arrogance and freedom in the history of literature. As a matter of fact, the poems attributed to Han-shan had few soul mates in his time of life. In the subsequent dynasties, although there is no shortage of admirers, his confusing life experience, the uninhibited form of his poems, and the colloquial content are hard to be accepted by the dominant ideology and dominant poetics that are characterized by orthodoxy and elegance. Coupled with the restraint and influence of subjective and objective conditions such as the conservative literary standpoint and the complicated literary interests of the literary patrons, the poet Han-shan and his Cold Mountain Poems have therefore long been absent from the catalog of literary canons.

## 0.2  From "Periphery" to "Center"

When Han-shan and his poems traveled across the border to the neighboring Japan in the 11th century, however, the plain language style, the secluded Zen realm, the detached hermit sentiment, and the ecological consciousness of back-to-nature in the poems won immediately the unanimous favor of both the intellectuals and ordinary people in Japan. A variety of translations, annotations, and journal articles of CMPs have been published, Han-shan's legendary anecdotes have been adapted into novels and plays, and the Zen image of Han-shan has become the most popular theme in Japanese paintings and religious circles.

Han-shan's legendary literary journey, however, has only just begun. After centuries of "Han-shan Fever" in the East Asian Sinosphere, the translation and research of the CMPs became the "favorite" of European Sinology in the 20th century. Across the Atlantic Ocean in the 20th century, this "crazy" Chinese poet almost became a household name of the American nation. The younger generation even idolized him as a soul mate and spiritual pioneer, and his poems became a classic of the "San Francisco Renaissance". Since the 1960s, the CMPs have been selected into many literature anthologies and widely quoted in college lectures of East Asian literature in America.

Han-shan, the once-frustrated Chinese poet, "accidentally" fulfilled his miraculous prophecy that "one day I'll meet someone with eyes, then my poems will plague the world." It is interesting that when the overseas "Han-shan fever" pushed the poet to prominence and world fame, Chinese people began to view Han-shan and his poems with new respect. Thus, the poet embarked on a new round of journeys to continue his dramatic life and legendary destiny in the history of literature and academic research of his native country.

As a matter of fact, when the honored "overseas traveler" returned home with heavy luggage, many subtle changes had taken place towards the "poor madman" in the Chinese academic circle from the psychological level in many fields other than literature. In May 2008, the International Symposium on "Han-shan-zi and Hehe (Harmony) Culture" named after the poet was held in Tiantai, Zhejiang Province. The unveiling of this big event made this change even greater. It is perhaps with regret for the Chinese academic circles to see this grand unveiling. We have to question: Why did a poet who always lingered outside the literary history and classical canon of his home country enter into the equally strict hierarchical literary history/canon of the host countries his poems found themselves in? How can Chinese literary critics let go of their commanding attitude and re-accept this literary "outcast" who has been frequently shunned by them?

In the introduction to *Six Dynasties Poetry*, Kang-i Sun Chang, a prominent Chinese-American sinologist and professor at Princeton University, wrote:

Only by consciously and diligently following the tradition of lyric poetry can a poet compete with or even surpass his predecessors. But sometimes, in order to redefine the tradition, a poet needs to break with the tradition. The change is so drastic that he risks himself being ignored or ridiculed by his contemporaries. The ultimate reward for such a poet, however, is that his works, as he believes firmly, will make him immortal; and that one day, as he feels strongly, there will be a "soul mate" among posterity. The desire to be understood by later generations is one of the most important determinants of the revival of Chinese literature.[6]

This statement may partially answer the readers' questions and doubts. It is not easy to rebel against literary traditions, but is it not just a trial of the law to persevere in and adhere to the unorthodox track of poetry? "Rebellion", however, in a sense, is to question and challenge the existing literary tradition and the current literary system. The "rebellion" and "disengagement" at both the formal level and the content level actually herald the possibility and new goals of literary innovation; the firmness and perseverance undoubtedly presuppose the Renaissance of Chinese literature to the greatest extent from the perspective of literature. In other words, the blatant challenge to the literary tradition is the inevitable precursor of the Renaissance and the new era of literature, and the faithful adherence to this kind of "disobedience" of poetic aesthetics may be an important and necessary step for this kind of temporary "peripheral literature" to enter the "literary limelight".

## 0.3 Research Background and Research Framework

Actually, the complicated life experience of the poet Han-shan, the colorful landscape of the CMPs, the intricate literary journey, the fantastic "Han-shan phenomenon" and the vicissitude of literary scene could have been important academic topics. The domestic academic research on Han-shan and his poems, however, has long been constrained to the traditional dimensions such as language, edition, content and addendum. The existing comparative studies and impact studies have mostly concentrated on the polysystem within Chinese literature; namely, the previous studies were either confined to the initial stage of introduction to basic information and data listing, or confined to the research on the translation and influence of the CMPs in the United States. In the meanwhile, it is noticeable that few scholars have made any substantive research and discussion on translations of the CMPs from the perspective of translation studies and cultural studies, while there is almost no research on the significance of the "Han-shan phenomenon" in terms of canon construction and the writing of (translated) literary history. These problems left over from Han-shan Studies are exactly the research background and research motivation of this book.

This book is intended to investigate the CMPs in a coherent global context. While giving due consideration to the "vertical" studies of the polysystem of Chinese literature, it shall highlight the "horizontal" influence of the CMPs. Furthermore, it shall discuss the making and developing of the "Han-shan phenomenon" and its implications for translation studies, travel writing, canon construction and Chinese literary historiography.

On the basis of literature research, this book is designed to review a variety of related materials of Han-shan Studies in detail, aiming to reveal the rich and colorful world of the CMPs to readers, which is not only a material world, real and full of vast historical materials, various legends, countless textual criticisms, and hypotheses, but also a spiritual world presented by the words of Han-shan. This book first examines the relevant discourses of Chinese and Western travel writing in Chapter 1 and Chapter 2, and at the same time, it puts forward the concepts and issues related to text travel and canon construction on the basis of examining "translation" as a travel metaphor. Afterwards, in Chapter 3, the book discusses the intralingual travel and acceptance of Han-shan and his poems within the norms of the source culture, and discusses subsequently the constraints and influences of the source culture and its literary norms on the canon construction. The fourth chapter provides in-depth perspectives on the interlingual literary journey of Han-shan and his poems, and investigates in detail how the CMPs in the literary polysystem of the departure stands out and takes the central position in the cultural polysystem of arrivals (the destination); moreover, the upsurge of "Han-shan Studies" in the East and the West driven by this shall be addressed accordingly. Chapter 5 deals with the canon construction of the CMPs in American translated literature from the theoretical perspectives of descriptive translation studies, such as polysystem theory and so on. As a consequence of the impact of "Han-Shan fever" from outside China, Chinese academic circles have regained their interest in Han-shan Studies, and the writing of Chinese literary history has begun to re-examine the literary status of Han-shan and his poems. Chapter 6 therefore outlines in detail the return journey of the CMPs and the current research situation in Chinese academic circles under the impact of Western "Han-shan fever". Meanwhile, it probes into the general situation of literary history writing and canonization of the CMPs in the polysystem of Chinese literary history from the 1960s to the present as well as its political and cultural implications. Chapter 7 is the concluding remarks of the book. On the basis of summarizing each chapter, this chapter re-examines the significant impact of the text travel and canon construction of the CMPs on theoretical travel, literary history writing and canon construction. In the meanwhile, it explores the future orientations of "Han-shan Studies" and reviews the explanatory power of the theory being employed.

The discussion on some issues of this book still needs to be further deepened due to the varied fields and disciplines involved, such as the history of literature, history of poetry, history of religion, history of linguistics, history of folklore, history of spirituality, history of culture, history of thought, as well as studies on classic Chinese literature, religion, linguistics, comparative literature and translation studies, which makes the research much more complicated and worthwhile.

## Notes

1 W. Liu & I. Lo (eds.). *Sunflower Splendor: Three Thousand Years of Chinese Poetry*. Bloomington and London: Indiana University Press, 1975: 549.
2 Zan-ning. *Biographies of Eminent Monks in the Song Dynasty*. Beijing: Zhonghua Book Company, 1997: 484–485. The citation here is translated by the translators of this book, and the citations that are not individually footnoted to indicate who translated them are the translators' own translation.
3 Frankel, Hans H. "T'Ang Literati: A Composite Biography." *Critical Readings on Tang China*, 2018, pp. 545–565. https://doi.org/10.1163/9789004380165_019.
4 Translated by Red Pine in *The Collected Songs of Cold Mountain*.
5 All CMPs in this book are quoted from Complete Tang Poems (Vol 860) and poems here are translated by Red Pine in *The Collected Songs of Cold Mountain*.
6 Kang-i Sun Chang. *Six Dynasties Poetry*. Princeton, NJ: Princeton University Press, 1986: 3.

# 1 Travel Writing and Translation Studies

With regard to the interconnections of translation and travel, Arthur Kinney once related that

> conceptually, then, translation and travel seem synonymous; what distinguishes them is the degree of abstraction. One emphasizes the abstract, the other the concrete. What both have in common—as idea and in practice—is a concentration on the relational and the referential alongside the self-referential. They both establish and then work by way of patterns, networks, or signifying systems to establish meaning; they rely on analogy, metaphor and simile explicitly or implicitly.[1]

Loredana Polezzi believes that travel writing, "like translation, has long been wrapped in the myth of faithfulness and objectivity (the traveler as eyewitness) while in effect being engaged in interpreting and representing reality according to specific ideologies and hierarchies."[2] In this sense, the roles and status of travel and translation, and travelers and translators in the polysystem of a country, are complementary, and also, to some extent, are subject to the specific polysystem. Meanwhile, they can also interact with each other and function through certain patterns, networks, fields, signifying systems and discourse systems.

## 1.1 The Role of Travel Writing and Translation Studies in China

From the etymological perspective of derived forms of "Lü" 旅, "Xing" 行, "You" 游 and "Guan" 观 described in ancient Chinese travel writings, as well as their discourse subjects and discursive practices, they are in a peripheral position in traditional Chinese cultural discourse, which is undoubtedly the same as the traditional status and role of translation and translators recorded in ancient Chinese translation discourse. As a matter of fact, the position of translation and translators, like that of ancient travel writing and the role of ancient travelers, is similarly peripheral in the polysystem of ancient Chinese indigenous cultures.

DOI: 10.4324/9781003415749-2

### 1.1.1  Etymology of "Lüxing" 旅行 (Travel)

In ancient Chinese travel writing, "Lüxing" 旅行 (travel) carried different meanings, and it was endowed with different ideological connotations in different historical periods. In ancient Chinese classics, the use of this compound could be traced back to the Spring and Autumn Period (770 BCE–476 BCE) and the Warring States Period (475 BCE–221 BCE), and it meant "group travel". From *The Question of Zengzi* in *Book of Rites* (《礼记·曾子问》), there is the record that "one should not be seen standing with others, or going along in a crowd."[3] In this record, "travel" (旅行) means "go along in a crowd". Similar sayings can be found in *Disputing Things* in *Garden of Stories* (《说苑·辨物》) by Liu Xiang (刘向, 77 BCE–6 BCE) in the Western Han Dynasty (202 BCE–8 BCE) that "the Kirin . . . are not gregarious and barely travel." The reason for the emergence of such an expression Lüxing is mainly due to the fact that in ancient China, large-scale individual travel activities were rare, except for a few individuals such as emperors, officials, scholars, merchants, and monks who had the opportunity to travel individually. People in early times had to resort to the whole tribe or several family groups within a tribe to solve many affairs because of low productivity and poor living conditions. Any kind of "travel" of moving to another place at that time, of course, can only be regarded as group migration, the major purpose of which is to seek higher productivity and better living conditions.[4]

However, Lüxing appeared significantly later than the two Chinese characters "Lü" 旅 (trip or travel) and "Xing" 行 (to travel, to walk, or to go), which were originally used as two independent but mutually referential words. The earliest denotation of the character "Lü" 旅 was a unit of an army, a brigade. The related record can be found in *The Overseer of the Masses* in *State Officials*, collected in *Zhou Rites* (《周记·地官·小司徒》) that "tens of thousands can be recruited to form an army. Five soldiers form a pent, five pents a quarter, four quarters a centum, five centums a Brigade." In *Shuowen Jiezi* (《说文解字》, *The Etymology of Chinese Characters*) (《说文解字》) by Xu Shen (许慎, 58–147) of the Han Dynasty (202 BCE–220 CE), there is a saying that "an army unit of five hundred soldiers is called a bridge." Thus there emerged the expression of "Xinglü" 行旅 (a brigade in travel), which is mostly related to the military. *Wen Xuan or Selections of Refined Literature*, by Xiao Tong (萧统, 501–531), known posthumously as "The Crown Prince of Resplendent Brilliance" (昭明太子), is one of the Chinese classics. The rhapsodies on travel in Volume 2 of this book are mainly based on the theme of military life, such as the verse "On me departure weighs heavily / About everything I feel nostalgic," and "Far and remote the frontier is / Nostalgic and dejected the soldiers are." Therefore, it can be suggested that there is a recurring theme, that a major purpose of travel is to fight and make battle.

Later, the word "Lü" 旅 (trip or travel) gradually obtained the derivative meaning of "way or road". In "Yugong" (禹贡, "The Tribute of Yu") in *Shangshu* (《尚书》, *Book of Documents*), there is a relative record that "the roads in Caishan Mountain and Mengshan Mountain have been repaired." Wang Yinzhi (王引之, 1766–1834)

of the Qing Dynasty (1644–1912), then explained in his book *Jingyi Shuwen* (《经义述闻》, *A Companion to Ancient Chinese Classics*) that "as for me, the word 'Lü' 旅 here meant 'road'." Similarly in *Erh-ya* (《尔雅》), there is a saying that "'Lü' (旅) means 'path' or 'road'." In *Zhouyi* (《周易》, *Zhou Changes*) appeared a sentence that "Lü intimates that (in the condition which it denotes) there may be some little attainment and progress. If the stranger or traveler be firm and correct as he ought to be, there will be good fortune,"5 from which we can know that the word "Lü" 旅 was used in the same way as now. In his *Zhouyi Zhengyi* (《周易正义》, *Interpretation of Zhou Changes*), Kong Yingda (孔颖达, 574–648) of the Tang Dynasty (618–907) then annotated that

> "Lü" 旅 means that one has to stay long in a place that is not his home, and this kind of sojourn is just a makeshift for survival. Despite losing his home, one can also go on a relatively smooth trip. Thus, in this case, one must behave himself during his sojourn to acquire luck and peace.6

As of today, the word "Lü" 旅 has included scores of established modern meanings such as "to live away from home", and "a traveler who lives away from home or who was on a long journey outside", "to stay at a place temporarily during a trip", and so on.

Just like "Lü" 旅, the word "Xing" 行 refers to the noun "road or path". A case at this point can be seen in *Shijing* (《诗经》, *Classic of Poetry*): "The girl with a basket on her arm walked along a path, picking mulberry leaves from time to time." "Xing" 行 can also be used as a verb; for example, there is a sentence in *Yijing* (《易经》, *The I Ching or Book of Changes*) that "Wind revolves in the sky," and in this case "Xing" 行 means "to revolve or blow through". Then, in *Zou Zhuan* (《左传》, *Spring and Autumn Annals*), "Xing" 行 includes the meaning of "to circulate or spread" in the saying that "words short of elegance won't spread far and wide." Then, in the Han Dynasty (202 BCE–220 CE), Xu Shen 许慎 in his book *Shuowen Jiezi* (《说文解字》, *The Etymology of Chinese Characters*) defined "Xing" 行 as "(human beings) walk," which is the earliest record currently available of the use of this word as a verb. Later, Ruan Yu (阮瑀, 65–212) in the Han Dynasty and Li E (厉鄂, 1692–1752) in the Qing Dynasty (1644–1912) employed "Xing" 行 as a verb, as the former wrote in his "Wei Caogong Zuoshu Yu Sunquan" (《为曹公作书与孙权》, "Letters addressed to Sun Quan for Cao Cao")—"The raging plague and drought claimed the lives of many soldiers"—and the latter composed the verse in his "Wanbu" (《晚步》, "Walking at Dusk")—"Water sparkles as the moon shines down, and petals fall down as the wind blows past."

Both "Lü" 旅 and "Xing" 行, to sum up, are more focused on the conception of geographical displacement. As mentioned earlier, it was rare for ancient Chinese to travel, as it was only emperors, government officials or monks who would travel. The reason for this is not related to just position in society, but also to the notion that societal norms and values such as "living in peace and stability" would render them "a life of happiness and commitment". Thus, they would not resort to moving away from their hometown unless wars wreaked havoc on the environment of their hometown or the government carried out immigration policies such as ethnic fusion and cross-regional water conservancy projects. For the Chinese, "travel" was by no means a physically or mentally pleasant trip, but was rife with ineradicable misery and tragedy. The sadness-ridden compound "Lüxing" 旅行 brought two major themes of ancient Chinese travel culture: sorrow for separation and hardships of fighting far away from home. The perfect examples of these two themes would be the earliest Chinese sentimental literature, "Gushi Shijiu Shou" (古诗十九首, "Nineteen Old Poems") of the Eastern Han Dynasty (25–220) and plenty of travel poems and frontier poems of the Tang Dynasty (618–907).

### 1.1.2  *History of the Word "You" 游 in Chinese Spiritual Culture*

Apart from "Lüxing" 旅行 and "Xinglü" 行旅, there is another vital concept in Chinese travel writing— "You" 游. In *Shuowen Jiezi* (《说文解字》, *The Etymology of Chinese Characters*), Xu Shen (许慎) explained that "You" 游 refers to the ribbon on the ancient flags. From "Huangong Ernian" (桓公二年, "The 2nd year of Duke Huan") in *Zou Zhuan* (《左传》, *Spring and Autumn Annals*), "Jade mat, sheath and its decorations, leather belt, the flag ribbon, and the belly band for the horse, all these are needed for formality." Gong Pengcheng (龚鹏程, 1956–) maintained that the word "Lü" 旅 can also be interpreted as "to travel with a flag at hand" in that it can be seen that in "Lü" 旅 and "You" 游 there is a word "Yu" 於 which resembles the shape of flags. "It seems that 'You' 游 means one person travels with a flag and 'Lü' 旅 two persons travel together," Gong explained.[7] His deduction, evidently, is yet to be certified. Some scholars, however, state that flags do have something to do with the meaning of "Lü" 旅. The formation of "Lü" 旅 can be traced back to the ancient totem time period when those congregated groups relied on totems to distinguish people of other tribes as they traveled outside together for hunting or fighting.[8]

Like "Lü" 旅 and "Xing" 行, the word "You" 游 also has its etymology connected to group travel and military expedition. Later, this word then included the meaning of "free wandering", and this kind of use can be seen in *Zhuangzi* (《庄子》, *Zhuangzi*). From "Zhibeiyou" (知北游, "Knowledge Wandered North"), there is a sentence that "knowledge wandered north to the banks of the Black Waters", and from "Qiushui" (秋水, "Autumn Floods") a sentence that "Zhuangzi and Huizi were enjoying themselves on the bridge over the Hao River."[9] In his book, Zhuangzi (庄子, 369 BCE–286 BCE) depicted a state of "free and easy wandering" in which "he eats his fill and wanders idly about. Drifting like an unmoored boat, emptily and idly he wanders along," which has been embraced as the acme of "travel" for thousands of years. Cao Pi (曹丕, 187–226), emperor Wen of the Wei Dynasty, in his poem "*Furongchi Zuo*" (《芙蓉池作》, "*On Lotus Pond*") composed a verse that "such a pleasing travel/Blesses me a long life." It is verified that "Lüyou" 旅游 originates from the poem "*Beizaixing*" (《悲哉行》, "*Sorrow of Departure*") by Shen Yue (沈约, 441–513), a poet who served in the Liu Song Dynasty (420–589),

Southern Qi Dynasty (479–502) and Liang Dynasty (502–557). In this poem, he wrote,

> In gorgeous spring travelers linger
> With beauty it greets them
> Through rosy clouds morning sunshine pours
> Beside river bank morning dew gathers
> The twitter of birds wakes flowers up
> The blow of breeze rouses the duckweeds
> Spring in the homeland is far away
> Only thought can carry the nostalgic soldier back.

Apart from *Zhuangzi* (《庄子》, *Zhuangzi*) of the Pre-Qin Dynasty (?–221 BCE), "Shanshuishi" (山水诗, nature poetry) of the Wei, Jin, Southern and Northern Dynasties (220–589) also plays a vital role in Chinese travel writing. This period of early medieval China witnessed social turmoil, political darkness and ruthless rule due to years of war and long-term disruption. Urged by the desire to escape the chaotic North, people for the first time in ancient history migrated southward in a large group. Innumerable amounts of people died of famine resulting from wars, those sensitive men of letters realized the weakness of human beings, the brevity of people's lives, and the fickleness of people's destiny in that stark society, and then they began to dedicate themselves to the Taoism philosophy of "Wuwei" (无为, inexertion, inaction or effortless action) and "Chushi" (出世, out of the world). The earlier-mentioned Taoism philosophy is well exemplified in *Zhuangzi* (《庄子》, *Zhuangzi*), such as "emptiness, stillness, limpidity, silence, inaction—these are the level of Heaven and earth, the substance of the Way and its Virtue"[10] from "Tiandao" (天道, "The Way of Heaven") and "to repair to the thickets and the ponds, living idly in the wilderness, angling for fish in solitary places"[11] from "Keyi" (刻意, Constrained in Will). Hence the third century CE witnessed a trend toward nature in the literary world. J. D. Frodsham (1930–2016), an Australian sinologist, maintained that

> the collapse of the ordered stable society of Han brought with it the eclipse of Confucianism. Faced with the ruins of their civilization the intelligentsia compensated themselves by taking refuge in a philosophy which denied any value to civilized society.[12]

It is owing to the cult of Taoism that "Shanshuishi" (山水诗, nature poetry) reigned supreme, hence numerous immortal rhapsodies and celebrated poets of this school at that time.

Xie Lingyun (谢灵运, 385–433), a poet of the Eastern Jin Dynasty (317–420), was generally thought to be the founder of nature poetry in the history of Chinese literature. Say, in *Zhongguo Shishi* (《中国诗史》, *Traditional Chinese Poetry*), Lu Kanru (陆侃如, 1903–1978) and Feng Yuanjun (冯沅君, 1900–1974) remarked that "Xie Lingyun, a travel lover, is the founder of Chinese nature poetry just as Tao Qian of Chinese fields and gardens poetry."[13] Yu-kung Kao (1929–2016) revealed,

> In the hands of Xie Ling-yun, "landscape poetry" acquired its own identity in both its formal and thematic components. The journey itself became its purpose rather than some fixed destination, and thus the visual and auditory pleasures of the journey were enjoyed for their own sake.[14]

Alternatively, Frodsham argued that "we see in fact that the essential characteristics of nature poetry existed within the corpus of the earlier Taoist *Hsüan-yen* 玄言 verse."[15] A closer look at the history of Chinese literature will prove the view of Frodsham. For instance, two poems by Zuo Si (左思, 250–305) of the Western Jin Dynasty (265–316), collected in *Wen Xuan or Selections of Refined Literature*, described "no need at all of silk or bamboo / For there is a pure music in the landscape itself."[16] Poems of Sun Chuo (孙绰, 314–371) and Xu Xun (许询) of the Eastern Jin Dynasty (317–420) also conveyed the Taoist idea of "keeping company with nature" and "experiencing and detaching the worldly affairs". Sun Chuo (孙绰) wrote, "I cast my line in woods and wilds / I have my friendships far from market and court."[17] As Xu Xun (许询) depicted, "pine trees are besprinkled with fresh dew / The land is strewn with Chrysanthemum petals." However, the Chinese poet Lin Geng (林庚, 1910–2006) held an opposing view that "many of their nature poems are marred by Taoist metaphysics, failing to reveal the natural splendor."[18]

Scholars differ widely about the origins of "Shanshuishi" (山水诗, nature poetry). Chen Yinchi (陈引驰, 1966–) argued that "the nature poetry (in Wei-Jin Period) should be attributed to the influence of the Jiangnan landscape on those scholars after the emperor moved the capital to Jiankang (now Nanjing)."[19] Lin Geng (林庚) held a different view, that nature poetry is derived from the employment of "Qi Xing" (起兴, a kind of rhetorical device used in Chinese poetry).[20] He further argued that "nature poetry came into being because of steady economic growth and convenient waterways in the Southern Dynasties, and then was developed in Tang Dynasty."[21] The poem "Guan Canghai" (《观沧海》, "*Looking at the Blue Sea*") of Cao Cao (曹操, 155–220) "was the first rhapsody with the theme of describing the nature which foreshowed the burgeoning of nature poetry".[22] Yuan Xingpei (袁行霈, 1957–) also agreed that the poem *Looking at the Blue Sea* should be considered the first real nature poem in Chinese literature.[23]

Some other scholars denied the aforesaid argument held by Yuan Xingpei (袁行霈) because they believed that there were many disputable questions. First, why did Cao Cao (曹操) write the first complete landscape poem in a period far away from the Western and Eastern Jin Dynasties (266–316) and the Liu Song Dynasty (420–589) more than 200 years ago when landscape aesthetics have been prevalent? What were the historical and personal reasons for Cao Cao to write this nature poem? In other words, how did Cao Cao (曹操) build an oasis of landscape poetry in the desert of the Han Dynasty (202 BCE–220 CE) when poets were obsessed with expressing emotions? Second, how come people deemed that "*Guan Canghai*" (《观沧海》, "*Looking at the Blue Sea*") ushered in nature poetry while they also assumed that Xie Lingyun (谢灵运, 385–433) in the Eastern Jin Dynasty (317–420) was the founder of nature poetry in the history of Chinese literature? In the hundreds of years from Cao Cao (曹操) to Xie Lingyun (谢灵运, 385–433), was it true that only Cao Cao (曹操) had the exclusive appreciation of nature represented by the sea? Were there any poems that bore the stamp of nature poetry rather than the unchanged emotion-expressing during this period? Third, why did not the poets in Jian'an era (196–220) attempt to imitate Cao Cao's nature poems as he laid the cornerstone of Jian'an poetry? Fourth, how should the fact be explained that before Cao Cao's nature poem there was a poem that "Green Green, River Bank Grasses" in "Gushi Shijiu Shou" (古诗十九首, "Nineteen Old Poems") as it was usually regarded as a work in the Eastern Han Dynasty (25–220)? Moreover, how did the nature theme wind its way to "Gushi Shijiu Shou" (古诗十九首, "Nineteen Old Poems")?[24] Despite a plethora of opinions, it seems that every Chinese is unconsciously influenced by the Chinese travel culture carried by "Shanshuishi" (山水诗, nature poetry).

Apart from "Shanshuishi" (山水诗, nature poetry), there also emerged another poetry genre embodying the Chinese travel culture: "Youxianshi" (游仙诗, poetry on the wandering immortal). This genre is a literary attempt by literati in troubled times to cultivate their minds and seek spiritual extrication through musing with Taoist ideas, and the works of those literati then mirrored their pursuit of longevity and even immortality through Taoist alchemy. If nature poetry is a sign and record of the "wilderness mean mountains and water",[25] then the Youxian poetry is for expressing feelings and thoughts by chanting the celestial journey. It is believed that its origin can even be traced back to *Chuci* (《楚辞》, *Songs of Chu, or Elegies of Chu*) of the Warring States Period (475 BCE–221 BCE), such as Qu Yuan's "Yuanyou" (《远游》, "Far-off Journey") and Xianzhenshirenshi (《仙真人诗》, "Songs of Immortals") written during the first emperor of the Qin Dynasty (221 BCE–206 BCE). These poems contain a plethora of depictions containing fairyland wanderings and are imbued with magnificent romanticism and fantastical imagination.

Youxian poetry in the Wei, Jin, Southern and Northern Dynasties (220–589) weighed heavily in the writing of social and literary history. *Wen Xuan or Selections of Refined Literature* recognized Youxian poetry as a distinct mode of poetry. In this category, it included eight poems by two poets in the Western Jin (265–316), He Shao (何劭,? –301) and Guo Pu (郭璞, 276–324). He Shao (何劭) depicted the unfettered state that transcended physical limitations in his verse "On the crane Prince Jin was riding / Over mountains and valleys they flew," and "For those immortals, I yearn / With celestial life I am obsessed." Most rhapsodies of Guo Pu (郭璞) were in line with the Taoism of Laozi (老子, 571 BCE–471 BCE) and Zhuangzi (庄子), and he disclosed his preference for the Taoist idea of "Chushi" (出世, out of the world) in his verses "The capital is a cave for wandering knights / Mountains and forests are hiding-places for hermits,"[26] and "Let me leave this wind and dust far behind / And bowing low, say farewell to Yi and Qi,"[27] and for the heavenly pleasure and detachment in "Good flyer should fly high above the sky / Good runner should run far and wide," and "The gigantic fish dove into the deep ocean / The huge waves blotted out the immortal abode." Obviously, those Youxian poems have enriched Chinese travel culture as well as Chinese travel writing and the writing of Chinese literary history. Moreover, with all its imagination and exaggeration, Youxian poetry has established a wonderful celestial world offering a temporary relief that was much denied by the tumultuous society and humans. Yu-kung Kao mentioned,

> For people of this age, escape from the misery and tragedy of this world could be possible only for an immortal. The early budding of "poetry on the wandering immortal" (yu-hsien-shih 遊仙詩) depended heavily on the objective description. However, with the gradual rise of popular Taoism and alchemy, the observer assumed the active voice of an immortal, which allowed him, the alchemist-hermit, the would-be immortal, to speak in the desired voice of the fully realized immortal. The poetry of both Ji Kang (嵇康, 223–262) and Guo Pu (郭璞, 276–324) moves freely between the personae of immortals and hermits and the poet speaking of himself.[28]

Nature poetry and Youxian poetry, in fact, originated and prospered in the Wei-Jin Period (265–420), and were popularized by a multitude of poets such as the "Three Cao",[29] Ji Kang (嵇康, 223–263), Ruan Ji (阮籍, 210–263), He Shao (何劭,? -301), Guo Pu (郭璞, 276–324), Shen Yue (沈约, 441–513), Yan Zhitui (颜之推, 531–591) and so on, all the way through the Sui Dynasty (581–619), Tang Dynasty (618–907) and Song Dynasty (960–1279). Nature poems were written by poets in the Tang dynasty such as Meng Haoran (孟浩然, 689–740), Wang Wei (王维, 701–761), Li Bai (李白, 701–762), Du Fu (杜甫, 712–770) and poets in the Song dynasty such as Yang Yi (杨亿, 974–1020), Zhang Yong (张咏, 946–1015), Wang Anshi (王安石, 1021–1086), Su Shi (苏轼, 1037–1101), Yang Wanli (杨万里, 1127–1206), Fan Chengda (范成大, 1126–1193), Liu Kezhuang (刘克庄, 1187–1269), Zhu Xi (朱熹, 1130–1200) and so on, and still retained vitality. Till the Ming and Qing dynasties (1368–1912), the appearance of travelogues, travel notes and travel novels once again enriched Chinese travel writing; just witness *Xu Xiake Youji* (《徐霞客游记》, *Xu Xiake's Travels*) by Xu Xia Ke (徐霞客, 1587–1641), *Wuyue Youcao* (《五岳游草》, *Visiting Five Mountains*) by Wang Shixing (王士性, 1547–1598) and *Lao Can Youji* (《老残游记》, *The Travels of Lao Can*) by Liu E (刘鄂, 1857–1909). Professor Leo Ou-fan Lee summarizes this genre well:

> The traditional Chinese travel literature (yu-chi) is a mixed genre. Closely connected with both prose and poetry, it is a flexible form that reflects man's closeness to nature. . . . Thus we find a wide range of writings from the poetic depictions of natural beauty, in which a Taoistic impulse of eremitism is manifest, to the encyclopedic accounts of environmental and geographical data.[30]

Thus it is safe to say that travels are the cultural products in the process of people experiencing nature, and there is no doubt that they contain richer travel speech than those before.

The sociocultural and spiritual connotations carried by "You" 游 are beyond the word "rich". Gong Pengcheng (龚鹏程) believes that, although the Chinese people are usually too attached to their native land to leave it, there is also a spirit of "travel" hidden deep in their minds. The ancient Chinese society bristled with all kinds of "travelers" and travel-related activities, and the spirit of "travel" was embodied in diverse fields of Chinese society and culture in varying degrees. The concept of "travel" is not only reflected in various activities such as games, travel, recreation, mind-wandering, sightseeing, study, and celestial roaming, but also in different kinds of people such as vagrants, scholars, heroes, rogues, prostitutes and others.[31] According to this, Guo Shaotang holds that "You" 游 in "Lüyou" 旅游 is part and parcel of Chinese travel culture as the word "You" 游 is subtler and more philosophical, reflecting some of the characteristics of Chinese cultural tradition.[32]

Together with the philosophically and socially meaningful "You" 游, "Lü" 旅 and "Xing" 行, which also bear the stamp of the ancient Chinese social culture and spiritual feelings, have jointly enriched Chinese travel culture and travel writing. Apart from the aforementioned three words, there is also another essential word in Chinese travel writing, that is "Guan" 观 (to view or to go sightseeing). In his *Shuowen Jiezi* (《说文解字》, *The Etymology of Chinese Characters*), Xu Shen (许慎) defines it as "the emperor goes sightseeing." This explanation somewhat proves that the original connotation of "Guan" 观 (to view or to go sightseeing) had something to do with the power and the privileged. People later also related this word to the act of "enjoying or looking at the beauty of the landscape from a high place", as witnessed in the verse in "Guan Canghai" (《观沧海》, "Looking at the Blue Sea") of Cao Cao (曹操) that "in the East, I stand on the Pillar Rock / And look at the blue sea."[33] The phrase "Guanguang" (观光, going sightseeing) can be traced back to "Guangua" (观卦, the Kwan Hexagram) in the *Yijing* (《易经》, *The I Ching or Book of Changes*), in which "the fourth line, divided, shows one contemplating the glory of the kingdom. It will be advantageous for him, being such as he is, (to seek) to be a guest of the king."[34] Different from this, "Guanguang" (观光, going sightseeing) nowadays refers to visiting and touring some scenic spots.

### 1.1.3 The Traditional Role of Translation Studies in Ancient China

In ancient Chinese translation discourse, "Fanyi" (翻译, translation or the act of translating) faces a situation similar to that of "Lüxing" (旅行, Travel). "Yi" 译 precedes "Fanyi" 翻译 just as "Lü" 旅 and "Xing" 行 precede "Lüxing" 旅行. In *Zhouli* (《周礼》, *Zhou Rites*), such descriptions can be found, like "'Xiangxu' (象胥, interpreting functionaries) interprets for people" and "reaching the royal court through relay-translation". It can be concluded that in these two sentences, "Yi" 译 is on a par with today's "intralingual translation" and concerns foreign affairs. From "Wang Zhi" (王制, "Royal Regulations") in *Liji* (《礼记》, *Book of Rites*), there is the record that

> in those five regions, the languages of the people were not mutually intelligible, and their likings and desires were different. To make what was in their minds apprehended, and to communicate their likings and desires, (there were officers),—in the east, called "Ji" (寄, transmitters); in the south, "Xiang" (象, representationists); in the west, "Didi" (狄鞮, Tî-tîs, functionaries whose job was to remain communication and diplomatic relations with neighbors of China in ancient times); and in the north, "Yi" (译, interpreters).[35]

which indicates that "Yi" 译 carries the meaning of "Yiguan" (译官, officers who take charge of translation). Such a conclusion thus can be reached that "Yi" 译 in ancient China is connected with government and its translation activities.

The appearance of the character "Fan" 翻 appeared a little later. According to Eva Hung, in those periods when translation movements burgeon, "Yi" 译 failed to cover various translation activities (translation and interpretation) and diverse translation methods (transliteration and sense-for-sense translation).[36] "Fan" 翻, therefore, emerged itself in the process of the Chinese translation of Buddhist sutras, "translating Hu-language into Chinese", "translating it into Chinese so as to rewrite it", and " 'Wu Bu Fan' (五不翻, The Five Untranslatables)" in *Chusanzangjiji* (《出三藏记集》, *A Collection of Records on the Emanation of the Chinese Tripitaka*). In the literature, "Fan" 翻 only literally means "language conversion", and the word of "Fanyi" 翻译, according to Eva Hung, was used as a compound word first in *A Collection of Records on the Emanation of the Chinese Tripitaka*, but it appeared only once in the whole book.[37] In addition, Hung pointed out that the "Fanyi" 翻译 in early ancient books was related to the translation of Buddhist scriptures, while "Yi" 译 was used only in the government's translation affairs. By the Qing Dynasty (1644–1912), the word "Fanyi" 翻译 had all kinds of implicatures of "Yi" 译 recorded in those early ancient books.[38]

Essentially, "Xing" 行 can be used to describe the whole translating process: the translation "spreads" first along a certain "road" and then gets itself "accepted" and "circulated". Indeed, that is the most ideal model in terms of the translating process, and sometimes it is possible for a travel text accepted by its readers to construct its canonical status in the target polysystem. In this sense, the transmutation of the meaning of "Xing" 行 in ancient Chinese discourse perfectly annotates the translation of travel texts.

From the perspective of translation studies, on one hand, the derived meaning of "road" and "path" from "Lü" 旅, in combination with the record that " 'Lü' 旅, a trip, must be taken placidly and carefully to get luck" in *Zhouyi* (《周易》, *Zhou Changes*), indicates that the travel text may come up against perilous sections. Qian Zhongshu (钱锺书, 1910–1998) once described such a situation:

> It is an arduous journey for a text to travel a long distance to reach another world, and it is also inevitable for it to suffer a loss of meaning from its original implication during this long and hazardous journey.[39]

On the other hand, such a statement coincides with the traditional description of the status of translated texts and translators in ancient China. Like the traveler, the travel text finally got to the target culture after a long and dangerous trip, only to find that it may end up in "toiling all day only for survival" as it is only "a wayfarer who lost his home and had to stay long in a foreign land". Those moralists regard the translation and translator as "participating in their environment in a small way, but obviously having no chances of creating great changes". Thus it can be seen that in Chinese traditional cultural norms, the role of translation is inferior just as that of "Lü" 旅 in *Zhouyi* (《周易》, *Zhou Changes*). The following description from "Xiaobian" 小辨 in *Dadailiji* (《大戴礼记》, *Elder Dai's Book of Rites*) can also exemplify that notion:

> Duke Ai of Lu 鲁哀公 (r. 494–467 BCE) said, "I intend to study the minor art of analysis and debate to help me manage the affairs of the state. Is that a worthy pursuit?" Confucius (551 BCE–479 BCE) said, "No, I don't think so. The head of state values time, and since time is limited, he will not preoccupy himself with the minor art of analysis and debate. That is the reason why the ancient kings studied the Way to manage state affairs. Today, the Son of Heaven studies music and poetry to acquaint himself with the prevailing customs; he sets down rites and regulations to govern his kingdom. The various dukes and rulers study the rites and regulations to oversee their officials and administer the land under the Son of Heaven. High officials study morals and absorb their essence so that they can tell the right from the wrong and act in the service of their rulers. Scholars study to be respectful and learn to use words with discrimination so that they can realize their aspirations. The common people obey the orders of their superiors, understand what is forbidden to them and work hard at farming. Even so, they are still afraid of not being able to accomplish their tasks. Such being the case, how much use is there in a minor art?"[40]

In addition, the "peripheral role" of translation can also be seen in the appellation of the translator at that time. During the Spring and Autumn period (770 BCE–476 BCE) of ancient China, the historian Zuo Qiuming (左丘明, 556 BCE–451 BCE?) had already depicted the humble status of the Sheren (舌人, "tongue-men", a common name for interpreters in ancient China) who are responsible for communicating with the various foreign tribes:

> The tribes of Rong 戎 and Di 狄 are bold, rash, reckless and brash, and forthright in their demands, and they do not yield or defer to others. They are untamed and uncouth, like animals. When they come to court to pay their tribute, they do not wait to be served fine and delicate food. So they are seated out of doors, and the tongue-men are ordered to give them whole chunks of meat.[41]

In his description, the tongue-men not only interpret but also have to engage in some menial jobs. According to Qian Zhongshu (钱锺书), in ancient Chinese discourse,

"Qianma" (牵马, leading a horse) was also used to describe the interpreter.⁴² Those appellations from "Xiangxu" (象胥, interpreting-functionaries) in *Zhouli* (《周礼》, *Zhou Rites*) to "Ji" (寄, transmitters), "Xiang" (象, representationists), "Didi" 狄鞮 (Tî-tîs; functionaries whose job was to maintain communication and diplomatic relations with the neighbors of China in ancient times) and "Yi" 译 (interpreters) in *Liji* (《礼记》, *Book of Rites*) all have shown that officials responsible for interpreting were regarded inferior. This kind of job was regarded by Confucius as a "minor" pursuit.

Some commentators have stated that these documents have shown that translation or interpreting before the Qin Dynasty (221 BCE–206 BCE) was functional in nature rather than an activity inspired by a genuine curiosity about other languages and cultures. The appearance of interpreters owed much to the state's administrative and communicative needs. Then interpreting was institutionalized as a minor government post, and for some was a means of livelihood.⁴³ Therefore, in such traditional Chinese translation discourse, the status and role of translation and translators are not recognized by the orthodoxy and mainstream culture.

### 1.1.4 Traditional Status of Travel Writing and Translation Studies in Ancient China

All kinds of records, either in the ancient Chinese travel writing or in the traditional Chinese translation discourse, reflect the same status and role of "travel" and "translation". Although both contribute to the dissemination and exchange of human knowledge and ideas, they are always peripheral in the Chinese polysystem. In essence, there are various determinants of their status such as the dominant ideology, hierarchy, power relations, geographical environment and traffic conditions.

First, the dominant ideology largely determines whether travel and translation are central or peripheral. China's ancient self-sufficient lifestyle, coupled with various political, economic and patriarchal forces, helped to shape the Chinese people's common nature, which is "attached to the land and unwilling to move". As some have remarked, the ancient Chinese regarded "being rooted down in a place never to migrate" as their attitudes towards life, and "therefore, they are prone to being conservative in that they will grieve for parting, demotion, exile, and migration, and are satisfied with their local society based on the ritual and patriarchal clan system."⁴⁴ Moreover, they also advocate what Laozi (老子) argued in *Daodejing* (《道德经》, *Tao Te Ching*):

> They are satisfied with their food. They are pleased with their clothes. They are content with their homes. They are happy in their simple ways. Even though they live within sight of another country and can hear dogs barking and cocks crowing in it, still the people grow old and die without ever coming into conflict.⁴⁵

Therefore, it will not take too much stretch of the imagination to conclude that the notions of "being rooted down in a place never to migrate" and "living in peace and contentment" featured in Chinese social culture, and it also played a deciding role in restricting the modernization of Chinese travel culture.

It is this cultural mentality and the social ideology of "being rooted down in a place never to migrate" that caused ancient China to lock itself in its cultural enclosure for a long time. The projection of this kind of psychology in cultural attitude and translation is that people were conservative and old-fashioned, taking a wait-and-see attitude towards or excluding the alien culture with suspicion and distrust. A spiritual product will find it difficult to get itself enthroned and revered by people as long as it is contrary to the dominant ideology and poetic tradition recognized by traditional forces. It is so strict for works within the system, let alone for the peripheral translations. As Martha Cheung (1953–2013) described the cultural mentality of the people in the Zhou Dynasty (1046 BCE–256 BCE),

> To the Zhou people, the notion of a civilized country did not include a deep intellectual curiosity in communicating with other peoples, let alone the ability to speak their languages. In their geopolitical view, the tribes and races residing in different parts of the known world had not developed an understanding and practice of rites and music, and hence were hardly people with whom one could have meaningful interaction.[46]

That is especially true of the period after the founding of the Qin Dynasty and the Han Dynasty (202 BCE–220 CE) when the pace of cultural exchange slowed considerably. For those regions beyond Qin's reign at that time, the introduction of Western culture and thoughts had never influenced traditional Chinese culture and thoughts.[47]

Moreover, the hierarchy, or the absolute separation of power, determines the actual status of travel and translation. In terms of ancient Chinese classics and historic cultural events, the non-mainstream state of "Lü" 旅, "Xing" 行, "You" 游 and "Guan" 观 gave rise to the peripheral role of "Lüxing" (旅行, travel), which consequently led to a situation that travelers at that time were as few as morning stars. Meanwhile, the majority of those travelers were frustrated and powerless people from all walks of life or were from the lower strata of the societal hierarchy. This relative closeness in geographic displacement eclipses the communicative functions of translation. Therefore, the translator responsible for communication could hardly find favor with the mainstream culture. In addition, the impact of "ethnocentrism" made translation limited to the necessity of government affairs for a long time before the translation of Buddhist sutras began. Despite its benefits to government operations, translation still failed to magnetize those cultural elites.

In the field of translation studies, the records of "coming to court to pay tribute with the help of 'Xiangxu' (象胥, interpreting functionaries)", "coming to court to pay tribute through relay-translation" and "'Yueshang' (越裳, a kingdom located to the south of Jiaozhi[48]), once came to court to pay tribute through relay-translation" in the early Chinese canon represent a certain condescending cultural mentality of being "Shangbang" (上邦, imperial kingdom). Eva Hung believes that relay-translation was so highly praised and recommended because it manifested the spread of China's national prestige, which made it necessary even for those remote foreign countries to overcome all difficulties and come to court to pay tribute. For the Chinese mainstream, it did not matter whether foreign countries could convey messages with language because the difficulty of expression was a problem that foreign countries (not China) had to solve. The more obstacles there were, the more distant those foreign countries came from, and thus it could be a greater proof of China's power and influence. Eva Hung holds that under the influence of such a cultural mentality, whether the translation was efficient or not was the concern of the Chinese mainstream in history.[49] Therefore, relay-translation in a third or fourth language apart from the source language and target language became the common expectation of the ancient Chinese officialdom and intellectual circles. As a result, the significance of translation had long been suppressed or even strangled by the mainstream culture.

As a result, many dynasties in ancient China relied on foreigners or newly migrated non-Han Chinese to perform translation tasks. Some argued that the lack of a large number of local translators in ancient Chinese translation activities was directly related to the fact that translation activities had not entered the cultural mainstream.[50] The early translation of Buddhist scriptures and political affairs at that time was therefore dominated by foreigners. For a long time, the cultivation of local translators had been difficult to be put on the formal agenda because of the disparagement and suppression of the dominant ideology and poetic tradition. This situation had long lasted roughly until the establishment of "Jingshi Tongwenguan" (京师同文馆, School of Combined Learning) in 1862. Moreover, due to the special status of foreign translators, local translators in every Chinese dynasty had been in a low position, which de facto rendered the translation official a fairly minor professional system. Therefore, the orthodox "Han" (Chinese Han nationality) intellectuals were ashamed to be translators; even though sometimes they translated, it was only for the sake of livelihood.[51] For example, Eva Hung once mentioned in her book *Translation in Asia: Past and Present* that Lin Shu (林纾, 1852–1924), a reputed translator in the late Qing Dynasty, translated a large amount of texts, which was in fact closely related to the income brought by his translations. His contemporary Bao Tianxiao (包天笑, 1876–1973) began translating novels in his early years also because it was a lucrative sideline.[52] In such a translation field and discourse system, the status and role of translation and translator have long been marginalized. For these reasons, the translation activities have always been difficult to carry out.

Furthermore, constraints of geographical environment and traffic conditions also determine the historical fate of travel culture and translation activities to be mainstream or to be peripheral. One of the reasons why ancient Chinese travel culture did not occupy a dominant position was because of its underdeveloped travel conditions. Ancient road and waterway transportation is relatively backward. "Difficult to travel" had been a consensus for travelers at that time. In addition, the risk and safety of the journey is also the biggest concern of travelers. For instance, from *Zhouyi* (《周易》, *Zhou Changes*), there are records like "The stranger (traveler) mean and meanly occupied. It is thus that he brings on himself (further) calamity";

"the stranger (traveler), burning his lodging-house, and having lost his child servants"; and "The stranger, (thus represented), first laughs and then cries out. He has lost his ox(-like docility) too readily and easily"[53]—all of which are all records about the safety and risks that travel brings. Hence, in ancient times, the farewell party set for relatives or friends was always pervaded by a mood of melancholy and sadness. Definitely, the inconvenience of transportation is actually the result of the ancient Chinese policy of valuing agriculture over commerce.

To conclude, such limitation of geographical environment and transportation is bound to affect the dissemination and reception of new knowledge and information. From *Shangshu Dazhuan* (《尚书大传》, *Amplification of the Book of History*), there is an account saying:

> The road is long. High mountains and deep valleys obstruct the way. To overcome the language problems encountered along the way, several yì 译 (official title of interpreting functionaries in charge of communicating with the regions in the north) has been sent to accompany your humble servant to pay tribute to Your Excellency.[54]

While the Silk Road originated from the Western Han Dynasty (202 BCE–8 CE) as well as the "Western Territories (or Xiyu 西域)" in both the Eastern Han Dynasty (25–220) and Eastern Jin Dynasties (266–316), they became collecting and distributing centers of trade and culture, which profited from their favorable geographical conditions and advantages of transportation. In essence, frequent immigration made these areas the place where new ideas and knowledge were accessible and could be exchanged. At the same time, the multilingual environment created by the travelers in these areas, including various accents from north and south, also provided a golden opportunity for the prosperity of translation activities and the emergence of outstanding translators. As a result, translators from these territories had been the nucleus in the translation of Buddhist scriptures at that time.

It is in such a travel writing discourse that the text fails to travel out of the country easily and that is the same case for foreign texts to travel inbound. For texts enjoying prestige, the situation was so harsh, not even to mention those texts regarded as "peripheral" in the prevailing cultural norms.

## 1.2 Western Travel Writing and Translation as a Travel Metaphor

When "travel" is used to explain various types of transformation and shift, then "translation", which includes language transformation and geographical displacement, is undoubtedly the most representative travel metaphor.

### 1.2.1 Etymology of "To Travel"

In Western countries, "to travel" is first referred to as "to labor", which is unquestionably synonymous with "to travail". Based on that, there were another two similar words, "travailen" and "travallen" coined in Middle English. Similar expressions like "traveiller" and "travaillier" were also found in French, later including the usage of "travailler" in today's French. And in the 13th century, there was a new word expressing the meaning of "travel", that is, "journey". The common origin or the common connection in the meaning of "travel", "travail" and "journey" can be traced back to the Latin word "tripalium" (an instrument of torture), which literally means "three stakes".[55] Due to this close affinity, Western people are accustomed to associating travel with specific experiences such as suffering, trial, torture and so on. Eric Reed (1942–) traced the historical extension of this lexical meaning in his book, *The Mind of the Traveler: From Gilgamesh to Global Tourism*:

> Travel is the paradigmatic "experience," the model of a direct and genuine experience, which transforms the person having it. We may see something of the nature of these transformations in the roots of Indo-European languages, where *travel* and *experience* are intimately wedded terms.
> 
> The Indo-European root of experience is *\*per* (the asterisk indicates a retro-construction from languages living and dead). *\*Per* has been construed as "to try," "to test," "to risk"—connotations that persist in the English word *peril*. The earliest connotations of *\*per* appear in Latin words for "experience": *experior* and *experimentum*, whence the English *experiment*. . . . Many of the secondary meanings of *\*per* refer explicitly to motion: "to cross space," "to reach a goal," "to go out." The connotations of risk and danger implicit in *peril* are also obvious in the Gothic cognates for *\*per* (in which *p* becomes an *f*): *fern* (far), *fare, fear, ferry*. One of the German words for experience, *Erfahrung*, is from the Old High German *irfaran*: "to travel," "to go out," "to traverse," or "to wander." The deeply rooted assumption that travel is an experience that tests and refines the character of the traveler is demonstrated by the German adjective *bewandert*, which currently means "astute," "skilled," or "clever" but originally (in fifteenth-century texts) meant merely "well traveled." These crossings of words and meanings reflect one of the first conceptualizations of travel as suffering, a test, an ordeal—meanings explicit in the original English word for travel: *travail*. . . . This ostensibly negative sense pervades ancient travel epics, including The Epic of Gilgamesh, the first work of Western travel literature (transcribed 1900 B.C.).[56]

Although in the West, the meanings of the word "trauel" were becoming separated in the 16th century, travel (journeying) and travail (toil, pain) are still interchangeable terms with the meanings closely associated.[57] When it comes to "travel", Western people always connect it with "hardship", "tribulation", "danger" and "unpredictable future" in their early consciousness. Even so, people still regard travel as a salutary "experience". James Clifford (1945–), an American travel theorist, once remarked:

> "Travel," as I use it, is an inclusive term embracing a range of more or fewer voluntarist practices of leaving "home" to go to some "other" place. The

displacement takes place for the purpose of gain—material, spiritual, and scientific. It involves obtaining knowledge and/or having an "experience" (exciting, edifying, pleasurable, estranging, broadening).[58]

The previous statement is also established on the traditional "travel experience" model in the West, a theory that is also recognized by Modern Tourism. John Urry (1946–2016), a British sociologist, holds the view that

> to be a tourist is one of the characteristics of the "modern" experience. Not to "go away" is like not possessing a car or a nice house. It has become a marker of status in modern societies and is also thought to be necessary for good health.[59]

Clifford and Urry's interpretation once again demonstrates that in the West, "travel" and "experience" in both traditional and modern senses are inextricably linked, while "travel", "knowledge acquisition" and "traveler's character improvement" are complementary.

### *1.2.2 Culture and Politics in Western Travel Writing*

As a matter of fact, in the Age of Exploration, especially when some descriptions regarding the Orient from Western missionaries were mystified, Western people's understanding of cross-border travel permeated with another kind of myth concerning colonialism and imperialism. The travel gaze to the "otherness", especially to Asian countries, was always based on condescending Orientalism. No matter from the perspective of earliest European travel writings represented by pilgrimage literature, or from the post-colonial discourse prevailing in the second half of the 20th century, the thoughts and theories respecting travel from Europe to other worlds unexceptionally arouse people's recollection of the concepts of exploration, expansion, colonization, plunder, salvation, conquest, enlightenment and so forth. As for the cultural and sociopolitical significance of this process, George Van Den Abbeele, a French travel theorist, made a euphemistic description in "The Economy of Travel", the preface of his book, *Travel as Metaphor*:

> Banal as it may be, travel is persistently perceived as exciting and interesting, as liberating, and as what "opens up new horizons." The dearest notions of the West nearly all appeal to the motif of the voyage: progress, the quest for knowledge, freedom as the freedom to move, self-awareness as an Odyssean enterprise, salvation as a destination to be attained by following a prescribed pathway (typically straight and narrow).[60]

Clifford, however, holds it differently:

> The traveler, by definition, is someone who has the security and privilege to move about in relatively unconstrained ways. This, at any rate, is the travel

myth. In fact, as studies like those of Mary Louise Pratt are showing, most bourgeois, scientific, commercial, aesthetic, travelers moved within highly determined circuits.[61]

From this point of view, the travel motif discussed by Van Den Abbeele is stated from another different aspect. When mentioning the previously given ideas, did he intend to avoid the strong political implication in Western travel history? Or are they entirely well-intentioned expressions of a humanist intellectual about travel writing in the capitalist society? Perhaps he just tried to make an explanation based on discourse regarding travel and leisure in Modern Tourism, or from the perspective of the traditional model of "travel experience".

Obviously, "tourism" is a modern concept hard to describe. With different purposes, there will be different ways to define "tourism". Between "tourism" and "travel", some made distinctions as followed:

> All tourism involves travel, yet not all travel is tourism; all tourism occurs in leisure, but not all leisure is given to tourist pursuits. Tourism is an activity that takes place when, in international terms, people cross a border for leisure or business and stay at least twenty-four hours.[62]

Rojek and Urry believe that "tourism" is a term to be deconstructed, which encompasses myriad various concepts. Thus, it's hard to explain its use as a term in social science. In addition, in the main tourism textbooks, tourism is regarded only as a set of economic activities.[63] Although Van Den Abbeele is reticent about the cultural politics underlying Western travel writing, Clifford is outspoken to say, "The long history of travel that includes the spatial practices of 'fieldwork' is predominantly Western-dominated, strongly male, and upper-middle class."[64]

Taking a brief review of the history of Western travel, it's not hard to find that the Western gaze on the object of travel (otherness) is always closely tied to certain social strata, power discourse, historical context, gender, and ethnic groups among other factors. As Daniel-Henri Pageaux said,

> There is no doubt that the image of a foreign country is subject to some mandatory rules, which can be explained by the position of the gazer culture and the power relationship between the gazer culture and the gazed culture.[65]

It is true not only when used to explain the tourist gaze between two different cultures, but also in the same cultural context. Urry once remarked that "before the nineteenth century few people outside the upper classes traveled anywhere to see objects for reasons that were unconnected with work or business."[66] In addition, he also recounted that in Imperial Rome, for example, a fairly extensive pattern of travel for pleasure and culture existed only for the elite. In the 13th and 14th centuries, pilgrimage had become a widespread phenomenon, but it often included a mixture of religious devotion and culture and pleasure. By the 15th century, there were regular organized tours from Venice to the Holy Land, and the Grand Tour had become firmly established by the end of the 17th century for the sons of the aristocracy and the gentry, and by the late 18th century for the sons of the professional middle class. In the 19th century, such a kind of "classical Grand Tour", with education as its main purpose, evolved into a much more private and passionate "romantic Grand Tour". In modern society, much of the population will travel somewhere else for reasons unconnected with work. In Britain, travel is thought to occupy 40 percent of available "free time".[67]

Regarding ethnic groups in travel and related historical narratives, Clifford once incisively pointed out, "In the dominant discourses of travel, a nonwhite person cannot figure as a heroic explorer, aesthetic interpreter, or scientific authority."[68] It is not difficult to think of the so-called "the white man as God syndrome" in cultural studies. Furthermore, the mainstream travel tradition in the West has always had women excluded. Clifford mentioned, "'Good travel' (heroic, educational, scientific, adventurous, ennobling) is something men (should) do. Women are impeded from serious travel. Some of them go to distant places, but largely as companions or as 'exceptions.'"[69] In reality, those very few female travelers are all white women in the upper class. Essentially, questions like "Who travels?" "Travel for whom?" "Where to travel?" "How to travel?" "Why travel?" "Travel writing for whom?" and "Compose what kind of travel diary?" are all tightly connected to power discourse and ethnic narrative. Intriguingly, there are similar power complexes and ethnic discriminations in ancient Chinese travel writing. Guo Shaotang once observed,

> The authors of ancient Chinese travel documents are mainly scholar-officials who had little interest in foreign countries and non-Han ethnic groups. . . . Starting from the ancient chronicles of emperors' inspection of the frontier, travel writing tends to focus on the description of the political mission around the Empire and tribes in the wilderness.[70]

Women's travel, however, seems not to be possible other than to marry far away. In fact, ancient Chinese women generally followed the social-ethical discourse pattern of "men traveling while women stayed in the boudoir", which resulted in the emergence of the distinctive "Boudoir Complaint Literature" in the ancient Chinese literature history.

Since the 20th century, the focus of cultural studies in travel writing has shifted to interpreting specific travel narratives from the perspectives of power, discourse, feminism, ethnicity, post-colonialism and so forth. Such kind of academic research has attracted not only geographers but also anthropologists, sociologists, scholars of cultural history and scientific history, as well as researchers of literary studies and translation studies. The academic field is not confined to travel writing in a narrow sense, but integrated into regional geography, maritime history, art history, cartography history, translation history, politics, pedagogy and many other disciplines. Seen from the earlier-mentioned statements, it is not difficult to find that "travel", in the eyes of Westerners, is invariably highly related to experience, knowledge and even the power discourse derived from it.

It can be concluded that the study of Western travel history is the study of the origin and evolution history of the Western culture, for a history of Western travel is undoubtedly a miniature landscape of Western culture. Eric Leed made a further explanation:

> The history of travel illuminates the history not only of the West but of the human species in general, suggesting that this is a story of the dispersal, aggregation, differentiation of the species and its adaptation to a variety of places, climates, soils, and topographies. In this, human society does not differ significantly from the history of other species that have evolved, preserved, and perpetuated variations that adapt a population to a "place", an ecological niche. Of course, human migrations are achieved not through "instinct" but through the imagination, through images of the mysterious and far-away, of sacred lands, lands of plenty and promises.[71]

Admittedly, it reminds us of Darwinism in the studies of travel when comparing human travel with the evolution of species, but such a statement on travel history is relatively objective. As a matter of fact, without a suitable ecological environment, human travel, even species' travel, and evolution can only encounter the fate of "failing to acclimatize" and "bearing unsatisfactory fruits". From "Kao Gong Ji Zongxu" (考工记总叙, "Introduction of Artificer's Record") in *Zhouli* (《周礼》, *Zhou Rites*), an ancient Chinese cultural classic, there is a record that

> if the mandarin trees are planted north of the Huai 淮 river, they change into the three-leaved tangerine. The crested myna never flies north beyond the Ji 济 river, the marten dies if he crosses the Wen 汶 river to the south. All this is caused by the Qi 气 of the earth! The knives from the principality Zheng 郑, the axes from the principality Song 宋, the scraping knives from the principality Lu 鲁 with which the script on bamboo strips is corrected, the swords from the principalities Wu 吴 and Yue 粤—all these are excellent products. They would not be so excellent if they are not made in these regions. This is also caused by the Qi 气 of the earth! The ox horns from the principality Yan 燕, the bows from Jing 荆, the arrow shafts from Fenhu 妢胡 and copper and tin from the principalities Wu 吴 and Yue 粤 count as top-quality materials. Nature has its time to grow and its time to die. Grasses and trees have their time to grow and their time to die. Rocks have their time when they develop crevices. The water has its time to freeze and it has its time to melt. All this is caused by the seasons of heaven!

There is a similar saying from "Neipianzaxia" (内篇杂下, "Miscellaneous", Part 2) in *Yanzichunqiu* (《晏子春秋》, *The Spring and Autumn Annals of Yan-zi*),

> When orange trees grow south of the river Huai they produce oranges but if they grow north of the river Huai they produce tangerines. (The same strain of citrus trees bears sweet and juicy citranges in the south of the River Huai

but puckery and bitter trifoliate oranges in the north.) Only their leaves look alike but their fruits taste differently. Why is this so? because the water and the soil differ.[72]

The process of text travel is similar to that of travel in a broad sense. Without imagination and curiosity about the culture of arrivals (the destination/the host culture), without the appropriate starting environment of the departure (the origin/the guest culture), without the process of "dissemination" (circulation), "plunder" (devouring) or "domestication" (localization), the text that departs/starts cannot "settle down" in the cultural polysystem of arrivals.

### 1.2.3  *Travel as a Metaphor*

People tend to hold misconceptions like: no matter when one is talking about "Lü" (旅, Trip or travel), "Xing" (行, To travel, to walk, or to go), "You" (游, To travel, to wander) or "Guan" (观, To view or to go sightseeing) in Chinese travel culture, or the Western "travel-experience" model, one believes that more emphasis is placed on the relationship between travelers and the spatial shift and displacement caused by travel itself. It is, actually, a narrow and one-sided understanding of travel research. Just as Chris Rojek and John Urry had discussed in their article *Transformations of Travel and Theory*, "peoples, cultures, and objects migrate.... It is now clear that people tour cultures; and that cultures and objects themselves travel."[73] Clifford even coined a new term "culture as travel" to express the omnipresence of travel. Hence, it is far from enough for travel studies to focus only on travelers as the subject of travel gaze.

As a matter of fact, "travel" has long been the main source of various metaphors in the field of cultural studies. In this regard, Leed made an explanation,

> The commonality and familiarity of travel may also be seen in the fact that travel is the most common source of metaphors used to explicate transformations and transitions of all sorts. We draw upon the experience of human mobility to define the meaning of death (as a "passing") and the structure of life (as a "journey" or pilgrimage); to articulate changes in social and existential conditions in rites of initiation (of "passage").[74]

Based on these initial meanings, an impressive array of travel metaphors is derived from various thoughts of modern critical theories, such as flow, flux, fluidity, mobility, exile, diaspora, displacement, nomadism, pilgrimage, migration, immigration, transgression, crossing boundary, hybridity, rootlessness, homelessness, etc.

There is no doubt that "travel" can also serve as a metaphor to denote the shift and change of space in cultural studies. For instance, in the Polysystem Theory of Itamar Even-Zohar (1939–), the position of translated literature is in a constant state of flux from the periphery to the center or from center to periphery. In addition, travel is also applied as a metaphor by scholars to refer to cross-border travel and translation of both knowledge and theories. Edward Said's "Traveling Theory",

Hillis Miller's "Performative Topographies" on literature and translation criticism and his theory of "Border Crossings" are good examples. It is assured that the text travel implies not only the spatial displacement but also the transformation of sign systems. Therefore, it is feasible to interpret and analyze translation phenomena from the perspective of travel.

*1.2.4 "Translation" as a Travel Metaphor*

The English word "to translate" derives from "translātus", a Latin verb and the irregular perfect participle of "transferre",[75] in which the root "ferre" means "to bear, to carry, to bring". "Translātus" means "to carry across" or "to transfer", and on this basis, the noun "translātiō" is derived, which refers to "transferring", also refers to "removal to heaven" and "a version".[1] In addition, Georgia Brown also traced its history, "In the Renaissance, the verb to translate also meant to transport or remove from one place to another."[76] Obviously, the etymology of "translation" presupposes a kind of geographic displacement. Moreover, like all travel metaphors, the etymology of "translation" also presupposes the shift and transfer of meaning. To sum up, the word "translation" in essence includes not only the shift of space and time but also the transformation of form and content.

Translation, in this respect, could be regarded as a special way of travel, a journey from the source text to the target text, and also a trip departing from the host culture to the guest culture. Arthur Kinney also pointed out in the preface of his book *Travels and Translations in the Sixteenth Century*:

> Conceptually, then, translation and travel seem synonymous; what distinguishes them is the degree of abstraction. One emphasizes the abstract, the other the concrete. What both have in common—as idea and in practice—is a concentration on the relational and the referential alongside the self-referential. They both establish and then work by way of patterns, networks, or signifying systems to establish meaning; they rely on analogy, metaphor and simile explicitly or implicitly.[77]

Kinney, of course, is narrowing the meaning of travel here. He however, could not be more correct in saying that both translation and travel depend, directly or indirectly, on analogy. The analogy is based on disanalogy. Obviously, both travel itself and translation, as one of the ways of travel, not only seek common ground among others, but also establish their own cultural identities through the examination of the differences in other cultures, which is of paramount importance anyway. Otherwise, what is the significance of travel? What is the significance of translation? However, both the translation as one way of text travel and the analogy sought by the travel itself have to be subject to some factors outside itself, so the analogy here is somewhat discounted. As Loredana Polezzi once said:

> The images and representations constructed by both travel writing and translation are frequently asymmetrical, due to the power relationships by which

they are framed. The travel writing tradition, like translation, has long been wrapped in the myth of faithfulness and objectivity (the traveler as eyewitness) while in effect being engaged in interpreting and representing reality according to specific ideologies and hierarchies.[78]

It is evident that travel and translation, as discourse practice, are not carried out in a vacuum. They are always selected and manipulated by manifold contextual factors and power relations. Hence, whether it is travel logs or translation products, there can only be an "asymmetric" correspondence between them and the constructed object. Clifford also remarked:

Today I've been working, overworking, "travel" as a *translation term*. By translation term I mean a word of apparently general application used for comparison in a strategic and contingent way. "Travel" has an inextinguishable taint of location by class, gender, race, and a certain literariness. It offers a good reminder that all translation terms used in global comparisons—terms like culture, art, society, peasant, mode of production, man, woman, modernity, ethnography—get us some distance and fall apart. Tradittore, traduttore.[79]

Clifford extends the denotation of translation to the level of comparative and contrastive meaning here. Since these "translation terms", like travel itself, are bound by class, power, race, etc., it is common that translation terms, including translation itself, always contain some sense of variation and betrayal. Such a statement is certainly defensible. Moreover, we can also say that it is variation and betrayal that, to some extent, promote and facilitate the migration and interaction of texts in different times and spaces. Assuming that there did exist two identical cultural contexts, then travel and translation would undoubtedly lose their premises and reasons of existence.

In conclusion, when the text as a traveler starts from the polysystem of the place of origin, passes through various spatio-temporal environments, spatial distance, and contextual pressure channels, and finally enters the polysystem of arrivals, it will always encounter the vigilance and resistance from the host culture of arrivals. In the process of gaining legitimacy, there are always a certain number of programs controlling, selecting, organizing, domesticating and reconstructing the new text and its loaded new discourse, which is an inevitable step in the process of text travel. Based on such understanding and judgment, the canon construction of translated texts must be tightly tied to truth, knowledge, belief and power. In essence, the process of text travel and canon construction is also a process of discourse practice, which presents no intention of questioning the meaning of text and discourse, but focuses more on the generation and practice of text and its attached meaning. In brief, this process is aimed at investigating the formation, metabolism (shift and transfer) and legitimization of the translated text which travels to the polysystem of arrivals.

## Notes

1. A. F. Kinney. Introduction. // M. Pincombe (ed.), *Travels and Translations in the Sixteenth Century: Selected Papers from the Second International Conference of the Tudor Symposium*. Hampshire: Ashgate, 2004: xiii.
2. L. Polezzi. Rewriting Tibet: Italian Travellers in English Translation. *The Translator*, 1998, 2(4): 322.
3. Translated by James Legge.
4. Much the same is true in the West. As Enzensberger pointed out, migration behavior in the West is also based on improving the ecological environment and economic conditions.

   > It was necessity, biological or economic in nature, that made people migrate. The treks of the nomads were due to geographic and climatic causes. The desire to travel never was a reason for ancient expeditions of warfare. The first people who left of their own will were merchants. In ancient Hebrew, the words for "merchant" and "traveler" are synonymous. With one exception which we will discuss later, travel was a matter for tiny minorities, subject to specific and tangible purposes. It was soldiers and messengers, statesmen and scholars, students and beggars, pilgrims and outlaws whom one found on the roads; but it was, above all, merchants dealing with spices and myrrh, gold and satin, weapons and pearls. Travel, as an end in itself, was unknown until well into the eighteenth century.
   >
   > H. Enzensberger. A Theory of Tourism. *New German Critique*, 1996 (68): 122

5. Translated by James Legge.
6. Kong Yingda. *Annotations of Book of Changes*. Beijing: Jiuzhou Press, 2004: 516. The text here is translated by James Legge.
7. Gong Pengchen. *A Spiritual and Cultural Historiography of Travel*. Shijaizhuang: Hebei Education Press, 2001: 153.
8. Huang Xunzhai. *Collected Writings on Chinese Characters*. Changsha: Yuelu Publishing House, 1998: 18.
9. Translated by Burton Watson.
10. Translated by Burton Watson.
11. Translated by Burton Watson.
12. J. D. Frodsham. The Origin of Chinese Nature Poetry. *Asia Major*, 1960, 8: 68–104.
13. Lu Kanru & Feng Yuanjun. *History of Chinese Poetry*. Jinan: Shangdong University Press, 1996: 285.
14. Yu-kung Kao. The Aesthetics of Regulated Verse. *The Vitality of the Lyric Voice*, 1987: 332–386. https://doi.org/10.1515/9781400858385.332.
15. J. D. Frodsham. The Origin of Chinese Nature Poetry. *Asia Major*, 1960, 8: 68–104.
16. Translated by John David Frodsham.
17. Translated by John David Frodsham.
18. Lin Geng. *A Comprehensive Study on Tang Poetry*. Beijing: People's Literature Publishing House, 1987: 70.
19. Chen Yinchi. *Buddhist cosmology*. Kunming: Yunnan people's Publishing House, 2001: 62.
20. Lin Geng. *A Comprehensive Study on Tang Poetry*. Beijing: People's Literature Publishing House, 1987: 66.
21. Lin Geng. A *Comprehensive Study on Tang Poetry*. Beijing: People's Literature Publishing House, 1987: 75.
22. Lin Geng. *A Brief History of Chinese Literature*. Beijing: Peking University Press, 1988: 114.
23. Yuan Xingpei. *A Study on Chinese Poetic Art*. Beijing: Peking University Press, 1998: 362.
24. Mu Zhai. *The Prospering of Jian'an Nature Poetry*. See http://muzhaiwenxue.bokee.com/4588198.html. [2006-09-29].

25 Translated by Red Pine.
26 Translated by David Knechtges.
27 Translated by David Knechtges.
28 Yu-kung Kao. The Aesthetics of Regulated Verse. *The Vitality of the Lyric Voice*, 1987: 332–386.
29 This term refers to Cao Cao曹操 (155–220), Cao Pi 曹丕 (187－226) and Cao Zhi曹植 (192–232).
30 Leo Ou-fan Lee. Lonely Traveler—Self-image in Modern Chinese Literature. *The Pursuit of Modernity*. Beijing: Joint Publishing, 2000: 70.
31 Gong Pengchen. Preface. *A Spiritual and Cultural Historiography of Travel*. Shijiazhuang: Hebei Education Press, 2001: 5.
32 Guo Shaotang. *Travel: Intercultural Imagination*. Beijing: Peking University Press, 2005: 44.
33 Translated by J. D. Frodsham.
34 Translated by James Legge.
35 Translated by James Legge.
36 Eva Hung. *Rewriting Chinese Translation History*. Hong Kong: RCT of the Chinese University of Hong Kong, 2005: 20.
37 Eva Hung. *Rewriting Chinese Translation History*. Hong Kong: RCT of the Chinese University of Hong Kong, 2005: 22.
38 Eva Hung. *Rewriting Chinese Translation History*. Hong Kong: RCT of the Chinese University of Hong Kong, 2005: 23.
39 Qian Zhongshu et al. *The Translations of Lin Shu*. Beijing: The Commercial Press, 1981: 19.
40 Wang Pinzhen. *Elder Dai's Book of Rites*. Beijing: Chung Hwa Book Co., 1983: 205.
41 Translated by Jane Lai.
42 Qian Zhongshu. *Seven Essays on Literature and Art*. Beijing: Joint Publishing, 2003: 79.
43 Martha P. Y. Cheung. *An Anthology of Chinese Discourse on Translation: Volume One—From Earliest Times to the Buddhist Project*. Manchester: St. Jerome Publishing, 2006: 46.
44 Gong Pengchen. *A Spiritual and Cultural Historiography of Travel*. Shijiazhuang: Hebei Education Press, 2001: 5.
45 Translated by Tolbert McCarroll.
46 Martha P. Y. Cheung. *An Anthology of Chinese Discourse on Translation: Volume One—From Earliest Times to the Buddhist Project*. Manchester: St. Jerome Publishing, 2006: 44.
47 Ma Honglu & Liu Fengshu. *Records of Chinese Transportation*. Chengdu: Sichuan Education Press, 1998: 9.
48 Before the Han Dynasty, "Jiaozhi" referred to the area circumscribed by the borders of the provinces of Hunan, Jiangxi, Guangdong and Guangxi (Hanyu dacidian, 1995 (2): 337).
49 Eva Hung. *Rewriting Chinese Translation History*. Hong Kong, China: RCT of the Chinese University of Hong Kong, 2005: 25.
50 Eva Hung & Yang Chengshu. *The Traditions and Modern Trends of Translation in Asia*). Beijing: Peking University Press. 2000: 30.
51 More details about the position and status of Chinese translators, see Eva Hung's *Rewriting Chinese Translation History*. Hong Kong: RCT of the Chinese University of Hong Kong, 2005: 129–130.
52 Eva Hung & Yang Chengshu. *The Traditions and Modern Trends of Translation in Asia*. Beijing: Peking University Press, 2000: 37.
53 Translated by James Legge.
54 Quoted in Martha Cheung, *An Anthology of Chinese Discourse on Translation, Volume One*.
55 A. Room. *NTC's Dictionary of Changes in Meanings: A Comprehensive Reference to the Major Changes in Meanings in English Words*. Lincolnwood, IL: National Textbook Co., 1996: 271.

56 E. Leed. *The Mind of the Traveler: From Gilgamesh to Global Tourism.* New York: Basic Books, 1991: 5–6.
57 E. Heale. Traveling Abroad: The Poet as Adverturer. // M. Pincombe (ed.), T*ravels and Translations in the Sixteenth Century: Selected Papers from the second International Conference of the Tudor Symposium.* Hampshire: Ashgate, 2004: 3.
58 J. Clifford. *Routes: Travel and Translation in the Late Twentieth Century.* Cambridge, MA and London: Harvard University Press, 1999: 66.
59 J. Urry. *The Tourist Gaze* (2nd edition). London: SAGE Publications, 2002: 4.
60 G. V. D. Abbeele. Introduction: The Economy of Travel. // *Travel as Metaphor: From Montaigne to Rousseau.* Minneapolis and Oxford: University of Minnesota Press, 1992: xv.
61 J. Clifford. *Routes: Travel and Translation in the Late Twentieth Century.* Cambridge, MA and London: Harvard University Press, 1999: 34–35.
62 R. Mill & A. Morrison. *The Tourism System: An Introductory Text.* Englewood Cliffs, NJ: Prentice-Hall, 1985: xvii.
63 C. Rojek & J. Urry. Transformations of Travel and Theory. // *Touring Cultures: Transformations of Travel and Theory.* London: Routledge, 1997: 1–2.
64 J. Clifford. *Routes: Travel and Translation in the Late Twentieth Century.* Cambridge, MA and London: Harvard University Press, 1999: 33.
65 Danial Henri Pageaux. Imagology Studies: From Literary History to Poetics (trans. Kuai YiPing). Meng Hua. *Imagology.* Beijing: Peking University Press, 2001: 210.
66 J. Urry. *The Tourist Gaze* (2nd edition). London: SAGE Publications, 2002: 5.
67 J. Urry. *The Tourist Gaze* (2nd edition). London: SAGE Publications, 2002: 4–5.
68 Clifford J. *Routes: Travel and Translation in the Late Twentieth Century.* Cambridge, Mass. & London: Harvard University Press, 1999: 33.
69 J. Clifford. Traveling Cultures. // L. Grossberg et al. (eds.), *Cultural Studies.* New York and London: Routledge, 1992: 105.
70 Guo Shaotang. *Travel: Intercultural Imagination.* Beijing: Peking University Press, 2005: 45.
71 E. Leed. *The Mind of the Traveler: From Gilgamesh to Global Tourism.* New York: Basic Books, 1991: 22.
72 Yan-zi. *The Spring and Autumn Annals of Yan-zi* (trans. & Annotated. Tang Hua). Beijing: Zhonghua Book Company, 2011: 403.
73 C. Rojek & J. Urry. Transformations of Travel and Theory. // *Touring Cultures: Transformations of Travel and Theory.* London: Routledge, 1997: 1.
74 E. Leed. *The Mind of the Traveler: From Gilgamesh to Global Tourism.* New York: Basic Books, 1991: 3.
75 [1] E. Partridge. *Origins: An Etymological Dictionary of Modern English.* London: Routledge, 1990: 725.
76 G. E. Brown. Translation and the Definition of Sovereignty: The Case of Elizabeth Tudor. // M. Pincombe (ed.), *Travels and Translations in the Sixteenth Century: Selected Papers from the Second International Conference of the Tudor Symposium.* Hampshire: Ashgate, 2004: 88.
77 A.F. Kinney. Introduction. // M. Pincombe (ed.), *Travels and Translations in the Sixteenth Century: Selected Papers from the Second International Conference of the Tudor Symposium.* Hampshire: Ashgate, 2004: xiii.
78 L. Polezzi. Rewriting Tibet: Italian Travellers in English Translation. *The Translator*, 1998, 2(4): 322.
79 J. Clifford. Traveling Cultures. // L. Grossberg et al. (eds.), *Cultural Studies.* New York and London: Routledge, 1992: 110.

# 2 Text Travel and Canon Construction

The lines of travel, according to Said Islam, do not exist in isolation; they are glued to each other in complex forms. "Each route corresponds to a specific spatial concept, boundary type, power relationship, organization method, and subjective mode."[1] As stated in the previous chapter, travel and translation, as some sorts of discourse practice, are usually influenced and restricted by contextual factors and power relations. In the process of various types of transformation and flow, text travel and canon construction, as two important forms of travel and translation, will inevitably involve the subjective attitudes of authors, travelers, translators and canon makers. The historical outlook and the destiny of the traveled text will change accordingly along with varied travel routes, writing perspectives, discourse selections, discursive patterns and transitions, historical narratives, spatial displacement, translation strategies and canon construction. It is the combined force of these contextual variables that defines the subject, orientations, causes and results of text travel as well as the object, ways and channels of canon construction.

## 2.1 Traveling Theory and Its Significance in Translation Studies

After crossing the boundary, the text of departure reaches its arrivals where the overall environment is different from the one where it departs. To achieve harmonious symbiosis with local culture, it will adapt itself to the local customs or be borrowed and rewritten. Thus, the original identity of the text, to some extent, is deformed or even undergoes an overall transformation. However, in translation studies, the identity variation in text travel has been less concerned. It is also rare for people to inquire into the host culture system to see how it drives translators to "create" "otherness" for their readers, and how to legitimize this "otherness" to be adapted to become a member of the host cultural system. Questions arise, such as: How does the text or the cultural meaning in the text travel between the two cultures? What are the elements contained in this travel process? What is the travel itinerary? Is it designed? How about the travel models? What are the models of arrivals? What is the result of this travel?

## 2.1.1  Traveling Theory

Edward Said (1935–2003), the world-renowned contemporary cultural critic, begins to think about the relationship between theoretical variation and spatial displacement after analyzing how the Paris context of Lucien Goldmann (1913–1970) weakened and degraded the radical rebellious consciousness and critical thoughts of George Lukacs (1885–1971). He observes:

> We are also recognizing the extent to which theory is a response to a specific social and historical situation of which an intellectual occasion is a part. Thus, what is insurrectionary consciousness in one instance becomes tragic vision in another, for reasons that are elucidated when the situations in Budapest and Paris are seriously compared.[2]

Therefore, Said puts forward the concept of "Traveling Theory". He points out that

> such movement into a new environment is never unimpeded. It necessarily involves processes of representation and institutionalization different from those at the point of origin. This complicates any account of the transplantation, transference, circulation, and commerce of theories and ideas.[3]

Said, however, still holds the view that the movement itself contains a discernible and recurrent pattern. The following are the four main stages of the traveling theory and thought he proposes:

> First, there is a point of origin, or what seems like one, a set of circumstances in which the idea came to birth or entered discourse. Second, there is a distance transversed, a passage through the pressure of various contexts as the idea moves from an earlier point to another time and place where it will come into new prominence. Third, there is a set of conditions—call them conditions of acceptance or, as an inevitable part of acceptance, resistance—which then confronts the transplanted theory or idea, making possible its introduction or toleration, however alien it might appear to be. Fourth, the now full (or partly) accommodated (or incorporated) idea is to some extent transformed by its new uses, its new position in a new time and place.[4]

The proposition of his theory aroused wide interest and heated discussions in academic circles. Zhao Xifang says,

> Despite Said's vagueness, his conception of "Traveling Theory" with its novelty still attracts the attention of Western academia. Linking "Traveling Theory" with translation issues enables people to think differently, thereby gaining new understandings of a series of academic propositions since the 1980s.[5]

Lydia Liu criticizes, however:

> His discussion does not go beyond the usual argument that theory is always a response to changing social and historical circumstances. And the traveling aspect of his theory is abandoned along the way. . . . Perhaps the notion itself lacked the kind of intellectual rigor needed for its own fulfillment. Indeed, who does the traveling? Does theory travel? If so, how? Granting theory such subjectivity leads to a further question: What is the means of transportation? Not only does the concept of traveling theory tend to affirm the primacy of theory (or Western theory in the context of Said's book) by endowing the latter with full-fledged, mobile subjectivity, but it fails to account for the vehicle of translation. With the suppression of that vehicle, travel becomes such an abstract idea that it makes no difference in which direction theory travels (from West to East or vice versa) and for what purpose (cultural exchange imperialism or colonization?), or in which language and for what audience.[6]

Interestingly, while the former reads the connections between "Traveling Theory" and translation and asserts that this theory will promote the development of translation studies, the latter questions the disconnection between the two that makes it difficult to justify the theory itself. The former's analysis is based on Benjamin and Derrida's thought of translation as a kind of "transformation" and "différance". He then introduces Said's discussion of time and space movement and theoretical variation, and with Said's referring to the problems of "misreadings" and "misinterpretations", the author naturally associates this theory with translation studies and uses it to analyze the rewriting and acceptance of Western literary texts in China.

Whether it is Benjamin's "afterlife" or Derrida's "différance", they both imply a metaphor about travel. The travel of the original text from "this life" to the "afterlife" undoubtedly contains various factors of transference, movement and transformation. It includes not only movement in form but also transference in content, which is consistent with the connotation of travel. The mobility and instability of the text are what Derrida calls "différance". Even in Said's view, the so-called "misreadings" and "misinterpretations" are nothing more than the transference of thoughts and theories in different contexts:

> We have become so accustomed to hearing that all borrowings, readings and interpretations are misreadings and misinterpretations that we are likely to consider the Lukacs-Goldmann episode as just another bit of evidence, even Marxists, misreads and misinterprets. I find such a conclusion completely unsatisfying. . . . It seems to me perfectly possible to judge misreadings as part of a historical transfer of ideas and theories from one setting to another.[7]

Lydia Liu, however, starts her analysis from the post-colonial metaphors of interlingual practice and travel. In the chapter "Traveling Theory and Postcolonial Critique", Lydia Liu repeatedly asks two questions: (1) What role do translation and related practices play in the construction of relations of power between the so-called First and Third worlds?[8] (2) What happens when theory produced in one language gets translated into another?[9] These two questions might be where Said has "vagueness". Therefore, Lydia Liu thinks that "Travel Theory and Travel Theorist", the special issue published on *Inscriptions* in 1989, is a collective effort of post-colonial travel theorists to practice and revise Said's theory. She says: "By focusing on the complexity of the self-positioning of the theorist in the post-colonial context, Lata Mani's move helps revise Said's original conception of traveling theory."[10]

According to Liu, "Since the modern intellectual tradition in China began with translation, adaption, appropriation and other interlingual practices related to the West, it is inevitable that this inquiry should take translation as its point of departure."[11] Therefore, in her book *Translingual Practice: Literature, National Culture and Translated Modernity—China, 1900–1937*, she emphasizes the role translation plays in interlingual practice and post-colonial context. In fact, translations, since the late Qing Dynasty have greatly enriched modern Chinese knowledge and the modern Chinese cultural system. Therefore, "translation" cannot be overlooked for its significance as a tool of text and traveling theory. Lydia Liu also pointed out that "interactions among different languages in translations and interlingual practices play a vital part in the historical process. Today, cross-cultural studies cannot get conducted without taking the complexity of historical exchanges among different languages into full consideration."[12]

### 2.1.2 Translation and Travel

Said's "Traveling Theory" is, first and foremost, a theory of cultural criticism, which originated in the background of the Second World War and economic crisis, as well as the resulting large-scale intellectual migration and ideological exile. It is undeniable that translation is a very important and ineluctable factor in the process of knowledge migration and thoughts exile or traveling theory. Theoretical and textual variation can be explained as the change of social and historical contexts, as what the text theory of deconstruction and Said have done. However, translators or/and interpreters, who play an important role in the process of theoretical or text travel, may be insusceptible to contextual changes due to their cultural position and political attitude. There are other reasons for the theoretical and textual variation, then. The key to the problem is to investigate the subjectivity consciousness of the translator and/or interpreter and the intended communicative purposes in interlingual practice.

Just as any travel cannot fail to take into account the gazees and the local customs of the destination, translation must also take into account the target audience and the context of arrivals. Discussions on Skopos theory and translation ethics, therefore, are extremely heated at present. According to Skopos theory, translation is an act, and all acting is goal-oriented, so translation is subject to its purpose. The most important factor that determines the translation's purpose is the target audience, that is, the intended readers of the translation. They have their cultural background, expectations for translations, and intended communication demands. The so-called "translating" by the Skopos theorists, therefore, is the act of producing a certain text for a certain purpose and target audience in the target context.

Hans Vermeer (1930–2010), a German functionalism theorist and the pioneer of Skopos, states that "translation cannot pursue the faithful reproduction of the source language's surface structure while ignoring the communicative purposes of target texts. Instead, it should try its best to serve for the purposes of the cultural background of the target language."[13] Doubtlessly, Skopos theory does not exclude the possibility that "loyalty" is also a reasonable purpose. It just opposes the viewpoint that regards literal translation as the only standard of "loyalty". Evidently, the emphasis of Skopos theorists on the target text and culture makes the status of the source text in this theory inferior to that of the start text in equivalence theory. The source text is no longer the priority in the translator's decision. It merely exists to provide the target audience with certain information they are willing to accept. Vermeer terms this as the "dethronement" of the source text. In this way, the relationship between the original text and translation is not the "mirror-image" model that the traditional translation studies have tried to display, because any kind of translation, more or less, includes rewriting and manipulation of the original text, as well as Said's mentioning of, "transformation to some extent by its new use and location in the new temporal and space".[14] To some extent, the localization, domestication or variation of theory and text in the process of travel are theoretically or practically normal and inevitable, therefore.

Contemporary translation studies, including Skopos theorists and deconstructionists, focus more on the text and culture of arrivals than on the text and culture of the departure. Susan Bassnett (1945–) commented on the "source text" that "the concept of the original is a product of Enlightenment thinking. It is a modern invention, belonging to a materialist age, and carries with it all kinds of commercial implications about translation, originality and textual ownership."[15] Santos further concludes, "We are in an era of skepticism about the origin. . . . We always insist that everything has been translated, and there is no such thing as the origin in the world."[16] The translation theorists of cultural school and German Functionalism, nevertheless, emphasize and value the communicative function of the translated text. Lawrence Venuti (1953–) reminds the readers that the authoritative status of the source text and the original author is deeply ingrained, but the translated text and the translator are in an embarrassing position.

> Translation is marginalized today by an essentially romantic conception of authorship. . . . The "original" is an unchanging monument of the human imagination ("genius"), transcending the linguistic, cultural, and social changes. . . . The "original" is a form of self-expression appropriate to the author, a copy of a copy, derivative, simulative, false, an image without resemblance.[17]

Travel log writing, similar to the cultural practice of translation, is also a reproduction of a copy. It can be imagined that in the process of translation, the translator will always subconsciously domesticate and reconstruct the original text out of "native consciousness" and "indigenous cultural tendency". However, with scruples about the authority of the original text and the original author, the translator always more or less or evasively claims that his or her translation is just to faithfully reproduce the original text. The loyalty that travelers and authors of travel logs demonstrate, similarly, is just to convince the reader that what they claim to be true is reality and truth, which is often not the case. As someone has claimed, the cultural experience gained by travelers in the travel process is, to a large extent, an unreal experience, a self-staged drama based on their cultural inclination. Even if what they see and hear is true, their cultural reflection can be distorted and transformed into a self-righteous action.[18] This kind of statement of cultural history and translation history has been already a cliché in postmodern historiography.

Bassnett has pointed out that

> map-making, traveling, and translating are not transparent activities. They are very definitely located activities, with points of origin, points of departure and arrivals. . . . The time has come not only for us to compare accounts by travelers, but to question the premise on which those accounts were written in the first place.[19]

The so-called "very definitely located activities" are just synonyms of "very definitely aimed activities" or "very definitely utilitarian activities", and the "premise" she refers to is the communicative purpose expected by these actors. Bassnett further emphasizes that

> the map-maker, the translator and the travel writer are not innocent producers of text. The works they create are not part of a process of manipulation that shapes and conditions our attitudes to other cultures while purporting to be something else.[20]

Polezzi has also repeatedly pointed out that the British discourse's appropriation of Italian texts is

> according to the conventions of English travel writing and put to the service of its interests, whether they were those of the imperial archive in the first half of this century, or serving the tourism industry interests of the second half of the century or those of the tourist industry in the second.[21]

The definite purpose and deliberate translation manipulation blur the boundary between translation and rewriting, translation and variation, translation and creation, translation and travel.

For these reasons, Clifford analyzes,

> I do think "postmodernism" can serve as a translation term, to help make visible and valid something strange (as modernism did for the early

twentieth-century primitivists discovering African and Oceanian "art"), but I want to insist on the crucial traduttore in the traditore, the lack of an equals sign, the reality of what's missed and distorted in the very act of understanding, appreciating, describing. One keeps getting closer and farther away from the truth of different cultural and historical predicaments. This reflects a historical process by which the global is always localized, its range of equivalences cut down to size. It's a process that can be contained temporarily, violently but not stopped.[22]

"Traduttore" can be tracked almost everywhere in text travel and translation practice, thus further widening the gap between texts and facts, texts and realities. In the meanwhile, the boundaries between translation and travel, translation and creation, and history and fiction are increasingly becoming blurred. As Clifford mentioned earlier, "global is always localized", and such human practices will never stop stepping forward. In other words, the localization and creative reconstruction emerging among text travel, on the surface, is a subjective choice, but in essence, it is a common practice in the process of human history.

## 2.2 Travel Model and Travel Route

Besides the "vagueness" problems in the process of translation, Said has also been criticized for his arguments in traveling theory.

> There is a set of conditions—call them conditions of acceptance or, as an inevitable part of acceptance, resistance—which then confronts the transplanted theory or idea, making possible its introduction or toleration, however alien it might appear to be.[23]

Lydia Liu has commented that

> Said's notion of traveling theory is generally interpreted as if the theory (or Western theory) were a hero from a European picaresque narrative who initiates the trip, encounters obstacles enroute, and always ends up being accommodated one way or another by the host country.[24]

The earlier-mentioned statement of Said may be appropriate if it is used to analyze and cite a single case. But there are an inherent incommensurability and lack of thoroughness in logic if it is to be extended to the height of universal theory. Secondly, Said's discussion of traveling theory is merely confined to the translingual travel of theory and ignores the synchronicity and diachronic travel of theory in the same cultural context.

### 2.2.1 Three Components of Travel

Admittedly, there never exists a theory that is perfectly constructed in form and content. Said has also stated, "Writings on theory, criticism, demystification, deconsecration, and decentralization are imperfect. Therefore, the theory is doomed to continue its travel, but always it will break free of fetters, move, migrate and maintain a certain state of exile."[25] Doubtlessly, the construction of a theory not only needs to be tested externally but also needs to be verified within its cultural norms for its validity and visibility. The response of the internal cultural system, at least, provides the initial environment for the theory's translingual travel. The external and internal parts are inherently linked, and therefore neither can be examined in isolation from the other. Only in the ever-changing social and historical context can the explanatory power and validity of the theory be comprehensively tested.

Regarding travel, Leed also input into this:

The history of travel is the study of a force—mobility—that has shaped human history and is observably at work in our present. Mobility is a force of change operating through distinctly different events that make up the structure of the journey: departure, passage, and arrival. The transformations of travel are an accumulation of effects derived from this sequence of distinctive situations: from departures that detach individuals from a familiar context: from passages that set them in motion across space; from arrivals that establish new bonds and identifications between strangers, creating a new union and coherence between self and context. Each of these events has its specific character and must be examined in its own right. . . . Each of these events, through many repetitions, produces and serves a particular set of needs. Departure may serve the need for detachment, purification, liberty, "individuality", escape, self-definition. Passage serves and generates a need for motion but may in turn generate other longings: for stability in a condition of disequilibrium, for fixed orientation in a world of flux, for immutability in the midst of transience. Arrivals serve a need for human association, for membership, definition, even confinement, and may, in turn, engender a growing desire for departure, liberty, and escape. In any one place and moment, these needs may be perceived as opposed and conflictual, but they are not when sequenced in the form of the journey. Here may lie the eternal appeal of travel, it resolves a logic of contradiction, a logic of place, into a logic of sequence, an order of change and transformation which serves and fosters a variety of human longings: for motion and rest, liberty and confinement, indeterminacy and definition.[26]

Travel means the acceptance of mobility and variation, while the travel model is shaped by the combination of departure, passage and arrival. In the travel process, however, the relations among various factors and forces are both hostile and harmonious. In the case of text travel, when the text as a traveler starts from the departure's cultural polysystem, traverses various time and space environments, spatial distances and contextual pressure passages, and enters the cultural polysystem of arrivals, it will always encounter the alienation and resistance from the mainstream culture of arrivals. In the process of breaking free from all sorts of constraints to gain legitimacy, a certain number of procedures to control, select, dissolve, organize, domesticate and reconstruct the travel text and its loaded new discourse is the key step in the process of text travel.

Regarding travel routes, the factors and issues involved are equally complex and diverse. Islam (1953–) reminds us in *Traveling Ethics* that "the lines of travel do not exist in isolation, they are glued to each other in complex forms. Each route corresponds to a specific spatial concept, boundary type, power relationship, organization method, and subjective mode."[27] Questions arise such as: who travels? for whom? why? where? when? The answers to these questions are ultimately to be sought in power relations, knowledge and beliefs, as well as discourse systems of the departure and arrivals.

### 2.2.2 *Intralingual Travel and Interlingual Travel*

In the 1950s, Roman Jakobson (1896–1982), based on the nature and characteristics of semiotic meaning, categorized translation into three different types in his seminal paper "On the Linguistic Aspects of Translation".

> 1. Intralingual translation, or rewording, is an interpretation of verbal signs by means of the same language; 2. Interlingual translation, or translation proper, is an interpretation of verbal signs by means of some other languages. 3. Intersemiotic translation, or transmutation is an interpretation of verbal signs by means of signs of a nonverbal sign system.[28]

"Intralingual translation" refers to the transference of verbal signs within the same language—for instance, the interpretation of ancient Chinese by modern Chinese. "Interlingual translation" specifically refers to the transference among different verbal signs—for example, the transference between Chinese and English, French and Italian. "Intersemiotic translation" refers to the transference among different sign systems—for example, the expression of words (linguistic symbols) is transferred into the expression of colors and shapes (pictorial symbols) in paintings, etc.

With regard to the "interferential" nature of "translation" and "travel", this book builds on Jacobson's concepts of "intralingual translation" and "interlingual translation" to put forward two categories of text travel: intralingual travel and interlingual travel. Unlike Jacobson's concerns about the action of translation and language transformation, the "intralingual travel" and "interlingual travel" in this book are broader in both connotation and denotation. They not only include translation and interpretation at the level of linguistic transformation, but also examine the constraints and influence of the subject cultural norms on the translational action, and on this basis explore issues such as circulation, dissemination and canonization of the text. In other words, we can roughly define "intralingual travel" as the circulation and dissemination of a start text within the same cultural polysystem. We can examine the text at the very beginning of its existence, and also discuss its translation, interpretation, circulation, dissemination and canonization in different historical contexts. The so-called "interlingual travel" thus refers to the translation, interpretation, circulation, dissemination and canonization of the departure text in the cultural polysystem of arrivals.

The discussion on intralingual travel of CMPs in this book focuses on its translation, interpretation, circulation, dissemination and canonization within the cultural polysystem of China where the text departs. The investigation on the interlingual travel of CMPs is primarily limited to its translation, interpretation, circulation, dissemination and canonization between the cultural polysystems of points of departure and of arrivals.

## 2.3 Canon and Canon Construction

It is self-evident that the so-called "canon" is the institutionalized text, which is highly related to power relations and mainstream discourse. The process of canon construction or canonization, on one hand, depends on the flow and shifts of power relations represented by dominant ideology, dominant poetics and literary patrons; on the other hand, it depends on the localization and reconstruction of translators in the process of text travel. That is to say, the various forces of "canonization" and "decanonization" are always in a state of waxing and waning.

### 2.3.1 Etymology of "Canon"

The word "canon" can be translated into Chinese as "Guifan" (规范, norm), "Zhengdian" (正典, canon), "Dianlü" (典律, law) and "Jingdian" (经典, classic). From its origin, nevertheless, the word can be traced back to the ancient Greek word "kanōn", meaning a "reed" or "rod", an instrument of measurement, and later its meaning extended to "rule" or "law". In early European languages, "canon" was used to refer to a particular text or author, but in later times it appeared in Christian creeds and literary principles, etc., especially in the books of the *Bible* and the early Christian theologians.[29] In Alexandrian Greece, literary critics used kanōn in rhetoric to refer specifically to some immaculate styles and writing norms, in a sense similar to the modern word "classic".

In ancient Chinese, "Jing" 经 and "Dian" 典 are originally two relatively independent but mutually referential concepts. According to Zhang Binglin (章炳麟, 1869–1936), "Jing", the woven silk threads, is called "Sūtra" in Sanskrit, and "Jing" in the early period should be "ribbons that weave the bamboo books".[30] Later, people called the vertical thread on the woven cloth "Jing" and the horizontal tread "Wei" 纬, as in "Qingcai" (情采, "Emotion and Literary Expression") of *Wenxin Diaolong* (《文心雕龙》, *The Literary Heart and the Carving of the Dragons*): "emotion is the wrap of literary pattern, linguistic form the woof of ideas. Only when the wrap is straight can linguistic form be meaningful."[31] Because of its implied meaning of "rule and law", "Jing" was later extended to the meaning of "Dianfan" (典范, model) and "Changdao" (常道, proper practice), for example, in "Jinxin xia" (尽心下, "Jinxin II") in *Mengzi* (《孟子》, *Mengzi*): "the superior man seeks simply to bring back the unchanging standard. If the standard is correct, the masses will rouse virtue. When they are so aroused, perversity and wickedness will disappear." "Jing" was also regarded as "external" and "supreme", as can be found in "Zongjing Disan" (宗经第三, "The Classics as Literary Sources") of *Wenxin Diaolong* (《文心雕龙》, *The Literary Heart and the Carving of the Dragons*): "the works dealing with the universal principles of the Great Trinity [heaven, earth, and man] are known as Jing. By Jing we mean an expression of the absolute or constant Tao or principle, that great teaching which is unalterable."

As for "Dian" 典, in ancient Chinese, people not only used it to signify "law", but also to describe writings with "norms" and "elegance" as "Dian" 典. For example, in "Da Xuanpuyuan Jiangsong Qiling" (《答玄圃园讲颂启令》, "Reply to Xuanpuyuan Ode "), Xiao Tong (萧统) commented that "the writing is Dian and flowery, elegant and refined." This interpretation of "Dian" 典 has already preset the criteria to select and define mainstream literary norms and canonical texts in ancient Chinese literary discourse. "The writing is Dian and flowery, elegant and refined" is the right path for literature, while the popular and low literature will undoubtedly suffer exclusion. Xiao Tong's (萧统) *Wen Xuan or Selections of Refined Literature* is just based on such a poetic standard. With Xiao Tong's prominent patronage status, this selection hence becomes a model for later literary anthologies to follow and naturally sets a golden rule for canonizers to take. Similar to "Jing" 经, "Dian" 典 is also endowed with the meaning of "Hengchang" 恒常 (constancy), for example, in "Shigu Shang" (《释诂》上, "Interpretation (Part One)") from *Erya* (《尔雅》, *Erh-ya*). "Dian" here was interpreted as "Being chang" (常也, being constant), together with "Fa" (法, standard), "Yi" (彝, norm), "Ze" (则, criterion), "Xing" (刑, punishment), "Fan" (范, model), "Ju" (矩, rule), "Yong" (庸, mediocre), "Heng" (恒, permanence), "Lü" (律, law), "Zhi" (秩, order), etc.

In the discourse of ancient Chinese literature, what "Jing" and "Dian" represent is the eternal and undisputed literary paradigm expected by canonizers. According to research, "Jingdian" (经典, canon) as an independent compound word was first written in "Sunbao Zhuan" (孙宝传, "The Biography of Sun Bao"), volume 77 of *Hanshu* (《汉书》, *The Book of Han* or *History of Former Han*): "the duke of Zhou is a great sage, so is the duke of Zhao. There was still discord between the two, which was recorded in the Confucian Jingdian, but it did no harm to the noble image of either." The "Jingdian" here refers to the classic as a model, and the so-called "Jingdian" in modern society primarily refers to "Jing" in terms of traditional Confucian classics.

As a matter of fact, since the Tang Dynasty (618–907), the classification of books in ancient China has had its own rule to carry on for generations, namely, "Jing" (经, classics), "Shi" (史, histories), "Zi" (子, masters) and "Ji" (集, collections), generally known as "Sibu" (四部, Four Categories) or "Siku" (四库, Four Treasuries). It is worth noting that in this classification, "Jing" has always been placed as the prior of the four, as the explanation in "Jingjizhi" (经籍志, "Catalogue") in *Jiutangshu* (《旧唐书》, *Old Book of Tang*), "Sibu is sequenced by "Jia" 甲, "Yi" 乙, "Bing" 丙, "Ding" 丁. "Jia" is "Jing" (经); "Yi" is "Shi" (史); "Bing" is "Zi" (子); "Ding" is "Ji" (集), through which the canonical status of "Jing" is displayed.

Actually, "once a text becomes a canon, it is expected to be of great significance. Especially in terms of politics and morality, it is supposed to be a model."[32] In ancient Chinese culture, *Shi* (《诗》, *Book of Odes*), *Shu* (《书》, *Book of Documents*), *Li* (《礼》, *Book of Rites*), *Yue* (《乐》, *Book of Music*), *Yi* (《易》, *I Ching or Book of Changes*), *Chunqiu* (《春秋》, *Spring and Autumn Annals*) were firstly defined as "canon". It was because for the canonizers these six Confucian books, known as the "Liujing" (六经, Six Canons) or "Liuyi" (六艺, Six Arts), were "canons of propriety and righteousness". When it comes to the historical background and social system, "the establishment of institutionalized study on Confucian classics in the Han Dynasty (202 BCE–220 CE) ensured the teaching, communication and annotation of Confucian classics."[33] The Confucian classics, therefore, have long been steadily held as "jing", and "Six Canons" becomes synonymous with main Confucian classics.[34] Later on, based on the "Six Canons", some literary and exemplary texts of Confucian books in the Pre-Qin Dynasty (?–221 BCE) were bestowed the status of "canon". Then, within the polysystem of the ancient Chinese literature, the concept of "literary canons" gradually came into being, as well as related works recognized by canonizers at that time, such as the earlier-mentioned *Wen Xuan or Selections of Refined Literature* compiled by Xiao Tong (萧统).

*2.3.2 Canon and Power*

The review of the etymology of "canon" only gives us a glimpse of its classical meaning. How then does the modern academic community reckon it? In 1972, Paul Lauter (1932–), an American literary historian, defined "canon" as "a set of literary works that are generally bestowed with cultural power, namely, collection of major philosophical, political, and religious texts".[35] In his essay "To Readers" from *The Heath Anthology of American Literature*, Lauter considered, "canon" as "a list of works and authors that people believe are important enough to be read, studied, written and taught".[36] Objectively speaking, Lauter's definition is vague because "no mention is made of the agency which makes the selection and expresses the value judgments, or prescribes the texts as reading matter in school."[37] His definition clearly fails to answer the question "whose canon?"

As for Confucian canons in China, the reason why some books and texts in the Pre-Qin Dynasty (?–221 BCE) could be called "Jingdian" (经典, Canons), according to some scholars, lies in two aspects:

> For one thing, it is owing to the division of officials and teachers and the appearance of private schools that canons were constructed through an oral tradition of recounting and retelling. For another, to highlight the status of their school, schools tended to elevate their important works to canons to make themselves prominent and competitive.[38]

It is evident that the birth of "canon" is closely related to the transition of social systems, power relations and competitions of interest. In other words, the construction of "canon" is by no means "innocent". At the same time, it can be noticed that "canon" is not the object of transcendental existence: "Whose canon is it?" is a question that needs to be examined in specific cases; and the canonical status of the author and work cannot be "constant", although ancestors expected it can, because "any literary tradition is a process of continual emergence and interpretation of canons."[39] Moreover, "the tensions between canonized and non-canonized cultures are universal. They are present in every human culture, because a non-stratified human society simply does not exist, not even in Utopia."[40] Due to the potential challenges of non-canonized texts and non-mainstream culture, as well as the competitions and struggles for the central order of the literary system in various fields, and the historical evolution of literary standards, the then-assumed canonical texts would in later years undergo a fundamental reversal of power and status, and thus suffer "decanonization". Its canonical status is very likely to be replaced by the non-canonized texts, which makes the "center" and "periphery" of the literary polysystem shift. Conversely, texts that were previously "marginalized" will also experience a migration from the "periphery" to the "center" as a new literary order and system emerge.

The unstable relations between canonization and non-canonization, center and periphery, mainstream and non-mainstream, primary and secondary mainly depend on the change of the whole social and cultural context, especially that of power relations, because "the canon will vary with the power rule."[41] The "power rule" and "power relation" mentioned here include not only political ideological factors but also mainstream poetic standards that do not contradict the dominant ideology, as well as other important motives that affect the construction of textual canons, such as literary patrons who maintain and formulate the authority of literary "game rules". For example, those "red canons" like *Linhaixueyuan* (《林海雪原》, *Tracks in The Snowy Forest*) and *Hongyan* (《红岩》, *Red Crag*), born in the era of Chinese revolution, were naturally placed at the center of the literary system when "political" and "revolutionary" were taken as aesthetic standards and canons were defined. In a new historical period, however, especially since the 1990s, the subjectivity of canonical reception has become prominent because of the opening up of politics: the roles of personal reading demands and perceptual experiences in the process of interpreting canons have been highlighted. What this brings is the ordinary state of mind towards the canon, that is, the spirit of equal dialogue and free exploration has replaced the admiring and eulogizing tradition in the past.[42] As a result, the "political" and "revolutionary" nature of these red canons is deconstructed, and the former "canons" are subjected to "decanonization".

### 2.3.3 "Canon" and "Canonization"

Traditional academic studies usually merely focus on the central class and official culture, and the mainstream literary historians in the past also just concentrate on a few writers and works that conform to mainstream values. Itamar Even-Zohar, an Israeli scholar of cultural studies and a representative of polysystem theory, however, argues that the historical study on the literary polysystem should not choose its research object according to the criterion of value judgement. That is to say, literary studies cannot be confined to the study of the so-called "masterpieces", for this kind of elitism is incompatible with the historical study of literature, just as ordinary history books can no longer equate with the biographies of emperors and generals.[43] When only the official products and literary "masterpieces" that meet the standard are studied, roles played by various constraints in the polysystem are often neglected. This naturally leads to the discussion of "canon" and "canonization".

It is undoubted that "canonization" and "canon" are two concepts that are both intrinsically connected and substantially different. With regard to texts and "canonization", Zohar believes that

> in the literary systems, texts, rather than playing a role in the process of canonization, are the outcome of these processes. It is only in their function as representatives of models that texts constitute an active factor in the systemic relations.[44]

In other words, textual canonization is far less concerned with the interior of the text. When it comes to the production of early Christian canonical texts, John Guillory relates that these canonizers

> were not concerned with how beautiful texts were, not with how universal their appeal might be. They acted with a very clear concept of how texts would "measure up" to the standards of their religious community or conformed to their "rule".[45]

It can be seen that the canonization of text is a very complex process of selection and exclusion, which involves many factors.

Zohar distinguishes between two kinds of "canonicity", static canonicity on the level of texts and dynamic canonicity on the level of models. The former means that "a certain text is accepted as a finalized product and inserted into a set of sanctified texts literature (culture) wants to preserve"; the latter "a certain literary model manages to establish itself as a productive principle in the system through the latter's repertoire." The second kind of canonization is the most crucial one for the system's dynamics, for "it is this kind of canonization that generates the canon, which may thus be viewed as the group of survivors of canonization struggles, probably the most conspicuous products of certain successfully established models."[46] Here, Zohar is trying to clarify the connotative meanings of "canonical" and "canonized". "Canonical" is the static "literary text", while "canonized" refers to the dynamic and active sociocultural factors that drive the text, particularly the "literary model" it represents, to enter into the canonized repertoire. Zohar mentions that the boundary between the two terms is rather blurred in some languages, especially in English. For some English and French critics, the former may imply that certain features are inherently "canonical", while the latter emphasizes that this canonical state is the result of a certain act or activity being exercised on certain material, rather than a primordial nature of this material "itself".[47]

The author presents two quite different views on the generation of canons. One is mostly represented by traditional literary critics, who hold that the production of "canon" is a pure literary process and that as long as a work is of high aesthetic value, it is bound to become a "canon". Harold Bloom (1930–2019), for example, says in *The Western Canon* that

> What makes the author and the works canonical? The answer, more often than not, has turned out to be strangeness, a mode of originality that either cannot be assimilated, or that so assimilates us that we cease to see it as strange. Walter Pater (1839—1894) defined Romanticism as adding strangeness to beauty, but I think he characterized all canonical writing rather than the Romantics as such.[48]

Such a way of expression is partly unjustifiable because even the recognition of the inherent and static aesthetic value of a text cannot be determined by the text itself. Then which texts or authors will be considered to be of greater preservation value than others? This is completely determined by "game rules" and the hidden rules of social culture set by the canon users and makers of a certain period. It is these "game rules" and hidden rules of society rather than the artistry of the text itself that manipulate the canonization of the text; it is also these "game rules" and hidden rules of society that determine the so-called value judgments on the text or the author.

Critics of the opposite, however, support the other view. They believe that the formation of the canon encompasses many extra-textual factors, such as politics, economy, gender, class, ethnic group, and power. Cai Zhenxing (蔡振兴) points out that "it is wishful to claim that Dianlü (典律, Law) is the sole, universal and aesthetic value. The existence of law has its history, and it presents itself in accordance with the evidence available in each era."[49] As a matter of fact, from the earliest selection process of canonical texts, it can be seen that the artistry of texts has been diluted or even discarded by canon users and makers from the very beginning. To regard the aesthetic value of texts as the standard to determine the canon, therefore, is merely a Utopian conjecture in the real world. Jane Tompkins (1940–), an American literary historian, also reminds us that

> the relationship between literary anthologies and historical phenomena . . . shows that "literary" value judgments do not rely solely on literary considerations, as the notion of "what is literary" is defined by the shifting historical conditions and resides in it. . . . Not only are works of art not chosen according to any constant criteria, but their nature is always changing according to the prevailing description and evaluation systems. Even if the "same" text keeps appearing in different anthologies, it is no longer the same text at all.[50]

Not all literary texts can turn into canons by virtue of their literary values, nor can they all become the measurement standards and selection benchmarks for outstanding literary works. The vast majority of texts mostly rely on a "powerful description and evaluation system", that is, the power norms and power relations, to achieve their canonical status. When these norms and relations change, the symptoms, criteria and limits of literature change accordingly, and each change gives birth to a new canonical text. For the departure text that travels across borders, if it can smoothly enter the cultural polysystem of arrivals through various contextual pressure channels, and, at the same time, if it can follow and conform to the power norms and discourse norms of arrivals, it is highly likely to achieve a canonical identity in translated literature.

## 2.4 Canon Construction of Translated Texts

Zha Mingjian once defined "translated literary canon" as outstanding translations in the history of translated literature; or translated masterpieces of world literature; or "canonized" foreign literature (translated literature) in the specific cultural context of the target language.[51] This is a more accurate statement, except that it does not include the translated literary canons shaped by intralingual translation. In terms of traditional Chinese translated literary discourse, nevertheless, the so-called "translated literary canon", in the eyes of the general reader and even of some researchers, only includes the first and second "canon" in the previously given definition. The focus of this book, however, is on the third type, that is, how translated texts complete their canon constructions in the literary system of their target language.

Generally accepted, the canonicity of most writers and works is influenced and shaped by power relations like dominant ideology and dominant poetics. Their canonicity, therefore, is in a constant state of being interpreted, deconstructed and reconstructed. Omar Khayyam (1048–1122), a Persian who lived in the 11th century, is perhaps a typical example. Though he is now acknowledged as the greatest Persian mathematician, astronomer and poet, for the Persians at his time he was best known as a scientist. He wrote mathematical monographs in Persian and Arabic, made astronomical charts and was appointed as the celestial official to revise the calendar. What he left were mostly mathematical monographs and astronomical and calendrical writings. Throughout the 11th and 12th centuries, there were no records of his poems, and in the 13th century, only one or two of his poems were mentioned sporadically. In the 15th century, however, he was found to have written more than 500 poems. It was not until more than 700 years after his death that his reputation as a poet was widely recognized. His poetry anthology, *Rubáiyát*, after being "localized" by Edward Fitzgerald (1809–1883), an English poet in the 19th century, achieved recognition and praise from literary patrons such as Dante Gabriel Roessetti (1828–1882), a famous Pre-Raphaelite poet, and Algernon Charles Swinburne (1837–1909).[52] Then *Rubáiyát*, almost forgotten by history, miraculously "came back to life" and "rose to fame" after traveling to the cultural context of arrivals. Nowadays, in the world's canonical literary repertoire, *Rubáiyát* has become one of the leading canons. It is said that there is a special collection room in the New York Public Library in the United States which keeps 500 different versions of Khayyam's *Rubáiyát*.[53]

In the history of Chinese literature, the fates of the obscure "CMPs" and their author have also gone through a process from the periphery to the center, from the layman to the royal, from the secular to the canonical. Due to the constraints of traditional literary norms, the CMPs have long been "marginalized" by Chinese literary historians and literary critics. As they embarked on their legendary interlingual literary journey, nevertheless, their literary quality and social value were explored and constructed to the greatest extent in cultural contexts of arrivals, and their author Han-shan thus gained a far greater literary reputation in arrivals than in his homeland. In the English-speaking world of the 1950s and 1960s, in particular, the CMPs even became the spokesman and the wind indicator of Chinese classical poetry. By the 1980s, in the preface to *25 T'ang Poets: Index to English Translations* (published in 1984), Stephen Soong (1919–1996), a famous translator, marveled that "the most famous Chinese poet, at least for lovers of poetry in the English-speaking world at present, is Han-shan, the monk poet."[54] In her book *Deep Layers of the Text: Cross-cultural Fusion and Gender Exploration* (published in 2018), Chung Ling (钟玲, 1945–) remarked that

> surprisingly, Han-shan fever has not waned in American cultural circles over the past thirty years. . . . As a result, the image of Han-shan is not only localized in the United States but has a new cross-cultural look that bridges the past and the present, as well as the two continents along the Pacific coast.[55]

The influence and dissemination of Han-shan and his poems are enduring and profound.

As stated earlier, compared with the two extra-textual factors of "ideology" and "patronage", the aesthetic value plays a negligible role in the canonized process of translated texts. It is even self-evident that the recognition of the sublime and inferior value of texts is, in actuality, entirely subject to these two extra-textual factors. It can also be noticed that although a translator's cultural attitude can affect his stance towards the dominant ideology and literary norms, his translation strategy is of great possibility to retrograde and deviate from the mainstream tradition. It is more frequent, however, that translators take advantage of the situation, follow the trend and actively adapt to the cultural norms, literary symptoms and power norms of the cultural field of arrivals. Like original authors, translators certainly hope that their translations can become literary canons and production modes of the canonical repertoire for future reference. Translators' discourse practice modes, which make the best use of the circumstances, can naturally contribute to the "canonization" of translated texts better. In that sense, "canon" is the reflection of the dominant ideology of the country and the nation. Therefore, the selection of the canons is inevitably involved in various power relations. As Zhou Yingxiong (周英雄, 1939–) said, "the selection of 'must-read canon' could not be generalized as the result of an administrative order; on the contrary, it has an intricate relationship with the reading community, ideology, commercial behavior, reading taste of the time, etc."[56]

Ordinarily, if a translated text travels to the arrivals where the cultural polysystem at a time is in a vacuum, in a weak state or at a critical turning point, the text then has the prerequisite for being accepted by the culture norms of arrivals. If the text bears aesthetic values, maintains reading interests that are recognized by the cultural polysystem of arrivals, conforms to its dominant ideology, dominant poetics as well as patronage's discourse field, and possesses qualified circulation and dissemination mechanisms, it is possible to become part of the canonical repertoire of this polysystem after being localized and discursively reconstructed by the translator. In other words, the study on the canonization of a translated text needs to focus on the following questions: Does the translated text possess aesthetic values recognized by the cultural polysystem of arrivals? Does it comply with the reading tastes of the reading community and the audience of arrivals at that time?

Does it represent or reflect the dominant ideology? Does it conform to the dominant literary norms and poetic traditions? Does it conflict with and denigrate the prevailing mechanism or not? Is there any sign of counterculture or counterpolitical power? Does it represent the literary interests of the makers and users of canons? Does it correspond to their literary pursuits? Does it have an unobstructed communication and dissemination channel? Does it meet the criteria for canonical selection by literary historians?

If reviewed from the perspective of translation study, the research on the canonization of translated texts needs to consider what Andrew Chesterman (1946–) calls "expectancy norms", that is, the aesthetic expectations on linguistic norms, social norms, and ideology that the target readers of the translated text and its the cultural polysystem of arrivals have. It also needs to take into account a series of "professional norms" that the translator chooses to follow in the translating process, for instance, the selection principles of texts to be translated, the selection criteria of translation policies, and the communication strategies of "appropriate similarity". If the "professional norms" chosen by the translator cater to the "expected norms" of target readers and the target culture to the greatest extent, the translated text will obtain an important prerequisite of being "canonized". Only when the translated text ends up in the history of popular literature or authoritative literary anthologies, as well as in the school classroom, is the process of "canonization" truly completed. Yet there is certainly a possibility that the "canonized" translated text encounters challenges from "de-canonized" discursive practice and falls back into the "non-canonized" sequence.

## Notes

1 S. M. Islam. *The Ethics of Travel: From Marco Polo to Kafka*. Manchester: Manchester University Press, 2000: 56.
2 E. Said. Traveling Theory. // *The World, the Text, and the Critic*. Cambridge, MA: Harvard University Press, 1983: 237.
3 E. Said. Traveling Theory. // *The World, the Text, and the Critic*. Cambridge, MA: Harvard University Press, 1983: 226.
4 E. Said. Traveling Theory. // *The World, the Text, and the Critic*. Cambridge, MA: Harvard University Press, 1983: 226–227.
5 Zhao Xifang. *Translation and Discourse Practice in the New Era*. Beijing: China Social Sciences Press, 2003: 4.

6  L. Liu. Traveling Theory and the Postcolonial Critique. // *Translingual Practice: Literature, National Culture and Translated Modernity—China, 1900–1937*. Stanford: Stanford University Press, 1995: 21.
7  E. Said. Traveling Theory. // *The World, the Text, and the Critic*. Cambridge, MA: Harvard University Press, 1983: 236.
8  L. Liu. *Translingual Practice: Literature, National Culture and Translate Modernity—China, 1900–1937*. Stanford: Stanford University Press, 1995: 21.
9  L. Liu. *Translingual Practice: Literature, National Culture and Translate Modernity—China, 1900–1937*. Stanford: Stanford University Press, 1995: 386.
10 L. Liu. Notes. // *Translingual Practice: Literature, National Culture and Translate Modernity—China, 1900–1937*. Stanford: Stanford University Press, 1995: 385.
11 L. Liu. Host Language and Guest Language. // *Translingual Practice: Literature, National Culture and Translated Modernity—China, 1900–1937*. Stanford: Stanford University Press, 1995: 25.
12 L. Liu. *Interlingual Writing: A Critical Outline of Writing History of Modern Thoughts*. Shanghai: Sanlian Bookstore, 1999: 30.
13 H. J. Vermeer. *A Skopos Theory of Translation (Some Arguments For and Against)*. Heidelberg: TextconText Verlag, 1996: 33.
14 E. Said. Traveling Theory. // *The World, the Text, and the Critic*. Cambridge, MA: Harvard University Press, 1983: 237.
15 S. Bassnett. When Is a Translation Not a Translation. // S. Bassnett & A. Lefevere (eds.), *Constructing Cultures: Essays on Literary Translation*. Clevendon: Multilingual Matters, 1998: 38.
16 S. Santos. A la Recherche de la Poesie Perdue: Poetry and Translation. // *A Poetry of Two Minds*. Athens: University of Georgia Press, 2000: 99.
17 L. Venulti. Introduction. // L. Venulti (ed.), *Rethinking Translation: Discourse, Subjectivity, Ideology*. London and New York: Routledge, 1992: 3.
18 Guo Shaotang. *Travel: Intercultural Imagination*. Beijing: Peking University Press, 2005: 67.
19 S. Bassnett. Constructing Cultures: The Politics of Traveller's Tales. // *Comparative Literature: A Critical Introduction*. Oxford and Cambridge: Blackwell, 1993: 114.
20 S. Bassnett. Constructing Cultures: The Politics of Traveller's Tales. // *Comparative Literature: A Critical Introduction*. Oxford and Cambridge: Blackwell, 1993: 99.
21 L. Polezzi. Rewriting Tibet: Italian Travellers in English Translation. *The Translator*, 1998, 2(4): 338.
22 J. Clifford. Traveling Cultures. // L. Grossberg et al. (eds.), *Cultural Studies*. New York and London: Routledge, 1992: 113.
23 Abozaid, Ahmed. "Re-reading Ibn-Khaldun in the 21st century: traveling theory and the question of authority, legitimacy, and state violence in the modern Arab world." *Arab Studies Quarterly* (2021).
24 L. Liu. *Translingual Practice: Literature, National Culture and Translated Modernity—China, 1900–1937*. Stanford: Stanford University Press, 1995: 21.
25 E. Said. Traveling Theory Reconsidered. // *Reflections on Exile and Other Essays*. Cambridge, MA: Harvard University Press, 2001: 451.
26 E. Leed. *The Mind of the Traveler: From Gilgamesh to Global Tourism*. New York: Basic Books, 1991: 21–22.
27 S. Islam. *The Ethics of Travel: From Marco Polo to Kafka*. Manchester: Manchester University Press, 2000: 56.
28 R. Jakobson. On Linguistic Aspects of Translation. // L. Venuti (ed.), *The Translation Studies Reader* (2nd edition). New York: Routledge, 2004: 139.
29 J. Guillory. Canon. // F. Lentricchia & T. McLaughlin (eds.), *Critical Terms for Literary Study* (2nd edition). Chicago and London: The University of Chicago Press, 1995: 233.
30 Quoted from Zhang Longxi. Culture, Tradition and Modern Interpretation. // *Beyond Cultures*. Beijing: Joint Publishing, 2004: 3.

31 Translated by Shi Youzhong.
32 Zhang Longxi. Culture, Tradition and Modern Interpretation. // *Beyond Cultures*. Beijing: Joint Publishing, 2004: 3.
33 Wang Zhongjiang. The Conditions of Being Classics: Taking Early Confucian Classics as Examples. // Liu Xiaofeng & Chen Shaoming (eds.), *The Power of Classics and Interpretations*. Shanghai: Joint Publishing, 2003: 23.
34 Wang Zhongjiang. The Conditions of Being Classics: Taking Early Confucian Classics as Examples. // Liu Xiaofeng & Chen Shaoming (eds.), *The Power of Classics and Interpretations*. Shanghai: Joint Publishing, 2003: 11.
35 L. Kampf & P. Lauter. *The Politics of Literature: Dissenting Essays on the Teaching of English*. New York: Pantheon Books, 1972: ix.
36 P. Lauter et al. *The Heath Anthology of American Literature*. Lexington: D.C. Heath and Co., 1994: xxxiii.
37 D. Fokkema & E. Ibsch. *Knowledge and Commitment, A Problem-oriented Approach to Literary Studies*. Amsterdam and Philadelphia: John Benjamins, 2000: 37.
38 Wang Zhongjiang. The Conditions of Being Classics: Taking Early Confucian Classics as Examples. // Liu Xiaofeng & Chen Shaoming (eds.), *The Power of Classics and Interpretations*. Shanghai: Joint Publishing, 2003: 12.
39 Huang Manjun. The Birth and Transmission of Modern Chinese Literary Classics. *Social Sciences in China*, 2004 (3): 149.
40 I. Even-Zohar. Polysystem Theory. *Poetics Today*, 1990, 11 (1): 16.
41 H. Adams. Canons: Literary Criteria/Power Criteria (trans. Zeng Zhenzhen). *Critical Inquiry*, 1988, 14(4): 748–764.
42 Huang Manjun. The Birth and Transmission of Modern Chinese Literary Classics. *Social Sciences in China*, 2004 (3): 149.
43 I. Even-Zohar. Polysystem Theory. *Poetics Today,* 1990, 11 (1): 13.
44 I. Even-Zohar. Polysystem Theory. *Poetics Today*, 1990, 11 (1): 19.
45 F. Lentricchia & T. McLaughlin. *Critical Terms for Literary Study* (2nd edition). Chicago and London: The University of Chicago Press, 1995: 233.
46 I. Even-Zohar. Polysystem Theory. *Poetics Today*, 1990, 11 (1): 19.
47 I. Even-Zohar. Polysystem Theory. *Poetics Today*, 1990, 11 (1): 16.
48 H. Bloom. Preface and Prelude. // *The Western Canon: The Books and School of the Ages*. New York: Harcourt Brace, 1994: 3.
49 Cai Zhenxing. Canon/ Right/ Knowledge. // Chen Dongrong&Chen Zhangfang. *Canon and Literature Teaching*. Taipei: Society for Comparative Literature/Department of English and American Languages and Literatures, National Central University, 1995: 63.
50 Quoted from Shan Dexing. *Creating Tradition: Literary Anthologies and Chinese-American Literature, Inscriptions and Representations: Chinese American and Cultural Studies)* Taipei: Maitian Press, 2000: 241.
51 Zha Mingjian. Cultural Manipulation and Utilization: Ideology and the Construction of Translated Literary Canons: A Study of Chinese Translated Literature in the 1950s and 1960s. *Comparative Literature in China*, 2004 (2): 87.
52 Tong Yuanfang. The English and Chinese Translation of *Rubáiyát*. // Luo Xuanmin & Tu Guoyuan (eds.), *Interpretation and Deconstruction*. Hefei: Anhui Literature and Art Publishing House, 2003: 105–165.
53 Fu Yuean. www.ylib.com/readit/tower/default.asp?DocId=STORY&SNO=159. [2007–04–13].
54 S. Soong. Introduction. // *Fung Sydney S K, Lai S T. 25 T'ang Poets: Index to English Translations*. Hong Kong, China: Chinese University Press, 1984: xi.
55 Chung Ling. *Deep Layers of the Text: Cross-cultural Fusion and Gender Exploration*. Taipei, China: "National" Taiwan University Press, 2018: 123.
56 Zhou Yingxiong. Canon, Subjectivity, Comparative Literature. // Chen Dongrong & Chen Zhangfang (eds.), *Canon and Literature Teaching*. Taipei: Comparative Literature Association and Department of English at National Central University, 1995: 2.

# 3 Cultural Norms of the Departure and Intralingual Travel of the CMPs

Regarding the poet Han-shan of the Tang Dynasty, the American translator Bill Porter, under the pen name Red Pine (1943–), once wrote in his translator's preface,

> If China's literary critics were put in charge of a tea for their country's greatest poets of the past, Cold Mountain would not be on many invitation lists. Yet no other poet occupies the altars of China's temples and shrines, where his statue often stands alongside immortals and bodhisattvas.[1]

Nevertheless, the most intriguing part is that even the label of "Tang Dynasty poet" is quite uncertain for academic research in that the truth of Han-shan's existence is still up in the air, let alone the time of his life and his real identity, as well as those many controversial poems that are attributed to him. Maybe it is the grotesque and gaudy literature description as well as the uninhibited poetic aesthetics that have made Han-shan and his poems excluded from the prevailing cultural norms and discourse system of the departure. For thousands of years, the intralingual literature travel of Han-shan and his poems in the Chinese literary polysystem could be described as the path to Cold Mountain that was mentioned in the poem at the outset: forgotten and neglected, at a loss of the shortcut home, and hard to trace their twists.

## 3.1 Prevailing Cultural Norms

Culture is a reflection of certain social values. Once the culture is formed, it will regulate and restrain the thinking pattern, mental state and social activities of its social members in many ways, thus influencing and shaping the material and spiritual products created by humans. Therefore, norms always have their own distinct character in the aspect of social morality. Essentially, the so-called prevailing cultural norms of the departure are norms of social behavior based on the dominant ideology, by which the behaviors, thoughts or ideas of a certain cultural group or social individual are measured to be "correct" and "ethical" or not.

### 3.1.1 Norms and Their Social and Ethical Attributes

"Norms" was originally a term widely used in sociological studies. Sociologists have treated norms as follows:

> Norms have long been regarded as the translation of general values or ideas shared by a community as to what would count as right or wrong, adequate or inadequate into performance "instructions" appropriate for and applicable to a concrete situation. These "instructions" specify what is prescribed and forbidden, as well as what is tolerated and permitted in a certain behavioral dimension.[2]

The concept was subsequently introduced into linguistics studies, and American linguist Renate Bartsch (1939–) defined it in his book *Norms of Language* as the "social reality of correctness notions".[3] Bartsch stressed "correctness" in this explanation. But people are always different on what kind of behavior or concept is correct. Chesterman adapted the definition of norms from Bartsch's notion:

Let S = a given society, C = a given set of condition, X = any individual belonging to S, A = a given act. Then: there exists a norm governing A if and only if all the following conditions hold:

1. Most members of S regularly do A under C.
2. If X does not do A, members of S may criticize X and other members of S will regard such criticism as justified.
3. Members of S use such expressions as "X ought to do A under C" or "it is the rule that under C, people in S do A" or "the right thing to do under C is A" in order to justify their own or others' action or criticisms.[4]

Chesterman further points out that norms stand between laws and conventions. Laws are objective, mandatory and legally binding; conventions are arbitrary regularities of behavior without any enforcement. Gideon Toury (1946–2016) indicates:

> In terms of their relative potency, constraints on any kind of behavior can be described along a scalable continuum anchored between two extremes: general, relatively objective rules on one hand, and idiosyncratic mannerisms on the other. Being intersubjective in nature, norms, therefore, occupy the central part of the scale, very often amounting to the whole continuum minus the small patches taken up by the two extreme points.[5]

Theo Hermans (1948–), the representative of the descriptive translation school and the professor of Dutch and Comparative Literature school in UCL, points out that "in essence, norms, like rules and conventions, have a socially regulatory function."[6] He ranks norms in the perspective of social constraint from weak to strong as conventions→norms→rules→decree. He believes that

> norms differ from conventions in that they have a binding character, carry some form of sanction, and may either grow out of customs or be issued by an authorizing instance. Rules are strong norms, usually institutionalized and posited by an identifiable authority, with or without the full assent of the individual subjected to them.[7]

Chesterman admitted that the norms he defined are nothing more than social norms. Toury also admits that

> norms are acquired by the individual during his/her socialization and always imply sanctions. . . . The centrality of the norms is not only metaphorical . . . rather, it is essential. Norms are the key concept and focal point in any attempt to account for the social relevance of activities.[8]

Both of them emphasize the interaction between norms and society.

Except for the social norms, norms have other different forms, such as Bartsch's ethical norms and technical norms. Technical norms can be divided into process norms, which regulate the behavioral process and stipulate the correct standard of behavior, and product norms, which make the judgment about what is the "correct" product. Toury regards norms' function as, "Within the community, norms also serve as criteria according to which actual instances of behavior are evaluated."[9] Based on Toury's conception, Chesterman then elaborates further:

> norms make life easier (for the majority at least). They do this (ideally) by regulating behavior in such a way that it is optimally beneficial to all parties, by creating and maintaining social order, by facilitating material and social interaction, even by facilitating cognitive processing.[10]

Whether sociologists, linguists, or researchers of translation studies, all emphasize the specific guiding significance of norms for social behavior without any exception.

### 3.1.2 Prevailing Cultural Norms

The concept of the cultural norm was therefore proposed:

> Cultural norms are an organic system with accepted beliefs and behaviors that shape every cultural group and are shared across generations. They provide reliable guidance to people's daily life and help to construct members' healthy physical and mental state. As correct and moral rules of behavior, cultural norms lead a harmonious and meaningful life. They are also a way of acquiring the sense of justice, security, and belonging. Normative beliefs and

related values and rituals together regulate and govern all aspects of social life. Without them, society would be in a chaotic or unpredictable situation.[11]

The "cultural norms" and the "norms" mentioned are not inconsistent with the function of norms. Just as Chesterman points out, thus far we have been looking at norms as positive phenomena, serving a useful purpose. Yet norms may also be felt more negatively as constraints, as restrictions to be challenged or overruled.[12] Toury also thinks that "non-compliance" with a norm in particular instances does not invalidate the "norm". At the same time, there would normally be a price to pay for opting for any deviant kind of behavior.[13] The so-called "standardized belief" and "corresponding values and etiquette" are nothing more than an expression of official ideology. The establishment of such cultural norms is just a way of maintaining normal and orderly social governance and domination by the ruler. Therefore, any ideas and behaviors that might lead to "chaos or unpredictability" are always "marginalized", or their potential negative impacts are eliminated permanently. Consequently, the spread and influence of material and spiritual products that are contrary to "standardized" cultural norms are inevitably interfered with and restricted by such cultural norms.

The prevailing cultural norms are the norms of social behavior set by the ruler according to the official ideology, by which the behavior, ideas or thoughts of a cultural community or individual are measured as "correct" and "ethical" or not. When it comes to the literature, in particular, prevailing cultural norms define and judge what is the "correct" and "ethical" literature, and then decide the destiny of literary texts in literary history based on the previous assessment.

It cannot be denied that prevailing cultural norms also change and transform in varying degrees with the change of time and space. From China's literary norms, one can see that the criteria for defining canonical literary texts by the cultural norms of the dominant culture have undergone constant evolution and adjustments in different periods. Due to the ardent admiration of Confucian classics in ancient China, especially the strong defense of the status of the Six Classics by ancient Chinese scholars, the early Chinese literary researchers and critics generally took the moral code of "moderation" as the standard and method to evaluate literary works and select literary classics. Later on, after the beginning of the emphasis on "literariness" of a literary works among the Confucian scholars, in particular, after the emergence of a vague to clear consciousness of "literariness" by famed scholars such as Cao Pi (曹丕, 187–226), Lu Ji (陆机, 261–303) and Liu Xiemeng (刘勰萌, 465–?), people of later generations started to regard the "literariness" of a literary text as the defining criterion of a classical text. The "literariness" is actually consistent with the assertion of "being reasonable in illustration and elegant in expression" proposed by Liu Xie. In the history of ancient Chinese literature, the "vivid and intriguing descriptions or narrations", which are "rich in vocabulary", are more likely to obtain a canonical status in that they are "prominent and echo down for generations" and "lighten people like the sun and the moon". Afterwards, due to the innovation and evolution of people's concept of "literature", especially the re-evaluation of "elegance" and "vulgarity" in contemporary cultural studies, some "little-known" literary genres that were denied and ignored in the long history of Chinese literature began to be valued, and then "climbed the ladder to enter the grand hall" with brand new roles as "canons".

It cannot be denied that in the process of the evolution of the standard of literary canonization, no matter the moral code, the quality of literariness or the final judgment of "elegance" and "vulgarity", it is always subject to the prevailing cultural norms of the dominant culture at that time. Once recognized by the cultural norms of the dominant culture, literary texts can prevail and thrive accordingly. On the contrary, they can only be cramped in the corner until "one day they meet someone with eyes and then plague the world."

## 3.2 The Poet Han-shan and His Cold Mountain Poems

There is no definite evidence about where Han-shan came from through to today. Rumor has it that he was a hermit who chose to live on a nearby hill called Cold Mountain or Cold Cliff in the Tiantai Mountains, and therefore he called himself Han-shan or Han-shan-zi. There is no final assertion of his real existence because the authentic material that can prove his real identity is always inaccessible. Japanese scholars in particular are suspicious of Han-shan's existence in general. For example, Yoshitaka Iriya (1910–1988), a leading expert in religious studies, asks, "What is exactly the prototype of Cold Mountain Poems? Can Han-shan be made up or not? There are many questions left."[14] Japanese historian Tsuda Yoshikichi (1873–1961) also points out that the existence of Han-shan as the hearsay believed is doubtful in his article "Remarks on Cold Mountain Poems, Han-shan and Shi-de" (寒山诗与寒山拾得之说话), which was published in 1944. He further points out that the CMPs and the legendary figure Han-shan can be regarded as different things. He even argues that Feng-gan and Shi-de did not exist either, and that they were in fact fictitious creations.[15] Daejeon Tisang also asserted in his article "Interpretation of Cold Mountain Poems" (寒山诗解说) that some people write poems in the name of Han-shan and Shi-de in an attempt to express their feelings and thoughts.[16] Until now, scholars are still far from reaching a consensus on Han-shan's identity and his poems.

### 3.2.1 The Poet Han-shan

Literary accounts about Han-shan are mingled with legends and myths, so scholars do not believe that they can be accepted as authentic documents. The Taoist Du Guangting (杜光庭, 850–933) in the Kindom of Qianshu (907–925) of the Five Dynasties and Ten Kingdoms (907–979) recorded the origin and spread of Han-shan and his poems in Volume 55 of *Xianzhuan Shiyi* (《仙传拾遗》, *Uncollected Biographies of Immortals*) of his book *Taiping Guangji* (《太平广记》, *The Extensive Records of Taiping Era*):

> No one knows who Han-shan-zi was. In the Dali period, he lived alone in Cuiping mountain of the Tiantai district. The mountain was deep and snowy

in the summer, so it was also called Cold Cliff. He named himself Han-shan-zi after the mountain. He enjoyed writing poems, and often wrote poems on bamboo, wood, stones and cliffs. Someone hunted up to more than three hundred of his poems. His many poems told about the reclusive life and natural scenery in the mountain, or satire about current affairs and warn the ordinary people. Xu Lingfu brought all poems together and made them into three volumes with a preface. Three volumes of poems disseminated among people for more than ten years, but then disappeared suddenly.[17]

*Xianzhuan Shiyi* (《仙传拾遗》, *Uncollected Biographies of Immortals*) firstly recorded Han-shan's identity with the "Dali Hypothesis" (an argument for Han-shan's lifetime during the Dali Reign, 766–799), which holds that Han-shan lived in the Middle Tang Dynasty. There are many proponents of this hypothesis, such as Hu Shi (胡适, 1891–1962), Yu Jiaxi (余嘉锡, 1884–1955) and so on, but they differ greatly in the assessment of the exact year of Han-shan's birth and death.[18] As for *Xianzhuan Shiyi* (《仙传拾遗》, *Uncollected Biographies of Immortals*), some indicate that Du Guangting's (杜光庭) narration is "a biography of fairies" or "a collection of dubiousness". Nevertheless, Yu Jiaxi (余嘉锡), Hu Shi (胡适), Sun Changwu (孙昌武, 1937–) and Xiang Chu (项楚, 1940–) all believed that the three-volume *Collection of CMPs* compiled in *Xianzhuan Shiyi* were all collected by Xu Lingfu. T. H. Barrett (1949–), a famous British sinologist and professor at the School of Oriental and African Studies at the University of London, doubts the real existence of Du Guangting (杜光庭), a Taoist from Qianshu (前蜀) in the Five Dynasties. He also argues that the name Du Guangting (杜光庭) exists only in the quote. Barrett further speculates that Du Guangting (杜光庭) may make up the whole story to discomfort contemporary Buddhists, and attributed his information to Xu. Therefore, he believes "it is unlikely to be Xu who firstly collected Cold Mountain Poems."[19] The current edition of *Anthology of Cold Mountain Poems* does not include Xu's preface, but only a preface signed with words: written by Lü Qiuyin, the governor of Taizhou.

> No one knows just what sort of man Han-shan was. Some old people knew him: they say he was a poor man, a crazy character. He lived alone seventy *li* west of the T'ang-hsing district of T'ien-t'ai at a place called Cold Mountain. He often went down to the Kuo-ch'ing Temple. At the temple lived Shih-te, who ran the dinging hall. He sometimes saved leftovers for Han-shan, hiding them in a bamboo tube. Han-shan would come ad carry it away; walking the long veranda, calling and shouting happily, taking and laughing to himself. Once the monks followed him, caught him, and made fun of him. He stopped, clapped his hands, and laughed greatly—Ha Ha!—for a spell, then left.
> 
> He looked like a tramp, his body and face were old and beat. Yet in every word he breathed was a meaning in line with the subtle principles of things, if only you thought of it deeply. Everything he said had a feeling of the Tao in it, profound and arcane secrets. His hat was made of birch bark, his clothes were ragged and worn out, and his shoes were wood. Thus men who have

made it hide their tracks: unifying categories and interpenetrating things. On that long veranda calling and singing, in his words of reply Ha Ha!—the three words revolve. Sometimes at the villages and farms he laughed and sang with cowherds. Sometimes intractable, sometimes agreeable, his nature was happy of itself. But how could a person without wisdom recognize him?

I once received a position as a petty official at Tan-ch'iu. The day I was to depart, I had a bad headache. I called a doctor, but he couldn't cure me and it turned worse. Then I met a Buddhist Master named Feng-kan, who said he came from the Kuo-ch'ing Temple of T'ien-t'ai especially to visit me. I asked him to recuse me from my illness. . . . I proceeded on a journey to my job at T'ai-chou, not forgetting this affair. I arrived three days later, immediately went to a temple, and questioned an old monk. It seemed the master had been truthful. . . . I ordered Tao-ch'iao and the other monks to find out how they had lived, to hunt up the poems written on bamboo, wood, stones and cliffs—and also to collect those written on the walls of people's houses. There were more than three hundred. On the wall of the Earth-shrine Shih-te had written some Gatha. It was all brought together and made into a book.[20]

Yu Jiaxi (余嘉锡) cited the register of appointed officers in Chen Qiqing's (陈耆卿, 1180–1236) *Jiading Chicheng Zhi* (《嘉定赤城志》, *Annals of Chicheng County During the Jiading Era*.)（Vol. 8）and stated, "In Zhenguan sixteen to twenty years (642–646), the governor of Taizhou is Lü Qiuyin. It corresponds to Zhinan's statement that Han-shan lives in the early years of the Zhenguan Reign."[21] Lü Qiuyin actually puts forward the "Zhenguan Hypothesis" (627–649) of Han-shan's identity in the preface, which had a profound influence and has the admiration of many supporters in ancient times and modern. For example, Zhi-nan (志南), an eminent monk of the Song Dynasty, was firstly confirmed in the preface "Tiantian Shan Guoqing Chansi Sanying Jiji" (天台山国清禅寺三隐集记) of *Han-shan Shiji* (《寒山诗集》, *Anthology of Cold Mountain Poems*), edited by him in the year that Han-shan lived in Zhenguan Reign (1189). In the fourth year of the Baoyou Reign (1256), Zhi-pan (志磐), an eminent monk of the Song Dynasty, corrected it to the seventh year of the Zhenguan Reign (633) in *Fozu Tongji* (《佛祖统记》, *A General History of Buddhism*); in the sixth year of the Xianchun Reign (1270), Ben-jue (本觉), an eminent monk of Song Dynasty, dated it to the 17th year of Zhenguan Reign in *Shishi Tonglan* (《释氏通览》, *Glossary of Buddhist Terms*); the second year of Zhizheng (1336), Shi Xizhong of the Yuan Dynasty proved it as the 16th year of the Zhenguan Reign in *Shishi Zijian* (《释氏资鉴》, *The Chronicle of Buddhism*). Wu Chi-yu (吴其昱, 1919–2011) examined the frequency of Buddhist allusions and terms that have been used in the CMPs and then concluded that nearly half of his Buddhist terms are also found in, if not derived from, the *Mahāparinirvāna-sūtra* (《大般涅槃经》, *Nirvana Sutra*), which was predominant before the middle of the seventh century.[22] Besides, Wu Chi-yu (吴其昱) indicated that Zhi-yan (智岩, 577–654), one of the eminent monks in Dao Xuan's *Xu Gaosengzhuan* (《续高僧传》, *Continued Biographies of Eminent Monks*), is the prototype of Han-shan. Based on Zhiyan's death in 675 at the age of 78 in *Xu Gaosengzhuan* (《续高僧传》,

*Continued Biographies of Eminent Monks*), it can be inferred that Wu Chi-yu (吴其昱) is a supporter of the "Zhenguan Hypothesis". He also claimed that Daoxuan (道宣, Tao-Hsuan) does not mention that Chi-yen (智岩, Zhi-yan) had written poems, nor does he specify where and when Lu-ch'iu (闾丘) had visited him.[23] In the article "The Resurrection of Poet Monk Han-shan", written by Hu Juren (胡菊人, 1933–), the author also considers Han-shan to be "a monk of Zhenguan Reign in the Tang Dynasty";[24] Huang Boren also supports the "Zhenguan Hypothesis" in that

> the preface of *Han-shan Shiji* (《寒山诗集》, *Anthology of Cold Mountain Poems*) written by Lü Qiuyin is the first-hand material collected by the witness of history, so there is no doubt that Han-shan lived in Zhenguan Reign of the early Tang Dynasty.[25]

Gary Snyder mentioned the "Zhenguan Hypothesis" in the preface of *Riprap and Cold Mountain Poems*: "He lived in the T'ang dynasty—traditionally A.D. 627–650, although Hu Shi (胡适) dates him 700–800."[26] What is worth mentioning is that because of the "Zhenguan Hypothesis", most contemporary textbooks of literature history place Han-shan and his poems in the literature of the early Tang Dynasty.

In volume 19 of *Tang Tiantaishan Feng-gan shi-de zhuan* (《唐天台山丰干拾得传》) of *Song Gaoseng Zhuan* (《宋高僧传》, *Biographies of Eminent Monks in the Song Dynasty*) which was compiled by Zan-ning of the Song Dynasty, the author doubts about Lü's way of wiring of "Feng-gan":

> A carpenter, who often travels between the capital city and market place, seems to be Feng-gan, but people cannot confirm that. "Feng (封)" and "Feng (丰)" have different meanings. The historian Wei Shu argues that "Feng (封)" means "enfeoffment"; three sages in Lü's preface assert that "Feng (丰)" means "harvest" however. It is unknown which one is right.[27]

For the real identity of Lü Qiuyin and his visit to Han-shan and Shi-de in the preface, Zan-ning (赞宁) also holds a different view in his *Song Gaoseng Zhuan* (《宋高僧传》, *Biographies of Eminent Monks in the Song Dynasty*). Based on doubts and verification, Zan-ning proposed the third hypothesis of Han-shan's identity, the "Xiantian Hypothesis" (712–713), which has few supporters and little impact. But his hypothesis leads to an examination of the authenticity of Lü Qiuyin's preface through the ages. "Tiantai Shan Guoqing Chansi Sanying Jiji" (《天台山国清禅寺三隐集记》), the preface of *Anthology of Cold Mountain Poems*) edited by the monk Zhi Nan (志南) of the Song Dynasty; *History of Vernacular Literature*, written by Hu Shi (胡适); and *Han-shan-zi Fu Feng-gan Shi-de Shiyi-juan* (《寒山子附丰干拾得诗一卷》, *The Collection of Han-shan's Poems with a Volume of Feng-gan's and Shi-de's Poems Attached*)" (Vol. 20 of *Siku Tiyao Bianzheng* (《四库提要辩证》, *Corrections to the Annotated Catalogue of the Imperial Library in Four Catalogues of the Imperial Library in Four Categories*)) recorded by Yu Jiaxi (余嘉锡) all suspect the authenticity of of Lü's preface as a literary and historical fact. Zhi Nan's preface records that "it is known that Han-shan has never held the hand of Lü Qiuyin, and Lü Qiuyin has never been to the Cold Cliff, and Shi-de perished after leaving the temple two *li*. The current hearsay is fallacious."[28] Hu Shi (胡适) however thinks that "Lü's preface is full of myths with a little truth and the story of Lü cannot be proved nowadays."[29] Yu Jiaxi (余嘉锡) even declares that "I would rather believe in the supplementary information of Du Guangting (杜光庭), instead of the pseudo preface of Lü Qiuyin."[30] He even suspects that Dao Qiao[31] (道翘) mentioned in Lü's preface "does not exist at all".[32] He even further concludes that the Zen master Ben-ji (本寂, 840–901) of Caoshan, who wrote *Duihanshanzishi* (对寒山子诗, *Commentary on Poems of Han-shan-zi*), is the real author of the pseudo-preface.

Lü's preface has been discussed passionately over time. The disagreement proposed by Hu Shi (胡适) and Yu Jiaxi (余嘉锡), which is mentioned earlier and mostly agreed, is a typical case. Wu Chi-yu (吴其昱) also considers Lu not to be the author of the preface, with proofs:

> T'ang-hsing, used three times in the preface, seems to have been an original part of it. That is to say, it is not a later insertion. Since Shih-feng was changed to T'ang-hsing in the second year of Shang-yuan (上元, 761 A.D.) under the reign of Su-tsung (肃宗), the preface must have been written after 761 A.D.... Besides, the term *ju-chu-jen* (汝诸人, "you many people") began to appear as a daily expression with the Dhyana masters in the *Ch'uan-hsin fa-yao* (《传心法要》) of Hsi-yun (希运), know as Huang-po Tuan-chi ch'anshih (黄檗断际禅师) with a preface written in 857 A.D. The preface of CMPs might not be earlier that this *yu-lu* (《语录》) (middle of the ninth century). Moreover, the official title of the preface writer may also afford a clue for the identification of the date. Only two periods are possible for T'ai-chou and *tz'u fei* (赐绯):721–242 A.D. and after 758 A.D. Finally, the preface does not conform to the ordinary formula of prefaces, to say nothing of its contradictions to the poems. And its end date was perhaps consciously avoided, and replaced by thirty-eight four-character lines. It might have been written after the model of Buddhist sutra, for instance, the *Lotus Sutra Saddharma-pundarika* (《妙法莲华经》) or the *pien-wen* (《变文》) which gives a summary in poetical from after the story in prose. The author seems to have been a Buddhist monk (Tao-ch'iao 道翘) rather than a learned official.[33]

Wu Chi-yu (吴其昱) also reminds us that the doubts about the preface do not deny the fact that there were some factual elements in the preface. The American sinologist Robert Borgen (1945–) had analyzed and advocated that

> one need not be a sensitive reader of Chinese prose to spot the solecisms. The most blatant is the repetitious use of the conjunction *nai* (乃). The narrative portion of the preface can be broken down into thirty-nine sentences, the word *nai* appears twenty-eight times. Yet the putative author is given a most

imposing official title. A man with so clumsy a prose style could not have passed his civil service examinations, much less risen to such a high position in Tang officialdom. The absence of the name of Lü Qiuyin from any reliable record of Taizhou prefects raises further doubts. . . . Other problems in the preface are more subtle. It claims to have been written by a contemporary of the poem's early Tang author, but Wu Chi-yu has noted that it employs terms that came into use in 761 or even later. Pulleyblank's linguistic analysis offers further evidence to support the view that the preface is a relatively late work, for he dates to the late Tang an ode in praise of Han-shan that concludes the preface. . . . The story shows several weaknesses. The events seem out of sequence. We are not startled by Han-shan's bizarre behavior when the narrator finally meets him, for the preface begins by noting his eccentricities. This is not good storytelling. Moreover, Shi-de's peculiar name is not explained. Worse, he is given two contradictory descriptions. . . . We never learned where the narrator is when he first meets Feng-gan nor do we find out what Feng-gan is doing there. And the preface lacks any dates, a starling omission from a Chinese biography. These features suggest that Han-shan was already a familiar figure when the preface was written. . . . These inconsistencies in the preface also suggest that it may have been based on three separate texts that were clumsily cobbled together at a rather late date.[34]

Du Guangting (杜光庭) whose works are included in *Taiping Guangji* (《太平广记》, *The Extensive Records of Taiping Era*), and Xu Lingfu (徐灵府), who "collected and wrote the preface" to the CMPs, were both Taoists. Dao Qiao (道翘), meanwhile, who "compiled the CMPs into volumes", according to Lü's preface, was a Buddhism monk. Scholars tend to believe that both Taoists and monks at the time were willing to draw Han-shan into their religious groups to use his reputation that grew out of the Cold Mountain to gather fame and attention. It poses the questions, Who was the real compiler of the CMPs?[35] Who was the real author of the preface? To whom could *Han-shan Shiji* (《寒山诗集》, *Anthology of Cold Mountain Poems*) be credited? No one has been able to explain the ins and outs of these issues, which, to some extent, makes Han-shan's identity even more confusing.

The mysterious preface and illusory legends have blurred Han-shan's existence, and scholars have therefore tried to find traces of his life experience from his poems, which gave rise to all sorts of stories and speculation about his identity. According to the following poem—

> From a lofty mountain peak,
> the view extends forever.
> I sit here unknown,
> the lone moon lights Cold Spring.
> in the spring there is no moon,
> the moon is in the sky.
> I sing this one song,
> a song in which there is no Zen.[36]

—the Chinese historian Qian Mu (钱穆, 1895–1990) analyzed that, "this poem is filled with Zen thoughts, and the poem quoted before mentioned 'greeting a guest talking Zen', so it is clear that Han-shan was born after Zen studies flourished in Tang Dynasty."[37] Xie Siwei (谢思炜, 1954–) also indicated that many of the CMPs discussed the Zen thought of self-purification and how to recognize one's nature to become a Buddha. Han-shan could only have talked of Zen thought in such a clear and voluminous manner after it had become more mainstream in the home culture.[38] Some even have made bold speculation about Han-shan's native place based on the so-called "self-narrative poems". For instance, Zhang Bowei (张伯伟, 1959–) deduced that "at this moment, Han-shan missed his hometown Xianyang very much,"[39] according to the following poem:

> I sit and gaze on tiffs highest peak of all;
> Wherever I look there is distance without end.
> I am all alone and no one knows I am here,
> A lonely moon is mirrored in the cold pool.
> Down in the pool there is not really a moon;
> The only moon is in the sky above.
> I sing to you this one piece of song;
> But in the song there is not any Zen.[40]

Xu Guangda (徐光大) furthermore concluded that Han-shan was a native of the nearby countryside of Xianyang, to which he had a special affection according to the lines "I thought about my youth" and "alas after less than a hundred years recalling the Capital hurts."[41] Qian Xuelie (钱学烈, 1944–), on the other hand, pointed out that Xianyang here actually referred to Chang'an, the capital of the Tang Dynasty. Previously given are two statements about Han-shan's native place. Robert Henricks (1943–), however, thought that "Chang'an" was the capital of both the Sui and Tang Dynasties, and Luoyang was an important city of both dynasties, so it is extremely common to mention these two places in Chinese poetry of any period. Thus he didn't consider it evidence of the native place of the author of the CMPs. From two lines, "alas after less than a hundred years, recalling the Capital hurts,"[42] Zhou Qi (周琦) assumed that Han-shan's hometown should be in Chang'an or Xianyang of Shaanxi Province. He further claimed that there is also a Cold Mountain in Chang'an, which is very similar to Cold Cliff in the Tiantai Mountains . . . It is no accident that Han-shan chose to live a reclusive life in Cold Cliff and disguised his real identity with the name of the mountain; instead, it is an expression of longing for his hometown at least.[43] Based on the lines "Mistress Tu of Hantan" and "This maid is from Hantan," Red Pine presumed that Han-shan was born in the ancient town of Hantan and his family moved to Chang'an when he was young.[44]

Some scholars have also tried to find clues or evidence of Han-shan's life experience from his poems. Qian Xuelie (钱学烈) inferred that "because he failed in the official career, Han-shan was desolate and condemned by his relatives and wife, and therefore broke away from home and retreated into privacy"[45] according to the poem in the following:

> When I was young I weeded book in hand,
> Sharing at first a home with my elder brothers.
> Something happened, and they put the blame on me;
> Even my own wife turned against me.
> So I left the red dust of the world and wandered
> Hither and thither, reading book after book
> And looking for some one who would spare a drop of water
> To keep alive the gudgeon in the carriage rut.[46]

Qian also believed that

Han-shan's choice of living in seclusion was not only related to the lifestyle of being a hermit at the time and the An Shi Rebellion (an armed rebellion led by An Lushan and Shi Siming in 755–763 in the Tang Dynasty) but also relevant to his family's neglect that derived from a hopeless prospect of being successful and famous. And he was profoundly influenced by the Taoist philosophy of returning to innocence, seeking carefree enjoyment, and combining the world with self that proposed by Laozi and Zhuangzi.[47]

Arthur Waley (1888–1966) also agreed with the statement, and he wrote in the preface of 27 translated CMPs that the

Chinese poet Han-shan lived in the eighth and ninth century A.D. He and his brothers inherited a farmhouse from their ancestors, but Han-shan abandoned his wife and children after a terrible quarrel with his family. He was full of intelligence but wandered far from home; he longed for rendering a service to a wise governor but had no opportunity to display his talent.[48]

On the contrary, Robert G. Henricks considered that it was Han-shan's wife who left Han-shan.[49] Zhao Zifan (赵滋蕃, 1924–1986) analyzed that "the alienation between Han-shan and his brothers, and the disharmony in Han-shan's family were caused by his honest, stubborn and innocent personality."[50]

From the stanza "Brothers young and old, 'together' in five commanderies; Fathers and sons, fundamentally one, though scattered now in three regions," Yan Zhenfei (严振非, 1943–) even concluded that Han-shan used to be the member of a prominent aristocratic family.[51] Moreover, according to "I live in a village in the countryside, without a father or a mother. With no name, no rank in my clan. Some people call me any old name. Some people call me Zhang Wang 张王," Yan deduced that Han-shan was originally named Yang Wen 杨温 (evolved from Zhang Wang), the fourth son of Yang Zan (杨瓒), who was one of the brothers of

Yang Jian (杨坚), the first emperor of the Sui Dynasty.⁵² Yoshitaka Iriya, however, believed that the prototype of Han-Shan could potentially be Pang Yun (庞蕴, 740–808) of the Middle Tang Dynasty.⁵³ Wu Chi-yu (吴其昱) suggested that Han-shan in the *Xu Gaosengzhuan* (《续高僧传》, *Continued Biographies of Eminent Monks*) seems to be the Buddhist monk Zhi-yan (智岩, 577–654), "a native of Tan-yang (Chiang-su), who was visited by Lü Qiuyin probably late in 623 A.D. or early in 624 A.D. in the T'ien-t'ai Mountains."⁵⁴ On the one hand, Zhou Qi (周琦) pointed out that the story in Lü's preface is very similar to that of Li Jingfang, who was the Cishi (an official name in ancient China) of Taizhou in the late Tang Dynasty (836–907); then he further concluded that Lü's preface should have been written by a monk in the late Tang Dynasty (836–907).⁵⁵ Sun Changwu (孙昌武), however, mentioned that some thought that Yi Ze (遗则, 754–830) of Niutou Zen (牛头宗), who "traveled south to Tiantai Mountains, then lived in the Cliff of Buddha Cave," may be the prototype of Han-shan, or one of the authors of the CMPs. He stated that

> the dissemination of CMPs nowadays is indeed created in the Tiantai district of Middle Tang Dynasty, and these poems are likely to be written by Niutou Zen masters, who are skilled in poetry because parts of poems express Zen thought.⁵⁶

Based on the internal evidence such as historical allusions, Zen quotations, historical figures, ancient rules and regulations, local customs and manners, dialects and slang in CMPs, scholars have attempted to sketch a more authentic and credible Han-shan for readers. Qian Xuelie investigated some terms, such as "Wu Daozi", "Master Wan-hui", "Monk Shan-dao", "regulated verse", "write name on Wild Goose Pagoda", "rent and taxes", "polish a brick and make it a mirror" and "South Hall", that were mentioned in Han-shan's poem.⁵⁷ Robert Henricks added a convincing appendix, "The Dates of Han-shan: the Internal Evidence", in his *The Poetry of Han-shan A Complete, Annotated Translation of Cold Mountain*, to reveal the connotative information in the lines of poetry, such as: "You may use all your strength polishing bricks, but can you ever turn into mirror?" "Cold or hot, we must judge for ourselves; never believe the lips of the servant," "What a poor scribe, who repeatedly comes to be tested at Southern Court!" and "There's a Mr. Wang, the *hsiu-ts'ai*."⁵⁸

Such efforts, however, have met with little success. The confirmation and investigation of Han-shan's identity have always been argued back and forth without an agreement. Ye Zhuhong (叶珠红, 1964–) concluded that

> in CMPs, except words like "I/my home", "lie alone/live alone", "usually live", "once", "recall" . . . and so on, which are used to describe his real life from a first-person perspective, there were also specific scenarios that were mentioned in poems, including Cold Cliff, where he lived in seclusion, and Guoqing Temple, where he went sometimes. The only two people who he fraternized with were Shi-de and the Zen master Feng-gan. Apart from that,

Han-shan did not mention any other friends in the poems which made it difficult to verify his surname and his living period, let alone the dates of his birth and death.[59]

What is interesting is that even the existing descriptions of his identity are varied and mixed. For example, Du Guangting, the author of *Xianzhuan Shiyi* (《仙传拾遗》, *Uncollected Biographies of Immortals*) calls him a "hermit"; in Lü's preface, he was described as a "poor but deviant poet"; in *Zutangji* (《祖堂集》, *Anthology of the Patriarchal Hall*), which is the first historical book of Zen in "Dengluti" (灯录体, Denglu Style), he is called a "Yishi" (hermit); Shi Zhecun (施蛰存, 1905–2003) named him "an anonymous talent"; Xiang Chu (项楚) confirms that Han-shan belongs to a "literatus class"; Gary Snyder regards him as a "tramp"; and Edward Schafer (1931–1991) considered Han-shan to be a "misanthrope".

Many researchers and numerous records in literary history tend to define Han-shan as a "monk-poet", but doubts about his belonging to religious sects have never disappeared. Based on the line "Ever since I left home, I've developed an interest in yoga" in Han-shan's poem, Yu Jiaxi (余嘉锡) deduces that "even though Han-Shan had converted to a religion and visited Guoqing Temple many times, he did not live there permanently. It is unknown whether he was a monk or a Taoist."[60] Tsuda Yoshikichi concludes from the line "I've developed an interest in yoga" that this free and easy life should be a Taoist way of life, not Buddhist. And a refined Buddhist monk should not cherish such a mental state.[61] Yoshitaka Iriya claims, "I think, the figure Han-shan, or more precisely, the author of *Anthology of Cold Mountain Poems* was not a monk."[62] Red Pine and Robert Henricks also expressed doubts about Han-shan's identity as a monk. From the stanza "Ever since I left home, I've developed an interest in yoga" and "I recall twenty years ago, my slow steps ending at Kuoching," Robert Henricks infers that "though we might safely call Han-shan a Buddhist recluse—or Zen recluse—he was never a purist."[63] John Blofeld (1913–1987), on the other hand, thinks that Han-shan was both a monk and a Taoist.[64] Paul Kahn argues that Han-shan was familiar with the three Chinese cultural traditions of Confucianism, Buddhism and Taoism.[65] Song Bainian (宋柏年) holds the same argument in his book *Chinese Classics in the Overseas*, and he believes that "Han-shan expressed Buddhist, Taoist, and Confucian thoughts at the same time, but he did not belong to a particular group."[66] Xiang Chu (项楚) concludes that

> Han-shan was generally regarded as a "poet monk" in the past. But in recent years, commentators incline to consider him as a poor hermit living in the Cold Cliff. From the poem "I have a coat," it is known that Han-shan once had a cassock and "in summer it serves as a shirt, in winter it serves as a shawl". Moreover, from the line "ever since I left home, I've developed an interest in yoga" (the 267th poem of *Anthology of Cold Mountain Poems*), it is known that Han-shan did not live a monk's way of life. Whether he was at one time a monk nonetheless, deserves further studies.[67]

It is unreliable to reconstruct the poet's life experience through their poems. Sun Qi points out that

> a poem is a creation of the poet, it could potentially be an autobiography or a self-analysis, but it is not identical with an autobiography or a self-analysis, "potentially be" does not mean "identical". . . . And a creative work can be made up from a third-person perspective, it does not necessarily involve the real character in life and real experience of the poet.[68]

Therefore, a cautious attitude must be taken when using poems as evidence to examine a poet's life; otherwise, it would be like what professor Luo Shijin said, "One would be inevitably trapped into the dilemma if he sought too much, and the scientific significance of academic research would be lost at the same time."[69]

### 3.2.2 Cold Mountain Poems

As previously mentioned, the uncertainty and confusion of Han-shan's life and identity have made the attribution of his poems a problem for a while. Wang Yao (王瑶, 1914–1989) once analyzed:

> Many of the works that have been passed down from ancient times are difficult to know who made them. . . . It is not only because the author was less-known or a long time passed, but also because in the feudal society, people's consciousness was not as strong as it was later. The public only emphasized the "words" or the "text" of a work, rather than the "author" who wrote these "words" or "texts".[70]

For a poet of uncertain identity and unknown reputation like Han-shan, it is not surprising that he and his poems are full of controversies and disputes. And from poems that have been passed down, we can find that the author of the CMPs does not comply with norms of the dominant culture and poetry aesthetics, both in terms of language using and writing style. So it is impossible to leave the name Han-shan in the history of literature. Without any records in the history of literature, it is inevitable that the assessment of Han-shan's life and identity is confusing and diverse. From the confusing personal information on Han-Shan's life and the inconsistent religious content in the CMPs, as well as the inconsistent elaboration, we have every reason to conclude that the CMPs were completed by more than one person. It would be a misdirection to try to present the author of the CMPs as one single person.

In the case of "Gushi Shijiu Shou" (古诗十九首, "Nineteen Old Poems"), Wang Yao (王瑶) analyzes that when these poems were made can be deduced, but who wrote them remains a mystery. Therefore, this book is a collection of poems by these nameless people. The CMPs are in the same situation.[71] Pulleyblank (1922–2013), a Canadian sinologist and president of the International Society for the Linguistics of Chinese, once remarked, "The poet Han-shan is a well-known figure in the history of Zen painting, but nothing is known about the real author of the collection of poems under his name, except for a few anecdotes."[72] He agreed with Yoshitaka Iriya and Burton Watson (1925–2017), maintaining the view that the CMPs cannot be written by only one author. After a deep study on rhymes used in the Poems, Pulleyblank even asserted,

> Obviously, some of CMPs are from the late Tang Dynasty (836–907), while a larger number of other CMPs refer directly to the early Tang Dynasty or even the Sui Dynasty in terms of rhyme . . . because this part of the poems is even stricter than the palace poems of the early Tang Dynasty in terms of rhyme cutting.[73]

As a result, he respectively named early and late poems in *Anthology of Cold Mountain Poems* Han-shan I and Han-shan II.

Shi Zhecun (施蛰存) has a similar view:

> Among the three hundred-odd poems, some extremely close to Wang Fan-zhi's (王梵志) poems can be considered works of the early Tang Dynasty (618–712); other five-word poems resembling the style of Meng Jiao (孟郊, 751–814) and Jia Dao (贾岛, 779–843) should be made before the late Mid-Tang Dynasty (766–835).[74]

Chinese scholars, such as Xiang Chu (项楚) and Chen Yinchi (陈引驰, 1966–), also believe that the author of the CMPs is more than one individual. After synthesizing the existing materials, Sun Changwu concluded,

> We can only be sure that a number of popular poems were circulated in the middle and late Tang Dynasties, and their authors were called "Han-shan-zi" or "Han-shan". In the process of the spread of the poem, a legend about the character of Han-shan has gradually formed. Lü Qiuyin and the story of his preface have also been created. As will be explained below, we can not exclude the fact that there was indeed a person called "Han-shan" at that time, he may also be one of the authors of the poem. It is certain that today's collection of Cold Mountain Poems is a collection of many authors' works that have been circulating for a long time, and it cannot be denied that there are works from earlier periods (such as the Kaiyuan period, 713–741). But generally speaking, the miscellany of Cold Mountain Poems should be formed after the Dali period (766–779).[75]

Judging from literary histories, we could say that the imitation of the ancients and falsification of the poems is not uncommon. Therefore, the claim of Han-shan authors might be valid.

Wang Yao talks about the phenomenon of imitating and faking the ancients' works in the Wei and Jin Dynasties (220–420) in his article *Nigu He Zuowei* (《拟古和作伪》, *Imitation of the Ancients and Falsification*). He argues that people did that for learning from and competing with their predecessors, as well as for following the trend that was a common tradition at that time. The original purpose of later writers was

> at most to make them similar in terms of words and style, rather than to pass them on to later generations or to mess with history. In that sense, it should be called imitation instead of faking; it was just a common phenomenon at that time, having nothing to do with angling for undeserved fame.[76]

The case of the CMPs is different. Firstly, its original author was just an unknown and his poems were not conformed to, even compatible with, the poetic tradition and ideology of his time, hence the argument that people imitated him for learning or competing is illogical. Their aim, at most, was to express themselves by imitating such a rebellious poetic style. Secondly, the CMPs were perhaps written by frustrated and unappreciated men of letters who were dissatisfied with reality. "In the turbulent and declining society of the mid and late Tang Dynasty (766–907), they rebelled and lived in seclusion for their beliefs."[77] Therefore, they gave vent to their "complaint" in poems, lamenting their poor destiny and the unfair reality. Of course, they also hoped that their poems would "one day meet someone with eyes, then their poems would plague the world" since they were confident in their talent in poetry. With these realistic utilitarian factors, coupled with recordings by those who may have been confused about the truth, imitations and fakes were possibly included in the CMPs. Yu Jiaxi (余嘉锡) once marveled that "since changes and misunderstanding may happen at any time, it is reasonable to say that there are pseudos in CMPs."[78]

As a result, the total number of CMPs has been a controversial topic for generations. According to *Song Gaoseng Zhuan* (《宋高僧传》, *Biographies of Eminent Monks in the Song Dynasty*), the number is more than 200; *Xianzhuan Shiyi* (《仙传拾遗》, *Uncollected Biographies of Immortals*) says it is more than 300; and Han-shan himself said that he had written 600 poems in total.

> Of five-character poems, I've written five hundred;
> With seven characters, seventy-nine.
> In three-character lines, twenty-one;
> Altogether that comes to six hundred shou.[79]

During the Yuanhe period (806–820) of the Tang Dynasty, Xu Lingfu (徐灵府) compiled three volumes of the CMPs. *Yiwenzhi* (《艺文志》, *Yiwen Record*), in *Xin Tangshu* (《新唐书》, *New History of the Tang Dynasty*) recorded them in seven volumes. Later, there was a seven-volume version with notes by the Zen master Ben-ji (本寂). None of them have been passed down, however; the Song version of *Anthology of Cold Mountain Poems* is the earliest surviving version by far, containing 313 poems. *Han-shan Shiji* (《寒山诗集》, *Anthology of Cold Mountain Poems*) edited by Zhi-nan (志南) in 1189, has 311 poems. *Annotation of Cold Mountain Poems (also Annotation of Shi-de's Poems)* (《寒山诗注（附拾得诗注）》), edited by Xiang Chu (项楚), contains 325 poems, 12 of which were anonymous at first but verified later. Qian Xuelie (钱学烈) maintains that the claimed "600 poems" is just the expectation of Han-shan, and hence it cannot be considered that Xu Lingfu (徐灵府) had omitted nearly 300 poems.[80] Sun Qi (孙旗, 1921–1995), on the other hand, states that "no poet has ever made a plan for the number of his compositions, let alone Han-shan. The dégagé poet even carved his poems on trees and stones. How these poems could be counted?"[81]

Victor Mair (1943–), an American sinologist in Dunhuang Studies, agrees with "more than 300 poems", believing that the number should be 311. His point of view relies on the number of poems in Robert Henricks's (1836–1902) complete translation, which is based on *Quan Tangshi* (《全唐诗》, *Complete Tang Poems*) and *Siku Quanshu Zongmu Tiyao* (《四库全书总目提要》, *Annotated Catalog of the Imperial Four Libraries*). Mair has an interesting explanation on "311":

> I am suspicious of the number 300 for the poems that are attributed to Cold Mountain. This immediately leads me to think of the number of poems in the *Shihching* (《诗经》, *Book of Odes*), which is also 300. Even more curious is the fact that in both cases 300 is merely a round number. The exact number of poems in both the Cold Mountain collection and in the *Book of Odes* is 311. It is beyond belief that Cold Mountain wandered around the Kuo-ch'ing si 国清寺 ("Temple of National Purity") on T'ien-T'ai 天台 ("Celestial Terrace") Mountain until he got to 311, and then stopped. Rather, the compiler must have wanted 311 unconventional Taoistic and Zen poems to act as a foil for the prototypical Confucian repository of verse. He may have picked up a portion of these poems from strange places, including the mouths of temple cooks and hangers-on as well as previous uncirculated collections of local versifiers. But to get exactly 311 poems, he or some later redactor probably would have had to write a considerable number himself. Perhaps, not entirely incidentally, the number of poems attributed to Wang Fanzhi is also somewhat over 300 and the most famous collection of the elite poetry of the T'ang dynasty, the *T'ang-shih san-bai shou* (《唐诗三百首》, *Three Hundred T'ang Poems*), obviously also clings to the same talismanic figure, despite its being compiled by a confessed Taoist in the Ch'ing period.[82]

It is difficult to reach a consensus on the number of CMPs since they have existed and circulated for more than a thousand years, during which many imitated and faked works were added to collections and records. This also shows the fact that Han-shan and his poems have always been two controversial topics. The existence of the poet is unclear, let alone verifying his origin, life and identity. As for the poems attributed to him, they are also confusing and difficult to distinguish. In that sense, this literary case is much of a "Goldbach Conjecture" in literature.

Nevertheless, the unique linguistic style and special aesthetic value of the CMPs attract many followers and backers among monks and the secular. There is a quote in Siku *Quanshu Zongmu Tiyao* (《四库全书总目提要》, *Annotated Catalog of the*

Imperial Four Libraries) from *Juyi Lu* (《居易录》, *Records of My Life*) of Wang Shizhen (王世祯, 1634–1711), a famous literary critic of the Qing Dynasty (1644–1912):

> CMPs are spoken highly for its language—some are written in serious polished words while some are in humorous colloquial language. For example: "teasing a parrot before the flowers, playing a lute beneath the moon, her singing echoes for months, thousands watch her briefest dance". These sentences show distinctive features of Tang poetry. Some poems seem to be from a Confucianist, like "they don't need Cheng Hsuan's comments, much less Mao Heng's explanations". Most of the poems are full of Buddhism thoughts. Despite various styles, all of the poems were written in seemingly casual words, thus cannot be restricted by poetry regulation. They are of enough great wit and wisdom to be regarded as life guidance.[83]

The CMPs are actually like an all-embracing social kaleidoscope. It not only reflected the artistic pursuit of mainstream poetry in the society at that time, but also enabled the vernacular style originated from both Buddhist scriptures translated in the Eastern Han Dynasty (25–220), Wei, Jin, Southern and Northern Dynasties (220–589) and Buddhist poems to be carried forward after being inherited by Wang Ji (王绩) and Wang Fanzhi (王梵志) in the early Tang Dynasty.

Chen Yinchi (陈引驰, 1966–) believes that

> there exist two different worlds or styles in CMPs. One is a simple and vernacular style like Wang Fanzhi's; the other, on contrary, shows a great literacy of the intellectuals, with rich allusions from *Shijing* (《诗经》, *Classic of Poetry*), *Zhuangzi* (《庄子》, *Zhuangzi*), "Gushi Shijiu Shou" (古诗十九首, "Nineteen Old Poems"), *Shi Shuo Xin Yu* (《世说新语》, *A New Account of Tales of the World*), *Liezi* (《列子》, *The Book of Lieh-tzu*), poems of Tao Yuanming (陶渊明, 365–427) and Xie Lingyun (谢灵运, 385–433), and so on.[84]

Chen Yinchi (陈引驰) may try to divide the CMPs into vernacular poetry and elegant poetry, yet allusions are also adopted in the vernacular poetry. The two kinds of poetry, therefore, cannot be considered opposite to each other. As for the relationship between the CMPs and Wang Fanzhi's (王梵志) poems, Xie Siwei (谢思炜, 1954–) holds that there are distinctive differences between them while the CMPs adopted Wang Fanzhi's style, "CMPs aim to express the poet's reflections on life, and are clearly influenced by the Zen Buddhism, while Wang Fanzhi's poems focus on preaching to normal people."[85] In terms of the vernacular poetry, objectively speaking, they are roughly similar. The CMPs are different from Wang Fanzhi's poems in that the former has two kinds of poems which the latter lacks: the mainstream poetry written by the secular, and the religious poetry written by religious people. Kuang Fu (匡扶, 1911–1996) attributes the unique reputation of the CMPs to the elements of its literati's poetry (文人诗), a type of genre of poem fitting for the Song Dynasty (960–1279). It is because of these elements that those poems were appreciated by later men and were then recorded and included in *Quan Tangshi* (《全唐诗》, *Complete Tang Poems*).[86] Liu Dajie (刘大杰, 1904–1977), a Chinese literary historian, argued, "CMPs and Wang Fanzhi's poems have a common characteristic of mixing verses with chants, yet the former, with wider themes and more descriptions of natural scenery, is more vivid and more telling than the latter."[87] Zhang Xihou (张锡厚, 1937–2005) agrees that Wang Fanzhi's poems are less extensive than the CMPs in theme.[88] Through comparing the vernacular poems written by Wang Fanzhi, Han-shan and Pang Yun (庞蕴, ?–808), Xiang Chu (项楚) finds that "Han-shan and Pang Yun share a characteristic in the use of slang and vernacular language, but the profound meaning the former carries is what the latter lacks."[89] From all this, it is clear that the CMPs are highly commended for their simple vernacular language and profound Zen ideas, as well as the fascinating poetic feeling they create and the rich thoughts they express. "Some are written in serious polished words while some in humorous colloquial language" and "of enough great wit and wisdom (of Confucianism, Buddhism and Zen Buddhism)". This is exactly the most comprehensive comment on the CMPs.

It may be safe to say that the emergence of the CMPs is a necessary historical stage and literary phenomenon during the development of Tang poetry, as well as a significant milestone in the history of Chinese poetry. It extends the mainstream poetry of the Tang Dynasty (618–907) and ushers in a new poetic style that significantly influences both the literature and poetry of later generations. Its representation of vernacular poetry style especially serves as a good opening shoot for the development of the vernacular literature of the Five Dynasties and Ten Kingdoms Period (907–960), the Song Dynasty (960–1279), the Ming Dynasty (1368–1644), the Qing Dynasty (1644–1912) and even the modern era (1840–1949). In the long-standing dispute between "elegance" and "vulgarity", many voices approving of such style emerge.[90] Such a phenomenon is not unique to secular literature. Writers of Buddhist poetry and "Dengluti" (灯录体, Denglu Style) have also used CMPs for reference. In that sense, it can be concluded that the CMPs can be divided into three sections according to their different poetic styles and artistic features: the "aspiring to beauty" mainstream poetry, the "simple" vernacular poetry and the "profound" religious poetry. Each of them shows obviously high literary value and great artistic appeal.

*3.2.2.1 Mainstream Poetry*

"Mainstream poetry" refers to the poems written by men of letters, or mainstream poets. They comply with mainstream cultural norms. For example:

> A moth-browed girl in town
> how her pendants chime
> teasing a parrot before the flowers
> playing a lute beneath the moon
> her singing echoes for months
> thousands watch her briefest dance

but surely this won't last
the hibiscus can't bear cold

Who takes the Cold Mountain Road
takes a road that never ends
the rivers are long and piled with rocks
the streams are wide and choked with grass
it's not the rain that makes the moss slick
and it's not the wind that makes the pines moan
who can get past the tangles of the world
and sit with me in the clouds

The Cold Mountain Road is strange
no tracks of cart or horse
hard to recall which merging stream
or tell which piled-up ridge
a myriad plants weep with dew
the pines all sigh the same
here where the trail disappears
form asks shadow where to

A group of girls play in fading light
wind fills the road with perfume
their skirts are embroidered with butterflies of gold
their hair is adorned with ducks of jade
their maids are dressed in red chiffon
their eunuchs in purple brocade
watching is someone who has lost his way
white temples and a trembling heart

Someone lives in a mountain gorge
cloud robe and sunset tassels
holding sweet plants he would share
but the road is long and hard
burdened by regrets and doubts
old and unaccomplished
called by others crippled
he stands alone steadfast[91]

Henricks once mentioned that the reason why there was an opinion that Hanshan could not be compared to great poets like Li Bai (李白), Du Fu (杜甫), Wang Wei (王维) and Bai Juyi (白居易) of the Tang Dynasty (618–907), and had always been ignored by Chinese literary historians, may be the fact that the CMPs were considered of low literary value.[92] This, of course, is an illusion, because people always think that the CMPs are nothing more than "vulgar" vernacular poetry written by a "mad monk" in slang and vulgar proverbs. In fact, not to mention that vernacular poetry has its own unique aesthetic value, in terms of this illusion, it is a hasty equation between the CMPs and vernacular poetry. However, perhaps such an illusion reflects the complexity of the style and content of CMPs. Therefore, in the beginning of his essay "A Glimpse into Cold Mountain Poems" (寒山诗管窥), Iriya Yoshitaka (1910–1976) states that

> what makes CMPs different from other Tang poems is not some unique poetic style or writing techniques, rather, it is characterized by its diversified nature. It is certainly good to be able to capture a certain point as a characteristic of CMPs, but it is not easy to do so.[93]

As mentioned before, the authors of the CMPs were probably literary scholars who were frustrated at their political careers and then lived in mountains or forests for seclusion. Being familiar with the poetic form strictly regulated by the authoritative examination, they made their poems not only formally meet the requirements of mainstream poetics for antithesis and rhythm but also ideologically conformed to poetic aesthetics advocated by Confucianism. As for the stylistic characteristics of poetry, Cao Pi (曹丕) addressed this in the following statement.

> Literature is the same at the root, but differs in its branches. Generally speaking, memorials and disquisitions should have dignity; letters and memorials should be based on natural principle; inscriptions and eulogy value the facts; poetry and poetic exposition aspire to beauty.[94]

The "Li" (丽, "Beauty") indicated the trend of the poetic tradition in later generations. Lu Ji (陆机) also mentioned in *Wenfu* (《文赋》, *The Poetic Exposition on Literature*) that

> The poem follows from the affections and is sensuously intricate;
> Poetic exposition gives the normative forms of things and is clear and bright;
> Stele inscription unfurls pattern to match substance;
> Threnody swells with pent-up sorrow[95]

The sentence "The poem follows from the affections and is sensuously intricate" means that poetry is created by the feeling of fluctuation; hence it requires beautiful language. From the previous poems, it is clear that the CMPs are not inferior to those of the immortal poets of the Tang Dynasty (618–907) in terms of "affection" and "intricacy". Iriya Yoshitaka commends the last poem previously given, which adopted "Chuciti" (楚辞体, Elegiac Style of *Chuci*), that

> even if its relations to poems of Li Bai (李白), Wang Wei (王维), Han Yu (韩愈) and Liu Zongyuan (柳宗元) are left aside, it is rather obvious that this poem is almost entirely composed of characters and lines taken from *Chuci* (《楚辞》, *Songs of Chu/Elegies of Chu*). What a gorgeous and stunning creation it is![96]

Xu Yi (许顗, 1091–?), a poet in the Song Dynasty (960–1279), also praised in his book *Yanzhou Shihua* (《彦周诗话》, *Yanzhou's Comment On Poetry*) that "even Qu Yuan (屈原, 340 BCE–278 BCE) and Song Yu (宋玉, 298 BCE–222 BCE) could not do better than Han-shan."

The relatively open religious policy of the Tang Dynasty (618–907) allowed Confucianism, Buddhism and Taoism to circulate in parallel. Growing up in such a multicultural society, the author(s) of the CMPs naturally knew the traditional requirement for the poetic form well and was (were) familiar with various classics of previous dynasties. Therefore, mainstream poems written by them do not lack quotations from classic books like *Wen Xuan or Selections of Refined Literature*, "Gushi Shijiu Shou" (古诗十九首, "Nineteen Old Poems"), *Liezi* (《列子》, *The Book of Lieh-tzu*) and *Shi Shuo Xin Yu* (《世说新语》, *A New Account of Tales of the World*), or poems of great poets like Tao Yuanming (陶渊明, 365–427) and Xie Lingyun (谢灵ff, 385–433).[97] There are also a large number of phrases and lines taken from Buddhist texts such as *Mahāparinirvāna-sūtra* (*Nirvana Sutra*), *Saddharma Puṇḍarīka Sūtra* (《妙法莲花经》, *Lotus Sutra*) and *Liuzu Tan Jing* (《六祖坛经》, *Platform Sūtra of the Sixth Patriarch*). There is a saying in *Wenfu* (《文赋》, *The Poetic Exposition on Literature*) that "he (successful writer) stands in the very center, observes in the darkness. Nourishes feeling and intent in the ancient canons,"[98] which means poetry also needs to focus on "the ancient canons" when "nourishing feeling". Out of question, Han-shan did it. His (their) insightful and aesthetic mainstream poems, therefore, would by no means be overshadowed, even in the star-studded Tang Dynasty (618–907). It could even be said that it was because of these mainstream poems with the characteristics of literati poetry that the CMPs were appreciated by later men of the letter and thus were passed on.

*3.2.2.2 Vernacular Poetry*

Vernacular poetry refers to poems of anti-tradition, anti-norm, anti-rhetoric and anti-mainstream in the CMPs. It endows CMPs with the most impressive characteristics. As Sun Changwu (孙昌武) said, the vernacular poetry neither uses simple nor shallow language to make itself understandable and accessible like the poems of Yuan Zhen (元稹, 779–831) and Bai Juyi (白居易), nor follows the mainstream poetic pursuit for refinement and dignity. It seeks to enlighten the mass with both vulgar language and simple meter.[99]

> Whoever runs into a ghost or spirit
> first of all don't be afraid
> be firm don't try to grab it
> call its name it'll leave
> petition the Buddha with incense
> bow down and ask a monk's aid
> a mosquito that lands on an iron ox
> finds nowhere to sink its beak

Pigs devour dead human flesh
humans savor dead pig guts
pigs don't mind human stink
humans say pork smells fine
throw dead pigs in the river
bury human bodies deep
if they ever stop eating each other
lotuses will bloom in boiling soup

A poor donkey is short by a bushel
a rich dog has three pints to spare
when poverty isn't equally shared
we separate comfort and hardship
but if we let the donkey fill up
we cause the dog to starve
I've weighed this for you carefully
it just makes me depressed

When an old man takes a young wife
how can she bear his thin hair
when an old woman weds a young man
how can he stand her dried-up face
but when an old man takes an old wife
neither abandons the other
and when a young girl weds a young man
both show the other affection

I see hundreds of dogs
and every one of them scruffy
lying wherever they please
rambling whenever the whim arises
but throw them out a bone
and watch them growl and fight
as long as bones are rare
a pack of dogs can't share[100]

Chinese traditional poetic aesthetics believes that poetry should be lyrical in nature, and "reserve" and "dignity" are regarded as the highest standards of poetry creation. "Ershisishipin" (二十四诗品, "The Twenty-Four Categories of Poetry") by Sikong Tu (司空图, 837–908), a famous poetic critic in the late Tang Dynasty (836–907), is a great comprehensive work on the pure artistic quality of poetry, representing the remarkable theoretical achievement of Tang poetry. It divides artistic techniques of poetry into 24 categories, such as potent and undifferentiated, reserve/accumulation within, lucid and wondrous, and the natural, decorous and

78  *Cultural Norms of Departure and Intralingual Travel of CMPs*

dignified. According to Sikong Tu, the "reserve/accumulation within" refers to the following:

> It does not inhere in any single word
> Yet the utmost flair is attained.
> Though the words do not touch on oneself
> It is as if there were unbearable melancholy.
> In this there is that "someone in control"
> Floating or sinking along with them.
> It is like straining the thickest wine,
> Or the season of flowers reverting to autumn.
> Far, far away, specks of dust in the sky;
> Passing in a flash, bubbles on the ocean.
> Shallow and deep, clustering, scattering,
> Thousands of grains are gathered into one.[101]

It fully shows the poetic aesthetics of "the image beyond image", "sound beyond sound" and "flavor beyond flavor" and thus has been valued by poets of all generations. Yuan Mei (袁枚, 1716–1798), a poet of the Qing Dynasty (1644–1912), is one example. The great poet expressed the same opinion in his poem "*Shenwu*" (《神悟》, *Enlightenment*), advocating that real poetry implicates thoughts rather than explicates them, hence the poet's need to pursue implication beyond language. As for the "decorous and dignified", Sikong Tu described it as that

> With a jade pot he purchases spring,
> Appreciates rain under a roof of thatch.
> Fine scholars are his guests,
> All around him, fine bamboo.
> White clouds in newly cleared skies,
> Birds from hidden places follow one another.
> A reclining lute in the green shade,
> And above is a waterfall in flight.
> The following flowers say nothing,
> The man, as limpid as the chrysanthemum.
> He writes down the seasons' splendors—
> May it be, he hopes, worth the reading.[102]

This kind of poetry gives priority to "classic majesty" and "calmly dignity". Contrary to literary norms and poetic aesthetics of the mainstream, the vernacular poetry of Han-shan is not lyric but didactic, and disregards "reserve" and "dignity". They were written in limpid and calm language and even pointed out the gist at the end of the poems. Different from other poems written in the dignified literary language in the Tang Dynasty (618–907), CMPs "disregards the classic form but adopts vulgar language". Such a composition principle has confused many Western scholars, such as Robert Henricks, who wrote in his book, *The Poetry of Han-shan: A Complete, Annotated Translation of Cold Mountain*, that

> Han-shan is a very odd poet. First of all, as is well known, on occasion he uses colloquial expressions and phrases in his poems, which would rarely be done in "good" verse. Moreover, in some cases, his "poems" are not poems at all. Rather, they are simply sayings, parables, or aphorisms. Many of them quite clever, that happen to be written in metric, rhymed lines.

Perhaps for maintaining the status of those poems in target readers' minds, Henricks added that "though, in my opinion, too much has been made of his use of the colloquial: many—I would say most—of his poems are written in good classical Chinese."[103] Such misunderstanding is caused by insufficient knowledge of traditional Chinese poetry. Some scholars mistakenly believe that Tang poetry is full of romanticism and vibrancy, failing to realize the fact that there is also plain and simple vernacular poetry created in the Tang Dynasty (618–907).

Like poems from Wang Ji (王绩, 585–644) and Chen Zi'ang (陈子昂, 661–702) in the early Tang Dynasty (618–712), the vernacular poetry of the CMPs developed in the ethos of rebelling against the decadent flowery "Gongtishi" (宫体诗, Palace Poetry) that derived from the Six Dynasties (222–589) and strict rules of prosody prevalent since the Qi and Liang Dynasties (479–557). This poetic genre was also a derivative for the ordinary people during the development of Buddhism, Zen Buddhism, in particular. Characterized as free and vivid colloquial or nearly colloquial language, even vulgar proverbs and slang, those poems "were not written for catering to the authority for a political career, which the palace poem always did, and was free from the constraint of rhyme and prescribed title."[104]

Such style is partly the result of poets deliberately differing themselves from others and refusing to follow the major poetic style of the day, which was, as Lu Kanru (陆侃如) and Feng Yuanjun (冯沅君) described, "shallow flamboyance, undignified frivolity and unnatural flowery". Han-shan wrote that

> Mister Wang the Graduate
> laughs at my poor prosody
> I don't know a wasp's waist
> much less a crane's knee
> I can't keep my flat tones straight
> all my words come helter-skelter
> I laugh at the poems he writes
> a blind man's songs about the sun
>
> Someone sighed Cold Mountain sir
> your poems possess no sense
> I said for the ancients

>            poverty was no disgrace
>            To this he answered laughing
>            such talk is poorly reasoned
>            Well sir then be as you are
>            with money your concern[105]

Both poems are evidence of the vernacular poetry of the CMPs tending to be anti-normative, anti-mainstream, anti-traditional and anti-rhetorical. One describes such vernacular poetry as "the first anti-rhetorical literature in the history of traditional Chinese literature" since it is contrary to the traditional poetic norm of illuminating thoughts in poems.[106] It could be true if he only generally comments on the vernacular poetry of the Tang Dynasty (618–907). Even in those CMPs, however, rhetorical devices like "Bi" (比, Parable) or "Xing" (兴, Atmospherical Introduction) are adopted many times.

In addition, the authors of the CMPs were from the lower classes. Being familiar with traditional conventions of oral literature such as folklores, Yue-fu poems and Buddhist chants, they preferred pure colloquial expressions to the so-called "new form", which was "superficial and cliched, florid and empty". Victor H. Mair (1943–) holds that

> the CMPs perhaps have a greater percentage of vernacular elements than those of almost any other Tang poets, except his spiritual brother and predecessor, Wang Fanzhi. Given Zen Buddhism prevailed in the society of that time, such a phenomenon is not surprising. In fact, the Zen Texts is one of the texts using the most colloquial language of ancient Chinese texts.[107]

Chen Dequan (程德全, 1860–1930), the provincial governor of Jiangsu during 1909–1911, wrote in the *Hanshanzishijiba* (《寒山子诗集跋》, *Postscript to the Collected Poems of Han-shan-zi*), "he expressed sorrowful and grievous emotions in poems in witty and abusive words, without conforming to any rules or norms."[108]

These colloquial vernacular poems have some regular syntactic structure, such as "我见XXX" ("I see . . ."), "余家XXX" ("I have . . ."), "昨见XXX" ("Yesterday I saw . . .") and "世有XXX" ("There is . . ."). These are all evidence of the popularization and vernacularization of these poems and suggest a purpose of "preaching" and "persuasion". Iriya Yoshitaka (1910–1976) believes that the first-person structure like "I see" indicates a stronger self-consciousness than that in Wang's poems. He relates it to the subjective spirit of Nanzong Zen and the strong critical spirit of the literatus out of the court. Xie Siwei (谢思炜, 1954–) holds the same view. From the perspective of grammatical structure, however, such structures only serve to introduce the object. With such colloquial structures, poems are more likely to meet readers' communication habits and aesthetic expectations both emotionally and psychologically. Similar structures are frequently adopted in the CMPs, such as "昨到XXX" ("Yesterday I went . . .") and "有人XXX" ("Someone . . .").

What makes this kind of poetry completely different from traditional metrical poems is that vernacular poetry has no strict rule on the number of words or sentences. Most of them are five-word poems, but there are also three-word poems and seven-word poems. Each poem may have four, six, eight, ten, twelve or twenty lines, and isn't limited by tone or antithesis. These poets, nevertheless, were apt at "Fengrenti" (风人体, Pun Poems) and the "Bangeti" (半格体, Semilattice Style). The "Fengrenti" was explained by Iriya Yoshitaka:

> The first line is a prelude to the next line where the gist is in. . . . This syntax often takes advantage of the feature of homophones to endow two different meanings to sentences because homophones are commonly used and easily derive other meanings, in another word, pun.[109]

In general, this method is mostly used in the last two lines of the poem. The "Semilattice Style" was exampled by Zhao Zifan (赵滋蕃) in Hanshanshi Pinggu (《寒山诗评估》, *Assessment of Cold Mountain Poems*):

> Semilattice refers to a poetic form that combines "Guti" (古体, Ancient Style) and "Qi-liang Ti" (齐梁体, Qi-liang Style). Made of half of the ancient style and a half of Qi-liang style, it is named "semi".[110]

He also argues that the one who created the semilattice style and took it as his own style is no one but Han-shan. Han-shan's poetic thoughts

> were expressed in a precise and concise, intricate and harmonious way by this new form; moreover, it gave Han-shan enough freedom of expressing that the musical characteristic and emotion of his language didn't lose even in the old meter form.[111]

Both "Fengrenti" and "Bangeti" are different from the mainstream aesthetics that emphasized rhetoric and meter, but they are, undoubtedly, more conducive to expressing feelings and thoughts and presenting popular themes.

Another notable feature of vernacular poetry lies in its inclusiveness. The poetry changes poetic themes from imperial life to mass, breaking with the tradition of early Tang poems by presenting ordinary people and their daily life. Characters in the CMPs are all-encompassing, ranging from the rich to the poor, the young to the old, the wicked and thieves to monks and Taoist priests, the lazy, hermits, philosophers and so on. Someone points out that "such change of objects suggests a dissatisfaction and rebellion of these monk-poets against the old regulations."[112] Xie Siwei (谢思炜) holds the same view:

> As a new social discourse, the vernacular poetry was a means for those who were stray and excluded in the feudal society of the Tang Dynasty (618–907). Those soreheads expressed their dissent to the major socio-political power by rebelling against the tradition of poetry.[113]

As a matter of fact, there is a saying in "Yanghuo" (阳货) of *Lun Yu* (《论语》, *The Analects of Confucius*) that "the odes serve to stimulate the mind. They may be used for purposes of self-contemplation. They teach the art of sociability. They show how to regulate feelings of resentment".[114] The poet Han-shan seems to understand better than many of his predecessors that poetry serves to "show how to regulate feelings of resentment". He gave a vivid account of and full details of his own hardship and troubles, as well as worries of the lower class in his vernacular poems. Weak and feeble though this resistance and complaint may be, they revealed misery and confusion of the common people. Moreover, the content, language and narrative approach of vernacular poetry show the poet's trait as the voice of the lower class, and his tendency to cater to the aesthetic interests of common people is suggested in the poetic style. That is why Xiang Chu (项楚) described Han-shan as "the guide of the lower class"; and Red Pine, the translator of *The Collected Songs of Cold Mountain*, said that "he wrote his poems for everyone, not just the educated elite."[115]

In addition to allegorical exhortation, there is no lack of poems expressing ecology, ethics filial duty, life philosophy and even worries about the country and the people. As for ecological problems, he wrote:

> I saw some trees by the river
> more weathered than I can describe
> a couple of trunks remained
> with thousands of ax-blade scars
> their dry yellow leaves had been stripped by the frost
> their rotten roots battered by waves
> but this is how habitats are
> why blame Heaven and Earth

With regard to social ethos, he depicted:

> I see people everywhere
> dignified and fond of form
> not repaying their parents' kindness
> square-inches of the smallest sort
> incurring debts to others
> not embarrassed until they have hooves
> caring for wives and children
> not supporting their parents

When dealing with the life philosophy, he incisively pointed out:

> Anger is a fire in the mind
> it can burn up a forest of merit
> if you travel the bodhisattva path
> forbearance keeps anger away

Cultural Norms of Departure and Intralingual Travel of CMPs   83

He even expressed his own unique views on how to run a country:

> A state relies on people
> just as a tree depends on soil
> if the soil is deep it thrives
> if the soil is thin it withers
> and if its roots are exposed
> its limbs produce no fruit
> draining a pond to catch fish
> gains only a short-term profit.[116]

All of those poems make the vernacular poetry of the CMPs, in particular in terms of content and realm, far superior to many other vernacular poems whose purpose is purely didactic.

In general, Han-shan's vernacular poems are eclectic and have a wide range of themes. They are full of laughter and scolding between the lines, showing the distinctive characteristics of folk vernacular poetry, which is in line with what Wang Shizhen (王世禎) commented in his *Juyi Lu* (《居易录》, *Records of My Life*), that the CMPs "were available at his fingertips," "cannot be measured by the meter of poetry" and "[are] brilliant wit and fun to be regarded as life guidance".

### 3.2.2.3  Religious Poetry

On the religious poetry of the CMPs, Iriya Yoshitaka points out that

> almost none have regarded CMPs as a work of a real poet. One reason is that most poems of *Han-shan-zi Shiji* (《寒山子诗集》, *Anthology of Cold Mountain Poems*) are written by religious people, not by poets.[117]

As a matter of fact, it is because of his purported identity as a monk and his religious poetry that Han-shan is mistakenly recognized by many scholars for a monk-poet:

> I see Tientai summit
> rising high above the crowd
> the rhyme of pines and bamboo in the wind
> the rhythm of the tide in the moonlight
> I see the mountain's green reach below
> white clouds discussing the unseen
> wilderness means mountains and water
> I've always loved friends of the Way
> Before the cliffs I sat alone
> the moon shone in the sky
> but where a thousand shapes appeared
> its lantern cast no light
> the unobstructed spirit is clear

the empty cave is a mystery
a finger showed me the moon
the moon is the hub of the mind

Spring water is pure in an emerald stream
moonlight is white on Cold Mountain
silence thoughts and the spirit becomes clear
focus on emptiness and the world grows still

For an image of life and death
consider ice and water
water freezes into ice
ice melts back into water
what dies must live again
what lives is bound to die
ice and water don't harm each other
both life and death are fine

Today I sat before the cliffs
I sat until the mist drew off
a single crystal stream
a towering ridge of jade
a cloud's dawn shadow not yet moving
the moon's night light still adrift
a body free of dust
a mind without a care

Steam some sand for your dinner
when you're thirsty dig a well
polish a brick with all your might
you still won't make a mirror
the Buddha said we're basically equal
we share the same true nature
figure it out for yourself
give up this useless struggle

The multitude of stars is the late night's light
alone above a cliff before the moon sets
the perfect luminescence the unpolished glow
hanging in the sky is my mind
Above Cold Mountain the moon shines alone
in a clear sky it illuminates nothing at all
precious heavenly priceless jewel
buried in the skandhas submerged in the body[118]

In the preface to the English translation of *Cold Mountain: 100 Poems by the T'ang Poet Han-shan*, Burton Watson (1925–2017) mentions:

> In the works of most first-rate Chinese poets, Buddhism figures vary slightly. . . . however, the CMPs is a striking exception to this rule. The collection of poetry attributed to him contains a certain number of sermons in doggerel. . . . But it also contains a large proportion of excellent poetry which is permeated with deep and compelling religious feelings. For this reason, he holds a place of special importance in Chinese literature. He proved that it was possible to write great poetry on Buddhist, as well as Confucian and Taoist, themes. . . . The surprising thing is that so few of his countrymen ever felt inclined to explore the paths he opened.[119]

The first half of this statement is undoubtedly accurate. The history of Chinese poetry has always paid little attention to religious poems. For a long time, such poems created by Han-shan and others were kept in seclusions and few people knew them. Of course, Watson's claim that none of the Tang poets dabble in religious poetry is too presumptuous. In fact, because the Tang Dynasty was the peak period of the development of Buddhism and Taoism in China, the literati and officials of the Tang Dynasty accepted the influence of both to varying degrees. As a result, not only monks but also men of letters, such as Meng Haoran (孟浩然), Wang Wei (王维), Li Bai (李白) and Bai Juyi (白居易), not only kept close contact with religious personages, but also excelled in writing poems on religious themes. Han-shan's religious poetry is the poetic reflection of the development and prosperity of Buddhist, Taoist and Zen thoughts in the field of poetry in the Tang Dynasty.

Stephen Owen (1946–) has a more convincing statement on the religious poetry of the Tang Dynasty:

> The Tang poets included many Buddhist monks. Most poet-monks worked entirely within the secular poetic tradition, though sometimes making reference to Buddhist terms or adopting a mode of reclusive or landscape poetry that vaguely suggested Buddhist values. In addition to these works, there is also a large body of doctrinal versification of little literary merit that is conserved in the corpus of Buddhist religious writing.[120]

As for the value of the CMPs, he argues that

> the closest thing to true "religious poetry" in the Tang Dynasty was a corpus of poems attributed to one Han-shan ("Cold Mountain"), and a smaller group of poems attributed to his companion, Shi-de.[121]

After the late Tang Dynasty (836–907), CMPs were used as Buddhist words spoken by Zen masters at Buddhism lessons and materials for spiritual enlightenment, and it was always imitated by Zen Buddhists. It can be seen from the previous material that Owen's statement is reliable.

Most religious poems of Han-shan were written for expressing thoughts of seclusion and Zen enlightenment. As the result of political turmoil and the prevailing wind of Taoism and Mohism, hermits of the Wei and Jin Dynasties (220–420) pursued a secluded life that was "tranquil and non-interventionist". Likewise, because of the An Shi Rebellion (755–763) and the influence of Zen Buddhism, the recluse began to seek a "natural and relaxing" life after the Mid-Tang Dynasty (766–835). In fact, the three major Chinese traditional cultures—Confucianism, Buddhism and Taoism—all applaud the practice of "seclusion". There is a saying in "Ji Shi" (季氏, "The Head of the Ji Family") of *Lun Yu* (《论语》, *The Analects of Confucius*), of "living in retirement to study their aims". Red Pine has a similar opinion:

> Throughout Chinese history, there have always been people who preferred to spend their lives in the mountains, getting by on lessons, sleeping under thatch, wearing old clothes, working on the higher slopes, not talking much, writing even less—maybe a few poems, a recipe or two. Out of touch with the times but with the seasons, they cultivated roots of the spirit, trading flatland dust for mountain mist. Distant and insignificant, they were the most respected men and women in the world's oldest society. No explanation has ever been offered or demanded for the admiration the Chinese have had for hermits. Hermits were simply there: beyond city walls, in the mountains, lone columns of smoke after a snowfall. As far back as records go, there were always hermits in China.[122]

More convincingly, Zen literature flourished during the Dali, Zhenyuan and Yuanhe periods of the Tang Dynasty (766–820), which may be the time when the CMPs showed up. Especially after the Mid-Tang Dynasty (766–835), "Hongzhou Zong" (洪州宗, Hongzhou Zen) founded by Ma Zudao (马祖道, 709–788/688–763) prevailed, turning the style of Zen Buddhism "from concise and sturdy into natural and relaxing"; the content "from the mixture of *Lankavatara Sutra* and *Prajnaparamita-Sutra* into the blending *of Prajnaparamita-Sutra* and Taoist"; the practice "from rational analyzing and intuitive meditating into natural experiencing"; the thought "from of self-restraint and self-adjustment to of freedom and following heart".[123] In that sense, it can be said that while hermits in the Wei and Jin Dynasties (220–420) merely took nature and idyll life as a refuge, or in terms of literature, a foreign object and a vehicle of metaphor, what the hermits of that time pursued was a loftier spiritual realm, that is, the ultimately enjoyable realm of unity between man and nature.

Such pursuit of leisure and a tranquil state of mind coincided with the Southern Zen's proposal of tranquility, contentment, self-satisfaction, "inner peace", "both mind and Buddha", and "neither mind nor Buddha". As a result, many poems that expressed the thought of seclusion and Zen enlightenment appeared. The frequent Buddhism imageries of "clouds" and "moon" in those poems are the best evidence.

## Cultural Norms of Departure and Intralingual Travel of CMPs   87

Ge Zhaoguang ever argues that "when the word 'cloud' came into the poems of the Mid-and-Late Tang Dynasties (762–859), it had already become a symbol of tranquil and undisturbed life, as well as an idle and free spiritual realm." When the Buddhist metaphor of "cloud" is applied to literary language, the mental state of "leisure" and "freedom" implied by it is also reflected in the CMPs, "trust the current like an unmoored boat"; "a boulder makes a fine pillow. Heaven and Earth can crumble and change."[124] "Moon" is also a common Buddhist metaphor, symbolizing emptiness, clarity and "no thoughts" of the state of harmony and Zen spirit. In the CMPs, there is a portrayal of "My mind is like the autumn moon, clear and bright in a pool of jade"; "Above Cold Mountain the moon shines alone in a clear sky it illuminates nothing at all."[125] As a matter of fact, the poet has broken away from the fetters of the mundane world and completely integrated himself into the clouds and mountains and moons, thus returning to the natural congenial and unencumbered state of his own. The poems in this part, with their beautiful imagery and confounding thoughts of Zen Buddhism, are also the most successful part of religious poetry. Sun Qi (孙旗) marveled that "these poems are as good as any of the great poets of the Tang dynasty."[126] Sun Changwu (孙昌武) even praised the CMPs as the one that "reflects Zen thought more clearly, achieves the highest artistic achievement and has a more profound influence on later generations."[127] In addition, Taoist poems in the CMPs expressing unrestrainedness and open-mindedness (such as "wilderness means mountains and water. I've always loved friends of the Way") and Buddhist poems full of Buddhist wisdom (such as "For an image of life and death, consider ice and water") are equally fresh and meaningful, leaving the reader with endless aftertaste.

Significantly, some of the poems are critical of the art of transcendence and alchemical arts, as well as monks' violation of discipline. For example,

> Emperor Wu of the Han they say
> and the First Emperor of the Ch'in
> both were fond of alchemical arts
> but failed to extend their years
> the Tower of Gold has been knocked down
> Sand Hill is no more
> Maoling and Liyueh
> today are nothing but weeds

> Buddhist monks don't keep their precepts
> Taoist priests don't take their pills
> count the sages who have lived
> all are at the foot of hills

> On Cold Mountain there's a naked bug
> its body is white its head is black
> its hands hold two scrolls
> in one is the Way in the other is Virtue

at home it makes no fire
for the road it packs no clothes
but always it carries the sword of wisdom
ready to strike troublesome foes

The Three-spoked Wheel is relentless
thought after thought it never stops
just when it seems you'll escape
you're dragged back down again
even if you get beyond no-thought
such karma still has its limits
unlike finding your true source
once there you're there forever

The homeless people I know
don't practice the homeless profession
you know when people are homeless
their minds are pure and detached
transparent without any secrets
free and naturally so
the Three Realms don't affect them
the Four Births don't restrict them
without any plans or cares
they wander forever content

I recently hiked to a temple in the clouds
and met some Taoist priests
their star caps and moon capes askew
they explained they lived in the wild
I asked them the art of transcendence
they said it was beyond compare
and called it the peerless power
the elixir meanwhile was the secret of the gods
and they were waiting for a crane at death
or some said they'd ride off on a fish
afterwards I thought this through
and concluded they were all fools
look at an arrow shot into the sky
how quickly it falls back to earth
even if they could become immortals
they would be like cemetery ghosts
meanwhile the moon of our mind shines bright
how can phenomena compare
as for the key to immortality

> within ourselves is the chief of spirits
> don't follow Lords of the Yellow Turban
> persisting in idiocy holding onto doubts[128]

These poems contain various themes, including the sermon, persuasion, Buddhist meditation, and life philosophy, presenting a distinctive poetic aesthetic. According to Ye Zhuhong (叶珠红), such a technique of "exhorting by satirizing" reveals the poet's "words from the bottom of his heart" in a special way and is far beyond the reach of ordinary monk-poets and men of letters. The religious poetry in the CMPs is irreplaceable in the history of Chinese poetry, both in terms of the poetic mood and linguistic expression.[129] It is also evident that the religious thoughts of those poems are not limited to any particular sect, and perhaps because of that, it is reasonable to question Han-shan's identity as an independent poet; all sects seem to find a good reason to claim him as their follower.

The appearance of CMPs is a necessary poetic phenomenon at some stage of the development of poetry, society and culture in the Tang Dynasty (618–907). It fully reflects the authors' ambivalence in the face of the mainstream cultural norms, that is, a complex state of mind of following the mainstream, of satirizing and criticizing the society with discontent and disappointment, and of detached peace and freedom after being secluded in the mountains and forests. The "aspiring to beauty" mainstream poetry, the "simple" vernacular poetry and the "profound" religious poetry all show a high literary level and great aesthetic value. Xiang Chu has summarized Han-shan's poetic style as "unconventional and straightforward, refined and general, interesting and charming".[130] Given these three different features created by the CMPs, this conclusion is generally correct. In fact, this style is named "Han-shan Ti" (寒山体, Han-shan style) by scholars of later generations.

The three sections of the CMPs (mainstream, popular, and religious poems) are all of great literary value, having a large readership among monks and the secular and being revered by prominent literary figures throughout the ages. Despite these facts, the CMPs still have long been excluded from the Chinese literary canon and rejected by the early feudal literary tradition. The fundamental reason for this is that the CMPs run counter to the prevailing cultural norms. Factors such as the legend of Han-shan, his mysterious life experience and the intense religious conflict in the poems made it difficult for the Confucian moralists, who "did not discuss strange occurrences, feats of strength, rebellion, the gods" to accept the "authentic" status of the CMPs; and many plain vernacular poems apparently excluded themselves from the classical texts defined by "literary quality". As a result, the intralingual literary journey of the CMPs has been stumbling. However, given the grotesque themes and the bumpy literary fate of the CMPs, the mysterious life of the poet, the juxtaposition of the secular poems and the religious poems, as well as the ups and downs of the elegance and vulgarity in the poems, it is no doubt a pity that such a significant and peculiar poetic phenomenon is despised or even ignored in the history of Chinese literature and Chinese poetry.

90  *Cultural Norms of Departure and Intralingual Travel of CMPs*

## 3.3 The Intralingual Travel of the CMPs

Regarding the dissemination and reception of CMPs in China, Shimada Kan (1879–1915), a Japanese sinologist, has this summary at the beginning of *Song Daziben Hanshanshi* ((《宋大字本寒山诗集》, *Anthology of Cold Mountain Poems in Bigger Chinese Characters, Song Edition*).

> Han-shan has been ignored for more than a thousand and two hundred years, so only a few of his poem collections have been handed down. Although there are many Buddhist canons in the Southern (1127–1279) and Northern Song Dynasties (960–1127), none of them included CMPs, nor did the Goryeo (ancient Korean, 918–1392) collection. The remained CMPs, which are included in the *Dushu Mingqiu Ji* (《读书敏求记》, *Reading and Researching Notes by Qian Zeng*) are also almost out of print. In the Qing Dynasty (1644–1912), the *Siku Zongmu* (《四库总目》, *Annotated Catalog of the Complete Imperial Library)* only included Wu Mingchun's (吴明春) block-printed edition of Ming Dynasty (1368–1644) in Xinan county; and the refined transcript and the foreign block-printed edition once possessed by Huang Wenpu (黄荛圃) are not known. There is a Goryeo block-printed edition in the Yuan Dynasty (1271–1368), a Fujian block-printed edition in the Ming Dynasty (1368–1644), and a recent Jinling edition, but there are many errors with them and none of the editions of the Song Dynasty (960–1279) survived. In short, CMPs are so poorly published that they are unable to be well passed on. People in the Tang Dynasty (618–907) disliked poetry of plain style, and people in the Song and Yuan Dynasties also contempt CMPs, seldom printing CMPs. It is no wonder that the CMPs have been forgotten and annihilated by the annals of time.[131]

Shimada Kan attributed the failure of the CMPs to both "poor printing" and "poor attraction to posterity". This, however, is not always the case. Actually, firstly, there is no shortage of admirers of the CMPs throughout the ages, and its publications have never been interrupted. Secondly, CMPs are not extinct but were just marginalized by the literary canon. When it comes to the vigorous vernacular literary movement of the first half of the 20th century, the CMPs merely served as "accompaniment" and "tool". In China, the real study of the CMPs began in 1958, with the publication of Yu Jiaxi's (余嘉锡) *Siku Tiyao Bianzheng* (《四库提要辨证》, *Investigation into Abstracts of the Imperial Four Libraries*), volume 20 of whose monograph on Han-shan marked the beginning of the era of academic research on the CMPs.

### 3.3.1 The Dissemination and Reception of the CMPs from the Tang and Song Dynasties to the Late Qing Dynasty

The three worlds of the CMPs all show extraordinary literary and aesthetic values. The poetic style of elegance and vulgarity and the eclectic poetic style should have won Han-shan a good fame in his lifetime and beyond, about which Han-shan himself also showed absolute confidence in his poems:

> When stupid people read my poems
> they don't understand and sneer
> when average people read my poems
> they reflect and say they're deep
> when gifted people read my poems
> they react with full-face grins
> the moment Yang-Hsiu saw *young woman*
> one look and he knew *mystery*[132]

Besides occasional references by a few poets such as Li Shanfu (李山甫, 836–900),[133] Guan Xiu (贯休, 832–912) and Qi Ji (齐己, 863–937), the CMPs did not impose any influence during the Tang and Five Dynasties (907–960). This is not only because the CMPs, at that time, were still in the state of being compiled, but also because Han-shan's expected literary fame was unfortunately lost in the flood of the poetry of the Tang Dynasty (618–907). "In the Tang Dynasty (618–907), the time Han-shan lived, there were so many great poets that Han-shan is not even among the top 100 poets."[134] The statement was by no means alarmist at the time. In addition, the CMPs could not attract people's attention at that time, in that Han-shan didn't have the literary identity accepted by authentic literature. Consequently, his poems were ignored. Those poems which were scrawled on trunks could only be a psychological catharsis for the poet's self-satisfaction, self-entertainment or self-healing.

Obviously, no one would pay attention to the life of Han-shan, a ragged man of letters, and his poetic sentiments. His poems are filled with too many rebellious voices, which, in the view of people at that time, were certainly disobedient to the main cultural value or cultural norm. Although "discontent can be expressed in poetry," if the complaining emotion is over-expressed, the poetry will be suppressed by the dominant ideology and poetics. Moreover, rulers and readers of China throughout the ages have always focused their interests in poetry on certain "dignitaries" who have superb knowledge of the art of poetry, and their identity as prominent officials has been recognized by dominant poetics. Therefore, "marginal poets" like Han-shan seemed to be unable to escape from the fate of being forgotten. In this respect, it was Han-shan's misfortune to be born in this great era of poetry, which, as a consequence, spawned the CMPs. That is to say, only in such a maternal environment could the very distinctive poems be produced, so it should also be a great fortune for Han-shan. From the current literary perspective, although the CMPs have a unique literary and artistic value, they were not accepted by the poetic orthodoxy at the time. And for centuries to come, such a "precious heavenly priceless jewel" could only suffer the fate of being "buried in the skandhas submerged in the body".[135] With the same destiny, the poet Han-shan could only lament alone, "I don't mind few understand me, those who know one's voice are rare."[136] Soon the loneliness and tranquility were remedied by the influx of admirers of the Song Dynasty.

Han-shan once wrote, "One day I'll meet someone with eyes, then my poems will plague the world."[137] According to the research by Ye Zhuhong (叶珠红), "someone" here most likely referred to Li Shanfu (李山甫), who lived in the period of 836–900 of the Tang Dynasty. Li Shanfu once said, "Han-shan is talented but unappreciated," and he was the first literatus to quote Han-shan in poetry. Apart from Li, literati in the Song Dynasty such as Wang Anshi (王安石, 1021–1086), Su Shi (苏轼, 1037–1101), Huang Tingjian (黄庭坚, 1045–1105), Lu You (陆游, 1125–1210), Zhu Xi (朱熹, 1130–1200), Liu Kezhuang (刘克庄, 1187–1269) and others all appreciated the CMPs. They expressed their appreciation by imitating, teaching, printing or commenting. Wang Anshi (王安石), a later soul mate of Han-shan and a great literary master of the Song Dynasty (960–1279), not only loved the CMPs but also created himself *Ni Han-shan Shi-de Ershishou* (《拟寒山拾得二十首》, *Twenty Poems in Imitation of Han-shan and Shi-te*), which bears a striking resemblance to the CMPs in terms of both language and theme.

In views of the circulation and dissemination of the CMPs, Ye Zhuhong (叶珠红) argues that except for Buddhists who inscribed and published CMPs, Huang Tingjian (黄庭坚) is the literary figure who contributed most to the spread of the CMPs, which is mainly reflected in two aspects: one is to widely deliver people the written transcriptions of the CMPs and to rewrite the poems arbitrarily as his own works.[138] The truth, however, is that the written copy and imitation imposed limited influence on promoting the circulation of the CMPs.

It was the printing industry in the two Song dynasties (960–1279) that really made Han-shan's poetry widespread and popular in the world. The high prosperity of economy and commerce at that time laid the foundation for the development of culture. With the flourishing of the reading culture, the demand for the publication, circulation and reading of books became more and more intense, which provided a natural opportunity for the robust development of the printing industry. In addition, the two Song dynasties inherited the imperial examination system of the Tang Dynasty, which further stimulated the enthusiasm of the intellectual. At the same time, convenient transportation, convenient currency, the maturity and popularization of woodblock printing technology, and the creation and invention of movable type printing made the printing industry of the Song Dynasty achieve great development, which became the golden age in the history of woodblock printing of our country in China. Hu Yinglin (胡应麟, 1551–1602) once said, "Engraving books dated from the Sui Dynasty (581–618), began in the Tang Dynasty (618–907), were popular in Five Dynasty and ameliorated in the Song Dynasties (960–1279)." In the history of block printing in China, three major woodblock printing systems, namely, official printing, private printing and workshop printing, were also established in the Song Dynasty.

It is under such a background that the CMPs have been printed and circulated many times. The "Tianlu Song" edition *Han-shan-zi Fu Feng-gan Shi-de Shiyijuan* (《寒山子诗一卷附丰干拾得诗一卷》, *The Collection of Hanshan's Poems with a Volume of Feng-gan's and Shi-de's Poems Attached*), printed from *Tianlu Linlang* (《天禄琳琅》, *Imperial Collection of Books*) in the Song Dynasty, is recognized as the earliest extant woodblock printed version of the CMPs at home and abroad. It is speculated that this version may be a collection of CMPs obtained from Guoqing Temple by Jōjin (1011–1081), a Japanese monk who came to China to visit Tiantai Mountain in the year 1072. In fact, it appeared in the diary of Jōjin (1011–1081), who left a detailed record, *San Tendai Godai San Ki* (《参天台五台山记》, *The Record of a Pilgrimage to the Tiantai and Wutai Mountains*) describing his encounter with the legend and poems of Han-shan on Tiantai Mountain. In the article *The Legend of Han-shan: A Neglected Source*, the sinologist Borgen (1945–) records that Jōjin (1011–1081) made "more reasonable" adjustments to the narrative of the preface by Lü Qiuyin (闾丘胤). First was the date, then the introduction of the three main characters of Tiantai Mountain, followed by the encounter of Lü Qiuyin (闾丘胤) with Feng-gan. The latter suggested Lü Qiuyin (闾丘胤) visit Han-shan and Shi-de. Lü Qiuyin (闾丘胤) did so, but Han-shan and Shi-de refused to see him. He then went to the Zen room where Feng-gan was living, only to find that Feng-gan had also disappeared. Additionally, Jōjin's (1011–1081) version of the CMPs has added dates and an explanation of the name "Shi-de". The wording of this version, however, is the synonymous with that of the preface by Lü Qiuyin (闾丘胤).[139]

In addition, another edition of the CMPs was the "Guoqing temple" edition (the original edition of the "Donggao Temple" edition and the "Wuwohuishen" edition), which was compiled by the monk Zhi-nan (志南) of Guoqing Temple in the year 1189. This edition is said to be "the most widely circulated and the most influential".[140] In the year 1229, the monk Wuyin (无隐) of Donggao Temple re-carved the CMPs on the basis of the previous version, which is known as the "Donggao Temple" edition. Subsequently, the monk Wuwohuishen (无我慧身) found a prologue by Han-shan and added it to the previous version, thus his "*Wuwohuishenben*". One more edition is the "Baoyou" edition published by a monk named Xingguo (行果) in the year 1255. According to the preface of *Song Daziben Hanshanshi* (《宋大字本寒山诗集》, *Anthology of Cold Mountain Poems in Bigger Chinese Characters, Song Edition*), published by the Japanese sinologist Shimada Kan (1879–1915) in Japan in the year of 1905, the "Baoyou" edition was introduced to Korea in the Yuan Dynasty (1217–1368) and was engraved and published by Park Gyeong-ryang (1320–?) and others as the "Goryeo" edition.[141] The previously mentioned "Wuwohuishen" edition, published between the "Donggao" edition and the "Baoyou" edition, has been proved to be the Song edition in the collection of the Japanese Imperial Household Agency. In fact, in addition to what was noted earlier, there are other editions of the CMPs printed in the Song Dynasty (960–1279), including the "Goryeo" edition as well as other editions.

It is noteworthy that the "Guoqing temple" edition has been misidentified as the earliest extant version of the CMPs by Chinese scholars Hu Juren (胡菊人) and Chung Ling (钟玲) as well as American scholars Robert Henricks (1943–) and Paul Kahn (1952–). However, in the "Tianlu Song" edition, there is a note below the last poem of Shi-de, "Woods and Springs Make Me Smile".[142] The note said, "this poem was added from another edition."[143] According to these records, Ye Zhuhon (叶珠红) claims, "Like the 'Guoqing temple' edition, the 'Tianlu Song' edition is also a conflation edition." After close examinations, Ye Zhuhong (叶珠红)

points out in *Critical Studies of Materials about Han-shan* (《寒山资料考辨》), that the "Tianlu Song" edition is better organized and more detailed than the poems of Han-shan, Shi-de and Feng-gan, and was published later than *Han-shan Shiji* (《寒山诗集》, *Anthology of Cold Mountain Poems*) in *Yongledadian* (《永乐大典》, *Great Encyclopedia of Yongle*, completed in 1408, the world's earliest encyclopedia), which does not include "the pseudo-preface by Lü Qiuyin (闾丘胤) ", "Zen master Feng-gan's record", or "Shi-de's record". The "another edition" mentioned in the "Tianlu Song" edition is most likely the "Shanzhong" edition, on which the edition of *Yongledadian* (《永乐大典》, *Great Encyclopedia of Yongle*) is based.[144] However, Lee Jongmee, a Korean scholar specializing in edition studies, argues that the earliest extant edition of the CMPs is the block-printed edition of the Song dynasty (960–1279) collected in the Beijing Library.[145] Undoubtedly, these block-printed books of the Song Dynasty greatly expanded the channels and scale of the circulation of the CMPs, pushing its dissemination in later times and laying a solid foundation for its intralingual travel.

Apart from the literati circle, the CMPs had many monk followers in the Song Dynasty. There are a large number of imitations of CMPs, among which, those by Zen Master Shanzhao (善昭, 945–1022) and Huaishen (怀深, ?–1131) are the most famous. Huaishen's *Ni Han-shan Shi* (《拟寒山诗》, *Imitations of CMPs*) include as many as 148 poems. Furthermore, CMPs were also frequently used as official words for Zen meditation and for the court. Those words are extensively recorded in Zen literature works such as *Zutangji* (《祖堂集》, *Anthology of the Patriarchal Hall*), *Wudenghuiyuan* (《五灯会元》, *Compendium of Five Lamps*) and *Jingdechuandenglu* (《景德传灯录》, *Records of the Transmission of the Lamp*).

Why were CMPs widely circulated among Buddhists and literati in the Song Dynasty? The first reason is that Zen Buddhist poetry started to arouse attention. The ideology of Neo-Confucianism formed under the influence of Zen Buddhism had driven the poetic style in the Song Dynasty toward reasoning. CMPs continued the dominant poetic tradition, and their popular and religious poems were not only composed in the form of verse and chant but were also essentially polemical and reasoning-based. This coincided with the Confucian ideology of "the righteousness of the mind" and "extension of knowledge by investigation of things" advocated in the Song Dynasty. Thus, the CMPs were generally favored by the monks and literati of the Song Dynasty (960–1279). Secondly, literary forms such as traditional Chinese opera and vernacular novels in the Song Dynasty gradually flourished and began to develop in parallel with high literature (雅文学). Since the middle of the Ming Dynasty (1368–1644), high literature (poetry, lyrics, etc.) has shown a trend of being extremely mature.[146] In this stylistic context, the part of the vernacular poetry in the CMPs naturally won a certain degree of popularity and recognition in due course.

When it comes to the Yuan (1217–1368) and Ming Dynasties (1368–1644), imitation of CMPs still continued. For instance, Xingduan (行端, 1254–1341), the poet monk of the Yuan Dynasty (1217–1368), had more than 100 poems imitating CMPs, and he titled them *"Han Shi Li Ren Gao"* (《寒拾里人稿》). Another monk, Zhongfeng Mingben (中峰明本, 1263–1323), also composed

*Nihanshanshi Guanglu* (《拟寒山诗广录》, *A Record of Imitations of CMPs*). Zhang Shouyue (张守约) in the Ming Dynasty published *Nihanshanshi Yijuan* (《拟寒山诗一卷》, *A Volume of Imitation of CMPs*) (the 27th book of Volume 6 in *The Collection of Uncollected Books of the Four Catalogues*). With the decline of Neo-Confucianism, however, the imitating trend in the Yuan (1217–1368) and Ming (1368–1644) Dynasties had gradually declined while the trend of block printing was surging. In the Yuan Dynasty (1217–1368), the Goryeo copy printed from the edition of the Song Dynasty (960–1279) was included in *Sibu Congkan* (《四部丛刊》, *Collectanea of the Four Categories*) and was widely circulated. Besides the "Chushi block-printed" edition in the year of 1416, the CMPs printed in the Ming Dynasty (1368–1644) also included the following currently known editions: the "Shengduzhai block-printed" edition printed by Liu Hongyi (刘弘毅) in the year of 1516, the "Shi Daohui (the head monk of Guoqing Temple)" edition printed in the year of 1525 (collected in the Hong Kong University Library, China), the "Eight-line" edition, the "Tulong" edition, the "Ganeryi" edition, the "Wu Mingchun (吴明春)" revised edition, the "Taizhou" edition (printed in the year of 1599, compiled by Ji Yiji [计益辑], the governor of Taizhou, prefaced by Zong Mu [宗沐]) *Hesansheng Shiji* (《和三圣诗集》, *Collection of the Poems of Three Sages*, printed by a Taoist priest named Shishu [石树道人]), the "Guangzhou Haizhuang Temple" edition (collected in Sun Yat-sen Library of Guangdong Province, China) and the edition in *Yongledadian* (《永乐大典》, *Great Encyclopedia of Yongle*) frequently referred to by scholars in recent years.

Despite the fact that many imitations and printings have been circulated in the world, and that the CMPs have been favored by literati throughout the ages, it is intriguing to note that from the 12th century to the early 18th century, the CMPs were marginalized by the orthodoxy. In other words, the CMPs had never been truly included in the literary anthology and literary history recognized by the literary orthodoxy. The CMPs are not found in books such as *Wanshou Tangren Jueju* (《万首唐人绝句》, *Ten Thousand Stanzas of Tang Poets*) edited by Hong Mai (洪迈, 1123–1202) and *Tangshi Jishi* (《唐诗纪事》, *Chronicle of Tang Poems*) by Ji Yougong (计有功) in the Song Dynasty (960–1279), *Tang Yin* (《唐音》, *Sounds of Tang*) by Yang Shihong (杨士) in the Yuan Dynasty (1217–1368), *Tangshi Pinghui* (《唐诗品汇》, *Collection of Tang Poem*) by Gao Bing (高棅, 1350–1423) in the Ming Dynasty (1368–1644), or *Tangshibiecaiji* (《唐诗别裁集》) by Shen Deqian (沈德潜, 1673–1769) in the Qing Dynasty (1644–1912). "The poems of Han-shan we can read today are only those separate editions printed privately."[147]

In the year of 1672, *Tiantai Sansheng Shiji Heyun* (《天台三圣诗集和韵》, *Poem Collection of Three Sages in Tiantai Mountain*) was published in the scripture workshop of the Lanyan Temple (楞严寺) in Jiaxing, Zhejiang Province. It is said that the original edition was the Japanese edition. It was only in the year 1707 that poems of Han-shan were officially included in *Quantanshi* (《全唐诗》, *Complete Tang Poems*), a collection of poems of the Tang Dynasty compiled in the Qing Dynasty (1644–1912), and were listed as the first Buddhist poems. Subsequently, in the 11th year of Yongzheng (1733), Emperor Yongzheng[148] personally selected

127 poems of the CMPs to be printed and handed down and made the preface *Han-shanzi Shixu* (《寒山子诗序》, *Preface to Poems of Han-shan-zi*). This edition records:

> More than 300 CMPs and more than 50 poems of Shi-de were collected by a local magistrate Lü Qiuyin (闾丘胤) in Tang Dynasty at Hanyan (Cold Mountain), circulating after that in religious circles. Readers regard its style as some sort of vernacular, or rhyming, or didactic, or Zen. Just like mani beads, they are not uniform in shape, but exquisitely carved everywhere, according to what people see. I think it is not vernacular, not rhyming, not didactic or not Zen, but rather is the straightforward words of ancient Buddas.[149]

The preface to Hanshan Zi's poems written by Emperor Yongzheng greatly enhanced the social status and influence of the CMPs. In addition, Yongzheng also granted Han-shan the title of "Saint of He (妙觉普度和圣)", Shi-de as "Saint of He (圆觉慈度合圣)", which is "Two Saints of Hehe (Harmony)". The image of "Two Saints of Hehe" represented by Han-shan and Shi-de thus became the symbol of "Hehe culture (Harmony Culture)" in China, and they also became the embodiment of happiness and harmony, and therefore were greatly worshiped by newly-weds. Despite the royal consent of the emperor and even being deified as the patron saint of marriage, thus entering thousands of households and temples, the CMPs, however, were not included in *Three Hundred Tang Poems* published in 1763; instead, Siku Quanshu (*The Imperial Four Libraries*, 1782), a large literature series that followed, included all the CMPs that could be found.

Supposedly, the CMPs have had their own readership in all generations, among which there were many prestigious literary critics, but why were they never recognized by the orthodoxy and the literati in the Chinese cultural polysystem before the Qing Dynasty?

Firstly, Consider the vernacular poems of the CMPs, which have always been an obstacle on its way to canonization. For thousands of years, the distinction between elegance in classical Chinese and vulgarity in vernacular Chinese has convinced people that "the Buddhist and the scholars should use the elegant language, while those who occupied low-class professions can only use the vulgar ones."[150] The authors of classical texts were mostly from the monastery and the scholarly world, while the authors of vernacular works were often unknown. The CMPs include many popular ones, so the CMPs were naturally classified by people as street talk and delusional words of the "low-class", which are far from the elegant orthodox literature. Such works find it hard to survive, not to mention to be accepted by the mainstream elite. Then why is the elegant mainstream part of CMPs also not in the canon? The reason is that Han-shan's inferior status led to all his poems being undervalued. The poet's literary status outside of orthodox literature makes it impossible for his poetry to enter mainstream poetics or to receive the attention of the canon makers. The poet's literary identity marginalized by orthodox literature has prevented his poetic works from catching the attention of mainstream poetics and classic makers.

Secondly, the CMPs started the trend of vernacular poetry, which was naturally a new temptation for literati who pursued innovation. This perhaps is also the reason why the literati scholars imitated the CMPs. In the past, there may have been the concern that "vernacular poetry is not valid," but since someone has set a precedent, they started to compose vernacular poetry without qualms. But for them, writing vernacular poetry was seemingly a pastime after official duties, and all these works were only for entertainment. They were well aware of the truth that "non-elegant words will not become popular." They did not have the delusion of spreading such poems of their own, so they had no intention of making the CMPs a canon. In their eyes, the CMPs may just be a topic of conversation after tea and dinner. Therefore, just as Zhang Zhongxing (张中行, 1909–2006) said, the CMPs were just "a side dish at a banquet whose status was not high though it is on the table."[151]

Thirdly, the literati who imitated CMPs, such as Su Shi (苏轼), Huang Tingjian (黄庭坚) and Wang Anshi (王安石), and those who compiled the ancient classical poems, such as Hong Mai (洪迈, 1123–1202) and Ji Youkong (计有功), all came from the scholarly circle, thus, for the sake of literary and official career, naturally having no intention to deviate from the dominant ideology of their times. Therefore, although they were in favor of the CMPs, they would undoubtedly maintain the original literary order once the literary interests within the ruling class were involved. In other words, no one was willing to take the risk of establishing a new order, so the original form of "periphery" and "center" was continued.

Fourthly, there is a kind of compatibility between the CMPs and Zen Buddhism after the Middle Tang Dynasty (766–835) and the Song and Ming philosophies, which include the argumentative vernacular poems and the religious poems filled with Zen meaning. But the reason why the CMPs still linger outside the canon is, perhaps, that religious literature has not been taken seriously in tradition. During the prosperous Tang Dynasty (731–766), although the confluence of Confucianism, Buddhism and Taoism was pursued, still, Confucianism's belief that "the Master did not discuss strange occurrences, feats of strength, rebellion, the gods" was the mainstream thought. And the vernacular tradition of religious literature and the elegant tradition of literary poetry were incompatible with each other. The traditional Chinese literary history is written by Confucian scholars and therefore had little to do with religious literature; thus the religious poems in the CMPs naturally had no place to stand. Moreover, because of the confusing religious ideas and conflicting religious views in the religious poems of the CMPs, the religious poems were also regarded as "hearsay" and were rejected by the classic religious text authors and elite.

It was not until 1707 that the 900-volume collection of Tang Dynasty poetry, *Quantanshi* (《全唐诗》, *Complete Tang Poems*), began to include CMPs and listed them as the first of Buddhist poems. In the 860th volume of *Quantanshi* (《全唐诗》,

*Complete Tang Poems*), CMPs took up a huge space of nearly 40 pages. Thereafter, CMPs started to receive attention from the literary orthodoxy. After the exhausting intralingual travel of nearly a thousand years, the CMPs finally found their long-lost "home" in the polysystem of Chinese literature and were recognized for the first time by the prevailing cultural norms,[152] receiving unprecedented attention in the public intellectual sphere.

On the one hand, thanks to the collection, comment, quotation and imitation of CMPs by monks and the secular people for generations, the CMPs' literary status was finally formed. After all, the generation of classics is a process of historical accumulation. Secondly, the emergence of many vernacular popular literary forms in the Ming Dynasty (1368–1644) produced a rare golden period for people to accept and appreciate CMPs. Moreover, the discussion of "reason" in the Song and Ming philosophies brought great attention and admiration to the reasoning poems in CMPs. Again, the approval of CMPs by Wang Shizhen (王世禎), the literary master of the early Qing Dynasty, in his work *Juyi Lu* (《居易录》, *Records of My Life*), was undoubtedly an important motivation for the poems to become a classic discourse. Meanwhile, it is worth mentioning that the Emperor's faith in Buddhism in the early Qing Dynasty was also one of the important reasons. Han-shan's status as "Manjushri" (文殊) in the preface by Lü Qiuyin (闾丘胤), as well as the large number of Buddhist and Zen poems included in the CMPs, were naturally praised by the ruler. The Emperor Yongzheng, who worshiped Buddhism, personally selected 127 CMPs and wrote the *Han-shan-zi Shixu* (《寒山子诗序》, *Preface to Han-shan-zi Poems*), which even more firmly established the literary status of CMPs. In terms of patronage theory, the supreme ruler of the trinity of ideology, economic interests and social status was undoubtedly the most powerful contributing factor in the process of textual canonization. The accumulation of history, the change of the prevailing cultural norms, the recommendation of authoritative literary patrons, the literary interests of the supreme ruler, and the literary interests of the ruling class have combined to achieve the literary status of Han-shan as well as his poems in the history of Chinese poetry.

In 1782, the *Siku Quanshu* (《四库全书》, *The Imperial Four Libraries*) also began to include the selection of CMPs. In addition, the contemporary literati of the Qing Dynasty (1644–1912) also showed great interest in the poems. Not only did Wang Shizhen (王世禎) comment on CMPs in *Juyi Lu* (《居易录》, *Records of My Life*), but also the famous documentarian Qian Zeng (钱曾, 1629–1701) included a volume of *Han-shan Shi-de Shi* (《寒山拾得诗》, *Han-shan and Shide's Poems*) copied from a Song engraving in his *Du Shu Mingqiu Ji* (《读书敏求记》, *Reading and Researching Notes by Qian Zeng*). Yu Yue (俞樾), a master of textual research during the Daoguang period (1821–1850), Lu Xinyuan (陆心源, 1838–1894), a bibliophile during the Tongzhi period (1862–1875), and Cheng Dequan (程德全, 1860–1930), the governor of Jiangsu Province during the Xuantong's reign (1909–1911), all admired the poems. However, because the literati in the early Qing Dynasty (1644–1912) were keen on the textual research that esteems the past over the present, the vernacular poetry represented by the CMPs was not popular then. It was not until the early 19th century that the thought of "study on ancient classics should meet present needs" against the textual research brought vernacular poetry more attention from the literati and readers of the Qing Dynasty (1644–1912). But except for the successful inclusion into *Quantanshi* (《全唐诗》, *Complete Tang Poems*) and *Siku Quanshu* (《四库全书》, *The Imperial Four Libraries*) in the Qing Dynasty (1644–1912), CMPs did not seem to receive the enthusiasm people should have for the canonical text. Even in the "poetry revolution" at the end of the Qing Dynasty (1644–1912), the CMPs were not known to the public.

In the late Qing Dynasty (1644–1912), when the literary polysystem was "peripheral" and "weak", translated literature began to move toward the center of the cultural polysystem. In this process, especially the translated novels with a strong political ideology gained the most central position. Perhaps because of the absence of political-ideological elements, the CMPs, which were generally regarded as vernacular poetry, did not attract much social reaction at that time. Besides, the legendary image of the crazy hermit poet, Han-shan, could not be accepted by the dominant ideology of the time, which preached radicalism and worldliness. As a result, the CMPs tended to be silent in the intralingual travel during this period.

### 3.3.2 The Dissemination and Acceptance of the CMPs from the Early Years of the Republic of China to the "Cultural Revolution"

When it comes to the early years of the Republic of China, the temporary silence was broken by the dramatic "Vernacular Literary Movement" and the "New Poetry Movement". The CMPs, which represented the vernacular and popular tradition, once again "climbed onto the stage." In 1919, the Commercial Press in Shanghai published *Han-shan Shi: 1 Juan, Feng-gan Shi-de Shi, Fu Cishou Ni Han-shan Shi* (《寒山诗：1卷、丰干拾得诗、附慈受拟寒山诗》, *Cold Mountain Poems: Volume 1, Feng-gan's and Shi-de's Poems, Cishou's Imitations of CMPs Included*), which was copied from the Goryeo collection by Zhai's family in Changshu, Jiangsu Province, China.

However, it was not until the publication of *History of Vernacular Literature* by Hu Shi (胡适) that Han-shan once again received more intensive attention. In 1921, when Hu Shi (胡适) was a professor at Peking University, he published *History of Vernacular Literature*, which for the first time clarified Han-shan as a "great poet of the vernacular", thus giving Han-shan a real identity as a poet in the poetry world for the first time.[153] In discussing the origin of vernacular poetry, Hu Shi (胡适) said, "Among the vernacular poets of the early Tang Dynasty (618–712), Wang Fanzhi (王梵志), Han-shan and Shi-de all made their debut by taking the path of mockery, and they all became famous by writing doggerel."[154] When speaking of the story of Shao Shuo (邵硕), a mad monk in the second half of the fifth century, Hu Shi (胡适) argued, "Under this trend of treacherous poetry driven by mad monks, three or five great vernacular poets emerged in the middle of the

7th century."[155] He first mentioned Wang Fanzhi (王梵志), Wang Ji (王绩) and the Four Masters of the early Tang Dynasty (618–712), and then Han-shan and Shi-de. Hu Shi (胡适) not only provided a detailed examination of Han-shan's life story but also demonstrated that Han-shan still followed the vernacular style of Wang Fanzhi (王梵志) according to nine of Han-shan's vernacular poems.

In the poetic climate of the time, Hu Shi (胡适) and his literary history work completely elevated Han-shan to the rank of mainstream Chinese poets, thanks to his position as a professor at Peking University and a leading figure in the New Literary Movement, and the fact that he was teaching *History of Vernacular Literature* to students at China's highest educational institutions. In Hu Shi's (胡适) opinion, "the history of vernacular literature is the central part of the history of Chinese literature, and if the history of vernacular literature evolution were removed, the history of Chinese literature would not be complete." He also considered the history of vernacular literature to be "the most lively, creative, and representative of the times" in the history of Chinese literature.[156] He said, "The history of Chinese literature over the past thousand years is a prosperous history of vernacular literature, but a declining history of ancient literature."[157] To sum up, it can be said that it was the Vernacular Literature Movement in the early 20th century and Hu Shi's (胡适) authoritative status that contributed to Han-shan's poet identity and classical status. From then on, the study of CMPs by contemporary Chinese scholars had begun. Since the 1920s, the number of publications of the CMPs began to far exceed that of the previous time; in 1924, the Zhou family in Jiande published *Jingsongben Han-shan shi* (《景宋本寒山子诗》, *Cold Mountain Poems of Jing Song Edition*); in 1926, the Zhang family in Wuxing published *Han-shan Shiji Fu Fenggan Shi-de Shi* (《寒山诗集:附丰干拾得诗》, *Anthology of Cold Mountain Poems: With the Poems of Feng-gan and Shi-de*) (written by Han-shan and collected by Zhang Junheng (张钧衡, 1872–1927), included in *Zeshiju Congshu* (《择是居丛书》, *The Zeshiju Series*). However, these two were both unofficial editions, and their circulation was relatively small, so their influence was quite limited. From the late '20s, *Sibu Congkan* (《四部丛刊》, *Collectanea of the Four Categories*), which was published by the Commercial Press, printed the CMPs two times in succession. The first is a copy of the Goryeo book collected by Huang Pilie (黄丕烈, 1763–1825) and Qu Yong (瞿镛, 1794–1846), and the second is a copy of the Song Dynasty's edition by the Zhou's family, that is, the edition of the Song Dynasty (960–1279) collected in Ji Guge (汲古阁). In 1931, relying on donation, Shanghai Fazang Temple printed an edition according to *He Sansheng Shiji* (《和三圣诗集》, *Collection of the Poems of Three Sages*) collected in Zangjingyuan in Yangzhou (扬州藏经院藏板), which was called *Heding Tiantai Sansheng Erhe Shiji* (《合订天台三圣二和诗集》, *Collection of Poems of the Three Sages of Tiantai*). It is Shanghai Buddhist Bookstore that published the most, with three editions and six titles in just ten years, from 1937 to 1947.

Following Hu Shi's (胡适) *History of Vernacular Literature*, Zheng Zhenduo's (郑振铎, 1898–1958) *History of Chinese Popular Literature* was first published by the Commercial Press in August 1938. The author arranged Han-shan in the part of Chinese popular literature and entitled him a "popular poet" for the first time. This book began by stating that "popular literature has become not only a major component of Chinese literary history but also the center of Chinese literary history."[158] He pointed out that "popular literature" is something supreme, all of which are masterpieces, unlike what other people imagine that popular literature is: something to be despised, something that is nothing.[159] In a chapter titled *Folk Songs in the Tang Dynasty* (《唐代的民间歌赋》), Zheng Zhenduo (郑振铎) pointed out:

> Although Bai Juyi's (白居易, 772–846) poems are said to be easy to understand, they are not vernacular poems at all: he did not dare to write exclusively for people, did not dare to quote dialects and colloquialisms in his poems, and did not dare to write in his poetry the opinions and emotions of ordinary people. The poems of the poets like Wang Fanzhi (王梵志) are the real vernacular poems. Because they can be understood and appreciated by people. . . . The monk poets in the Tang Dynasty, such as Han-shan, Shi-de, and Feng-gan, were all influenced by him.
>
> (Wang Fanzhi)[160]

What Zheng Zhenduo (郑振铎) emphasized is the characteristics such as "writing specifically for the people", "quoting dialects and colloquialisms into the poems" and "expressing the opinions and emotions of the people" etc., which are all fully presented in Han-shan's vernacular poems. Afterward, Zheng Zhenduo (郑振铎) quoted one of the CMPs, "People Laugh at My Poems",[161] and said, "This is a poem of the popular poet to offer an explanation to save his face in response to the ridicule of the classic poet."[162] Han-shan's identity as a poet was further established here. However, due to the political situation in China at the time and the support for anti-war literature, Zheng's literary history did not attract much response at the time. Like Hu Shi's (胡适) *History of Vernacular Literature*, it was written by intellectuals of the May Fourth Movement period for cultural enlightenment and literary innovation. Although it was somewhat utilitarian, Hu Shi (胡适) and Zheng Zhenduo (郑振铎), in any case, combined their efforts to bring Han-shan and other vernacular poets to the forefront of modern and contemporary literary studies.

However, the ensuing war against Japan and the preference for left-wing literature (revolutionary literature) during this period caused the CMPs to fall out of favor once again. Twenty years later, in 1958, when the American poet Gary Snyder published his significant translation of 24 CMPs in *The Evergreen Review*, the famous Chinese bibliographer Yu Jiaxi's (余嘉锡) *Siku Tiyao Bianzheng* (《四库提要辨证》, *Investigation into Abstracts of The Imperial Four Libraries*) was published in the same year. Volume 20 (Collection I) of this book, which was a meticulous examination of Han-shan's life, and proved the falsification of *Han-shan-zi Shixu* (《寒山子诗序》, *Preface to Han-shan-zi Poems*) caused great responses in the Chinese mainland, Taiwan and Hong Kong. Yu's monograph is believed to be an important milestone in the study of the CMPs, a truly meaningful academic study of the poems.

In 1959, Qian Mu (钱穆) published 读书散记两篇•读寒山诗 ("Two Essays on Reading—Reading Cold Mountain Poems") on the first issue of *Hong Kong's New Asia College Academic Yearbook*. The article cited several of the CMPs and made bold assumptions about the poet's life based on the poems. Qian's article did not have much impact on the Chinese mainland academic circle at the time.

In 1963, Ruo Fan's (若凡) essay, 寒山子诗韵 (附拾得诗韵) ("Poetic Rhymes of Han-shan-zi (with poetic rhymes of Shi-de)") was included in *the Linguistic Series* (5th series), which was edited by the Chinese Department of Peking University and published by the Commercial Press. This monograph analyzes the rhymes of Han-shan's and Shi-de's poems to discover the characteristics of their rhymes and the actual phonetic situation of the time they reflect. In the introduction, the author uses Zheng Zhenduo's (郑振铎) terminology, calling Han-shan and Shi-de the "monk-poet" and claiming that their story was rendered divine and grotesque. The author's comment on the poems of Han-shan and Shi-de, however, is not so positive. He said,

> Their works should be more accurately called "Buddhist chant" rather than poems because their content and form are similar to the Buddhist chant or hymn. And most of the content is to preach Buddhist philosophy, and there are some descriptions of the natural world, which are not very desirable.[163]

Why, then, does the author explore the CMPs? This is precisely because of the plain and simple language of the poems. Ruo Fan (若凡) concludes in his study that the rhyming system of Han-shan and Shi-de's poems

> not only differs greatly from the rhyming system in "Qieyun" (切韵, a Chinese rhyme dictionary) which mainly focuses on "appreciating the pronunciation", but also does not meet the requirements of imperial examination regulations in the Tang dynasty (618–907). . . . These facts indicate that the use of rhyme by Han-shan and Shi-de was not influenced by the "official rhyme" of the time, thus can reflect the reality of the language.[164]

It should be told that the publication of this monograph has greatly enriched the perspective of the study of the CMPs and perhaps inspired later researchers such as the Canadian sinologist Pulleyblank's (1922–2013) study "Linguistic Evidence for the Date of Han-shan" in 1978, as well as a series of phonetic studies of CMPs by Chinese scholars such as Qian Xuelie (钱学烈) and Zhu Rulue (朱汝略, 1952–) in the 1980s and 1990s and beyond. In the late 1960s, because of political ideology among other reasons, the publication and study of the CMPs declined in the Chinese mainland.

## 3.4 Prevailing Cultural Norms and the Literary Fate of the CMPs

The fundamental reason why CMPs were rejected by the literary orthodoxy before the 18th century was that the poems were incompatible with the prevailing cultural norms and were against the dominant poetics and literary values. Therefore, before the 18th century, the dissemination and acceptance of the CMPs in the local cultural polysystem was purely a non–cultural elite act. A series of activities, such as collecting, proofreading, publishing, commenting and imitating, were all carried out and continued by secular folk forces and unofficial monks under the premise of not violating the main cultural norms.

In fact, Han-shan's "bizarre" legends, his "tangled" life experience, and the large number of "vernacular poems" despised by mainstream poetics, as well as the intense religious conflicts in the poems, make it difficult for official traditionalists of orthodox literary and moralists to accept it as "authentic" and "classical". Only in the year 1707 did the *Quantanshi* (《全唐诗》, *Complete Tang Poems*), a 900-volume collection of Tang poetry, begin to include the CMPs and list them as the first Buddhist poems. After that, the CMPs began to truly receive public readers' attention. Besides the inclusion of CMPs in *Siku Quanshu* (《四库全书》, *The Imperial Four Libraries*) in 1782, the CMPs did not renew their glory. In the late Qing Dynasty, when the cultural polysystem was "peripheral" and "weak", the translated literature was at the center of the polysystem. And the value and status of novels that had long been regarded as "unorthodox" were re-examined and re-evaluated. However, according to literary value criteria at the time, the "popular novels" seemed to be identified as a new literary model for "saving the country" and as a new form of linguistic expression that imported advanced new ideas. Thus, the status of the creation of local popular novels can't be matched with that of the translation of the foreign novel. Naturally, there is little interest in vernacular poems, especially in those of the local cultural tradition. Although the so-called "poetic revolution" was advocated, Han-shan's image as a retired hermit in the mountains and the "poisonous thoughts", advocating a sequestered life, in his poems were obviously not eulogized by the initiators and organizers of the movement in this period. Although popular literature gained an unprecedented literary status in Chinese literary history of the late Qing Dynasty (1644–1912), the CMPs, which were recognized as a popular genre in tradition, did not attract the slightest attention in the literary context and political discourse of the time.

At the beginning of the Civil War when the vigorous "Vernacular Movement" and "New Poetry Movement" happened, the local popular culture tradition was pursued and valued. And the movement itself showed the literary and political value in terms of the language revolution. Thanks to all these factors, Han-shan's "role as a vernacular poet" was highlighted. Particularly, the publication and lecture of Hu Shi's (胡适) *History of Vernacular Literature* in 1921 brought Han-shan and his poems to people's attention once again. The CMPs, representing the vernacular and popular tradition, paced into the pantheon of literary classics in literary history written by Hu Shi (胡适), hence the promotion of Han-shan into the ranks of mainstream Chinese poets. In 1938, Zheng Zhenduo (郑振铎) traced the tradition of Chinese popular literature in his *History of Chinese Popular Literature*. He once again affirmed the supremacy of CMPs in popular literature as the "center of Chinese literary history". However, due to socio-historical reasons such as the cooling of the "New Culture Movement" and the subsequent Anti-Japanese War, Hu Shi's (胡适) and Zheng Zhenduo's (郑振铎) literary histories were known only in limited literary circles at the time, having little influence on the general readers and the public. The passage of time, however, brought about changes in literary concepts and a paradigm shift in academic research. In 1985, the publication of the famous Chinese bibliographer Yu Jiaxi's (余嘉锡) *Siku Quanshu* (《四库全书》, *The Imperial Four Libraries*) won the unanimous approval of the academic community in the Chinese mainland, Taiwan and Hong Kong, thus ushering in an era of academic research of Han-shan and his poems in the true sense. Then, in 1959 Qian Mu's (钱穆) "Two Essays on Reading—Reading Cold Mountain Poems" (读书散记两篇•读寒山诗) was published in the first issue of *New Asia College Academic Yearbook* in Hong Kong, and in 1963, Ruo Fan's (若凡) essay on the CMPs, "Poetic Rhymes of Han-shan-zi (with Poetic Rhymes of Shi-de)" (寒山子诗韵 (附拾得诗韵)) was published, both of which were the practical fruits of that influence.

Of course, before the "New Culture Movement" to the 1960s, there were several publications of CMPs. The truth, however, is that except for the fleeting "big hit", the CMPs remained a peripheral role in the dominant ideology of the time. Therefore, the CMPs were still not well known until the 1960s. Moreover, from the late 1960s on, the publication and study of the CMPs in Chinese mainland fell off again. This decline, nonetheless, was like the darkness before the dawn. The temporarily silent scene did not last long, and then was broken by the overseas "Han-shan fever", which made the CMPs enter into the magnificent palace of translated literature canon in the world. In comparison, this fever from overseas is much fiercer than the expectations of the departure. The influence of Han-shan and his poems is almost everywhere. The CMPs traveled from our neighboring Japan and Korea to the distant Sweden of Scandinavia, from the British and French in Western Europe to the United States in North America, from the small European countries, Belgium and the Czech Republic, to the powerful Holland and Germany. In fact, in the history of Chinese literature, the textual journey of the CMPs indicated that Han-shan is more famous abroad than at home. Owing to such a unique and magnificent "Han-shan phenomenon", the history of Chinese and Western literature has to re-examine a series of interactions between text travel and canon construction.

In fact, in the history of Chinese literature before the first half of the 20th century, the CMPs have always been a "subsidiary tool". The attention and study of CMPs are also limited to utilitarian interests. This long-term embarrassed identity is contributed by the tension between the CMPs and the prevailing cultural norms. Because of the tension, they inevitably contradict and conflict with each other. Because of the conflict and contradiction, the poems' intralingual literary journey is bound to be full of frustrations. For a long time, the unrestrained, plain, deviant CMPs had been ignored because they were not in line with the shared literary quality, moral codes, poetic aesthetics and cultural norms of the mainstream society.

The poems accordingly have been wandering outside of the orthodox literary history and the dominant literary discourse.

In the Qing Dynasty (1644–1912), the poems were included in the *Quantanshi* (《全唐诗》, *Complete Tang Poems*), the classical Chinese poetry, and in the Vernacular Movement of the early 20tha century, Han-shan was "invited" into Chinese literary history by Hu Shi (胡适) and Zheng Zhenduo (郑振铎) as a "vernacular poet" and "popular poet". Perhaps because the idea of actively engaging in the world advocated by the literary orthodoxy and by the May Fourth Movement is opposite to the "negative avoidance" thoughts that repeatedly appeared in the CMPs, especially when the critical spirit of the poems as vernacular literature was gradually forgotten by the "revolutionary" propagated by Marxism, however, CMPs once again became a historical relic. As some commentators said, "But when it was studied, analyzed in depth and grasped comprehensively, people saw the gap and deviation between its tendencies and the politics, ideology and culture of the time, so they naturally abandoned it."[165]

As mentioned earlier, given the constraints of prevailing cultural norms in China, the CMPs had suffered from a poor reception during the thousands of years of intralingual literary journey in Chinese literary history. Even if Han-shan was occasionally favored, he mostly served as a tool of manipulation, and his poetic achievements were still shrouded in the shadow of vernacular poets of the Tang Dynasty, such as Wang Ji (王绩) and Wang Fanzhi (王梵志). If Yu Jiaxi's (余嘉锡) *Siku Tiyao Bianzheng* (《四库提要辨证》, *Investigation into Abstracts of the Imperial Four Libraries*) (the 20th volume of Collection I) in the 1950s is to be regarded as the very outset of the genuine academic study of Han-shan and the CMPs, it could be told that the CMPs had been absent in Chinese academic circles for more than 1,200 years since they were first circulated in the eighth century.

**Notes**

1. R. Pine. *The Collected Songs of Cold Mountain*. Port Townsend: Copper Canyon Press, 2000: 3.
2. G. Toury. *Descriptive Translation Studies and Beyond*. Amsterdam and Philadelphia: John Benjamins Publishing Company, 1996: 54–55.
3. R. Bartsch. *Norms of Language: Theoretical & Practical Aspects*. London and New York: Longman, 1987: xiv.
4. A. Chesterman. *Memes of Translation: The Spread of Ideas in Translation Theory*. Amsterdam and Philadelphia: John Benjamins Publishing Company, 1997: 54–55.
5. G. Toury. *Descriptive Translation Studies and Beyond*. Amsterdam and Philadelphia: John Benjamins Publishing Company, 1996: 54.
6. T. Hermans. Norms and the Determination of Translation: A Theoretical Framework. // R. Alvarez & M. Vidal Carmen-Africa (eds.), *Translation, Power, Subversion*. Clevedon and Philadelphia: Multilingual Matters Ltd., 1996: 26.
7. T. Hermans. Norms and the Determination of Translation: A Theoretical Framework. // R. Alvarez & M. Vidal Carmen-Africa (eds.), *Translation, Power, Subversion*. Clevedon and Philadelphia: Multilingual Matters Ltd., 1996: 32.
8. G. Toury. *Descriptive Translation Studies and Beyond*. Amsterdam and Philadelphia: John Benjamins Publishing Company, 1996: 55.

9. G. Toury. *Descriptive Translation Studies and Beyond.* Amsterdam and Philadelphia: John Benjamins Publishing Company, 1996: 55.
10. A. Chesterman. *Memes of Translation: The Spread of Ideas in Translation Theory.* Amsterdam and Philadelphia: John Benjamins Publishing Company, 1997: 55–56.
11. Cultural Norms. www.answers.com/topic/cultural-norms-1. [2007–03–14].
12. A. Chesterman. *Memes of Translation: The Spread of Ideas in Translation Theory.* Amsterdam and Philadelphia: John Benjamins Publishing Company, 1997: 56.
13. G. Toury. *Descriptive Translation Studies and Beyond.* Amsterdam and Philadelphia: John Benjamins Publishing Company, 1996: 55.
14. Y. Iriya. A Glimpse into Cold Mountain Poems (trans. Wang Shunhong). // *Collation and Research of Ancient Books* (Issue 4). Beijing: Zhonghua Book Company, 1989: 234.
15. Quoted from Zhang Mantao. Evaluation and Interpretation of Cold Mountain Poems by Japanese Scholars. // *Death of The Japanese.* Taipei: Liming Press, 1976: 100–108.
16. D. Tisang. Interpretation of Cold Mountain Poems. // *Southeast Culture* (Special Issue of Tiantai Mountain Culture), 1990 (6): 125.
17. Li Fang. *Taiping Guangji (A Collection of Ancient Novels in China).* Beijing: Zhonghua Book Company, 1961: 338.
18. For instance, Hu Shi believed that the birth and death of Han-shan should be 700–780; see Hu Shi. *History of Vernacular Literature.* Hong Kong: Yingzhong Publishing House, 1949: 175. Yu Jiaxi believed that his birth and death year should be 691–793; see *Investigation into Abstracts of the Imperial Four Libraries.* Hong Kong: Zhonghua Book Company, 1974: 1255–1256. Qian Mu verified it as: 680?–810?; see Qian Mu. *Two Essays on Reading: Reading Cold Mountain Poems. Journal of New Asia College,* 1959 (1): 12. Chen Huijian thought that his life spanned 710–815; see *Han-shan-zi Studies.* Taipei: Dongda Book Company, 1984: 267. Sun Changwu presumed that it was 750–820; see Han-shan Legends and Cold Mountain Poems. *Nankai Literature Studies,* 1987; Zhang Bowei supposed that it could be 708?–810?; see Cold Mountain Poems and Zen Buddhism. *Zen and Poetics.* Hangzhou: Zhejiang People's Publishing House, 1992: 229–234. Qian Xuelie identified as 725–830; see *Commentary on Cold Mountain Poems and Shi-de Poems.* Tianjin: Tianjin Ancient Books Publishing House, 1998: 25. Luo Shijin deduced it as 726–826; see *The Evolution of Tang Poetry.* Nanjing: Jiangsu Ancient Books Publishing House, 2000: 111. Ye Zhuhong judged it as: 710–827; see *Examination of Cold Mountain Data.* Taipei: Xiuwei Information Technology Co., Ltd., 2005: 172. Red Pine, the translator of the complete English translation of the CMPs, puts the date of his birth and death at 730–850. See Red Pine. *The Collected Songs of Cold Mountain.* Port Townsend: Copper Canyon Press, 2000: 13. Someone held that the *Anthology of Cold Mountain Poems,* a collection of *The Imperial Four Libraries* compiled by Ji Yun, was in favor of the "Dali Hypothesis", but it is not true. Ji Yun in *The Abstract of Cold Mountain Poems* actually mentioned not only Xu Lingfu's Anthology of Cold Mountain Poems in *Uncollected Biographies of Immortals,* but also the so-called anecdote of Lü Qiuyun of Taizhou governor meeting the three sages (Feng-gan, Han-shan and Shi-de). The *Abstract* ended: "There is no way to investigate further." It can be seen that Ji Yun's examination of the birth and death of Han-shan is fundamentally fuzzy and ambiguous.
19. T. H. Barret. Han-shan's Place in History. // P. Hobson (ed.), *Poems of Han-shan.* Walnut Creek: Altamira Press, 2003: 127.
20. Han-shan. *Cold Mountain Poems (The Song Dynasty Edition).* Hong Kong: Hong Kong Society for Permanent Release, 1959: 1–5.
21. Yu Jiaxi. *Investigation into Abstracts of The Imperial Four Libraries.* Hong Kong: Zhonghua Book Company, 1974: 1246–1247.
22. Wu Chi-Yu. A Study of Han Shan. *T'oung Pao,* 1957 (XLV): 400.
23. Wu Chi-Yu. A Study of Han Shan. *T'oung Pao,* 1957 (XLV): 409.
24. Hu Juren. The Resurrection of the Poet Monk Han-shan. *Ming Pao Monthly* (Hong Kong), 1966, 1(11): 3.

25 Huang Boren. Preface. // *Han-shan and His Poems*. Taipei: Xinwenfeng, 1981: 1.
26 G. Snyder. *Riprap and Cold Mountain Poems*. San Francisco: Grey Fox Press, 1965: 33.
27 Zan-ning. *Biographies of Eminent Monks in the Song Dynasty*. Beijing: Zhonghua Book Company, 1997: 484.
28 Han-shan et al. *Anthology of Cold Mountain Poems: Poems of Feng-gan, Chu-shi, Shi-de and Shi-shu Included*. Taipei: Wenfeng Press, 1970: 64.
29 Hu Shi. *History of Vernacular Literature*. Hong Kong: Yingzhong Bookstore, 1959: 173.
30 Yu Jiaxi. *Investigation into Abstracts of The Imperial Four Libraries*. Hong Kong: Zhonghua Book Company, 1974: 1260.
31 There are different opinions about Dao Qiao. Wu Chi-Yu suspected he was the author of the pseudo-preface; David Hawkes, a renowned translator, broadly agrees with this opinion and speculates that Dao Qiao probably did not know who Han-shan was, but he did collect poems. The hermit who wrote the poem had died about 15 to 20 years earlier, so all Dao Qiao knew about Han-shan was a legend told by superstitious peasants. See David Hawkes. Book Review: *Cold Mountain: 100 Poems by the T'ang Poet Han-shan*, Translated and with an Introduction by Burton Watson. pp. 122. New York: Grove Press, Inc., 1962: 596–599. *Journal of the American Oriental Society*, 1962, 82(4): 596. Ye Zhuhong, based on Li Yong's (678–747) preface to *The Monument of Guoqing Temple*, believed that Dao Qiao was a real person:

According to his age, Dao Qiao still existed in the year of 747, while Han-shan had not yet lived as a hermit in Cold Mountain, who secluded himself there in the era of middle Dali reign (about 766–779). How can Dao Qiao collect poems before Han-shan created more than 300 poems on bamboos, woods and stone walls and on the walls of houses in villages? Therefore, we know that "Monk Dao Qiao" is a real person, but he did not collect any poems at all.
    Ye Zhuohong. *Investigation of Anthology of Cold Mountain Poems*.
    Taipei: Literature, History and Philosophy Press, 2005: 10–11

Victor Mair speculated that the compiler Dao Qiao was the real author of the CMPs:

Given the lack of literary polish in both the poems and the preface, Tao-ch'iao, an undistinguished local monk who seems not to have fully mastered Classical Chinese, would be an eligible sort of person for the task. Not being completely conversant with Classical Chinese, the compiler/author (?) of the Cold Mountain poems would have had a natural predilection to rely on MVS. ... To provide some sort of justification for his collection, Tao-ch'iao may have created Cold Mountain, Foundling, and Feng-kan 豐干 ("Broad Shield"), the person who allegedly introduced them to Lu-ch'iu Yin, as characters in a poetic fable. He may even have borrowed Lu-ch'iu Yin, the presumed Prefect of T'ai-chou 台州, to lend legitimacy to his humble enterprise.
    Mair Victor. Script and Word in Medieval Vernacular Sinitic.
    *Journal of the American Oriental Society* 112.2, 1992

Daejeon also believes that "there are zen monks and Taoist priests, who write poems to express their feelings and ambitions under the pseudonym of Han-shan and Shi-de, in the hope that their contemporaries could view them as madmen" (Daejeon Tisang. Interpretation of Cold Mountain Poems. *Southeast Culture* (Special Issue of Tiantaishan Culture) 1990 (6): 125).
32 Yu Jiaxi. *Investigation into Abstracts of The Imperial Four Libraries*. Hong Kong: Zhonghua Book Company, 1974: 1254.
33 C. Y. Wu. A Study of Han-shan. *T'oung Pao*, 1957, XLV: 397–399.
34 R. Borgen. The Legend of Han-shan: A Neglected Source. *Journal of the American Oriental Society*, 1991 (3): 576–578.
35 Ye Zhuhong believed that Han-shan himself was the first person to compile his poems. The author also believes that Xu Lingfu was the first person besides Han-shan to compile the CMPs. Ye Zhuohong. *Investigation of Anthology of Cold Mountain Poems*. Taipei: Literature, History and Philosophy Press, 2005: 14. The period of his compilation of the

CMPs, according to Ye, ranged from the completion of Tongbai Temple (829) to the first year of Huichang before he was recruited (841). Ye Zhuohong. *Investigation of Anthology of Cold Mountain Poems*. Taipei: Literature, History and Philosophy Press, 2005: 10.
36 Translated by Red Pine.
37 Qian Mu. Two Essays on Reading—Reading Cold Mountain Poems. *Journal of New Asia College*, 1959 (1): 6.
38 Xie Siwei. *Zen and Chinese Literature*. Beijing: China Social Sciences Press, 1993: 110.
39 Zhang Bowei. Cold Mountain Poems and Zen Buddhism. // *Zen and Poetics*. Hangzhou: Zhejiang People's Publishing House, 1992: 230.
40 The poem here is translated by Arthur Waley.
41 Xu Guangda. Han-shan, Shi-de and Their Poems. // *Annotations of the Poems of Han-shan-zi: Shi-de's Poems Attached*. Xi'an: Shanxi People's Publishing House, 1991: 5.
42 R. Henricks. *The Poetry of Han-shan: A Complete, Annotated Translation of Cold Mountain*. New York: State University of New Work Press, 1990: 9.
43 Zhou Qi. *Cold Mountain Poems and Its History*. Hefei: Huangshan Press, 1994: 17.
44 Red Pine. *The Collected Songs of Cold Mountain*. Port Townsend: Copper Canyon Press, 2000: 13.
45 Qian Xue-lie. On Confucianism and Taoism in Cold Mountain Poems. *Chinese Cultural Studies*, 1998 (Summer volume): 103.
46 The poem here is translated by Arthur Waley.
47 Qian Xuelie. Preface. // *Commentary on Cold Mountain Poems and Shi-de's Poems*. Tianjin: Tianjin Ancient Books Publishing House, 1998: 59.
48 A. Waley. Poems by Han-Shan. // *Chinese Poems*. London: Unwin Paperbacks, 1982: 105.
49 R. Henricks. *The Poetry of Han-shan: A Complete, Annotated Translation of Cold Mountain*. New York: State University of New Work Press, 1990: 9.
50 Zhao Zifan. Han-shan-zi and His Poems. // Sun Qi. *Han-shan and Hippies*. Taichung: Putian Press, 1974: 133.
51 Yan Zhenfei. Han-shan-zi's Life History. *Southeast Culture*, 1994 (2): 213–214.
52 Yan Zhenfei. Han-shan-zi's Life History. *Southeast Culture*, 1994 (2): 213–214.
53 Y. Iriya. A Glimpse into Cold Mountain Poems. // Wang Shunhong (trans.), *Collation and Research of Ancient Books* (Issue 4). Beijing: Zhonghua Book Company, 1989: 248.
54 Wu Chi-Yu. A Study of Han Shan. *T'oung Pao*, 1957, XLV: 411.
55 Zhou Qi. *Cold Mountain Poems and Its History*. Hefei: Huangshan Press, 1994: 9–10.
56 Sun Changwu. *Traces of Buddha in Literature*. Beijing: Zhonghua Book Company, 2001: 216.
57 Qian Xuelie. *Commentary on Cold Mountain Poems and Shi-de's Poems*. Tianjin: Tianjin Ancient Books Publishing House, 1998: 18–22.
58 R. Henricks. *The Poetry of Han-shan: A Complete, Annotated Translation of Cold Mountain*. New York: State University of New Work Press, 1990: 419–421.
59 Ye Zhuhong. *Investigation of Anthology of Cold Mountain Poems*. Taipei: Literature, History and Philosophy Press, 2005: 14.
60 Yu Jiaxi. *Investigation into Abstracts of The Imperial Four Libraries*. Hong Kong: Zhonghua Book Company, 1974: 1256.
61 Quoted from Zhang Mantao. Evaluation and interpretation of Cold Mountain Poems by Japanese Scholars. // *Death of The Japanese*. Taipei: Liming Press, 1976: 110.
62 Y. Iriya. A Glimpse into Cold Mountain Poems. // Wang Shunhong (trans.), *Collation and Research of Ancient Books* (Issue 4). Beijing: Zhonghua Book Company, 1989: 240.
63 R. Henricks. The *Poetry of Han-shan: A Complete, Annotated Translation of Cold Mountain*. New York: State University of New Work Press, 1990: 11.
64 J. Blofeld. Introduction. Porter Bill. // *The Collected Songs of Cold Mountain*. Port Townsend: Copper Canyon Press, 2000: 32.
65 P. Kahn. Han Shan in English. *Renditions*, 1986 (Spring): 141.
66 Song Bainian. *Chinese Classical Literature Abroad*. Beijing: Beijing Language and Culture Institute Press, 1994: 230.
67 Xiang Chu. Reading Notes of Cold Mountain Poems. *Studies on Ancient Chinese Books* (Vol. 1). Shanghai: Shanghai Ancient Books Publishing House, 1996: 131.

68 Sun Qi. *Han-shan and Hippies*. Taichung: Putian Press, 1974: 3.
69 Luo Shijin. *The Evolution of Tang Poetry*. Nanjing: Jiangsu Ancient Books Publishing House, 2000: 116–117.
70 Wang Yao. Imitation of the Ancients and Falsification. // *On the History of Medieval Literature*. Beijing: Peking University Press, 1986: 208.
71 Wang Yao. Imitation of the Ancients and Falsification. // *On the History of Medieval Literature*. Beijing: Peking University Press, 1986: 209.
72 E. Pulleyblank. Linguistic Evidence for the Date of Han-shan. // Ronald C. Miao (ed.), *Studies in Chinese Poetry and Poetics*. San Francisco: Chinese Materials Centre, Inc., 1978, No. 1: 163.
73 E. Pulleyblank. Linguistic Evidence for the Date of Han-shan. // Ronald C. Miao (ed.), *Studies in Chinese Poetry and Poetics*. San Francisco: Chinese Materials Centre, Inc., 1978, No. 1: 164–165.
74 Shi Zhecun. Han-shan-zi: Eleven Poems. // *On the Tang Poetry*. Shanghai: East China Normal University Press, 1996: 585.
75 Sun Changwu. Cold Moutain Poems and Zen. // *Zen Mediation and Poetic Sentiment*. Beijing: Zhonghua Book Company, 1997: 258.
76 Wang Yao. Imitation of the Ancients and Falsification. // *On the History of Medieval Literature*. Beijing: Peking University Press, 1986: 204.
77 Sun Changwu. Cold Moutain Poems and Zen. // *Zen Mediation and Poetic Sentiment*. Beijing: Zhonghua Book Company, 1997: 258.
78 Yu Jiaxi. *Investigation into Abstracts of the Imperial Four Libraries*. Hong Kong: Zhonghua Book Company, 1974: 1259.
79 The poem here is translated by Robert Henricks.
80 Qian Xuelie. *Commentary on Cold Mountain Poems and Shi-de's Poems*. Tianjin: Tianjin Ancient Books Publishing House, 1998: 31.
81 Sun Qi. *Han-shan and Hippies*. Taichung: Putian Press, 1974: 15.
82 V. Mair. Script and Word in Medieval Vernacular Sinitic. *Journal of the American Oriental Society*, 1992, 112(2): 271.
83 Han-shan. *Anthology of Cold Mountain Poems in The Imperial Four Libraries*. The intranet edition in the library of Hong Kong Baptist University. No page. All poems in the quotation here are translated by Red Pine.
84 Chen Yinchi. Two Worlds of Han-shan. // *The Great World: Buddhist Literature*. Kunming: Yunnan People's Publishing House, 2001: 192.
85 Xie Siwei. *Zen and Chinese Literature*. Beijing: China Social Sciences Press, 1993: 110.
86 Kuang Fu. The Prose- and Argumentation-styled Poems of Wang Fanzhi and the Song Dynasty. // Zhang Xihou (ed.), *Studies on Wang Fanzhi's Poems*. Shanghai: Shanghai Classics Publishing House, 1990: 120.
87 Liu Dajie. *History of the Development of Chinese Literature*. Taipei: Huazheng Books, 1980: 405.
88 Zhang Xihou. On the Colloquial Tendency of Wang Fanzhi's Poems. //*Studies on Wang Fanzhi's Poems)*. Shanghai: Shanghai Classics Publishing House, 1990, 135.
89 Xiang Chu. The Vernacular Poetry School in the Tang Dynasty. *Jiangxi Social Science*, 2004 (2): 40.
90 More details can be read in the following four articles: 1. Xu Sanjian. The Circulation and Influence of CMPs. *Southeast Culture: Special Issue of Tiantai Mountain Culture*, 1990 (6): 113–120; 2. Chen Yaodong. On the quotation and imitation of CMPs: A study on the influence of CMPs in the Zenand the Literary Field and Their Editions. *Journal of Jishou University*, 1994 (6); 59–66; 3. Cao Xun. The Bosom Friend of Cold Mountain Poems in the Song Dynasty—Also on the Circulation and Influence of Cold Mountain Poems in the Song Dynasty. //. *Chinese Classics & Culture Essays Collection* (4th edition). Beijing: Zhonghua Book Company, 1997: 121–133; 4. Sun Changwu. Cold Mountain Poems and Zen Buddhism. //*Zen Mediation and Poetic Sentiment*. Beijing: Zhonghua Book Company, 1997: 268–273.
91 Translated by Red Pine.

92 R. Henricks. *The Poetry of Han-shan: A Complete, Annotated Translation of Cold Mountain*. New York: State University of New Work Press, 1990: 12.
93 Y. Iriya. A Glimpse into Cold Mountain Poems//. Wang Shunhong (trans.), *Collation and Research of Ancient Books* (Issue 4). Beijing: Zhonghua Book Company, 1989: 241.
94 Translated by Stephen Owen.
95 Translated by Stephen Owen.
96 Y. Iriya. A Glimpse into Cold Mountain Poems // Wang Shunhong (trans.), *Collation and Research of Ancient Books* (Issue 4). Beijing: Zhonghua Book Company, 1989: 233.
97 For details, see the articles of Iriya Yoshitaka and Sun Changwu as well as the annotation by Qian Xueli 钱学烈 and Xiang Chu 项楚.
98 Translated by Stephen Owen.
99 Sun Changwu. Cold Mountain Poems and Zen Buddhism. // *Zen Mediation and Poetic Sentiment*. Beijing: Zhonghua Book Company, 1997: 263.
100 Translated by Red Pine.
101 Translated by Stephen Owen.
102 Translated by Stephen Owen.
103 R. Henricks. *The Poetry of Han-shan: A Complete, Annotated Translation of Cold Mountain*. New York: State University of New Work Press, 1990: 12.
104 Chen Yan & Li Hongchun. *Tang Poems in the Context of Confucianism, Buddhism and Taoism*. Beijing: Kunlun Press, 2003: 32.
105 Translated by Red Pine.
106 Xie Siwei. A Study on Tang Vernacular Poetry. *Chinese Social Sciences*, 1995 (2): 162.
107 V. Mair. Script and Word in Medieval Vernacular Sinitic. *Journal of the American Oriental Society*, 1992, 112(2): 271. The earliest extant lamp record is *Anthology of the Patriarchal Hall* 祖堂集 compiled by two Zen masters Jing 静 and Yun 筠 of Zhaoqing Temple in Quanzhou, in the tenth year of the reign of Li Jing of the Southern Tang Dynasty (952). This anthology is colloquial in both vocabulary and grammar. Jing &Yun. *Anthology of the Patriarchal Hall* (Proofread by Zhang Hua). Zhengzhou: Zhongzhou Ancient Books Press, 2001: 471.
108 Ye Changchi. *Chronicle of Han-shan Temple*. Nanjing: Jiangsu Ancient Books Publishing House, 1986: 116.
109 Y. Iriya. A Glimpse into Cold Mountain Poems // Wang Shunhong (trans.), *Collation and Research of Ancient Books* (Issue 4). Beijing: Zhonghua Book Company, 1989: 238.
110 Sun Qi. *Han-shan and Hippies*. Taichung: Putian Publishing House, 1974: 168.
111 Sun Qi. *Han-shan and Hippies*. Taichung: Putian Publishing House, 1974: 176.
112 Chen Yan & Li Hongchun. *Tang Poems in the Context of Confucianism, Buddhism and Taoism*. Beijing: Kunlun Press, 2003: 28–29.
113 Xie Siwei. A Study on Tang Vernacular Poetry. *Chinese Social Sciences*, 1995 (2): 157.
114 Translated by James Legge.
115 Porter Bill. *The Collected Songs of Cold Mountain*. Port Townsend: Copper Canyon Press, 2000: 15.
116 Poems in this section are translated by Red Pine.
117 Y. Iriya. A Glimpse into Cold Mountain Poems // Wang Shunhong (trans.), *Collation and Research of Ancient Books* (Issue 4). Beijing: Zhonghua Book Company, 1989: 233.
118 Translated by Red Pine.
119 B. Watson. *Cold Mountain: 100 Poems by the T'ang Poet Han-shan*. New York: Grove Press, Inc., 1962: 11.
120 S. Owen. *An Anthology of Chinese Literature: Beginnings to 1911*. New York: Norton, 1996: 404.
121 S. Owen. *An Anthology of Chinese Literature: Beginnings to 1911*. New York: Norton, 1996: 404–405.

122  R. Pine. *Road to Heaven: Encounters with Chinese Hermits*. San Francisco: Mercury House, 1993: 1.
123  Ge Zhaoguang. *A History of Chinese Zen Thought: From the 6th to the 9th Century*. Beijing: Peking University Press, 2000: 333.
124  Translated by Red Pine.
125  Translated by Red Pine.
126  Sun Qi. *Han-shan and Hippies*. Taichung: Putian Publishing House, 1974: 18.
127  Sun Changwu. Cold Mountain Poems and Zen Buddhism. // *Zen Mediation and Poetic Sentiment*. Beijing: Zhonghua Book Company, 1997: 247.
128  Translated by Red Pine.
129  Ye Zhuhong. *Papers on Cold Mountain Poems*. Taipei: Showwe Information Co. Ltd., 2006: 212–213.
130  Xiang Chu. Preface. // *Annotation of Cold Mountain Poems: Shi-de's Poems Included*. Beijing: Zhonghua Book Company, 2000: 14.
131  Quoted in Xiang Chu. Appendix II. // *Annotation of Cold Mountain Poems: Shi-de's Poems Included)*. Beijing: Zhonghua Book Company, 2000: 953.
132  Translated by Red Pine.
133  Ye Zhuhong. *Papers on Cold Mountain Poems*. Taipei: Showwe Information Co. Ltd., 2006: 215.
134  Wang Qingyun. On CMPs and Its Influence in East and West. *Journal of Yantai Normal College (Philosophical and Social Edition)*, 1990 (1): 52.
135  Translated by Red Pine.
136  Translated by Red Pine.
137  Translated by Red Pine.
138  Ye Zhuhong. *Papers on Cold Mountain Poems*. Taipei: Showwe Information Co. Ltd., 2006: 220–222.
139  R. Borgen. The Legend of Han-shan: A Neglected Source. *Journal of the American Oriental Society*, 1991, 111(3): 578.
140  Liu Yucai. Photocopied notes on *Anthology of Cold Mountain Poems*. // *Anthology of Cold Mountain Poems*. Beijing: Threadbare Books, 2001: 6.
141  Quoted in Xiang Chu. Appendix II. // *Annotation of Cold Mountain Poems: Shi-de's Poems Included*. Beijing: Zhonghua Book Company, 2000: 954.
142  Translated by Red Pine.
143  Ye Zhuhong. *Investigation of Anthology of Cold Mountain Poems*. Taipei: The Liberal Arts Press, 2005: 14.
144  Ye Zhuhong. *Critical Studies of Materials about Han-shan*. Taipei: Showwe Information Co. Ltd., 2005: 172.
145  Lee Jongmee. A Systematic Examination on Ancient Printed Versions of CMPs. *Compilation of Papers from the International Symposium on Han-shan-zi and Harmony Culture*, 2008: 125.
146  Wu Zilin. The Reproduction of the Canon: A Case Study on the "Canonization" Process of the Novel in the Ming and Qing Dynasties. *Literary Review*, 2003 (2): 121.
147  Chung Ling. *The Literary Status of Han-shan in Eastern and Western Literary World*. Taipei: Wenfeng Press, 1970: 3. The original article appeared in the supplement of *Central Daily* of Taiwan in March 8 to 12, 1970.
148  Emperor Yongzheng 雍正 (1678–1735) was an emperor of the early Qing Dynasty who had a close relationship with Buddhism. During his vassal period, he often communicated with Zen monks about Buddhist theories. He has studied Buddhism thoroughly and written several relevant books.
149  Emperor Shizong 雍正. *The Selected Imperial Quotations of Yongzheng* (Vol. 1). Complied by The Palace Museum. Haikou: Hainan Publishing House, 2001: 41.
150  Zhang Zhongxing. *Classical and Vernacular Chinese*. Harbin: Heilongjiang People's Publishing House, 1995: 159.

151 Zhang Zhongxing. *Classical and Vernacular Chinese*. Harbin: Heilongjiang People's Publishing House, 1995: 160.
152 It is worth mentioning that Wang Zhifan's 王梵志 poems, which had a greater and profounder influence before the Qing (1644–1912) and Ming Dynasty (1368–1644), seldom appeared in *Quantanshi*全唐诗 (*Complete Tang Poems*). *Ribenguo Xianzai Shumulu* 日本国见在书目录 (*The Catalogue of Chinese Literary Works in Japan*), which was complied in the year of 784–897, included the *Collected Poems of Wang Zhifan*. Early in the Tang Dynasty (618–907), therefore, Wang Zhifan's poems have traveled to Japan, while the CMPs were hardly found in famous anthologies and poem collections, and the time it traveled to Japan was even later. See more information: http://edit.ndcnc.gov.cn/datalib/2004/Character/DL/DL-20031211143158. [2007–06–01].
153 There is no clear and definite records of Han-shan's life experience in *Quantanshi* 全唐诗 (*Complete Tang Poems*), Han-shan is only defined as "Manjushri" 文殊, which originates from the preface by Lü Qiuyin 闾丘胤. That is the reason, in some aspects, the CMPs can be topped among Zen poems.
154 Hu Shi. *History of Vernacular Literature*. Hong Kong: Ying Zhong Book House, 1959: 157.
155 Hu Shi. *History of Vernacular Literature*. Hong Kong: Ying Zhong Book House, 1959: 161.
156 Hu Shi. *History of Vernacular Literature*. Hong Kong: Ying Zhong Book House, 1959: 9.
157 Hu Shi. *History of Vernacular Literature*. Hong Kong: Ying Zhong Book House, 1959: 4.
158 Zheng Zhenduo. *A History of Chinese Vernacular Literature* (Vol. 1). Shanghai: Shanghai Bookstore, 1984: 2.
159 Zheng Zhenduo. *A History of Chinese Vernacular Literature* (Vol. 1). Shanghai: Shanghai Bookstore, 1984: 6.
160 Zheng Zhenduo. *A History of Chinese Vernacular Literature* (Vol. 1). Shanghai: Shanghai Bookstore, 1984: 124–125.
161 Translated by Red Pine.
162 Zheng Zhenduo. *A History of Chinese Vernacular Literature* (Vol. 1). Shanghai: Shanghai Bookstore, 1984: 125.
163 Ruo Fan. *Poetic Rhymes of Han-shan-zi (with poetic rhymes of Shi-de). Linguistic Series* (Vol. 5). Beijing: The Commercial Press, 1963: 99.
164 Ruo Fan. *Poetic Rhymes of Han-shan-zi (with poetic rhymes of Shi-de). Linguistic Series* (Vol. 5). Beijing: The Commercial Press, 1963: 130.
165 Ruo Fan. *Poetic Rhymes of Han-shan-zi (with poetic rhymes of Shi-de). Linguistic Series* (Vol. 5). Beijing: The Commercial Press, 1963: 130.

# 4 Cultural Polysystem of Arrivals and Interlingual Travel of the CMPs

Compared with the cold reception in Chinese literature, the CMPs, when they had traveled to China's eastern neighbors Japan and Korea, instantly gained a popularity that dwarfs almost all Chinese "mainstream poets". Not only had various translations, notes and commentaries of the CMPs been published, but various mythical legends about Han-shan also had been adapted into novels, and the image of Han-shan entered the painting and the altar, with its influence lasting for centuries. In the 20th century, translations and studies pertaining to the CMPs were given particular preference by European sinology: scholars and translators from Western, Central and Northern European countries such as England, France, Germany, the Netherlands, Belgium, Sweden and the Czech Republic showed great enthusiasm and interest in the CMPs. At the same time, across the Atlantic, the Chinese poet Han-shan became the spiritual leader that was greatly venerated by the younger generation in the United States, and his poems became the classics of the "San Francisco Renaissance". Since then, CMPs were included in major American literary anthologies and universities' East Asian literature halls. In fact, all this "belated" glory is actually the result of the "harmonious" discourse field constructed between the CMPs and the cultural polysystem of arrivals, namely, the host countries. Therefore, what Said (1935–2003) called "channels crossing all context pressure" proves to be accessible to the CMPs' interlingual travel. The interlingual literary travel, as a result, was surprisingly smooth, and the CMPs miraculously fulfilled the prophecy of "one day I'll meet someone with eyes, then my poems will plague the world."[1]

## 4.1 Cultural Polysystem and Status of Translated Literature

To address the cultural polysystem and cultural status of the translated literature, Itamar Evan Zohar (1939–), a representative of the Manipulation School in Israel, should be mentioned. His polysystem theory, proposed in the early 1970s, drawing on the positive elements of Russian formalism and Czech structuralism, treats translated literature as a subsystem of the literary polysystem of arrivals, and objectively describes the reception and influence of translated literature in the cultural polysystem of arrivals, attempting to "make functional interpretation of various forms of writing from the canonical texts that are central to a given culture to the most peripheral non-canonical texts".[2] According to Zohar, various symbolic phenomena, such as culture, language, literature and society, are not a mixture of unrelated factors, but an organic system composed of interrelated factors. So literature should also be examined in the context of the cultural polysystem. The researcher, in fact, should not only focus on the text itself, but also on other related constraints. It is widely known that it is always the non-textual factors that govern and manipulate the creation, distribution, translation and reception of literary works. Zohar points out that these systems are not equal, but hierarchized within the polysystem.[3] Some items are at the center, while other items are located at the periphery of the same polysystem. According to Zohar's explanation, polysystems are not static and immutable. On the contrary, there is a constant tension between the center and the periphery, and various literary genres are always in the competition for the center. Some systems thus may have to undergo status change from the center to the periphery, or from the periphery to the center, due to changes in specific sociocultural contexts.

When it comes to the translated literature, Zohar thought that the translated literature not only serves as an integral system within any literary polysystem, but as a most active system within it. Whether it serves as innovatory ("primary") or conservatory ("secondary") depends on the specific sociocultural context of the polysystem under study. In his essay "The Position of Translated Literature within the Literary Polysystem", Zohar proposed that there are three major cases that can help promote the translated literature's central position: First, when a polysystem has not yet been crystallized, that is to say, when a translated literature is still young. Second, when a translated literature is either "peripheral" (within a large group of correlated works of literature) or "weak", or both; and third, when there are turning points, crises or literary vacuums in a translated literature.[4]

To say that translated literature maintains a central or primary position in the literary polysystem means that it participates actively in shaping the center of the polysystem. In such a situation, it is by a large integral part of innovatory forces, and is to be identified with major events in literary history. In such a state when new literary models are emerging, translators are likely to become one of the means of elaborating the new repertoire.[5] Through the foreign works, translation not only helps to establish new literary repertoire, but also introduces into the home literature new poetics, linguistic forms, writing pattern and skills. In this situation, no clear-cut distinction is maintained between "original" and "translated" writings, and translators tend to convey the "adequacy" of the original text, that translation will be faithful to the content and structure of the "original" writings. And it is notable that it is the leading writers, or members of the avant-garde who act as translators that produce the most conspicuous or appreciated translated works. In this situation, writers play the role of translators.

However, when translated literature is in a secondary position, it is modeled according to norms already conventionally established by a dominant type in the target literature and subject to norms rejected by the newly established center. Translation, in this situation, becomes a factor of conservatism.[6] In this case, translators try to accommodate the target reader by using established linguistic expressions and familiar linguistic structures and even contents to consolidate the existing aesthetic norms, so the "adequacy" of the translation is obviously insufficient.[7]

The condition of cultural polysystem of arrivals, to a large extent, decides the status of translated literature in the literary polysystem: primary or secondary, central or peripheral. The translated literature's status, central or peripheral, will exert direct influence on the interlingual travel of text travel: smooth or difficult. In addition to the constraints of the attributes and representations of translated literature in the overall cultural polysystem, whether the interlingual travel of the proposed translated text will be smooth or difficult, and whether it eventually occupies the center or the peripheral position in the translated literature depends on a number of other factors. For example, despite the peripheral position of translated literature in the target culture, its interlingual travel will still be smooth if there is no ideological (poetic tradition) conflict with the target culture norms, or even if it contributes to, manifests and reflects the dominant ideology. Furthermore, the interlingual travel of the translated literature would also be smoother if the translated text follows the worldwide trend in scholarship, either in form or in content; or if it is introduced pioneeringly by a well-established scholar in the target culture for his strong personal interest in the text. Or, because of the great influence of the translated text in academic research and social life worldwide, researchers began passive study in their own cultural fields, triggering a larger research frenzy in their own academic and intellectual circles, as a result. Besides, the cultural charm and culture promotion policy of the "intermediary (country)" will deeply influence the "third party (country)", and the potential literary and social values of the text are explored in depth based on the introduction and translation of the text. These objective conditions also can contribute to the central position of translated text in the target language's cultural context and the form of its literary identity as a literary classic or translated literary classic on this basis. In fact, all the previously mentioned factors and the text's central position they contribute to get proved in this chapter by the interlingual literary travel of the CMPs in the East and West.

## 4.2 Interlingual Travel of the CMPs in Eastern Asia

Given the historical origin of Japanese and Chinese culture, the CMPs, which had been repeatedly marginalized in China, has gained long-lasting preference for the polysystem of target culture because of the openness and inclusiveness of the target language and culture. Various translations, notes and commentaries of CMPs have been published in Japan, various myths and legends about Han-shan have been adapted into novels, and the image of Han-shan has entered into Japanese painting and the altar of God. Due to the geographical position and accessible transportation, coupled with the historical connection in language, and writing and the ancient cultural exchanges, Chinese cultural classics mainly take the Korean countries as the "travel intermediary" and travel to Japan, and then take Japan as the "transit station", travel to Europe and the United States. In fact, the transmissions of ancient Chinese culture mostly followed this travel route for a long time; hence Korea became an important inheritance and historical witness of Chinese culture

116   *Cultural Polysystem of Arrivals*

moving forward. Since their introduction to Korea in the 13th century, the CMPs have gained great popularity in all walks of society.

### 4.2.1   Intralingual Travel of the CMPs in Japan

In fact, since their introduction to Japan in the Northern Song Dynasty, the CMPs have had a positive and significant impact on Japanese language, literature, religion, art and even the study of spiritual history, and they have thus acquired a "canonical" and "central" literary status in their cultural context. In addition to the linguistic and cultural proximity between the two countries and the host country's openness as a featured cultural attitude, the literary status of the CMPs also results from their extraordinary impact on Japanese society for their simple linguistic style, their mystical Zen realm, their seclusion from the world, and their ecological awareness of returning to nature.

#### 4.2.1.1   Origin of China–Japan Cultural Exchange and Text Travel of the CMPs

Over 2,000 years ago, China and Japan began their friendly relations across the ocean barrier. In *Houhanshu* (《后汉书》, *The Book of the Later Han*), there are records that Japan sent tributary envoys from the year 57 to 107. The full exchange between the two countries dated back to the late Eastern Han Dynasty (184–220) and the Wei Dynasty (220–266). According to *Weizhi* (《魏志》, *The History of Wei*), Japanese envoys came to the Wei Kingdom four times, and envoys of the latter twice went to Japan. The ancient Japanese belong to the East and Northeast Asian cultural circle centered on Chinese characters. Throughout the various periods of Japanese history, Chinese literature has been ceaselessly introduced into Japan through various means. The earliest recording of Chinese texts being introduced to Japan is dated to the third century. This record is found in "Yingshen Tianhuang" (应神天皇, The Emperor Ōjin), one of the volumes of *Kojiki* (《古事記》, *Records of Ancient Matters*), written in the year 712, which is the earliest surviving written document in Japan that includes oral myths and historical legends:

> The Japanese emperor ordered envoys from Paekche, "Any man of virtue from your country should be summoned here. Then Wani-kishi was summoned, and he also presented the Japanese emperor ten volumes of *Lun Yu* (《论语》, *The Analects of Confucius*) and one volume of *Qian Zi Wen* (《千字文》, *The Thousand Character Classic*)."[8]

If the *Kojiki* (《古事記》, *Records of Ancient Matters*) is only a book of myths and historical legends and thus cannot be considered credible, it is an indisputable fact that before the Taika period (645–650), Japanese culture and education were mainly based on Confucianism and education in Chinese texts.[9] The *Seventeen-Article Constitution* written in pure Chinese by Prince Shōtoku (574–621), the leader of Japanese politics and intellectual communities during the Suiko Tennō period (593–628), demonstrates the deep influence of Chinese culture to Japan at that time. It not only reflects the "harmony"-based spiritual idea of Chinese culture in its statute law, but also shows apparent imitation to Chinese characters both in language and allusion.

Since 607, Japan had sent ambassadors five times to China, then in the Sui Dynasty (581–619). After the fall of the Sui Dynasty, it sent "ken-toh-shi" (遣唐使, ambassadors sent to Tang) from the year of 630. According to Yue-him Tam (谭汝谦, 1941–) in his "Sino-Japanese Cultural Interchange: Aspects of Literature and Language Learning", Japan sent "ken-toh-shi" (遣唐使, ambassadors sent to Tang) 19 times (three of which failed) and unofficial groups to the Tang Dynasty six times, in total 25 times (the exact number of times is still in disputation), or about once every 12 years on average during 280 years of the Tang Dynasty.[10] The prosperity of cultural exchange between China and Japan during this period was unprecedented, and there were famous Japanese students and learned monks such as Abe no Nakamaro (698–770), Kibi no Makibi (695–775), Kūkai (774–835),[11] and Saichō (767–822).[12]

In the field of poetry, the earliest extant collection of Chinese poetry in Japan, *Kaifūsō* (《怀风藻》, *Florilegium of Cherished Airs*), was published in the third year of the Tenpyō-shōhō era (751). It contains 120 poems (116 extant poems) by 64 Han poets from the late Asuka era and the early Nara periods. It highly values Confucianism and Taoism in mindset, aesthetics, and wording and phrasing. The poetic style is based on the ancient five-character quatrain of *Wen Xuan or Selections of Refined Literature* in Six Dynasties, mainly featuring eight stanzas, with four and twelve stanzas as the subsidiary.[13] In terms of cataloging, *Kaifūsō* (《怀风藻》, *Florilegium of Cherished Airs*) is also an imitation of the style of *Wen Xuan or Selections of Refined Literature*, such as in chapters that express emotions, sightseeing, etc. So it has a strong Chinese poetic flavor. More than ten years after the publication of *Kaifūsō* (《怀风藻》, *Florilegium of Cherished Airs*), the first collection of Japanese waka, *Manyoushu*, was born. It uses Chinese characters as a phonetic script to record the waka, and thus the "Man yōgana" was created. In addition to the preface of the song written in Chinese, some of the familiar words in the "Manyoushu" waka was also written in ideographic Chinese characters. In addition, the odd number of five or seven tones in the short song form was clearly influenced by the five or seven characters of Chinese poetry. Because of these origins, this example of ancient Japanese waka, which had much to do with Chinese poetry, was reputed as the "Japanese Book of Songs". Japanese monk Kūkai, after returning from his stay in Tang Dynasty, took *Wenxin Diaolong* (《文心雕龙》, *The Literary Heart and the Carving of the Dragons*) as a reference and compiled poetic works such as *Xindingshige* (《新定诗格》, *New Style of Poetry*), *Shige* (《诗格》, *Rhyme of Poetry*) and *Shiyi* (《诗仪》, *Comment on Poetry*) into the Six Dynasties poetry theory collection *Wenjingmifulun* (《文镜秘府论》, *On Chinese Poetry*), and followed the traditional Chinese poetic thought that "poetry is mainly to express emotion and mindsets." For one time, "Han poetry and literature overwhelmed everything, and many songs and treatises were imitated from *Wenjingmifulun* (《文镜秘府论》, *On Chinese Poetry*)."[14] During the Heian period (794–1192), there was a trend of pursuing Chinese poetry throughout the whole society, especially in the early Heian period, when Japanese culture continued to be nourished by Tang culture and Sinology was recognized as the most flourishing time.

According to some studies, the number of Chinese literature books in circulation in Japan in the ninth century was said to be 50.1% of those belonging to the Sui Dynasty and 51.2% of those belonging to the Tang Dynasty. That is to say, half of the Chinese literature had already spread eastward to Japan.[15] It was during this period that *Baishichangqingj* (《白氏长庆集》, *Bai Juyi's Poetry*) by Bai Juyi (白居易), the great poet of the Tang dynasty, was brought to Japan by Tang merchants and Japanese monks who studied abroad, gaining great popularity in Japan.[16] Bai's new *yuefu* poems, being direct and relevant, got popular in all walks of Japanese society.[17] After the middle of the Heian period (794–1192), "Japanese Sinology became almost exclusively of the Bai Juyi school."[18] *Baishichangqingj* (《白氏长庆集》, *Bai Juyi's Poetry*) thus replaced *Wen Xuan or Selections of Refined Literature* as the new model of Chinese literature in the eyes of Japanese. Although Japan stopped sending ambassadors to China ("ken-toh-shi" 遣唐使) in the sixth year of Kanpyō (894) in an attempt to weaken the penetration of Chinese culture to its native culture, communications between China and Japan had never been broken off.[19] Japan still had close civil trades with the Song Dynasty, but mostly in the form of smuggling.

There were many official exchanges between Song and Japan in the field of religion. There were many Japanese monks who went to China to study Zen and Ritsu Buddhism; some even stayed in China for several years or ten-plus years. According to the statistics, since the reign of Emperor Taizong (976–997) in the Song Dynasty, Japanese monks came to China successively, including Fujiwara no Chōnen (938–1016) during the reign of Emperor Taizong (627–649), Jakushō (962–1034) during the reign of Emperor Zhenzong (997–1022), Qingsheng 庆盛 during the reign of Emperor Renzong (1010–1063), Jōjin (1011–1081) and Zhong Hui during the reign of Emperor Shenzong (1048–1085). According to *Wushan Shiseng Zhuan* (《五山诗僧传》, *Accounts of Gozan Monks*), there were 37 Japanese monks who came to China in this period to seek Dharma, and there were 21 Zen monks who went to Japan during the Song Dynasty (960–1279) and the Yuan Dynasty (1271–1368).[20] The Japanese monks who went to China in the Song Dynasty brought back to Japan not only a lot of translated works of Chinese Buddhist scriptures in both the Tang and Song Dynasties, but also a large number of Chinese Confucianism classics and poetry and literature collections,[21] which made great contributions to the introduction of Chinese culture to Japan in this period.

In the reign of Emperor Shenzong (1048–1085), on his tour to Tiantai mountain, the Japanese monk Jōjin went on a tour to Tiantai Temple, where he received a copy of the CMPs from Yu Gui, a monk of Guoqing Temple, and in the year that followed he ordered Lai Yuan and five of his other disciples to bring this copy back to Japan. Since then, the CMPs began to spread in Japan. Jōjin's own *San Tendai Godai San Ki* 参天台五台山记 (*The Record of a Pilgrimage to the Tiantai and Wutai Mountains*) also recorded this anecdote. It is worth mentioning that Tong Xian Iridao (1106–1159), a book compiler in the 12th century, also had this book in his catalog. In fact, the *Han-shan Poetry* given by Yu Gui was more than 100 years earlier than the "Guoqing temple" edition engraved in 1189. Qian Xuelie (钱学烈) believes that this edition might be "the earliest Song engraved edition of CMPs extant at home and abroad", that is, the so-called the "Tianlu Song" edition. Ye Zhuhong 叶珠红, however, in her *Critical Studies of Materials about Han-Shan* (《寒山资料考辨》), clearly points out that

> the methodical Tianlu Song edition, is better than the poems of Han-shan, Shi-de and Feng-gan, which are not subdivided, and are all without the "Lü Qiuyin's Pseudo-Preface", "Feng-gan's Zen Poems" and "Shi-de's Poems". The so-called "other edition" in the "Tianlu Song" edition is more likely to be *The Yongle Canon* edition of CMPs, which might be the older Shanzhong edition that *The Yongle Canon* edition is based on.[22]

Regardless of whether the edition of CMPs brought back to Japan by Jōjin's disciples was the "Tianlu Song" edition or whether it had any actual connection with the older Shanzhong edition, the Northern Song edition was undoubtedly the first version of the CMPs circulating in Japan, and its introduction has since opened the curtain of Japanese Han-shan studies.

*4.2.1.2 Circulation, Dissemination and Reception of the CMPs in Japan*

According to the statistics, in addition to the "Jōjin" edition, Japan's CMPs include a volume of CMPs in the Joseon edition printed in 1296, a volume in the Gozan edition published by Zongze Channi in 1325 (in the Dagok University Library),[23] a volume of CMPs in the 11th year of the reign of Emperor Yongzheng (1722–1735), and a volume of CMPs (with poems by Feng-gan and Shi-de in the first collection of *Zeshiju Congshu* (《择是居丛书》, *The Zeshiju Series*) by Zhang Junheng (张钧衡, 1872–1927) in the fifth year of the Republic of China (1916), a volume of printed Song edition of CMPs in 1928, and a volume in *Sibu Congkan* (《四部丛刊》, *Collectanea of the Four Categories*) by Commercial Press in 1929, and so on.

In addition to collections, annotations and proofs of CMPs have also become popular in Japan, and a variety of commentaries have been in spread for centuries. Daejeon Tisang says in his *Interpretation of Cold Mountain Poems* (《寒山诗解说》), that

> among the commentaries in Japan, there are three volumes of *The Annotated Cold Mountain Poems* (《首書寒山詩》) from the Kanmon period (1661–1672), six volumes of (《寒山詩管解》, *On Cold Mountain Poems*) by monk Jiao Yi (交易和尚) from the Genroku period (1688–1703), three volumes of *Annotated Cold Mountain Poems* (《寒山诗阐提记闻》) by the monk Deji (白隐慧鹤禅师) from the Yanxiang period (1744–1747), and three volumes of *Annotated Book of the Collected Poems of Han-shan* (《寒山詩索颐》) from the Bunka period (1804–1817). *Annotated CMPs* (《寒山诗阐提记闻》) is unsurpassed in detail, *The Annotated Cold Mountain Poems* (《首書寒山詩》)

is simple, and *Annotated Book of the Collected Poems of Han-shan* (《寒山詩索頤》) is detailed. The monk Deji's annotation are probably based on *On Cold Mountain Poems* (《寒山詩管解》). After the Meiji period (1868–1911), there were also a number of explanations or speeches, among which the "New Interpretation to CMPs" by Shih Ching-tan is of great value.[24]

In addition, during the Meiji period (1868–1911), there was also *Remarks on Han-shan* (《寒山诗讲话》) edited by Kenji Wada.

Since the 20th century, the CMPs have continued to circulate in Japan. In the 38th year of Meiji (1905), the Southern Song edition at the Japanese Imperial Palace was reprinted, with a preface by Shimada Han. This edition contains 304 poems by Han-shan, 2 by Feng-gan, and 48 by Shi-de, less than the "Tianlu Song" edition that does not distinguish between five-character poems and seven-character poems. Different from the first line of the "Tianlu Song" edition "All you who read my poems",[25] the first line of this edition is "Towering cliffs were the home I chose."[26] In addition, the first page of the volume was printed with the words "there are only 500 copies of this edition, and this is the first copy." It has been studied that this edition is a third version of the "Guoqing Temple" edition, which was the "Wuwohuishen" edition published between the "Donggao Temple" edition of 1229 and the "Baoyou" edition of 1255. In the preface, Shimada Han attributes the poor circulation of CMPs to poor publication and dislike of later generations. However, Shimada Han thinks highly of the artistic achievements of CMPs: "Full of wit and rhyme, CMPs are superior in artistic achievements to those of Jiao Ran (720–803), but inferior to those of Dao Xian. They are well accepted by religious personage and its loss is therefore particularly deplorable."[27]

The translations, commentaries and other research results of Japanese scholars made on the CMPs since the Showa period (1926–1989) are described in Zhang Mantao's article "Japanese Scholars' Evaluation and Interpretation of CMPs" (日本学者对寒山诗的评价与解释): (1) *Cold Mountain Poems* (by Daejeon Tisang); (2) *CMPs* (by Kenao Harada); (3) *Translation of Cold Mountain Poems* (by Yanwon Okawa); (4) *Commentary on the First Volume of Cold Mountain Poems (by Sōgen Asahina)*; (5) *Han-shan* (by Iriya Yoshitaka). (6) *Han-shan Poetry and the Speech of Han-shan and Shi-de*; (7) "View on Cold Mountain Poems" (by Iriya Yoshitaka); (8) "Han-shan's Poetry" (by Eiichi Kimura); (9) "An Interpretation of Cold Mountain Poems" (by Toshio Fukushima); (10) "Miscellaneous Thoughts on Cold Mountain Poems" (by Takashi Nakagawaguchi). Zhang Mantao (张曼涛, 1933–1981) considers these to be a fruitful achievement in the evaluation and interpretation of the CMPs by a generation of Japanese academics and religious circles since the Showa period (1926–1989).[28]

But in fact, the study results on the CMPs go far beyond this. Fumio Kusu also mentions other commentaries and research papers since the Meiji period (1868–1911) in his book *Han-shan and Shi-de* (《寒山拾得》). Others include Wakasa Kuniei's *Lectures on Cold Mountain Poems* (《寒山诗讲义》), Sei Ching-Tan's *New Interpretation of Cold Mountain Poems* (《寒山诗新释》), Watanabe Haiku's *Remarks on Han-shan* (《寒山诗讲话》), Ichikawa Takeda's "Cold Mountain

Poems" (寒山诗), Hidetori Hiroyama's "Zhengzhong Edition of CMPs" (正中版寒山诗集), and Matsubara Taichō's "Wandering Youth: The World of *Cold Mountain Poems*" (青春漂泊—寒山诗之世界).²⁹ Among the many translations and annotations, *Han-shan* (《寒山》)—the one published by Iwanami Shoten in 1958, translated and annotated by the famous Japanese sinologist Iriya Yoshitaka (1910–1998)—has been the most influential in sinology circles. There are 126 poems in this translation, and they were included in the *The Newly Revised Anthology of Chinese Poets* (《新修中国诗人选集》) in 1984.³⁰ Because of its outstanding academic values, the Western versions of CMPs are held in high esteem in many languages.³¹ It is also the most comprehensive Japanese annotated edition of CMPs, with 306 by Han-shan, 2 by Feng-gan and 55 by Shi-de. According to *A Comprehensive Catalogue of Japanese Translations of Chinese Books* (《日本译中国书综合目录》) edited by Yue-him Tam (谭汝谦, 1941–), another Japanese translation of CMPs in the 1970s is *Cold Mountain Poems and Its Translations* (《寒山诗和訳》) by Fumiji Yoda (代田文誌) in 1977.³²

In the 1980s, Japanese translations of CMPs were published in two volumes by Fumio Kusu, on November 25, 1985. The book was translated and annotated on the reference of the author's teacher, Shun'ō Fukushima (1898–1981), and the translations of CMPs by Iriya Sensuke (1933–2003) and Matsumura Aki (1938–). In addition, on March 20, 1986, Chikuma Shobo published a translation of CMPs by Keiji Nishitani (1900–1990), a famous Zen master of the Kyoto School of Japan, and the book was included in *Zen Writers' Discourses II* (《禅家语录II》) edited by Keiji Nishitani (1900–1990) and Seiyama Yanagida (1922–2006) in Volume 36B of Chikuma Shobo's *The Complete World Classics* (《世界古典文学全集》) in February 1974.

Notably, in 2018, Kazuaki Tanahashi (1933–), a renowned Japanese calligrapher, Zen master, writer, environmentalist and translator, translated *The Complete Cold Mountain: Poems of the Legendary Hermit Han-shan* (《寒山全集：传奇隐士寒山的诗歌》) in cooperation with Canadian Zen master Peter Levitt (1946–). In the opening paragraph of "Introduction", Levitt states:

> In a most beautiful poem, where pines sway in the wind and bamboo stalks rustle beneath a moon that rises above the solitary magnificence of Tiantai Peak, the legendary hermit poet Han-shan ("Cold Mountain") who had left behind what he called "the dusty world" of delusion to live a life of wandering and solitude among the mountains he loved, makes a confession that I find quite moving:
>
> Scanning the green slopes below,
> I discussed the profound principle with the white cloud.
> Though the feeling of the wild is in the mountains and waters,
> truly, I long for a companion of the way.³³

In addition, Levitt believes that the poet traditionally called Han-shan may actually have been at least three people who wrote under the same name. Nonetheless, Levitt says, because of the consistency of heart and mind found in the CMPs, that he would like to speak of Han-shan as one person. "Perhaps it is the shared quality of mind that the collective Han-shan poets possess that allows me to speak in this way,"³⁴ he adds.

As a matter of fact, in commentaries and essays, Japanese scholars always tended to consider Han-shan to be a fictitious person imagined in religious mythology and legends, and thus they have been skeptical about the existence of poet Han-shan. Iriya Yoshitaka (1910–1998), for example, once argued, "What is the prototype of CMPs? Whether Han-shan is formulated or not? In fact, it is still a big question."³⁵ The Japanese historian Sōkichi Tsuda (1873–1961), in his 1944 article "Remarks on Cold Mountain Poems, Han-shan and Shi-de" (寒山诗与寒山拾得之说话), also expressed his dubious opinion whether Han-shan really exists as the legend says. He pointed out that the CMPs and their supposed author Han-shan, a legendary figure, are totally different. He even further argued that Feng-gan and Shi-de are not real either.³⁶ Another Japanese scholar Tizo Ota's *Explanation of Cold Mountain Poems* also maintained that "there were Zen monks who assumed the names Han-shan and Shi-de and wrote poems about their feelings, so that common people of the time saw them as mere madmen."³⁷ As a result, Japanese scholars were being skeptical about the single individual authorship, Thus, they are not as enthusiastic about the date of Han-shan's birth and death as the Chinese mainland academic circles are, which, nonetheless, has not hindered the Japanese people from being fond of Han-shan and his poems.

In addition to annotations, translation and commentaries, Han-shan and his poems have also become popular in the creation of Japanese artworks and novels. The image of Han-shan and his companion Shi-de has been highly favored by Japanese painters of each generation. In August 1977, Japan issued a set of engraved "national treasures" stamps, one of which, for 50 yen, was a portrait of the poet Han-shan. Some commentators suggested that the design on this stamp is a painting of Cold Mountain by the 16th-century Japanese painter Hasegawa Tōhaku (1539–1610). Others thought that it is by the 14th-century Japanese painter Kao (?–1345). However, both Hasegawa Tōhaku (1539–1610) and Kao (?–1345) are renowned artists in the history of Japanese art.³⁸ This vivid and simple painting of Han-shan the celebrity is considered a "national treasure" in Japan.³⁹ In addition, Japanese painter Sesshū Tōyō (1420–1506), the most outstanding representative of ink-and-wash painting and landscape painting in the Muromachi period (1336–1573), and Kanō Motonobu (1476–1559), the master of the most influential Kanō school in the history of Japanese painting, both employed Han-shan and Shi-de as the subject of their paintings. The former has portrayed *Han-shan and Shi-de* (《寒山拾得图》), while the latter has drawn *Han-shan, Shi-de and Feng-gan* (《丰干·寒山拾得图》). Notably, during the Kamakura period (1185–1333) in Japan, the works of Liang Kai (梁楷, 1150–?), a famous landscape painter of the Southern Song Dynasty (1127–1279), and Indra (1114–1193), a famous Zen monk painter of the Yuan Dynasty (1271–1368), were introduced to Japan along with Zen Buddhism, leading to the formation and development of Japanese Zen ink painting, both of whom have been enjoying a high position in Japanese painting circles,⁴⁰ and both of whom have painted portraits of Han-shan and Shi-de. The latter's

*Han-shan and Shi-de* (《禅机图断简寒山拾得图》) was also awarded the title of "National Treasure of Japan".[41]

In the field of literature creation, Tsubouchi Shōyō (1859–1935), the pioneer of modern Japanese novel theory known for his book *The Essence of the Novel* (《小说神髓》), wrote a dance script called *Han-shan and Shi-de* (《寒山拾得》) with the theme on Han-shan and Shi-de, which was staged at Waseda University in 2005 to commemorate Tsubouchi Shōyō. In addition, Ogai Mori (1862–1922), one of the founders of modern Japanese literature and a pioneer of Japanese Romantic Literature, wrote the short story *Han-shan and Shi-de* (《寒山拾得》) in 1916 based on the preface of Lü Qiuyin (闾丘胤). It was considered one of the best short stories in modern Japan and was translated into English by two American translators, D. A. Dilworth (1934–) and J. T. Rimer (1910–?), in the 1970s and was published in the 26th issue of *Monumenta Nipponica* in 1971.[42]

In addition to the love and admiration to Han-shan in the academic community, the Japanese public has shown great interest in various legends of Han-shan and all the things related to him. Like the academic community, the Japanese public's love for Han-shan can also be summarized as "fanaticism". Although the Han-shan Temple and the poet Zhang Ji (张继,?–779) have nothing to do with Han-shan and his poems, in Japan, people are happy to make a connection between them.[43] Zhang Ji's "Maple Bridge Night Mooring" was circulated in Japan from early times, and Japanese people are no less familiar with this poem than any Chinese people. According to *Newly Restored Chronicle of Han-shan Temple* (《新修寒山寺记》) by Yu Yue (俞樾, 1821–1907), a great master in classic Chinese cultures:

> There are more than one thousand temples in Wu regions, but due to this poem by Zhang Ji, Han-shan Temple gained great popularity in both China and Japan. I have been living in Soochow for a long time, and I have witnessed that when men of Japanese literature came here, they would always talk about Han-shan Temple. Furthermore, it is said that even three feet tall Japanese children can recite this poem.[44]

Even today, "Maple Bridge Night Mooring" is still included in Japanese school textbooks and Japanese tourists often regard Han-shan Temple as a site of pilgrimage. The Japanese tourists who visit China tend to go to Soochow to pay homage to Han-shan and Shi-de, which are almost household figures in Japan, and visit the Maple Bridge described in Zhang Ji's poem. Moreover, during the Chinese Lunar New Year, many Japanese also like to go to Han-shan Temple to listen to the "Han-shan Temple bell", which they believe can remove troubles and bring good luck.

*4.2.1.3 Cultural Polysystem of Arrivals and Canon Construction of the CMPs in Japan*

The question is, how did the CMPs, a collection of poems that found no place in Chinese mainstream literature during their conception, instantly gain long-lasting popularity in Japan after being travelled to and culturally exchanged? Some scholars believe it is because the colloquial vernacular language style could be easily understood by readers in the East Asian cultural circle, in which Japanese is also included. The popularity of *Baishi Wenji* (《白氏文集》, *Bai Juyi's Poetry*) by Bai Juyi (白居易) in Japan is a typical example. According to Sun Changwu (孙昌武), the CMPs should have appeared around the year of 780 at the reign of Emperor Dezong[45] (780–805) in the Tang Dynasty.[46] Although it was produced earlier than Bai's Poetry, it was introduced into Japan more than 200 years later than Bai's poetry. Therefore, it is undeniable that the popularity of Han-shan poetry in Japan owes to the lasting influence of the simplicity and vernacular style of the earlier Bai's poetry in Japan. In addition, some commentators believe that religion strongly characterizes the Japanese literary traditions, and that many of the leading Japanese poets and scholars were monks, such as the "sage of song" Saigyō (1118–1180) in the 12th century and the "sage of haiku" Matsuo Bashō (1644–1694) in the 17th century. "As the Japanese have a tradition of appreciating religious poetry, the Buddhist and Taoist mindsets ubiquitous in CMPs have made Han-shan popular in Japan."[47]

Except for the language, culture and religious traditions, the following factors cannot be ignored in promoting the intralingual travel of the CMPs in Japan:

First, during the Kamakura period (1185–1333), Zen Buddhism, which was introduced from China and had little to do with the old Japanese religion and was originally popular among lower-class monks, became popular due to the dual needs of aristocratic rule and civilian beliefs. From the time when Zen became influential, the mysticism was used to train samurai to fight alone, and Zen helped produce a large number of Japanese politicians, swordsmen and university students who wish using Zen to achieve secular goals.[48] This quest for secularism is reflected in the monumental work entitled *The Promotion of Zen for the Protection of the Country* (《兴禅护国论》) by Eisai (1141–1215), the founding father of the Rinzai sect of Zen Buddhism in Japan. In fact, the influence of Zen on Japan was not only reflected in political purposes, but also in many aspects of social life. D. T. Suzuki (1870–1966), a leading Japanese sinologist, Buddhist scholar, and specialist on the history of Zen Buddhism, once cautioned that

> to have an all-round perception to the Japanese cultural life, including their love of nature . . . , a penetrating study on the mysteries of Zen Buddhism is necessary. . . . If we have a perception of Zen, we can at least enter the deepest of the colorful spiritual life of the Japanese.[49]

The Kamakura and Muromachi in Japan were the periods that featured the closest cultural exchanges between Chinese and Japanese Buddhism, represented by Zen Buddhism. Although the CMPs had been introduced to Japan earlier (the late Heian period), it is believed that the popularity of Zen Buddhism during this period made the part of CMPs that is rich in Zen wit, the Zen enlightenment poems and the image of Han-shan as a Zen master, more attractive to the nobles, samurai, monks and the general public at this time. This enabled a new found appreciation for the CMPs and allowed them to continue to grow in popularity and also gain further assimilation into Japanese culture. With the reverence for the Zen master's arrogant and unconventional character, his contempt for tradition, his scolding of the Buddha and his ancestors, his sharp wit, and his punches and punches, as well as Bai Juyi's poetic view of "wild words" in his later years, it was only natural that Japanese literature accepted and revered Han-shan's unrestrained character and his uncommon poems. Moreover, the Japanese admired for Bai's poetry during the Heian period, so much so that Bai Juyi was revered as "Mañjuśrī" and Han-shan is also called "Mañjuśrī" in the preface, which brought favors to Han-shan and the CMPs.

Secondly, Han-shan's carefree and unfettered life philosophy of "moon and breeze is always in my company" coincides with the "elegant" literary view of "no worldly turbid, seeking no fame and wealth" advocated by the literary communities in the Heian, Kamakura and Muromachi periods in Japan. The Taoist style and hermit's sentiment that features in the CMPs were obviously attractive in the unprecedented social turmoil of the mid-to-late Heian and Kamakura periods. A famous short poem by Dōgen (1200–1253), the founder of the Tso Dong sect of Zen Buddhism in Japan, expresses people's life orientation at that time.

> Between the world of life and death I would like to travel,
> Between ignorance and epiphany I wander.
> Only one thing haunts me
> The pitter-patter of rain I can hear.
> This is a lonely night in Fukakusa.[50]

Let us take a further look at that, the Japanese cultural tradition of nature and the "mountain complex" also attracted Japanese people to the seclusionist lifestyle and the return to the natural state of life reflected in the CMPs. D. T. Suzuki (1870–1966) once analyzed: "The Japanese's love of nature, I usually think, is related to Mount Fuji in the center of the main island of Japan."[51] In fact, the Japanese have a special affection for mountains and forests, especially Mount Fuji, the national symbol; the poet Han-shan lived in seclusion among the cold rocks and secluded forests of Mount Tiantai in Zhejiang Province, so most Japanese monks also regard Mount Tiantai as their ancestral temple of Buddhism. The combination of affection for mountains and forests, as well as the religious sentiments attached to them, thus gave rise to an irresistible natural affinity for the Japanese people in terms of Han-shan's ecological thinking, his life attitudes and the mystical moods depicted in his poems. As a result, Han-shan and his poems have gained literary fame lasting for centuries and countless followers in Japan. Futhermore, the endearing love for Han-shan in Japanese fine arts community has been consistent. This and what has been mentioned earlier is a reason for the CMPs' long-lasting popularity in Japan since its introduction.

The reason that Japanese interest in Han-shan and his poems since the Showa period also lies in the "scholarly fever towards the medieval ages" triggered by the discovery of the Mogao Caves in Gansu's Dunhuang of China, at the beginning of the 20th century (June 22, 1900). More than 50,000 pieces of Buddhist scriptures, social documents, embroideries, silk paintings, ritual implements and other relics from the fourth to eleventh centuries were excavated in the Mogao Caves. This discovery provided an extremely large number of valuable materials for the study on ancient Chinese and Central Asian history, geography, religion, economy, politics, ethnicity, language, literature, art, science and technology. The Japanese have always attached importance to Dunhuangology, and showed a keen interest from the very beginning of the discovery of the Sutra Cave. When Tachibana Zuicho (1890–1968), the famous modern Japanese explorer, followed British archaeologist Marc Aurel Stein (1862–1943) and French orientalist Paul Pelliot (1878–1945) to Dunhuang, he used unscrupulous means to take a large number of artifacts and scripture scrolls from the guardian of the Sutra Cave, Taoist priest Wang Yuanlu (王圆箓, 1849–1931). In October 1912, Japanese explorer Koichiro Yoshikawa (1885–1978) and his associates fraudulently bought more than 400 volumes of Dunhuang manuscripts with 350 taels of silver. Japanese academics have always been pioneering in the study of Dunhuangology and ancient Chinese academic study, and have achieved many remarkable results. To this day, they still regard Dunhuangology as a pride in their Oriental historiography.

Although not a single trace of Han-shan or his poems was found in the cave, 28 original volumes of poems of Wang Fanzhi (王梵志), an important pioneer of vernacular poems in the Tang Dynasty, were unearthed. Since then, these five-word vernacular poems, which had been buried for over a thousand years, were finally unveiled and revived in the Tang poetry world, and thus sparked people's interest in the subject. In 1933, the book *Interpretation of Mingsha* (《鸣沙余韵解说》) by Yabuki Keiki (1879–1936) was published, which first introduced Wang Fanzhi (王梵志) and his poems to Japanese readers. Thereafter many experts specializing in Wang Fanzhi studies, such as Sennosuke Uchida, Iriya Yoshitaka, Kiichiro Kanda and Kanaoka Shoko, gained prominence in the Japanese academic community due to their studies and expertise on Wang Fanzhi. Though Han-shan's vernacular poems inherited Fanzhi's poetic style, their art dwarfs Fanzhi's in artistic achievements—despite the fact that Wang Fanzhi (王梵志), Han-shan and Pang Yun (庞蕴, 740–808) all belong to the same genre of vernacular poetry. Xiang Chu (项楚), a Chinese expert of Dunhuangology, once said, "CMPs contains both slang and vulgar words, which are similar to those of Wang Fanzhi and Pang Yun, but the slightly deeper and more delicate aspect of it makes Wang Fanzhi's and Pang Jushi's poems look clumsy."[52] Thus, when attention was drawn to Fanzhi's poems, it was also naturally directed to poems of Han-shan, which in fact had already enjoyed a high reputation among Japanese readers for centuries. As a result, owing to Japanese passion for Chinese medieval literature, the long-standing religious element in the traditional Japanese literature, coupled with the profound influence of Sŏn (禅, Chinese: Chan; Japanese: Zen) in Japan, the craze on CMPs was rekindled in all Japanese circles after Fanzhi's poems. This conclusion can be easily drawn from the numerous achievements of the study on Han-shan and his poems since the Showa period (1926–1989).

In short, for its plain language style, mysterious Zen realm, unworldly eremitic sentiment and ecological consciousness of returning to nature, the CMPs have won lasting affection from both professional readers and ordinary people in Japan. The development of cultural studies in the 20th century, however, gradually dissolved the distinction between elegance and vulgarity in literature. Literary classics thereby ushered in a post-canonical era in which various voices are mixed, and elegance and vulgarity coexist. Because of the Japanese reinterpretation of vernacular literature and the view of the traditional canonical status in Japan, the CMPs have been firmly established in Japan for centuries, and the poems still hold a large literary reputation even in modern Japan.

It seems that the interlingual travel of Han-shan and his poems in Japanese literature and translated literature has been quite smooth. The CMPs not only were favored by people from all walks of life after the travel, but also achieved a prominent canonical literary status.

### 4.2.2 CMPs on the Korean Peninsula

Research shows that the CMPs were first introduced into the Korean peninsula during the Song and Yuan Dynasties in the 13th century, and gained immediate dissemination throughout the peninsula thereafter. Apart from the ancient engraving, collecting, reviewing and imitating, modern and contemporary studies of Han-shan on the Korean peninsula reveal a pluralistic trend of translation, annotation, revision and review, and have thus even caught attention from the academic community.

#### 4.2.2.1 Cultural Exchange between China and Korea and the Dissemination of CMPs on the Korean Peninsula

According to some early Chinese and Korean documents, the first dynasty on the Korean Peninsula was founded by Jizi (箕子,?–1082 BCE), a sage minister in the late Shang Dynasty of China. The story of Jizi's eastern travel is recorded in the *Shangshu Dazhuan* (《尚书大传》, *Amplification of the Book of History*), "Songweizi Shijia" (宋微子世家, "The House of Song Weizi") in *Shiji* (《史记》, *Records of the Grand History*), and "Dili Zhi" (地理志, "Regional Administration") in *Hanshu* (《汉书》, *Book of Han*). It is said that there is a lineage of Jizi (箕子,?–1082 BCE) on the Korean Peninsula, and is believed to be the ancestor of today's Taewon Seonu clan, but some historians suspect that it is a falsification, and no archaeological confirmation has been made yet. There are also many scholars among Japanese and Korean historians who do not recognize the existence of Ji Zi Joseon, but it is an accepted fact that the exchanges between China and Korea started as early as the Shang (1600 BCE–1046 BCE) and Qin (221 BCE–206 BCE) Dynasties.

In ancient times, the communication between the two nations mainly manifested in the continuous flow of immigrants. Large-scale immigration began around the end of the Warring States period in China. As the unification war of Qin accelerated, the people of Yan, Qi, Zhao and other states began to flee to the

Korean Peninsula on foot via the east of Liaoning province or by ferry from the Yellow Sea through in order to escape from the war. After the unification, many Qin people continued to flee to the Korean peninsula to get out of hard labor due to the oppressive policies of the Qin dynasty. The scale and frequency of emigration became greater than before with the outbreak of the peasant uprising at the end of the Qin Dynasty.[53] Undoubtedly, the flood of many immigrants and the advanced Han culture that came with them largely facilitated the civilization and accelerated the enlightenment in the Korean Peninsula. In the early Western Han Dynasty, Wei Man (卫满) of Yan Kingdom led more than 1,000 subordinates to the Korean Peninsula and established the Wei's Joseon (194 BCE–108 BCE). During the reign of the Wei, the country actively and passively imported Chinese culture as a result of the emigration. This led to a rise of cultural and physical power in the reign of Wei Man. The rising power in the east across the ocean threatened Emperor Wu of Han (156 BCE–87 BCE), who then led his army in 108 BCE to destroy the Wei Man Kingdom and set up a vassal state in the former territory. He had direct control over the northern part of the Korean Peninsula for more than 400 years. During these 400 years, China's culture and influence was continuously imported and adopted. It is said that as early as 17 BCE, King Yuri of Goguryeo (?–18 BCE) on the Korean peninsula composed a poem entitled *A Song of Yellow Bird* (《黄鸟歌》) in Chinese characters to express his longing for his Chinese concubine, Chihui (雉姬), who had left him after a quarrel. The following statement is what King Yuri of Goguryeo supposedly wrote: "Aloft the yellow birds flutter, females and males count on each other. My desolation I brood over: with whom would I return, I wonder?" Although it is difficult to verify whether the poem was actually written by King Ryul or not, it does suggest that lyrical poetry did exist in Korean peninsula before that time.[54] "*A Song of Yellow Bird*" is composed in the four-character poetic style of ancient Chinese, and it is easy to see the traces of the *Shijing* (《诗经》, *Classic of Poetry*) in both its form and content. Later, during the Silla era (57 BCE–935 CE), an ancient country on the Korean Peninsula, created a form of poetry called "Hyangga". The language which Hyangga is composed of is commonly known as "idu", a hybrid of both Chinese and Korean. The form of this language is completely composed of Chinese characters, and most of the content words in the text are in Chinese, while most of the function words are in Korean (with Chinese phonetic notation), and the syntax is mainly from Korean. This language applies the ideographic and phonetic functions of Chinese characters to the Korean language, with some syllables in its words being pronounced in the borrowed phonetic form, some in the Korean ideographic form, and some in a combination of the two methods. In fact, the history of borrowing Chinese characters for writing continued until the reign of King Sejong the Great (1419–1450) in 1446, when he created the nation's own phonetic alphabet, Chosŏn'gŭl in North Korea (Hangul/Hangeul in South Korea). The poetic form of poetry in South Korea is defined by the number of syllables in a line and the number of lines in a verse, rather than by tone. The most common form of "Hyangge" is in ten lines.

Studies show that Chinese poetry was first introduced to the Korean Peninsula around the sixth century CE, just after the unification of Korea by Silla. The envoys and students sent by Silla to the Tang Dynasty were the first group of people to accept and imitate Tang poems. Some poems of Silla poets, like Choi Chi-won (857–900), Wang Ju-in and Kim Chijiang (696–794), were included in *Quantanshi* (《全唐诗》, *Complete Tang Poems*). Among them, Choi Chi-won (857–900) is the most accomplished Silla poet and is regarded as the founder and pioneer of Korean Chinese poetry. The famous poet Yi Gyubo (1169–1241) of the Goryeo Dynasty (918–1392) stated in his novel *A Novel of White Clouds* (《白云小说》) that "Cui went to the Tang palace and stayed there as an official, and was famous for his writing."[55] In terms of poetics, the Korean peninsula did not have its first monograph on poetic discourse until in 1260 when Yi In-ro's (1152–1220) *Appreciation of Poems* (《破闲集》) was published. In addition, with the creation of the unique alphabet "Chosŏn'gŭl", translations of Chinese poetry into Chosŏn'gŭl were born. The most emblematic one is the 25 volumes of *Classification and Explanations of Du Gongbu's Poems in Chosŏn'gŭl* (《分类杜工部诗谚解》) issued in 1481. There is also the *Transcriptions and Explanations of a Hundred Couplets* (《百联抄解》), a collection of a hundred Lianju poems in seven lines.[56]

During the Song and Yuan Dynasties (960–1368), the cultural and personnel exchanges between China and the Korean Peninsula were not very close due to the obstruction of the Liao Kingdom and Jin Kingdom. The exchange of books between the two countries was mostly confined to non-political areas such as poetry, Buddhist scriptures, and medical and legal documents. It is believed that the CMPs were introduced to the Korean peninsula during this period. According to the preface of *Anthology of Cold Mountain Poems in Bigger Chinese Characters, Song Daziben Hanshanshi* (《宋大字本寒山诗集》, *Anthology of Cold Mountain Poems in Bigger Chinese Characters, Song Edition*) published in 1905 (the 38th year of the Meiji era) by Japanese Sinologist Shimada Kan (1879–1915), in the Yuan Dynasty (1271–1368), the "Baoyou" edition printed by Xing-guo (行果) in 1255 was introduced to North Korea. Park Gyeong-ryan (1320–?), together with other scholars, recopied the "Goryeo" edition, a copy of the "Baoyou" edition. According to Kim Young-jin (1962–), the earliest existing version of CMPs in Korea is a copy of the "Bongeunsa" edition printed in the Joseon Dynasty (1392–1897). The "Bongeunsa" edition can be traced back to Guo's Book Shop in the Song Dynasty (960–1279). It was first printed in 1296, and the "Bongeunsa" edition in 1856. It is now kept in the libraries of Dongguk University and Koryo School in South Korea.[57] Moreover, according to Lee Jongmee of Yeungnam University, there is a common feature for the Joseon version system: it is the earliest compilation of both the CMPs and some imitating poems by the monk Cishou's of the Song Dynasty (960–1279). The "North Korean copy of Yuan" edition (in 1574, collected in the Institute of Spiritual Culture of Korea) is the earliest version of the CMPs and the imitating poems of Monk Cishou. On this basis, a number of other versions have been derived, for example, the "Sillokwiki" edition (or the Korean Edition, collected in Beijing Library), the "Bongeunsa" edition (collected in Institute of Spiritual Culture of Korea, printed in 1856) and the "New North Korean" edition based on the "Bongeunsa" edition (collected in Beijing Library). Lee Jongmee pointed out that there has never been any Chinese copy of both Han-shan and Monk Cishou's combined version. This version is circulated only in South Korea.

130  *Cultural Polysystem of Arrivals*

*4.2.2.2  Circulation, Dissemination and Reception of the CMPs in the Koreas*

In the Goryeo Dynasty (918–1392), the first person that had introduced the CMPs was Chin'gak Hyesim (1178–1234), the State Preceptor during the Goryeo dynasty (918–1392). He was well versed in Korean and Chinese Zen thought and Zen literature and was able to use the CMPs freely and create his own unique literary works based on them. His masterpiece, the famous *Biography of the Chinul* (《冰道者传》), holds an esteemed place in the study on the history of ancient Korean novels. The words and Zen practices of Han-shan have been widely disseminated as Zen actions by eminent Korean monks of all generations such as Zen Master Koryo-ryun, Cheon Oh, Taego Bou, Zen Master Jong-jung Seo Kyung-bok, and Zen Master Jong-jung Jung-seo. Besides the Zen field, CMPs were also favored by famous officials and scholars from the Goryeo Dynasty (918–1392) to the Joseon Dynasty (1392–1897). For example, in the collection of poems by the famous Goryeo prime minister Yi Jehyeon (1287–1367), there are poems with the theme of the three saints (Han-shan, Shi-de and Feng-gan), such as *The Three Saints of Tiantai Mountain Sleeping Besides the Tiger* (《天台三圣傍虎同眠》) and *Feng-gan Subduing the Tiger* (《丰干伏虎》). The one who was most profoundly influenced by the CMPs was the Joseon writer Jo Uk (1498–1557), who wrote a number of poems that were similar to the CMPs in styles and tones. In modern times, many Korean poets have taken the CMPs as their spiritual soil and used them either directly or indirectly in their works, poets such as Jeong Ji-yong (1902–1951), Yi Wŏnsŏp, Kim Yŏng-dal, Kim Kwan-sik (1934–) and Park Tu-jin (1916–1998).[58]

In contemporary Korea, works that translate and annotate CMPs are *Cold Mountain Poems* (《寒山诗》), translated by Kim Tal-chin, a professor in the Department of Korean Literature at Dongguk University (Beop Bowon, 1964), and was reprinted by Hongbeopwon in 1970; *Cold Mountain Poems* (《寒山诗》), translated and annotated by Kim Tal-chin and interpreted by Choi Dong-ho (World Society, 1989, 1995); *Cold Mountain Poems* (《寒山诗》), translated and annotated by Kim Tal-chin and edited by Choi Dong-ho (Literature Village, 2001), and *Lectures on CMPs*, compiled by Yi Jeong-ik (Seoul Cultural Society, 1982).[59] Among them, Kim Tal-chin's version is the most famous one, which contains the original Chinese within its total 320 pages and contains a wealth of knowledge for studying the CMPs. There is also *Cold Mountain: 301 Poems* (《寒山诗：301首》) (1989), translated by Jaihiun Kim (1934–), a Korean scholar and translator, published by Hanshin Express Co., Ltd in Seoul. Like Kim Tal-chin's version, within its total 232 pages, the original Chinese texts were presented, in conjunction with a 13-page preface in this version. Undoubtedly, the modern and contemporary Korean translations and annotations of CMPs play a very important role in the understanding and recognition of Han-shan and his poems by the Koreans, and to a certain extent, they have spawned various interests in the CMPs among other fields.

As a matter of fact, the CMPs have not only attracted great interest in the Korean poetry and translation circles, but also in the fiction and academic fields. In 1994, the Korean press Jeonin published a Buddhist novel *Han-shan and Shi-de* (《寒山拾得》) by the novelist Ko Un (1933–) based on their story. In the following table,

Cultural Polysystem of Arrivals 131

one can see that there is interest in the CMPs in the Korean academic field. The first table contains doctoral dissertations and postdoctoral research reports. Table 4.2 contains master's dissertations. The specific information on their research can be found in each respective table.

In terms of the topic selection of the dissertations, Zen poetry is the most common research perspective of the CMPs, with one doctoral thesis and four masters' thesis; the second frequently selected topics of CMPs are from the perspective of edition science, with one doctoral thesis and one masters' thesis. Other topics selected include one doctoral dissertation that explores the artistic characteristics

*Table 4.1* Doctoral Dissertations and Postdoctoral Research Reports on the CMPs in Korea

| Author | Title | Graduating University | Time of Graduation |
|---|---|---|---|
| Lee Iljae | "A Study on Han-shan's Poetry World (Based on Zen Literature)" | Dongguk University (Korea) | 1994–02 |
| Kim Young-jin | "A Study on Vernacular Poetry in Tang Dynasty (Centered on Wang Fanzhi and Han-shan)" | Sichuan University (China) | 2000–07 |
| Lee Jongmee | "A Study on the Editions of Han-shan Poems" | Peking University (China) | 2001–11 |
| Lee Jongmee | "A Study on the Systematic Origin of the Han-shan Poems' Versions (Postdoctoral Research Report)" | Zhejiang University (China) | 2004–12 |

*Table 4.2* Master's Dissertations on the CMPs in Korea

| Author | Title | Graduating University | Time of Graduation |
|---|---|---|---|
| Park Seok | "A Study on Han-shan's Zen Poems" | Seoul National University (Korea) | 1985–02 |
| Park Roo-hyeon | "A Study on Cold Mountain Poems and Their Editions" | "National" Chengchi University (China) | 1986–02 |
| Kim Hyeonu | "A Study on Cold Mountain Poems" | Kookmin University (Korea) | 1988–02 |
| Oh Yuns | "A Comparative Study on the Poems of Wang Wei and Han-shan (Centered on Zen Quest)" | Sungkyunkwan University (Korea) | 1988–02 |
| Kim Gyeongyeop | "A Study on Han-shan and His Zen Poems" | Chung-Ang University (Korea) | 1990–02 |
| Yoo Ji Won | "A Study on Han-shan's Zen Poems" | Korea University (Korea) | 2002–08 |
| Sung Myeongs | "A Study on the Portrait of Han-shan and Shi-de in China and Japan" | Hongik University (Korea) | 2002–08 |

and literary influence of Han-shan's vernacular poems from the perspective of archeography, and one master's dissertation that studies CMPs from the perspective of their content composition, linguistic characteristics, and transmission (Kim Hyeon-woo's *Study on Cold Mountain Poems* (《寒山诗研究》). It's worth mentioning that another master's dissertation investigates the circulation and influence of Han-shan and Shi-de as a painting subject in the history of Chinese and Japanese art from the perspective of Eastern art historiography.[60]

The data in the tables seem to indicate that the research methods on CMPs studies in the Korean academic community range from traditional approaches such as exploring linguistic forms, rhetorical features, and content analysis, to influential studies that examine the circulation and transmission of Han-shan and his poems from specialized fields such as bibliography, edition science, and art history. These research papers are of great academic value and pioneering significance in terms of documentation and research methodology. Korean "Han-shan Studies" has thus earned respect from its peers around the world.

Similar to the case of doctoral and master's dissertations, Korean academic journals hardly saw any articles on "Han-shan Studies" until the 1980s. Only a few research findings that can be found were not from Chinese literature either, but mainly from Korean literature and Buddhist circles, for example, Kumsung's "The Poets and Philosophizers on Earth: Lives of Han-shan and Shi-de" (the 29th set of *Buddhism*, May 1941), Kim Un Hak's "Han-shan's Poems: A Kind of Literature that Keeps Buddhism Alive" (*Modern Literature* 8th set, September 1962), Kim Kwang-rim's *Han-shan and Shi-de* (《寒山拾得》) (*Korean Literature* 36th set, Korea Literature Agency, October 1976), and Seitsu Yamaguchi's "Studies on Han-shan Poems" (*Studies on Indological Buddhism*, March 1970).[61]

Since the 1980s, this situation has seen radical change. The most representative researchers are Professor Yoo Sung-Joon and Professor Kim Tae-Khôn. The series of researches they published in the 1980s launched studies on "Han-shan" in Korea. Among them, Prof. Yoo Sung-Joon authored "Han-shan's Zen Poems" (1981) and "Han-shan and His Poetry" (1982). Professor Kim Tae-Khôn authored "Study on the Han-shan's Life Change Process" (1987) and "The Thought in Cold Mountain Poems" (1988). Besides, in the late 1980s, Professor In Kwon-Hwan of the Department of Korean Literature at Korea University published a book review "The Fresh Impact of Cold Mountain Poems", specifically on CMPs translated by Kim Tal-chin and interpreted by Choi Dong-ho, in *Modern Literature*, No. 249 (1989).[62] These reviews, together with Kim Tal-chin's translation and annotation of CMPs, laid a good foundation for the further dissemination and acceptance of "Han-shan Studies" in South Korea in the 1990s and the 21st century.

Around the 1990s, South Korea has made progress in "Han-shan Studies", not only in the number of papers and researchers but also in the scope and quality of papers. Among the academic papers published in Korean academic journals during this period, the quintessential one is "The Influence of Han-shan Poetry on Zen Poetry and Modern Poetry" (1994) by Professor Choi Dong-ho of the Department of Korean Literature, Korea University. Moreover, professor of Pai Chai University (Daejeon), Lee Sun-Hee's series monographs on "Han-shan Studies" also had a good academic impact. These monographs include *The Context of 'Cold Mountain' in Cold Mountain Poems* (1993), *The Spiritual World of Han-shan-zi in his Poetry* (1997), *Han-shan-zi's Tragic Consciousness* (2006), and *Han-shan-zi's View of Life and Death* (2005). Park Roo-hyeon, who wrote *A Study on Han-shan's Poetry and its Versions* (1986), published the following papers during this period: "A Study on Cold Mountain Poems: Centering on the Content" (1990), "A Study on Buddhist Thought in Cold Mountain Poems (1994) and Cold Mountain Poems with Confucianism and Taoism" (2001).

In addition, there is also Lee Il-jae's "The Symbolism and Fundamental Use of the Green Hills and White Clouds of Hansan's Poetry" (1992), Lee Ting-jo's "Study on Han-shan's Poetry" (1992), Joo Jang-hwan's "Study on Han-shan's Life and Thought" (1994), and Kang Jung-man's "A Preliminary Study on Master Han-shan's Buddhist Thought" (1998), Kim Young-jin's "The Influence of Han-shan's Poetry on Japan" (2002), "The Influence of Cold Mountain Poems on Korean Classical Literature" (2002), "On the Influence of Cold Mountain Poems on Korean Zen Masters and Literati" (2002), Sung Myung-sook's "Study on Portrait of Chinese Han-shan and Shi-de in the 13th and 14th centuries" (2002).[63] In addition, there is Lee Jongmee's series of researches: "The Circulation of Cold Mountain Poems from the Catalogs of the Past Generations" (2003), "On the Version Systems of Cold Mountain Poems" (Postdoctoral Report of Zhejiang University, 2004), "Study on the Origin and Version Systems of the Cold Mountain Poems in the Korean System" (2005), "Study on the Origin and Version Systems of the Cold Mountain Poems in the Guoqing Temple" (2005), etc.

To sum up, in the 1990s, Korean research papers on "Han-shan Studies" focused mainly on their poetic conception, especially the literary connection between the CMPs and Confucianism, Buddhism and Taoism; however, in the 21st century, some new trends emerged, with influence studies and edition studies being the two major centers during this period. The research results of Drs. Kim Young-jin and Lee Jongmee are quite representative. In fact, they have provided new research ideas and paths for Korean "Han-shan Studies" in the new era. In general, these research results from the 1990s and the research teams from different fields of expertise, have not only contributed greatly to Korean "Han-shan Studies", but enabled the immediate and wide circulation and dissemination of Han-shan and his poems in Korea, and gained momentum for the related "Han-shan Studies" in Korea.

Why are the CMPs so popular in the inter-lingual travel arrivals of Koreas? The reason is roughly similar to what happened to the CMPs in Japan. The first is linguistic affinity. The Koreas have long adopted Chinese characters for writing. Moreover, due to the convenient transportation between China and Koreas, the Han culture has been continuously imported into the Korean Peninsula since the ancient immigration wave, and Chinese poetry is one of the source of Korean classic poetry, so at all times in their histories, both Koreas are quite fond of Chinese poetry, and are therefore quite familiar with Chinese culture. Specifically, CMPs, whether their mainstream poetry, vernacular poetry or religious poetry, have a high literary value, which naturally has a certain appeal to the Korean readers who love

Chinese poetry. Second, Koreans' interests in Buddhist literature, especially Zen literature, are far greater in both Koreas than in China. Take the aforementioned "Hyangge Literature" as an example: its source was substantially religious culture; its subjects were mostly monks and Buddhist believers; its content reflected mainly religious thoughts. Therefore, the hermit of Zen, Han-shan, together with his poems, words and conducts were deeply attractive to readership. The imitation, review, annotation and translation of the CMPs have continued from generation to generation, as evidenced by the fact that five of the ten existing dissertations analyze the CMPs from the perspective of Zen. Thirdly, since Korean literary patrons, such as famous monks, literary scholars and even important officials in the imperial court, had made great promotion, imitation and commentary on the CMPs, their prevalence after traveling to Korea should come as no surprise. Regarding why Korea is interested in the CMPs in the 20th century, the reason may be concluded as the rise of popular cultural studies and Zen studies worldwide, as well as the attraction of the second wave of overseas "Han-shan fever" to China's neighbors, South Korea and North Korea.

## 4.3 CMPs in Europe

The translation and study of classical Chinese poetry have always been the "beloved" of Western sinology since the 19th century. With the help of the "Imagists" in the early 20th century and the remarkable creative work of poets and scholars such as Ezra Pound (1885–1972) and Arthur Waley (1889–1966), classical Chinese poetry was at the height of its influence in the Western sinological circle. Since the 1950s and 1960s, the translation and research of classical Chinese poetry have become the exclusive domain in the Departments of East Asian languages and literature of Western universities, in order to meet the needs of teaching East Asian and Chinese literature courses in these universities. This undoubtedly provides an excellent opportunity for the interlingual travel of classical Chinese poetry, like the CMPs, to enter the cultural polysystem of its destination. In such a discourse environment, the CMPs successfully ventured into the European sinology field and were thus added on the list of canonical translated literature. As a matter of fact, from the 1950s to the present day of the 21st century, the CMPs have never stopped their interlingual travel in Europe. Moreover, they have almost become the focus of the translation and research of classical Chinese poetry in European Sinology.

### 4.3.1 CMPs in the United Kingdom

The first foreign confidant of Han-shan in England, the destination of his interlingual travels, turned out to be the famous British sinologist Arthur Waley. Since the publication of Waley's translated poems of Han-shan in 1954, the CMPs have aroused the interpretation and academic research interest of many sinologists and translators in Britain. Therefore, the CMPs have become popular in Britain and even the whole Western world, and gradually established their canonical status in Western translated literature.

*1. Arthur Waley and the CMPs*

Arthur Wiley was a renowned sinologist and translator, fluent in both Japanese and Chinese. He translated a large number of Chinese and Japanese literary works, including *The Nō Plays of Japan* (1921); *The Tale of Genji* (1925), a masterpiece of classical literature by the Japanese author Murasaki Shikibu (973–1014); *The Pillow-Book of Sei Shōnagon* (1928); and translations of Chinese poetry, canons and artworks, like *A Hundred and Seventy Chinese Poems* (1918), *An Introduction to the Study on Chinese Painting* (1923), *The Way and Its Power* (1934), *The Book of Songs* (1937), *The Analects of Confucius* (1938), *Monkey* (An Abridged translation of *Journey to the West*) (1942), *Zen Buddhism and Its Relation to Art* (1959), *Tunhuang Manuscripts: Ballads and Stories from Tun-huang* (1960). In addition, he also wrote some biographic monographs on Chinese poets Li Bai (李白, 701–762) (*The Poetry and Career of Li Po*, 1950), Bai Juyi (白居易, 772–846) (*The Life and Times of Po Chü-I*, 1949), and Yuan Mei (袁枚, 1716–1791) (*Yuan Mei: Eighteenth Century Chinese Poet*, 1956).

Objectively speaking, when compared with his previously mentioned translated works and studies, Waley's translation on the CMPs is a bit inferior in terms of both the scale and its actual impact, however, his rendering of the 27 poems by Han-shan, published on *Encounter* (《相遇》), vol. 12, September 1954, inadvertently initiated the translation and study of the CMPs in the Western world. The Chinese poet and his CMPs, after being translated by this highly regarded English sinologist, became the focus of much attention in the Western world. Gary Snyder (1930–), an American poet, claimed that it was due to these 27 poems' stimulation and motivation that he began his own translation of the CMPs. In 1958, Snyder published his version of 24 CMPs on the *Evergreen Review*, a propaganda camp of the Beat writers (The American Hippy Movement). His version is still recognized as the most influential one in academic circles.

The 27 CMPs published by Waley on *Encounter* are mainly those that reflect family life, secular life, Zen enlightenment, and reclusive life, with the latter taking up about two-thirds of the total. In 1961, these 27 poems, translated and republished by Waley, were included in the *Chinese Poems* (《中国诗选》). In 1970, four of the 27 poems and a short preface were also included in Waley's biography, *Madly Singing in the Mountains*[64]*: An Appreciation and Anthology of Arthur Waley*, edited by Ivan Morris (1925–1976).

Nevertheless, how Waley discovered Han-shan and his poems is still unknown to the academic world. Neither Waley nor experts that study him have ever disclosed it, whether in the preface, biographies or other places. Perhaps because poetry in China's Tang Dynasty is too dazzling, and the awareness and evaluation of classical Chinese poetry in Western sinology at that time was still basically the same as that in the Chinese critical and academic world, no one would have paid attention to the "marginal" poet Han-shan and his "unwelcoming" poems, which were not even found in the history of canonical Chinese poetry. Perhaps Waley himself had no intention of arguing for or redeeming this "disillusioned" Chinese poet, so it makes sense that there is no documentation of how this "literary marriage" was made.

136  *Cultural Polysystem of Arrivals*

The academic community, however, is still inclined to the statement that Waley "probably discovered Han-shan in Japan."[65] Today, it seems that there is certain persuasiveness in this statement. As previously mentioned in this book, the CMPs are widely circulated in Japan and have had a profound influence on Japanese literature and art. Since Waley is an expert in both Chinese and Japanese literature, art and philosophy, the enduring enthusiasm of the Japanese literary and art world on Bai Juyi and Han-shan is certainly not unknown to Waley. Actually, the poetic aesthetics Bai Juyi rendered in his poems was so influential that Waley's version of *The Tale of Genji* was profoundly affected by it, and he even published a monograph for Bai Juyi, *The Life and Times of Bai Juyi*, before translating the CMPs. Following Bai Juyi, Han-shan and his poems were later introduced to Japan in the early 11th century, where they earned admiration from generations of sinologists, art historians and artists. Waley must have noticed that. In addition, Waley's vast translations reveal his familiarity with the Chinese vernacular poetic tradition and his keen interest in Zen culture and Dunhuang literature, all of which are well represented in the CMPs. It is therefore entirely possible that Waley, in the course of his translation and study of Chinese Zen culture and the vernacular poetic tradition, made occasional references to the CMPs. In fact, in Walley's time, the research Japan developed, and the emphasis Japan put on Han-shan and his poems, were unparalleled by China.

Taking these factors into account, we believe that Japan is an important intermediary for the interlingual travel of the CMPs to the Western world, and Waley most likely encountered Han-shan and his poems in Japanese literature.[66] The currently available information reveals that Waley was the first "British discoverer" of Han-shan, and the first to have discovered and translated the CMPs in the United Kingdom.

*2. The Translation of the CMPs in the United Kingdom*

Perhaps because of the previously mentioned reasons, and influenced by the traditional poetic evaluation system, not any version of the CMPs, which is characterized by mixed styles and runs counter to the mainstream poetic standards, was found for nearly a decade after Waley in Britain.

It was only in the 1960s that Reginald Horace Blyth (1898–1964), a British expert on Haiku and Zen, mentioned Han-shan and his poems in his monograph *Zen and Zen Classics*, and translated two of the CMPs, Maodong Yerenju (《茅栋野人居》, "A Mountain Man Lives Under Thatch") and Kexiao Han-shandao (《可笑寒山道》, "The Cold Mountain Path is Strange"). Whereas, Blyth's five-volume series was published by the Hokuseido Press in Japan, so his translations and treatises had little effect in England at the time.

Then, more than a decade later, in 1976, Yale University Press published both in London and New Haven the famous sinologist Hans Frankel (1916–2003)'s *The Flowering Plum and the Palace Lady: Interpretations of Chinese Poetry*. The CMPs are only briefly mentioned in this book. Only three poems by Han-shan, "Laoweng Qushaofu" (《老翁娶少妇》, "When An Old Man Takes a Young Wife"), "Dongjia

Yi Laopo" (《东家一老婆》, "In the house to the East Lives An Old Woman"), and "Yushi Shengsipi" (《欲识生死譬》, "If You Want to Know a Simile for Life And Death") were included in the collection, with minor impact. In the same year, *A Golden Treasury of Chinese* in a series of the *Renditions*, published by the Chinese University of Hong Kong Press, China and edited by the Translation Research Center of Sun Yat-sen University, was published simultaneously in London and Seattle by the University of Washington Press. The preface of this book listed one poem of Han-shan, which was translated by the famous translator John Turner (1909–1971), named *No Title*. But John Turner wrote in his preface that he didn't like the CMPs very much because

> the author is unknown. They were chosen for their eccentricity and lack of the "majesty and magnificence" that is customary in Tang poetry. People have always held the bias that all Chinese poetry is majestic and uniform in its content. The "incidental purpose" of my translation on Chinese poetry is to disabuse this bias, and this simple and unadorned poem is exactly what I needed.[67]

Objectively speaking, because of the influence of political ideology at that time, China's domestic literature in the 1970s had grown stagnant. The West at that time was far more interested in the domestic political situation of China than in its literature. Moreover, the two versions' introduction to the CMPs in 1976 was so simple and superficial that British people made little acquaintance with Han-shan and his poems. Even when in 1980, the well-known British poet and translator, James Kirkup (1918–2009)'s version—*Cold Mountain Poems: 25 Poems by Han-Shan*, was published, it did not make any difference to this situation. Though his version had Chinese cross-references, they were actually published and distributed by Kyoto Editions in Kyoto, Japan.

For nearly two decades thereafter, the CMPs fell silent again in England. Nevertheless, the great Dunhuang discoveries in the 20th century, the remarkable work the British explorers and archaeologists have made in this field, especially the worldwide trend of Zen studies in the 1990s, led British poets and scholars to look at Chinese and Japanese Zen poetry with special respect, which was plain in words but exquisite in artistic conception. In 1999, the *Zen Poems* (compiled by Pete Harris), a collection of Zen poems by Chinese poets Xie Lingyun ((谢灵运), Dajian Hui Neng (六祖惠能), Wang Wei (王维), Liu Changqing (刘长卿), Liu Zongyuan (柳宗元), Han-shan, Shi-de, Jiaoran (皎然), Jia Dao (贾岛) and Su Dongpo (苏东坡) went public. In addition, Japanese poets and Zen monks such as Dōgen Kigen (1200–53), Gidō Shūshin (1325–88), Matsuo Bashō (1644–94), Hakuin Ekaku (1686–1769), and Ryōkan Taigu (1758–1818) were also included. 16 of the CMPs and 3 of Shi-de's poems were selected into the selection of Chinese Zen poems, just after Wang Wei (18 poems) and Su Dongpo (18 poems). Only 7 of Bai Juyi's poems were included. The 16 CMPs were translated by Harris (two poems), Waley (three poems), Snyder (three poems), Watson (six poems), Edward Schafer (one poem), and Robert G. Henricks (one poem). The three poems of Shi-de were all selected from *Sunflower Splendor: Three Thousand Years of Chinese Poetry* (1975) by James Hargett (1948–), a professor at the State University of New York. In the Foreword of *Zen Poems*, Harris presented that

> a number of remarkable poets in China and Japan were indeed Zen monks or people who led a reclusive existence. In China, the best known of them is Han-shan, "Cold Mountain". Like other Chinese poets with an interest in Buddhism, Han-shan had a strong influence on later generations of Zen monk poets in Japan, including Ryokan,[68] an outstanding poet-recluse.[69]

In 2006, the British translator A. S. Kline (1947–) published his own version, *Words from Cold Mountain, Twenty-Seven Poems by Han-shan* on the Internet, and it was available for free download by researchers for non-commercial circulation and dissemination. This version consists of three parts: Introduction, The Poems, and Index by First Line. Kline wrote in the short preface that

> Han-shan, the Master of Cold Mountain, and his friend Shi-de, lived in the late-eighth to early-ninth century AD, in the sacred Tiantai Mountain of Chekiang Province, south of the bay of Hangchow. The two laughing friends, holding hands, come and go, but mostly go, dashing into the wild, careless of others' reality, secure in their own. As Han-shan himself says, his Zen is not in the poems. Zen is in the mind.[70]

The following translation starts with "Don't You Know the Poems of Han-shan?", and ends with "Cold rocks, no one takes this road". The vast majority of the poems selected by Kline are those associated with the poet's hermitage, the Cold Mountain. Kline's version is mainly a literal translation, with concise, lively and strong colloquial language.

From Waley's first version of the CMPs in 1954 to the publication of Kline's version in 2006, the dissemination and translation of the CMPs in the United Kingdom spanned more than fifty years. Although the journey was stumbling, and the vulgar and simple CMPs did not receive a positive response in the British cultural context at that time, Waley's interpretation and study of Han-shan and the CMPs, and his concerns on the norms in the translating process were so distinctive to Sinologists that they were highly recognized by professional readers. Although the CMPs are not as glamorous in the UK as they are in the American cultural polysystem, the world-renowned sinologist Waley's translation has led to a boom in the translation and study of the CMPs throughout the Western world. In fact, Waley's version has, more or less, nourished, inspired too, and influenced several other translations of the CMPs that are widely circulated in the Western world.

*3. British Monographs on "Han-shan Studies"*

In 1962, when American sinologist Burton Watson's *Cold Mountain: 100 Poems by the T'ang Poet Han-shan* was published by the Columbia University Press,

David Hawkes (1923–2009), a leading British sinologist and translator, also published a review of Watson's translation in the *Journal of the American Oriental Society* in the same year. It is not only a book review, but also a fascinating monograph on "Han-shan Studies". Hawkes points out that, despite the long-held belief that the Preface was a forgery, the lingering superstitious idea didn't come out of vacuum. For instance, many people still assume that Han-shan was a Buddhist monk, but the research on the internal evidence of the CMPs is very different from this conclusion. Hawkes mentioned the research of Wu Chi-yu and supported the claim that Dao Qiao (道翹) was the author of the pseudo-preface. He even speculated that Dao Qiao might not know who Han-shan was, but Dao Qiao did collect the poems. The hermit who wrote the poems had died about 15 to 20 years before and Han-shan's image in Dao Qiao's mind was from a legendary story told by the local superstitious crofters.[71] This book review has, to some extent, enriched the English-speaking world's understanding of Han-shan and his poems. But because of the British academy's rejection on such poems, and the interest of the British translation and sinology community in Chinese poets was still largely confined to the traditional poets in the Chinese poetic history, the CMPs did not gain much literary fame in the British academic world in the 1960s and for the forty years thereafter.

Whereas, in 2003, two important articles on Han-shan Studies: *Han-shan's Place in History* and *Han-shan in Translation* appeared in Peter Hobson (1949–)'s *Poems of Han-shan*, both of which are written by T. H. Barrett, an internationally renowned sinologist and professor of East Asian history at the School of Oriental and African Studies, University of London. They are seminal research findings on Han-shan and the CMPs in the British academic circle, and outstanding contributions British scholars made to the world's "Han-shan Studies", which marked the beginning of a real era of academic research on Han-shan and the CMPs in the British academic community. Therefore, they are milestones to be recognized in the field of British "Han-shan Studies", and even in the field of East Asian studies in the entire Britain. In the first of *"Han-shan's Place in History"*, the beginning of "The Religious Poetry Tradition in East Asia", Barrett addresses:

> The traditions of East Asian literature deriving from China represent an impressive stretch of continuous literary consciousness, spanning about three thousand years into modern times. One of the most striking differences between this continuum and the time-span covered by Western literature is the relatively unimportant role played in it by religious literature. There are, of course, exceptions, and Han-shan is one of them. But to understand just how and why Han-shan is exceptional requires some background information on how the literary tradition developed in China, and how its values came to differ from those that are presumably more familiar to the reader of English.[72]

Starting with Qu Yuan (340 BCE–278 BCE), a patriotic poet of Chu (a vassal states in the Yangtze Valley) at the end of the Warring States Period (476 BCE–221 BCE), Barrett talks about the later Taoist literature and the rise of religious poetry in China, and in the third part of his essay he probes into the relationship between "mountain" and "poetry". According to Barrett, "mountain" is one of the most commonly used words in the elite poetry of the Tang Dynasty. The name "Han-shan" is only a pseudonym of the poet. He also mentions Han-shan's predecessor Wang Fanzhi (王梵志), arguing that "Wang Fanzhi's work is mentioned in a Dunhuang manuscript which turns out to be of Taoist provenance.' This willingness to mix ideas from different traditions is, of course, one of Han-shan's characteristics, too."[73]

Barrett also described in his book that

> China's mountains offered an environment for learning that was at once tranquil, bracing and aesthetically pleasing. And, what is more, in China one's chances of employment were improved by education. The Tiantai Mountains where Han-shan made his home were very much a location of the "university" type, long famous for their association with Buddhism and also with legends of the immortals. . . . It may be that there was already a spot there named "Cold Mountain" before our poet arrived, but it is equally possible that he chose this name for his dwelling as well as for himself . . . and the Wenxuan: the latter work is a standard literary anthology compiled in the early sixth century, in which the phrase "Cold Mountain" occurs several times. So it would not be an obscure choice for a name, and indeed we find that Jiao Ran uses it as well. By the second half of the eighth century, too, we find near the city of Soochow a "Cold Mountain Monastery", mentioned in a poem of the period by Zhang Ji (712/715–779) that was anthologized by the end of the century.[74]

There is no denying about the author's insightful examination of the "mountain" and the verification of the name "Han-shan". In fact, Eastern and Western readers, when reading his articles, will catch a glimpse of his perceptive understanding of the Chinese and Western literary traditions, the status of religious literature, and the origins of Eastern Asian literature. By virtue of this narrative strategy, Barrett is intended to show the reader that Han-shan and his poems did not emerge out of nowhere, but that they were nurtured and flourished in a certain literary context. In a word, Barrett's approach to the study on Han-shan and his poems in this literary context and the conclusions drawn from it, are useful both for the study on Han-shan and Han-shan's poetry itself and for the study on Chinese literature, Eastern Asian literature and history as a whole.

In the next section, "Who was Han-shan", Barrett refers to the examination of Han-shan's origins by scholars such as Wu Chi-yu (France), Edwin Pulleyblank (1922–2013) (Canada) and Robert Henricks (The United States), as well as the polemic over Han-shan between the Taoists, represented by Du Guangting (杜光庭) and Xu Lingfu (徐灵府), and those of the later Zen religion. The authors then arrive at the following conclusion:

> My own conclusion would be that Han-shan could be clearly identified with neither group. This explains my introduction of the category of "mountain

man" as the most appropriate background against which to understand Han-shan himself, despite the picture created by later legend. But, whether I am right or wrong, it cannot be denied that Han-shan's influence on later literature was exercised through his legendary image as a man of Zen. How and why that image came into existence is therefore an essential preliminary to any discussion of his place in the further history of religious verse in East Asia.[75]

The author then discusses the circulation and reception of Han-shan and his poems in Eastern Asian countries such as Japan, Korea and Vietnam. In the final section of his book, "On Cold Mountain", the author argues that the immortality of the CMPs owes much to the imitation of later generations, a view in line with the claim of Walter Benjamin (1892–1940) that the "afterlife" of a literary work should be credited to the translation and translator. The author also notes that "But in Han-shan's case wholesale imitation took place, and this is perhaps a clue to the nature of his impact." At the end of this section, the author summarizes:

It is precisely when he is distracted from the literati tradition by the realities of his existence that his poetic gaze becomes utterly individual: clear, direct and even startling. What is more, this clarity of vision prevents his religious insights from becoming mere preaching—something which the religious poets obviously envied, but did not always succeed in duplicating. For Nishitani Keiji (1900–1990) is probably right: if there is a touch of Zen in the genuine Han-shan, it is not because he was a follower of that movement. Rather, the likelihood is that the movement followed him and Zen underwent a touch of Han-shan.... Although "Zen verse" suggests writing infused with the insights of enlightenment, we must accept (as Nguyen explicitly does for Vietnamese Zen poetry) that much of it was just as conventional as mainstream, elite verse, though in another way. Simplicity and directness, especially when allied to the predictability of a structured monastic environment rather than the alarming vicissitudes of a solitary hermit life, often produced at best mere charm, and at the worst pointless insipidity. But Han-shan's verse remained, and remains, a challenge.[76]

Barrett's discussion of Han-shan and his poems is very captivating, especially his analysis and commentary on the theme of "mountain" in Chinese literature, Han-shan's poetic style, and the literary status of the CMPs in Zen poetry. It is believed that this monograph will be of great academic value and reference significance to the study on Han-shan and his poems, and even to the study on Chinese religious literature. And Barrett also puts forward one powerful and compelling argument that "if there is a touch of Zen in the genuine Han-shan, it is not because he was a follower of that movement. Rather, the likelihood is that the movement followed him and Zen underwent a touch of Han-shan," which somehow attests to the great academic value and influence of Han-shan and his poems in literary and religious studies.

142  *Cultural Polysystem of Arrivals*

In another article, "Han-shan in Translation", Professor Barrett compares the surviving translations of the CMPs, which renders those CMPs lovers access to making comparative studies so that they can better understand Han-shan and his poems. The author summarizes that "It seems likely that in Han-shan scholarship and appreciation, 'one hundred flowers' will continue to blossom."[77] In fact, Barrett's two monographs on "Han-shan studies" are certainly two gorgeous and distinctive blossoms of this garden.

In conclusion, Arthur Waley's translation of the CMPs in the 1950s has been followed by a number of sinologists and translators in Britain, but perhaps because of the conservative nature of British cultural norms and literary traditions, as well as the differences between the vulgar CMPs and the refined poetry of academic style pursued by those British academics, the academics have never considered making serious research on the folk poets represented by Han-shan and his poems. As Father Zbigniew Wesołowski SVD (1957–), Director of the Centre for Chinese Studies in the School of Foreign Languages at Fu Jen Catholic University in China, said, "There is a utilitarianism-oriented tradition of sinology in Britain that places too much emphasis on real politic and economic values, which can be detrimental to so-called 'classical' sinology."[78] Indeed, Tang poetry, a kind of classical Chinese literature, barely found favor with those British scholars. Thus it does not take too much stretch of the imagination to think that the CMPs in Britain were just like a few sporadic stars in the starry sky of British mainstream poetry. What those British scholars failed to predict, however, was that these little sparkling stars would light up so many European countries, say, the neighboring France which then became a major European center for sinology. Then many other European countries followed suit such as Germany, Belgium, the Netherlands, Sweden, and the Czech Republic, and this craze of "Han-shan fever" eventually came back to Britain, luring many later British scholars into the translation and study of the CMPs, with Peter Harris's *Zen Poems* and Barrett's two research monographs, and Klein's *Twenty-Seven Poems by Han-shan* as the representative products.

*4.3.2 CMPs in France*

In France, thanks to the "Chinese culture fever", Dunhuang studies, Free Verse Movement, the Beat Movement, existentialist philosophy, and the worldwide Zen fever, the interlingual travel of Han-shan was almost spared from any contextual pressure from the target polysystem so that the CMPs were widely circulated and disseminated in France, a major European capital of sinological studies.

*1. Cultural Exchanges between France and China*

The exchanges between France and China, for some historical reasons, and obvious geographical reasons, lagged behind those between France and its neighbors, such as Spain, Portugal and Italy. However, the writings of those Western missionaries on China planted the seeds of an "ideal country" in the minds of those French, and then their yearning for the mysterious Chinese culture drove them to communicate with China. Cultural exchanges between France and China took place finally as six French Jesuit priests traveled to China in the 17th century under the title of "King's Mathematicians". Then 1742 saw the start of the teaching of Chinese studies at the Royal Academy of Chinese Studies, and 1796 witnessed the establishment of the Institut National des Langues et Civilisations Orientales (Institute of Oriental languages and Civilizations in Paris). As some commentators have pointed out, "Although French Sinology was inspired initially by the neighboring countries such as Italy, it occupied the central position soon in France."[79] It was to the writings of these early Jesuits on Chinese culture that the Chinese cultural fever in 18th-century France and throughout Europe owed a lot. This Chinese cultural fever led people from all fields and walks of life to look to Chinese culture for useful solutions to their own development. In the first half of the 19th century, Chinese cultural fever took a steady course as classical Chinese literature in France became one of the century's most striking cultural sights. In 1814, the French Academy decided to include Chinese as a subject in the highest French academies, thereby opening the way for the training and development of specialists in sinology, and even German scholars were trained in Chinese here due to the limitations of their own academic facilities in their country at the time. This was the beginning of unprecedented activity in the translation of Chinese literature in France. In the 1940s, however, France was caught in the quagmire of the Second World War, and the study on sinology then came to a complete standstill and even regressed. Fortunately, the early 1960s saw a strong resurgence of sinology, with the emergence of Chinese language courses in many French universities and secondary schools and the training of Chinese language personnel. At the same time, a series of Chinese studies institutions were expanded and established, and a large number of specialists in various fields of Chinese studies emerged, hence a new heyday of Chinese studies in France. The interlingual journey of Chinese culture and literature naturally went smoothly in the midst of such cultural syndromes.

There were some sporadic translations by French sinologists of classical Chinese poetry in the 17th and 18th centuries, with some being more influential such as a fragmentary translation of *Shijing* (《诗经》, *Classic of Poetry*) which was acclaimed as "the first of the Five Classics". After the nineteenth century, the translation and study of Chinese poetry then began to flourish. Exemplary Translations sprang up such as *Poesies de L'epoque des Thang* (《唐诗》, *Tang Poems*) (1862) by the famous sinologist Le Marquis d'Hervey-Saint-Denys (1823–1892), and *Le Livre de Jade* (《玉书》, *A Collection of Selected Poems by Ancient and Modern Chinese Poets*) translated by the outstanding poetess Judith Gautier (1845–1917) assisted by her Chinese teacher Tin Tun Ling (丁敦龄, 1831–1886). Le Marquis d'Hervey-Saint-Denys collected 97 Tang poems by 35 Chinese poets, including Li Bai (李白), Du Fu (杜甫) and Wang Wei (王维), while Judith Gautier collected and translated 110 poems by 35 poets (including eight unknown ones) from the Zhou Dynasty down to the Qing Dynasty. The translated poems are divided into eight categories according to their subject matter: 42 poems on love, 9 on the moon, 7 on travel, 6 on the court, 8 on war, 8 on wine, 16 on autumn, and 14 on poets. Of these, 19 poems are by Li Bai (李白), 17 by Du Fu (杜甫), 8 by Su Dongpo (苏东坡), 7 by Zhang Ruoxu (张若虚) and 6 by Li Qingzhao (李清照).

The 20th century witnessed great progress in Sinology in France. With the improvement of sinology educational institutions and the discovery of the Dunhuang Caves in Gansu province, China, there were more frequent cultural exchanges between France and China, and sinology studies in France also began to enter the era of full prosperity. During this period, there emerged some experts of sinology with worldwide influence—Edward Chavannes (1865–1918), "the European luminary in Sinology", Henri Maspero (1883–1945), a leading expert on Chinese ancient history, Marcel Granet (1884–1940), a reputed sociologist, Paul Pelliot (1878–1945), a pioneer of Western Dunhuang studies, P. Demieville (1894–1979), a renowned specialist in Dunhuang studies and his disciple Jacques Gernet (1921–2018), a well-famed sociocultural historian (1921–2018), Yves Hervouet (1921–1999) and Wu Chi-yu (1919–2011), authoritative experts on Fu poetry of Sima Xiangru (司马相如, 179 BCE–117 BCE), Max Kaltenmark (1910–2002), an outstanding specialist of Taoist texts, and his disciple K. Schipper (1934–), a world-famous expert on Taoist Canon, Andre H. Lévy (1925–), a distinguished scholar on Chinese fiction, Donald Holzman (1926–), a leading scholar on Ruan Ji (阮籍, 210–263) studies, Jean-Pierre Diény (1927–2014), an authoritative specialist on ancient Chinese characters and thoughts, Francois Cheng (1929–), a world-class scholar on Chinese poetry, Claudine Salmon (1938–), a key expert on Chinese Nanyang (an old name for southeast Asia) literature, and Alain Peyraube (1944–), a prominent scholar on Chinese language studies.

As for classical Chinese poetry, *Fêtes et Chansons de Anciennes de La Chine* (《中国古代祭礼与歌谣》, *Festivals and Songs Of Ancient China*) by Marcel Granet was published in 1911, and the sinologists enthusiastically acclaimed its thorough study on *Shijing* (《诗经》, *Classic of Poetry*) and the translation of "Guofeng" (国风, "Airs of the States") in *Shijing* (《诗经》, *Classic of Poetry*). From the 1920s to 1950s, however, French translations and studies of classical Chinese poetry were relatively quiet for obvious historical reasons (WWI and WWII). But this stalemate was broken in 1962 by the publication of *Anthologie de la poésie Chinoise classique* (《中国古诗选》, *Selected Ancient Chinese Poems*) under the direction of Professor Demieville, and in this anthology, he translated a total of 374 poems by 204 poets, from the primitive ages to the Qing Dynasty (1644–1912). The following 1960s and 1970s saw the appearance of a large number of translations and research monographs on classical Chinese poetry. For example, Yves Hervouet's *Un Poète de cour sous les Han: Sseu-ma Siang-jou* (《汉代宫廷诗人——司马相如》, *Han Dynasty Court Poet: Sima Xiangru*), Jean-Pierre Diény's *Les Dix-neuf Poimes anciens* (《古诗十九首》, *Nineteen Old Poems*), *Pastourelles et magnanarelles. Essai sur un theme litteraire chinois* (《牧女与蚕娘》, *Pastourelles and Magnanarelles*), Donald Holzman's *La vie et la pensée de Hi K'ang* (《嵇康的生平和思想》, *The Life and Thought of Ji Kang*), *Poetry and Politics: the Life and Works of Juan Chi*, and Francois Cheng's *Chinese Poetic Writing*, to name but a few. Such a large number of high-standard studies and translations of classical Chinese poetry enabled France to play an increasingly vital role in sinology around the world. It was in this context that the interlingual travel of the CMPs in France made its debut.

## 2. The Circulation, Dissemination, and Reception of the CMPs in France

The translation and study of the CMPs in France began with a monograph on Han-shan Studies by the renowned Dunhuang expert Wu Chi-yu in 1957 and experienced a brief period of silence. Thanks to the renewed enthusiasm for translating classical Chinese poetry in the 1960s, the CMPs regained scholarly favor in the 1970s. One case about that was *Le Clodo du Dharma: 25 poèmes de Han-shan* (《达摩流浪者：寒山诗25首》, *The Dharma Bums: 25 CMPs*), translated by a leading contemporary French sinologist Jacques Pimpaneau (1934–2021), and published by the Centre de publication Asie orientale (East Asia Publication Centre) in Paris.[80] Then the 1980s featured the translations of Tang vernacular poets. First came the publication of P. Demieville's *L'œuvre de Wang le zélateur* (《王梵志诗全译本》, *The Complete Translation of Wang Fanzhi's Poems*) in 1982, followed by the two translations of the CMPs in 1985—*Han-shan: Merveilleux le Chemin de Han-shan* (*Han-shan: Wonderful Cold Mountain Path*) by Cheng Wing fan and Hervé Collet and *Le Mangeur de Brumes: L'oeuvre de Han-shan, Poète et Vagabond* (*Clouds Thick, Whereabouts Unknown: The Collected Works of the Wanderer Poet Han-shan*) translated by Carré Patrick (1952–). Besides, *Le Recueil de la Falaise Verte: Kôans et Poesies du Zen* (《碧岩录：语录与禅诗》, *The Blue Cliff Record*)[81] published in 2000 by Éditions Albin Michel included 27 CMPs translated by Maryse et Masumi Shibata.

The translation and study of the CMPs in France is marked by an English monograph, *A Study on Han-shan*,[82] published in English in *T'oung Pao* in 1957 by Wu Chi-yu, a French-Chinese specialist in Dunhuang studies and vernacular literature, which represented the highest level of scholarship on Han-shan and the CMPs at that time. Wu Chi-yu explores in detail the various legends and biographies of Han-shan and ventures to theorize that the prototype of Han-shan may be Zhi-yan (智岩, 577–654), the monk in Dao Xuan's (道宣, 596–667) *Xu Gaosengzhuan* (《续高僧传》, *Continued Biographies of Eminent Monks*). In addition to translating some anecdotes related to Han-shan, Wu Chi-yu has also selected and translated 49 poems of Han-shan and one poem by Shi-de (many articles mistakenly refer to 50 CMPs). The appendices to the article consisted of four parts—"A Table of More Important Events in Chih-yen's Life", "The Place-names: Shih-feng and T'ang-hsing and T'ang-hsing", "The Editions of Han-shan poems", and "The Authenticity of the Hou-chi Hsu Kao-seng chuan". It must be mentioned that his documentary examination is impressively meticulous and thorough.

Wu Chi-yu also believes that the preface attached to the CMPs is not written by Lü Qiuyin (闾丘胤). He expounds on it as follows:

> T'ang-hsing (唐兴), used three times in the preface, seems to have been an original part of it. That is to say, it is not a later insertion. Since Shih-fêng (始丰) was changed to T'ang-hsing (唐兴) in the second year of Shang-yüan（上元, 761 A.D.）under the reign of Emperor Suzong of Tang (肃宗, 756–762), the preface must have been written after 761 A.D. . . . Besides, the term ju-chu-jen (汝诸人, "you many people") began to appear as a daily

expression with the Dhyâna masters in the *Chuanxin Fayao* (《传心法要》, *Transmission of the Dharma Mind*) of Huangbo Xiyun (黄檗希运,?–850), (with a preface written in 857 A.D.).[83] The preface of CMPs might not be earlier than this account in the middle of the ninth century. Moreover, the official title of the preface writer may also afford a clue for the identification of the date. Only two periods are called tz'û fei (赐绯), 721–742 A.D. and after 758 A.D. Finally, the preface does not conform to the ordinary formula. At its end the date was perhaps consciously avoided, and replaced by thirty-eight four-character lines. It might have been written after the model of Buddhist sûtra, for instance, the *Saddharma Puṇḍarīka Sūtra* (《妙法莲花经》, *Lotus Sutra*) or the pien-wên (变文) which gives a summary in poetical form after the story in prose. The author seems to have been a Buddhist monk (Dao Qiao (道翘) rather than a learned official.[84]

Wu Chi-yu also examines the use of Buddhist texts and Buddhist terminology in the CMPs. He points out that nearly half of the terms in those poems about Buddhist ideas are quoted from the *Mahāparinirvāna-sūtra* (*Nirvana Sutra*)[85], which was most prevalent before the mid-seventh century. This approach to the study on Han-shan's life and the linguistic features of his poems based on historical sources largely inspired the later "Han-shan Study". Wu Chi-yu's translations of the CMPs have also been criticized by scholars like Paul Kahn (1952–), who said that, "Wu's (Wu Chi-yu) translations are pedantic and short of sentimentality of English poems. Those translations are, on the whole, poor poems."[86] What we must admit is that Wu's Han-Shan Studies, with its investigation of Han-shan's life and the internal evidence of the CMPs have pioneered and pushed forward later studies of Han-shan and his poems. *CMPs: Being the Legends and Poems Attributed to the T'ang Dynasty Hermit Han-shan*, a single volume of English translations of the CMPs by Wu Chi-yu, was published by Clear Light Free Press (Shirley, Surrey) in the United Kingdom. This slim book with only 32 pages, together with Wu Chi-yu's monograph on Han-shan Studies, paved the way for the interlingual travel of the CMPs in France and Europe, and in particular for the circulation and dissemination of them in a number of major European sinological towns. In this respect, Wu should be credited with a great deal.

Wu Chi-yu pioneered "Han-shan Studies" in France, but it took 18 years for the first French translation of the CMPs to arrive. In September 1975, *Le Clodo du Dharma: 25 poèmes de Han-shan*, translated by Jacques Pimpaneau, was published by Centre de publication Asie orientale. The title of the book is apparently taken from the novel of the same name, *The Dharma Bums*, by Jack Kerouac (1922–1969), the spiritual leader of the Beat Generation. It is worth noting that Kerouac's novel is also dedicated to his ideal hero, Han-shan. Pimpaneau remarked in his long preface to this French translation in June 1974 that

> Han-shan was a Chinese poet who lived around the seventh century AD and whose name is always associated with Zen. There are 311 poems attributed to him. This legendary figure in rags was always cheerful. He had a companion

called Shi-te (拾得). He had the hippie air of his time about him. Today his words and actions have become a trendsetter for a distinctive lifestyle.[87]

His statement seems to suggest that Pimpaneau chose to translate the CMPs because he noticed the similarity in image and temperament between Han-shan and the 20th-century hippie. In this preface, Pimpaneau mentions Waley's translation, Snyder's translation, Wattson's translation and Kerouac's *The Dharma Bums*, but mistakenly dates the publication of Snyder's translation to August 1956. He also discusses the promotion of Zen Buddhism in the United States by Alan Watts (1915–1973) and D. T. Suzi (1870–1966) in the United Kingdom, and the reverence of the younger generation for Han-shan in the meantime. The translator then briefly presents the life of Han-shan and the reception of his poems in China and Japan.

Pimpaneau's translation is distinctive in that each poem is accompanied by the original Chinese text inscribed in various forms of soft calligraphy by China's calligrapher Li Guorong (李国荣, 1929–). In his translation, each original poem in Chinese is translated into French in two ways—a word-for-word translation and a natural, smooth translation. The translation is also particularly well illustrated: on the front cover is a portrait of Han-shan and Shi-de painted by the famous Qing Dynasty painter Luo Ping (1733–1799), and there is a stone carving by him:

The poem "*The Incarnations: Han-shan and Shi-de*" reads: "Ho, ho, ho! If I am happy from my heart, all troubles will turn into happiness. There is no use worrying in that Tao lies in happiness. A nation can prosper in the happy union of the king and the subjects, and a family can thrive in happy harmony between the father and his son, brothers and sisters, and the husband and his wife. The host is on good terms with the guest; the upper is at peace with the lower. All is happy! All is well! Ho, ho, ho!" Han-shan and Shi-de are said to be the incarnations of two Chinese Bodhisattvas, Manjusri (Wenshu) and Samantabhadra (Puxian). Now Han-shan and Shi-de are known as *the He-he icons*.

The painting on the back cover is a picture of Shi-de by the famous painter Yan Hui (颜辉) in the late Song and early Yuan Dynasties, which is now in the Tokyo National Museum. In short, the combination of book, painting, text and translation is the greatest highlight of this translation, and this typically "Chinese flavor" naturally appeals to Western readers.

In the 1980s, there were two French translations of the CMPs, both of which were published in 1985. The first was translated by Cheng Wing fan and Hervé Collet as *Han-shan: Merveilleux le Chemin de Han-shan* (*Han-shan: Wonderful Cold Mountain Path*), and the second was translated by Carré Patrick as *Le Mangeur de Brumes: L'oeuvre de Han-shan, Poète et Vagabond* (*Clouds Thick, Whereabouts Unknown: The Collected Works of the Wanderer Poet Han-shan*). The former was published by Moundarren. The number of poems translated is mistakenly put at 108 by both T. H. Barrett and Qian Linsen (钱林森), the author of *La Littérature*

148  *Cultural Polysystem of Arrivals*

*Chinoise en France* (*Chinese Literature in France*), but this figure is in fact inaccurate because the translators have selected a total of 111 CMPs for translation. Of these, 97 are in five lines, nine in seven lines and five in three lines. In the preface, the translator begins with the "epiphany" of Sakyamuni (623–543) and briefly traces the history of Zen Buddhism up to the life of the Sixth Patriarch Hui Neng (惠能). Cheng Wing fan and Hervé Collet describes Han-shan as follows:

> Hui Neng passed away in 713 AD. At that time China was at the dawn of a glorious era of culture. In this century lived the great poets Li Bai (李白), Du Fu (杜甫), Wang Wei (王维) and Bai Juyi (白居易). In addition to Hui Neng, the great Zen masters included Nan Yue (Huai Rang) (南岳怀让, 677–744), Ma Zu (Dao Yi) (马祖道一, 709–788), Huang Bo (Duan Ji) (黄檗断际, ?–850) and Lingzhi (灵智). Zen was at its height, and it exerted considerable influence on both the monks who dotted the monasteries of China and the lay monks who sometimes wanted to get away from the world and retreat to the mountains. Some of them chose to remain in the monasteries or to become hermits, living a carefree, pure-hearted life in the great and peculiar Chinese hermit tradition. Of them all, Han-shan is perhaps the most famous, having also lived in that great age. After a brief family life, he travelled in all directions, finally retiring to the state of Yue. There he consulted two masters of Southern Zen: Nan Yue (Huai Rang) and Ma Zu (Dao Yi), and finally settled on Mount Tiantai, where the world called him Han-shan. According to his name, if man and mountain are united as one, etymologically, they reveal a divine and immortal style. Man + mountain = immortal too. Tiantai (Heaven's Terrace) is a mountain range at the eastern end of China, south of Hangzhou Bay adjacent to the Chinese coastline. On the slopes of Tiantai are mountains of laurel trees, symbols of the immortality of life. In this isolated area there are many temples and Taoist temples. The most famous is Guoqing Temple, where the Zen master Feng-gan (丰干), riding on the back of a tiger and singing, lived. . . . Han-shan and his companion, the monk Shi-te of Guoqing Temple, later became a popular subject in the history of Zen painting—Han-shan holds a scroll of poetry, while Shi-te holds a broom. They are happy and far from the mundane world. The portrait of Han-shan on the cover of the book is a copy of a painting of Han-shan by the great fourteenth-century painter Yan Hui (颜辉). It is said that Han-shan carved his poems on trees, rock walls and walls. The preface to CMPs was written by a high-ranking official named Lü Qiuyin (闾丘胤), who compiled the poems, but, contrary to Chinese tradition, the preface does not indicate the date on which it was written. However, all the poems collected by Lü are now lost and untold. The trajectory of Zen, la confiance, le doute and la persévérance gave direction to the poet Han-shan on the summit of Cold Mountain and enriched his life. His search for the true human nature, following the natural way, led him to freedom in the end.[88]

As can be seen, the translators are quite familiar with the history of Chinese Zen Buddhism and the tradition of hermits in ancient Chinese culture. In addition, like most scholars, they also doubt whether the CMPs preface was written by Lü Qiuyin (闾丘胤), and their reasoning is similar to that of previous scholars. However, Cheng Wing fan and Hervé Collet claimed that Han-shan once studied under the guidance of Nan Yue (南岳) and Ma Zu (马祖), a view which has not yet been discussed. Despite their skepticism, they still translated accurately the preface which was generally deemed to be written by Lü Qiuyin (闾丘胤), but they left out the ode in the preface. The translation is mainly a straightforward one, simple and fluent, and without any relevant commentary. The translation is also accompanied by the original Chinese text inscribed by one of the translators, Cheng Wing fan, which naturally makes it easier for the reader to read and study in comparison. This translation, first published in June 1985, was reprinted in December 1992. It is worth mentioning that in this series of French translations of Chinese poetry, there are also translations of Chinese poets such as Tao Yuanming (陶渊明), Li Bai (李白), Wang Wei (王维), Du Fu (杜甫), Bai Juyi (白居易), Su Dongpo (苏东坡) and Yang Wanli (杨万里).

In 1985, the Parisian publisher Phebus published a French translation of the CMPs by Carré Patrick, *Le Mangeur de Brumes*: *L'oeuvre de Han-shan, Poète et Vagabond*. The book is thought to be 311 pages long, but the accurate number of the translated poems by the translator is not clear to me as there are varying ideas among scholars. However, Professor Qian Linsen (钱林森) briefly mentioned the translation of the CMPs in France:

In 1985, two translations of CMPs were published in France: one book, entitled *Han-shan*, contains 108 of CMPs; the other book, entitled *L'oeuvre de Han-shan, Poète et Vagabond*, includes 331 CMPs.[89]

Considering the actual number of extant CMPs, Qian may have mistaken 311 for 331.

In the 1990s, no new translations of the CMPs appeared in France, except for the translation of *Han-shan: Merveilleux le Chemin de Han-shan* by Cheng Wing fan and Hervé Colletr, which was reprinted in December 1992. The first French translation of CMPs in the 21st century was published in 2000 by the Parisian publisher Editions Albin Michel and translated into French by the Japanese scholars Shibata Maryse and Shibata Masum, *Le Recueil de la Falaise Verte: Kôans et Poésies du Zen*. The title of the book is taken from the eponymous book of discourses, *Biyanlu* (《碧岩录》, *The Blue Cliff Record*) written by the famous Song Dynasty Zen monk Master (圜悟克勤, Huanwu Keqin), known as the "First Book of Zen".

*Le Recueil de la Falaise Verte: Kôans et Poésies du Zen* (《碧岩录：语录与禅诗》, *The Blue Cliff Record: Quotations and Zen Poems*) is divided into four parts. The first part is a selection of translations from *Biyanlu* (《碧岩录》, *The Blue Cliff Record*), which is subdivided into four subparts—"Nan-ts'iuan", "Tchao-tcheou",

"Éventail, danse et neige", and "Le Zen poétique et un doigt omnipotent". In these chapters are records of stories and discourses of many Chinese Zen masters such as Nan-ts'iuan (南泉普愿, 748–834, Nansen in Japanese), Tchao-tcheou (赵州从谂, 778–897, Jôshû in Japanese), Yen-kouan (盐官齐安, ?–842, Enkan in Japanese), Kin-nieou (金牛和尚, Kingyû in Japanese), Ta-kouang (大光和尚, Daïkô in Japanese), Le laic P'ang (庞居士, ?–815, Hô-koji in Japanese), Tch'ang-cha (长沙景岑, ?–868, Chôsha in Japanese), Kiu-ti (俱胝和尚, Gutei in Japanese), and others. The second part, entitled *La Montagne froide, poésies du Tch'a*, contains a selection of 27 poems by the Tang poet Han-shan. The third and fourth parts are a selection of the deeds and Zen poems of two Japanese Zen masters with the former being "Le monde est lamentable et mélancolique: Le Père Gen par Kunnikida Doppo" ("The Mundane World Is Sad and Melancholy: Doppo Kunikida's Poems")[90] and the latter being "Le monde est éphémère Mais je suis joyeux: Poèmes de Sengaï" ("The World Is Transient, But I Am Happy: Sengai Gibon's Poems").[91]

As for the CMPs, the 27 poems they selected are mainly poems that are good at reasoning and commentary, most of which contain some Buddhist thoughts, such as exhortations to good deeds and reincarnation. These poems account for almost two thirds of the total number of translated poems, and there are 21 in total.[92] The order of these 21 poems in the translation is "Fan Duwoshizhe" 凡读我诗者 "Whoever Reads My Poems" ("To the Reader"), "Yiwei Shujianke" 一为书剑客 "A Book and Swordsman" ("I Am Old"), "Yutang Gua Zhulian" 玉堂挂珠帘 "Inside the Jade Hall is a Curtain of Pearls" ("A Beautiful, Charming Woman"), "Zhizhe Jie Paowo" (智者皆抛我 "The Wise Ones Ignore Me" ("The Wise and the Foolish All Ignore Me"), "Chen Shi Xinzhonghuo" 嗔是心中火 "Anger Is a Fire in the Mind" ("Anger"), "Tanren Hao Jucai" 贪人好聚财 "A Greedy Man Who Gathers Wealth" ("Gathering Wealth"), "Dongjia Yi Laopo" 东家一老婆 "An Old Lady to the East" ("Wealth Gathers, Wealth Disappears"), "Cuican Lujianv" 璀璨卢家女 "The Beautiful Lady Lu") "A Rich Man Can Die"), "Chengzhong Emeinv" (《城中娥眉女》"A Moth-browed Girl in Town" ("A Beautiful Girl Singing and Dancing"), "Shuijia Chang Busi" 谁家长不死 "Who Will Not Die" ("About Death"), "Ruo Renfengguimei" 若人逢鬼魅 "Whoever Runs Into a Ghost" ("Running into a Ghost"), "Wendao Chou Nanqian" 闻道愁难遣 "It's Hard to Get Rid of Sorrow" ("Sorrow for His Life"), "Shengqian Dachiyu" 生前大痴愚 "Too Dumb the Life Before" ("Reincarnation"), "Junjie Mashanglang" 俊杰马上郎 "A Fine Young Man on Horseback" ("An Old Boy"), "Youjiu Xiangzhaoyin" 有酒相招引 "Call Friends Over When You Have Wine" ("A Young Man Must Work Hard"), "Haohao Huangheshui" 浩浩黄河水, "The Water of the Yellow River" ("The River and People"), "Yourenxi Shanxing" 有人坐山陉 "Someone Lives in a Mountain Gorge" ("Sorrow for Old Age"), "Laoweng Qu Shaofu" 老翁娶少妇 "An Old Man Takes a Young Wife" ("Four Kinds of Marriages"), "Zuoye Menghuanjia" (昨夜梦还家 "Last Night I Dreamed of Returning Home" ("The Woman in the Dream"), "Geshi Shuijiazi" 个是谁家子 "Who on Earth is That a Man Everyone Hates" ("The Abominable Man"), and "Chengbei Zhong Jia Weng" 城北仲家翁

"Old Zhung North of Town" ("Old Zhong"). In addition, the translation includes six poems of Zen enlightenment written after the poet's retirement from the cold rocks, these are the poem translated, "Yaoyao Han-shan Dao" 杳杳寒山道 "The Trail to Cold Mountain is Faint" ("The Trail to Cold Mountain"), "Baiyun Gaocuoe" 白云高嵯峨 "The White Clouds From High Rugged Crags" ("Passionate"), "Bijian Quanshui Qing" 碧涧泉水清 "Spring Water is Pure in an Emerald Stream" ("Empty and Still"), "Yi Xiang Han-shan Zuo" 一向寒山坐 "Once I Reached Cold Mountain" ("The Death of My Friend"), "Zhongyan Wobuju" 重岩我卜居 "Towering Cliffs Were the Home I Chose" ("The White Clouds and the Rocks"), and "Kexiao Han-shan Dao" 可笑寒山道 "The Road to Cold Mountain is Strange" ("The Road to Cold Mountain"). The poems selected by the translator are all five-character poems, except for "Yourenxi Shanjing" (有人兮山径, "There Are People Who Are in a Mountain Defile") in the form of Chuci (Elegies of Chu). In addition, each translation is followed by the translator's commentary on the original poem, and some of the translations also quote the poems by Japanese Zen masters for comparative study.

In terms of translation strategies, it can be seen that the translators have mainly adopted the technique of paraphrase. For example, in Poem 2, "寄语钟鼎家" was translated as "J'avertis les familles opulentes" in which "钟鼎家" (literally "families with bronze vessels") was translated into "les familles opulentes" (the opulent families); in Poem 15, "黄泉无晓日" was translated as "Dan l'autre monde/Il n'y a ni aurore ni soleil" in which "黄泉" (literally "yellow spring") was translated into "l'autre monde" (the other world). Throughout the work, literal translation was employed sometimes, but those poems under such translation method were usually poorly understood. In the 18th poem, for example, "生前大愚痴" was rendered as "Avant ma naissance j'étais t naissance j'étais tres ignorant" in which "生前" (my past life) was misunderstood as "before birth" and "今生" (this life) as "today". Similarly, in Poem 20, the translators failed to get the meaning of "一向" (for a long time) and "坐" (live in). As a result, they translated the verse "一向寒山坐" as "Une fois je m'étais assis/Face à la 'Montagne froide'" in which "一向" was misunderstood as "Face" (face toward) and "坐" as "étais assis" (were sitting). The translation by Shibata Maryse and Shibata Masumare, though arranged in lines of poetry, is more like prose. Moreover, although allusions are scattered in the original CMPs, their translation has only one explanatory note in Poem 3. However, we can never doubt the important role of this anthology of Zen poetry in the popularization of the CMPs in France in the 21st century.

Taken as a whole, the text travels and canon constructions of the CMPs in France were largely driven by the following contextual factors:

Firstly, the "Chinese cultural fever" in Europe. It began in the eighteenth century in Europe and flourished after the two world wars when Ancient Chinese civilization and rich culture became a remedy for the wounds of society and war. French sinology, therefore, has achieved remarkable successes in the wake of this "Chinese cultural fever" with its translation and study of classical Chinese poetry has been at the forefront of sinology in the world.

Secondly, the development of Dunhuang studies.[93] Those French sinologists, while noting the poetry written by the Tang Dynasty vernacular poet Wang Fanzhi (王梵志) in the Dunhuang Cave, naturally began to pay attention to his successor Han-shan. For instance, *A Study on Han-shan* by Wu Chi-yu in 1957 and P. Demieville's *L'Oeuvre de Wang le Zélateur* (*A Complete Translation of Wang Fanzhi's Poems*) in 1982, etc.

Thirdly, the commencement of vers libres (free verse).[94] Then researchers in the French literary world began to take interest in studying the new Chinese poetry as well as the vernacular movement in China. Thus, Chinese free verse, symbolic poetry and hazy poetry were well translated in France with poems by Li Jinfa (李金发, 1900–1976), Dai Wangshu (戴望舒, 1905–1950) and Xu Zhimo (徐志摩, 1897–1931) being translated in large numbers. Actually, the popular tradition represented by the poets and poetry since the Chinese New Poetry Movement could find its origin in the Tang poets Wang Ji (王绩), Wang Fanzhi (王梵志), Han-shan and Shi-de. In fact, the West, including France, was far more interested in classical Chinese poetry than in new Chinese poetry, although the latter had its roots in the free verse while at the same time incorporating indigenous Chinese classical traditions. The underlying reason for the French's great interest in popular and liberal poetry such as the CMPs was that Chinese classical poetry was some sort of the origin of the "free verse" of the French symbolic poetic tradition and the so-called "imagist" poetry in America. Hence it is perhaps under this influence that the translations of the 1970s and 1980s came into being.

Fourthly, the Beat Movement. This movement originated in the United States and also spread to Europe and, naturally, to France. The "rebellious" nature of existentialist philosophy was exaggerated to its utmost due to the combination of the Beat Movement and the youth's attachment to the most representative philosophical trend of the first half of the 20th century, existentialism under the banner of Sartre. "Gradually, the Hippies became existentialists, and the Hippie and existentialist movements reached complete harmony."[95] The anti-traditional, anti-cultural, anti-mainstream and anti-secular young generation was bound to find comfort in CMPs. As Jacques Pimpaneau (1934–2021) remarked in his *Le Clodo du Dharma: 25 poèmes de Han-shan* in 1975, "He (Han-shan) has the hippie air of his time. Today, his words and deeds have become the guideposts of a nontraditional way of life." Obviously, the ancient hippie Han-shan has influenced American youth as well as those equally energetic French youngsters.

Finally, it should be noted that in the early 20th century, with the discovery of a large number of Zen texts in the Dunhuang writing, Zen studies attracted great attention from scholars in China and abroad. Immediately afterward, Zen thought was introduced to Europe and the United States by Japanese scholars such as D. T. Suzuki (1870–1966), and immediately aroused the interest of Western scholars, resulting in a worldwide Zen craze that is still going strong today, making Zen studies the "prominent discipline" of the 20th and 21st centuries. Han-shan and his poetry, which is reminiscent of Zen, have naturally become the subject of much interest among Western scholars. The dissemination, translation and study of the CMPs in France, and indeed worldwide, is undoubtedly a product of this Zen craze, and the translation and study of the CMPs in France, a major center of Chinese studies, in particular, has thus become a trendsetter for "Han-shan studies" in Europe. Under the influence of France, many European countries such as Germany, Belgium, the Netherlands, Sweden and the Czech Republic have also begun to translate and study the CMPs.

*4.3.3 CMPs in Other European Countries*

The CMPs, starting its interlingual journey from England and then prospering in France, finally put down roots in many other European countries. In 1974, Stephan Schuhmacher's translation *Han-shan: 150 Gedichte vom Kalten Berg* was published in 1974. Published by Diederichs in Dusseldorf-Koln, Germany, this translation of 150 CMPs is 177 pages in length. Schumacher's translation has had its influence in Europe, as the 1996 Czech translation of the CMPs was based on it.

In 1977, *Gedichten van de Koude Berg: Zen-poezie*, translated in Dutch by a world renowned sinologist Wilt. L. Idema (1944–), was published by De Arbeiderspers in Amsterdam, the Netherlands.[96] This translation contains a total of 200 CMPs and some related material. The origin translation of classical Chinese poetry in the Netherlands was traced back to 1838. *De Gids*, the most influential Dutch literary journal of the time, published in volume 2 a Chinese narrative poem, "Nigu Sifan" (尼姑思凡, "The Nun Sifan"), "Mulanshi" (木兰诗, "De dochter soldaat: Chinese ballade") and Du Fu's "Jiangcun" (江村, "De terugkomst in het dorp").[97] However, while there was little interest in Chinese poetry in the Netherlands in the 19th century, the 20th century, especially after the 1940s, saw the appearance of a large number of translations of Chinese poetry from other European languages, but of varying quality. Furthermore, in the 1970s and 1980s, as the number of Dutch students studying in China increased, there was a breakthrough in the translation and study of Chinese poetry. Wilt L. Idema, undoubtedly a top expert in the field of Dutch translations of Chinese poetry, has translated not only 200 CMPs but also a large number of poetic works by Tang poets such as Meng Haoran (孟浩然), Wang Wei (王维), Li Bai (李白), Du Fu (杜甫), Bai Juyi (白居易) and others. In 1986 and 1989, he published Dutch translations of 100 poems by Bai Juyi (白居易) and 144 poems by Du Fu (杜甫).

In 1985, in Belgium, one of the center of comparative literature and translation studies, the publishing house Thanh-Long in Brussels published a book, *Han-shan, Ermite Taoiste, Bouddhiste, Zen*, by Georgette Jaeger (1920–), a renowned expert on Tang poetry.[98] The translation is in French, the official language of Belgium, and contains around 100 Han-shan poems. It is worth noting that in 1987, Jaeger also translated *Tangshi Sanbaishou* (《唐诗三百首》, *Three Hundred Poems of the Tang Dynasty*). This book was compiled and selected by Hengtang Tuishi (蘅塘退士,

Master of Hengtang) of the Qing Dynasty (1636–1912), and was published and distributed by the China International Culture Publishing Corporation.

In Sweden, another major European country in sinological studies, two eminent scholars, Lars Bergquist and Li Keqian (李克前), translated and published a work entitled *Skuggspeo, klara vatten: Tangdikter* in 1990. The translation, published by Norstedt in Stockholm, focuses on a selection of poems by Tang poets with roots in Buddhism, Taoism, and Zen. The translation includes 17 poems by Han-shan, 2 poems by Shi-de, 16 poems by Li Bai (李白) and 10 poems by Wang Wei (王维), Du Fu (杜甫) and Bai Juyi (白居易) respectively.[99]

In addition, the CMPs were well translated in the Czech Republic in Central Europe, thanks to its excellent linguistic tradition and its love of Zen studies. In the 1970s, Oldřich Král (1930–2018), a leading translator of Chinese literature and a leading figure in Czech sinology, selected several CMPs for translation in his 1971 translation *Tao: texty stare Číny*, which was published by the Prague publishing house Ceskoslovenský Spisovatel.[100] In 1987, Marta Ryšavá, an eminent Czech scholar and translator, translated and published *Chan Šan: Nad Nefritovou tůní jasný sviit*.[101] She has been translating Tang poetry since the late 1950s, such as poems by Li Bai (李白), Wang Wei (王维), Bai Juyi (白居易), Meng Haoran (孟浩然), Han-shan and Shi-de, and it took her nearly 25 years to translate the poems of Han-shan and Shi-de. Her translations are rhymed, sometimes even more so than the original. But because of her excessive use of rhyme, her translations have attracted some criticism in the Czech Republic. Nevertheless, she has indeed been a crucial player in the circulation and dissemination of Tang poetry in the Czech Republic.

In 1996, another Czech translation of the CMPs, *Han-Šan: Basne z Ledove hora*, emerged. It was translated by Alena Bláhová and prefaced by Olga Lomová, a leading specialist in Czech Tang poetry studies.[102] The translation is based on Stephan Schumacher's German translation. Olga Lomová, the editor of the translation, added commentary and notes to the translation. At the beginning of the preface, Olga Lomová translated the original preface by Lü Qiuyin (闾丘胤) and some anecdotes about Han-shan, followed by her commentary, which runs to 18 pages. In the postscript to the translation, the editor and translator mentioned the translation of the CMPs in Czech, the three Czech translations, and Schumacher's German translation. In addition, she mentioned *Han-shan Poems: An Annotated Version in Full Translation*, published by State University Press in 1990 and translated by Robert Henricks, and *Han-shan-zi Shi Jiaozhu* (《寒山子诗校注》, *Annotations of the Poems of Han-shan-zi*) by Xu Guangda (徐光大), published by Shaanxi People's Press in 1991. It is evident that the translator has referred to the earlier-mentioned editions in her translations. The fact that nearly all the 151 selected poems by Han-shan are annotated by Olga Lomová certainly makes it more of a scholarly translation than its predecessor. Moreover, the translation is accompanied by 17 pictures on related subjects which complement the translated poems. Because of its academic rigor and high-quality translation, the book won wide acclaim and was reprinted in 1998.

Compared with its text travel and canon construction in Japan and the United States, it is not difficult to find that for more than half a century, the journey of the CMPs to Europe was mainly confined to sinological and religious circles, thus leading to limited attention to and dissemination of the CMPs. Objectively speaking, the route and mode of the CMPs' text travel appear to be monotonous, and it does not even complete the real canon construction. Therefore, its influence, circulation and dissemination are relatively limited. However, it should be pointed out that without the translation and research of European sinological and religious circles, then Han-shan Studies in Europe or other countries and regions would definitely miss the chance of a so-called "afterlife" by Benjamin (1892–1940), and there would be also no way to meet the poet's expectation of "plague the world".

## 4.4 CMPs in the United States

Beginning with the translation of the CMPs by the ecological poet Gary Snyder, the inclusion in *Anthology of Chinese Literature: from Early Times to the Fourteenth Century* by the renowned scholar Cyril Birch (1925–2018) and other literature anthologies, and then the emergence of complete translations, documentaries, travel notes, the publication of American native poets' imitation of the CMPs, as well as the inscription on the "Poetry Path" in Berkeley, all of this, present the most legendary and colorful text travel and canon construction of the CMPs. Different from the situation in European countries, the travel routes and patterns of the CMPs in the United States are diversified and multi-dimensional, and even recognized by school education and included in the institutionalized context of syllabus and curriculum arrangement, thus completing a series of canon construction activities, such as being circulated, disseminated, copied and taught.

### 4.4.1 *The Translation of the CMPs in the United States*

Objectively speaking, the translation of the CMPs in the United States has been a great success through the efforts of sinologists, poets, professors, freelance translators, freelance writers, publishers, monks, Buddhists and Zen masters. From manifold perspectives of material selection and interpretation, these translations have greatly enriched the perception of the CMPs in the cultural pluralistic system of the destination, and have laid an important foundation for the actual canon construction of the CMPs in the host cultural norms.

#### 4.4.1.1 *CMPs in the Pre-1960s United States*

In 1933, American Sinologist Henry Hart (1866–1945) first introduced the CMPs in *Poems of the Hundred Names*, in which a popular poem was included. And the translator also added the title "The House of Chung" to the poem. The reason why Hart chose to translate this Cold Mountain poem might have to do with the description of Han-shan in Hu Shi's work *History of Vernacular Literature*, because he mentioned this book in the foreword of his translation.[103] However, this short poem did not attract much attention at that time, which may be attributed to the fact that Sinology in the United States was still in its formative stage in the 1930s and 1940s. By 1936, there were fewer than 50 people in colleges and universities across the United States who focused on Chinese studies.[104] Therefore, the interlingual literary travel of the CMPs in the United States, though more than 20 years earlier than that in Britain and France, had not had any substantial impact. After the end of World War II, however, and especially in the 1950s and 1960s, sinological studies in the United States gained rapid momentum.

In 1955, under the guidance of the famous Sinologist Professor Chen Shih Hsiang (陈世骧), Snyder began to translate the CMPs. During this period, he also received guidance from Achilles Fang (1910–1995), a professor of Chinese literature at Harvard University, and Iriya Yoshittaka (1910–1998), a renowned Japanese scholar. In 1958, when the Chinese scholar Yu Jiaxi (余嘉锡) published *Siku Tiyao Bianzheng* (《四库提要辨证》), *Investigation into Abstracts of The Imperial Four Libraries*, Gary Snyder, a 28-year-old young American poet on the other side of the Pacific Ocean, published 24 translated CMPs in *Evergreen Review*, the second volume, the sixth issue, a propaganda outlet for the Beat Generation. This English translation is currently recognized as the most influential one.[105]

In those special years after the end of World War II, Han-shan, a poet of the Tang Dynasty translated by Snyder, was shaped into the spiritual leader of the young generation of the United States. And his CMPs, which had been marginalized for a long time in the Chinese literature system, made a splash in the fierce "Beat movement", emerging as a classic of the "San Francisco Renaissance". The following year, in 1959, Snyder published his collection *Riprap and Cold Mountain Poems*, into which he incorporated his translation of the CMPs.

Just as Michelle Yeh (奚密) has remarked Han-shan's life style of "thin grass for bedding/blue sky for quilt" has become a symbol of the "Beat Generation" and the model of hippies. The translated Hanshan became a fascinating archetype of American literature and had a wide influence on European and American culture.[106] Snyder's success in reviving the Chinese poet Han-shan in the minds of American readers also catapulted him to fame and earned him a nickname "American Han-shan".

It is generally believed that the great turning point of the destiny of the Tang poet Han-shan and his poems appeared at this time. Robert Kern once looked back:

> In this context, Snyder's Han-shan, Tang Dynasty Chinese poet and "mountain madman", becomes a Beat hero and countercultural role model, as well as, to borrow Davidson's phrase, an "oppositional sign", while CMPs itself, like Cathay in Kenner's view of it as a war book, becomes a Cold War book.[107]

Significantly, Han-shan had become a countercultural pioneer in American society at that time, and the CMPs had also begun to make their way into the hall of fame and become a bona fide bestseller. Therefore, it is axiomatic that Snyder's translation of the CMPs had gained wide influence. Obviously, his translation of 24 CMPs had won high recognition first and foremost in sinological circles. Coupled with the call for oriental wisdom from the cultural polysystem of the post-war American society, and the translator's deliberate misinterpretation and indigenized reconstruction in the process of translation, the CMPs won the unanimous acclaim of both professionals as well as the general public from all walks of life at the same time. Moreover, it also played a great role in spiritual salvation and literary enlightenment in American society at that time. Snyder's English translation to this day remains one of the most influential translations of the CMPs. Against the background of the "Beat Movement" and San Francisco Renaissance, the Zen state of mind, ecological consciousness, philosophy of life, and state of being revealed in the CMPs, to a great extent, echoed the dominant ideology and poetics of post-war America, and healed the psychological trauma and spiritual distress of the American public. Since then, the interlingual travel of the CMPs in the United States had achieved a soaraway success. Taking this opportunity, Han-shan and his CMPs embarked on their most legendary literary journey in the history of American translated literature.

*4.4.1.2 CMPs in the 1960s United States*

In 1961, the venerable Thomas Y. Crowell Company in New York published *A Casebook on the Beat*, edited by Thomas Parkinson, a scholar at the University of California. This book contains 24 of the CMPs translated by Snyder (pp. 138–47). As a matter of fact, the collection edited by Parkinson is an earlier source of authentic materials recording the life and creation of the "Beat Generation", thus it enjoys a good reputation in the academic circles and is also deeply recognized for its superb historical value. For that reason, it has always been a critical source for research on the "Beat Generation" as well as American society and culture in the 1950s and 1960s, and Snyder's translation of the CMPs is among them. By virtue of the introduction of this book, the interlingual travel of the CMPs gained wider circulation and acceptance in the early 1960s.[108]

In 1962, American Sinologist Burton Watson (1925–2017) published *Cold Mountain: 100 poems by the Tang Poet Han-shan*, which came off the Grove Press. This is the first Chinese classical poetry anthology translated by Watson, which included the largest number of translated CMPs at that time. It was reprinted twice, in 1970 and 1972, using a colloquial and "localized" translation method in contemporary American oral English. It is worth noting that Watson's translation also influenced and inspired later translations, studies, and imitations of the CMPs. In 1983, the whole translation of the CMPs by the American translator Red Pine was published with the help and encouragement of Watson's translation, and so did Robert Henricks's whole translation in 1990. In 2007, the American poet

158  *Cultural Polysystem of Arrivals*

Lenfestey's collection *A Cartload of Scrolls: 100 Poems in the Manner of Tang Dynasty Poet Han-shan* was published, also inspired by Watson's translation.

In 1963, Professor Edward H. Schafer (1913–1991) of the University of California published *The Golden Peaches of Samarkand: A Study on Tang Exotics*, in which two of the CMPs were included. As for "Han-shan", he wrote in the appendix to his 1975 collection *Sunflower Splendor: Three Thousand Years of Chinese Poetry* as follows:

> Han-shan means "Cold Mountain". It is the name of a place, but also the name of a person. Little is known for certain about the man who made that mountain his place of refuge, the symbol of his spiritual aspirations, and his own pseudonym. . . . Centuries after his death he became a Ch'an myth, especially in Japan. In these later times he was frequently represented in art as a freak in tattered garments, grinning imbecilely, a happy social reject. It is hard to relate this popular image to the contents of the poems attributed to him.[109]

It is also worth noting that the theme and description of a mad social reject who has become a Zen icon that meets readers' expectations and is quite attractive to read. The superficially derogatory rhetoric, therefore, provokes a more enthusiastic reading interest.

As a matter of fact, Watson was inspired to embark on the translation of Cold Mountain by the annotated version by Iriya Yoshitaka (1910–1998). The inclusion of the CMPs in the other two works of the 1960s, however, was heavily influenced by the "Beat Movement" of that time. Especially the Berkeley area of California was the birthplace of the hippie movement at the time, so naturally, California and nearby university campuses bore the brunt of it. Therefore, it is no wonder Han-shan, the acknowledged pioneer of hippies at the time, appeared in the writings of two professors at the University of California. And the attention as well as the literary writing of the academics and literary patrons undoubtedly contributed to the circulation and dissemination of the CMPs in the United States and was somewhat of a prerequisite for the canonization of the text.

In 1969, the first master thesis on the CMPs was released at the University of Wisconsin-Madison in the United States. It was entitled *The Cold Mountain: Han-shan's Poetry and Its Reception in the West*, written by Chung Ling (钟玲), a Chinese scholar who was studying at this university then. The publication of this paper marked the formal entry of "Han-shan Studies" into American scholarly discourse in the late 1960s.

*4.4.1.3  CMPs in the 1970s United States*

In 1974, Hart's collection of translated poems, *The Charcoal Burner and Other Poems*, included three of the CMPs: "The sky is the Everest high", "Life is not a hundred years" and "Reward your monk". The three poems chosen by the translator are all Buddhist poems with a strong didactic purpose. *Sunflower Splendor*, published in 1975 and edited by renowned scholars Liu Wu-chi (柳无忌, 1907–2002) and Irving Yucheng Lo (罗郁正, 1922–), contains four untitled CMPs translated by Edward Schafer and Eugene Eoyang. In 1976, Hans Frankel (1916–2003), in his book *The Flowering Plum and the Palace Lady: Interpretations of Chinese Poetry*, published by Yale University Press, also included three Cold Mountain poems relating the worldly life and the Samsara philosophy: "An Old Man Takes a Young Lady", "In the House to the East Lives an Old Woman" and "If You Want to Know a Simile for Life and Death". Also in 1976, *The View from Cold Mountain*, an anthology of poems translated by Jim Hardesty and Arthur Tobias, was published in English and Chinese. The translation is a slim book of 21 pages, but it was published by the prestigious White Pine Press. In 1977, the Juniper Press in La Crosse, Wisconsin, published *Guffawing in the Wilderness: 13 Poems*, an adaptation by George Ellison, which was based on the English translation of the CMPs by Arthur Waley and other translators. The influence of this translation was comparatively more subdued than that of the other Cold Mountain translations of the 1970s.

In 1978, *The White Crane Has No Mourners: From the Chinese of Han-shan* (42 pages) was published by the Stone Press in San Francisco, also translated by Hardesty and Tobias, who had published *The View from Cold Mountain* in 1976. In the same year, the translation was also incorporated into a collection of translated poems, *The White Crane Has No Mourners: from the Chinese of Han-shan/Honking Geese: from the Japanese of Basho & Etsujin of Basho & Etsujin*, in which *Honking Geese* included works by the Japanese haiku master Basho（1644–1694）and his disciple Etsujin. In fact, the haiku portrays the same artistic mood as that of the CMPs, with many commonalities in their depiction of natural scenery, life's mysteries, and the Zen realm. In addition, the haiku makes extensive use of folk words (witticisms) and things with a rich flavor of life as expressive subjects. Therefore, the juxtaposition of the haiku and the CMPs can be seen as complementary and helpful in terms of circulation and dissemination.

It is worth noting that in the 1970s, the "Han-shan Studies" began to be noticed by the American academics on a larger scale. There were three doctoral and master's theses on the CMPs during this period: *Leaves of Mist/Flowers of Snow: A Comparative Study on the Translations of the Chinese Poet Han-shan* (1973) by Anna Frances Holley at the University of Texas-Austin; *The Transmission of Buddhism in the Poetry of Han-shan* (1974) by S. H. Ruppenthal at the University of California-Berkeley; and *The Poems of Han-shan Collections* (1977) by Robert Stalberg at Ohio State University, which provided a more comprehensive discussion of the CMPs from the perspectives of literature, religion and translation studies.

*4.4.1.4 CMPs in the 1980s United States*

Following the momentum of the academic studies of the 1970s, Arthur Tobias's master thesis, "Han-shan, the Cold Mountain Poems" (1980), was completed at

Cornell University. Also in 1980, David Lattimore (1900–1989), a famous professor and poetry translator at Brown University, selected one poem of the CMPs: "Has Your House Got Cold Mountain Poems" into his collection *The Harmony of the World*.

In 1982, *The View from Cold Mountain: Poems of Han-shan and Shih-te*, translated by Tobias et al., contains 34 of the CMPs and 19 of Shih-de's poems translated by Tobias. Same as *The View from Cold Mountain* published in 1976, this book was also published by the White Pine Press. This translation, however, differs from the previous one in that it includes a translation of Shi-de's poems.

In his foreword to the book, the editor Dennis Maloney writes, "Their poems (Han-shan and Shih-de) are no longer merely sermons in the religious sense, but encompass a profound and striking spirituality. In addition, they maintain a distinctly personal character in terms of vision and narrative."[110] In the essay "Han-shan" which precedes the translation of poems, Tobias introduces the poems by saying,

> To be honest, we don't know much about Han-shan. His real identity and life are still a mystery. . . . Han-shan, like so many mountain hermits in Chinese history, took the mountain as his name. . . . My personal feeling is that Anthology of Cold Mountain Poems is both a true record of the journey and a glimpse of the outcome. Each poem has its statement, and it depends largely on the reader's perception of the poem. The poems we have selected for translation are for me a microcosm of the whole collection.[111]

And the translator ends humorously with "Happy climbing". The poems chosen for this collection are all about the reclusive life of Han-shan, and the most striking feature of the translation is the almost word-for-word literal translation. In this respect, it seems to be better than any of the previous translations.

In 1983, Red Pine's complete translation of *The Collected Songs of Cold Mountain* was published. As the first complete translation of the CMPs in the English-speaking world, it is thus of special significance in the field of translations and studies of the CMPs. In addition to the translation, this version is also carefully and meticulously annotated by the translator. In 2000, a revised edition of this translation was published.

In 1986, the journal *Renditions* by the Chinese University of Hong Kong published an article by Paul Kahn, *Han-shan in English*. This article traces the circulation history of the CMPs in both the East and the West, and makes a contrastive study on the characteristics of four translations of the CMPs by Waley, Snyder, Watson and Red Pine. The essay concludes with an account of Han-shan Temple, the poem "Maple Bridge Night Mooring" by Zhang Ji, and Snyder's "At Maple Bridge", which was written during his visiting of Han-shan Temple.[112] This research paper on "Han-shan Studies" is of high documentary and academic value.

*4.4.1.5 CMPs in the 1990s United States*

In 1990, Robert Henricks published *The Poetry of Han-shan: A Complete, Annotated Translation of Cold Mountain*, which was the second complete English translation of the CMPs following Red Pine's translation. Similar to Red Pine's translation, Henricks's edition is richly illustrated with quotations, notes, and examinations, as well as an extensive appendix and index.

In 1993, *The Ways of Religion*, edited by Roger Eastman, included nine of Snyder's translated the CMPs in Chapter Three, "Zen Buddhism: The Sound of One Hand". In 1994, *A Drifting Boat: An Anthology of Chinese Zen Poetry*, co-edited by Maloney and Jerome Seaton, a professor and translator of Chinese at the University of Northern California, also included twenty-two poems translated by Tobias. In 1995, Oxford University Press published *Chinese Religion: An Anthology of Sources* compiled by Deborah Sommer, a leading American sinologist in religious studies. This anthology of religious readings includes nine CMPs translated by herself, with a short translation preface regarding Han-shan and his poems. The book has been used as an introductory textbook for Chinese religion courses at universities in the United States.

In 1996, *Encounters with Cold Mountain: Poems by Han-shan, Modern Versions* by Peter Stambler was published in Beijing and released worldwide. Stambler selected and translated a total of 134 poems by Han-shan. Interestingly, he said in his preface that the reason why he titled his translation is because the poems he made were not translation in the literal or scholarly sense. They are rather, *encounters*, perhaps conversations, between a Tang Dynasty master and a 20th-century American poet.[113] In the process of translation, Stambler therefore did not seek for the mechanical mapping at the semantic level, but made full use of creative rewritings to make the translated poem and the original poem accomplish a high degree of cognition iconicity and aesthetic coherence. In August 1996, The *Roaring Stream: A New Zen Reader*, edited by Nelson Foster and Jack Shoemaker, two of Counterpoint's general editors, was published by the Ecco Press and distributed simultaneously in Canada. This reader features a selection of Zen texts spanning over a thousand years, including works by Chinese Hui Neng (638–713), Seng Ts'an (510–606), Huang Po (?–850), Han-shan and Ma Tsu (709–788) and works by Japanese Dōgen (1200–1253), Ryōkan (1758–1831), Bashō (1644–1694), Hakuin (1686–1769) and Ikkyū (1394–1481). The book is prefaced by Robert Aitken (1864–1951), a leading contemporary American ecologist and a Zen master. In his foreword, Aitken wrote, "It is both an ideal point of entry for those exploring Ch'an and Zen for the first time and an essential sourcebook for those with a long-established interest."[114] This reader contains a selection of 18 poems by Han-shan.

In 1999, *The Clouds Should Know Me by Now: Buddhist Poet Monks of China*, edited by Red Pine and Mike O'Connor, selected on the title page the eighth Cold Mountain poem translated by Snyder, "Climbing up the Cold Mountain Path". The editors intended to use the last two lines of the poem, "Who can leap the world's ties and sit with me among the white clouds?" to echo the title of the book and thus set the tone for the translation of monastic poetry throughout. In the introduction, Andrew Schelling classifies the CMPs as "rock-and-bark poetry", and traces the legend of Lü Qiuyin (闾丘胤) collecting scattered poems of Han-shan. The commentator states that translations by R.H. Blyth, Gary Snyder, Red Pine and Burton Watson have made Han-shan well-known in recent decades.[115] In May of the same year, an essay *Selected Han-Shan Poems for Hippie Reading* written by Yogi C. M. Chen a former president of the Buddhist Association of America, was posted on his personal website. This article pointed out that although the hippies claimed to have learned from Han-shan, they had in fact seriously misread and distorted Han-shan and his poems. Chen translated nearly 80 CMPs and contrasted the differences between the two in terms of their words and actions in three aspects: Drop Out, Turn On and Tune In. The article is very insightful and has had a great impact on the religious community.[116] In October of the same year, *Chinese Zen Poems: What Hold Has This Mountain*, published by Bottom Dog Press, including a collection of more than 100 Zen poems by Han-shan, Shih-de, Wang Wei (王维), Du Fu (杜甫), Bai Juyi (白居易), Jiao Ran (皎然), Su Shi (苏轼) and other Chinese poets. The compilers are Larry Smith, Professor of Humanities at Bowling Green State University, and Huang Meihui (黄美惠), a Chinese schola. As can be seen, Han-shan and his poems continued to be popular in the United States in the last five years of the 20th century, especially as people explored the Zen thought, Buddhist philosophy and linguistic features of his works from both literary and religious perspectives.

*4.4.1.6 CMPs in the 21st-Century United States*

The interlingual travel of Han-shan and His Poems in the new century continues to be a smooth one. In 2000, Columbia University published *Classical Chinese Literature: An Anthology of Translations* (Volume I: From Antiquity to the T'ang Dynasty), co-edited by renowned translator John Minford (闵福德, 1946–) and Joseph S. M. Lau (刘绍铭, 1934–), which contains Snyder's preface to his translation and 14 of his translated poems.

In 2002, *Mountain Home: The Wilderness Poetry of Ancient China*, published by Counterpoint Press and compiled by David Hinton, included 13 CMPs. In 2003, *Poems of Han-shan* (106 poems), selected and translated by Peter Hobson (1949–), was published. In addition, the translation is accompanied by two monographs of Han-shan Studies, *Han-shan's Place in History* and *Han-shan in Translation* by Barrett of the School of Oriental and African Studies at the University of London, thus giving the translation a good academic and historical value.

In 2004, *The Poetry of Zen*, edited and translated by American poet Sam Hamill and Jerome Seaton, a professor of Chinese at the University of North Carolina at Chapel Hill, was published by Shambhala Press. On the copyright page of the collection are two lines from a Cold Mountain poem translated by Seaton, "My heart is like the autumn moon, Pure and Unsullied on the Blue-green Pool". This collection of Zen poems consists of two main parts. The first is a collection of Chinese

Zen poems translated by Seaton, including poems by Lao Zi (老子), Tao Yuanming (陶渊明), Xie Lingyun (谢灵运), Wang Fanzhi (王梵志) Han-shan, Shi-de, Li Bai (李白), Wang Wei (王维), Du Fu (杜甫), Jiao Ran (皎然), Bai Juyi (白居易), Du Mu (杜牧), Su Shi (苏轼), Yuan Mei (袁枚) and others; the second is a collection of Japanese Zen poems translated by Hamill, including works by Saigyō, Budai Monk, Dōgen, Bashō, Ryōkan and others, as well as some Chinese poems and Japanese haiku. In his "Introduction to the Chinese Poems", Seaton wrote,

> Wang Fanzhi (王梵志), like the legendary pair of madmen, Han-shan and Shi-de, was a ragged wanderer. It is quite possible that none of these three ever officially joined a monastery, even though Han-shan and Shi-de worked in the kitchen of the famous Tien-t'ai monastery and are celebrated in Ch'an as reincarnations of the Indian bodhisattvas Manjushri and Samantabhadra.[117]

This anthology of Zen poetry contains a total of ten CMPs translated by Seaton.

In 2005, Andrew Hegeman completed his 124-page master dissertation, *Moving Mountains: Han-Shan's Poetic Body Crossing Ocean, Lands, and Time*, at Western Washington University, USA. Also in 2005, a booklet entitled *Cold Mountain: Transcendental Poetry by the Tang Zen Poet Han-shan* was printed in the United States. The translator, who calls himself the Wandering Poet, is a monk from Northern California. The book acknowledges his friend Yao Xiao Ying, who assisted him with the translation. In a short preface to the translation, the translator wrote, "No one knows who composed these CMPs. We know nothing about the author of the poems except the poems themselves."[118] Among other things, the translator referred to Watson's 100 translated CMPs and Snyder's 24 translated poems. The translation contained a total of 33 CMPs, including six triple-word poems from Cold Mountain poetry. Five of the poems were translated literally from the original, while the remaining 28 poems were mostly paraphrased. The booklet was reprinted in January 2008, with the translator revising and expanding the original translation to include 77 CMPs.

In July 2009, another anthology *Cold Mountain Poems: Zen Poems of Han-shan, Shih Te, and Wang Fan-chih* was published by Shambhala Press, still respectably translated by the veteran of his field Jerome Seaton, with a mainly literal and colloquial method. The title page of this poetry anthology, however, describes Wang Fan-chih as a Zen monk who came out centuries after Han-shan, which is at odds with the traditional understanding of the scholarly community. Similarly, the copyright page misrepresents Han-shan (寒山) as one of the four great monks of the Ming Dynasty, Hānshān (憨山), and therefore his years of birth and death were incorrectly given as 1546–1623. This book was reprinted in May 2019.

In 2010, Snyder's *Riprap and Cold Mountain Poems* was reintroduced in a 50th-anniversary edition published by Counterpoint Press as one of the most important poetry collections of the 1950s and 1960s, a testament to the monumental status and enduring influence of Han-shan and his CMPs in the minds of target language

164  *Cultural Polysystem of Arrivals*

readers. There is no doubt that this edition would revive the shared cultural memory of Americans of that era, while also would stir a new generation of readers with its simple, lucid poetic aesthetic and ubiquitous Chinese wisdom. In the same year, *Clouds Thick, Whereabouts Unknown: Poems by Zen Monks of China* translated by Charles Egan of San Francisco State University was published by Columbia University Press. This collection is part of the "Translations from the Asian Classics" series, which included Egan's translation of old Mountain poems. In 2011, *After Many Autumns: A Collection of Chinese Buddhist Literature*, published by California's Buddha's Light Publishing, also included CMPs. This anthology was compiled by John Gill, Susan Tidwell, and John Balcom.

In 2015, Paul F. Rouzer, Professor of Chinese Literature at the University of Minnesota, first published the monograph *On Cold Mountain: A Buddhist Reading of the Han-shan Poems*. It is a book of literary criticism that offers a comprehensive reading of the Han-shan poems from the perspective of a Buddhist. The book is divided into three parts: "The Poet", "The Poems" and "Reading Buddhists". In 2017, Rouzer followed up with a translation of *The Poetry of Han-shan (Cold Mountain), Shi-de,* and *Feng-gan*. The translation is part of the Library of Chinese Humanities, whose general editorial list includes the celebrated Stephen Owen.

In summary, the interlingual travel of the CMPs in the 1960s United States was mainly influenced by the "Beat Movement" and the "San Francisco Renaissance", while the literary travel of the 1970s and 1980s was mainly in response to the teaching needs of East Asian and Chinese literature courses in American universities. The influence of the CMPs during the 1990s United States was mostly confined to the study and research of the religious community. In the 21st century, the CMPs continued to be included in various poetry anthologies, while at the same time it began to enter various anthologies in a comprehensive manner, accompanied by new interpretations and translations.

*4.4.2 CMPs in Literary Anthologies*

In 1965, *Anthology of Chinese Literature: From Early Times to the Fourteenth Century*, edited by Cyril Birch of the University of California, Berkeley, included all 24 CMPs translated by Snyder, as well as the preface to the poems of Han-shan by Lü Qiuyin (闾丘胤) governor of Tai Prefecture. Published by Grove Press, this literary anthology was well received from the outset and became a designated textbook in many American universities and it was later included by UNESCO in its series of representative Chinese works. With the inclusion and teaching of this classic anthology, the CMPs were formally established as a canon in American translated literature.

In 1984, Watson's *The Columbia Book of Chinese Poetry: from Early Times to the Thirteenth Century* included 25 CMPs translated by Watson. It is noteworthy that Watson places Han-shan in the chapter "Major Tang Poets", alongside the famous Tang poets Han Yu (韩愈) and Bai Juyi (白居易). In the preface, the translator stated, "Underlying them throughout is the Zen—or more correctly, the

Mahayana Buddhist—conviction that these very experiences of daily life, painful or peaceful, harsh or serene, are the stuff that enlightenment is made of."[119] In fact, this history of Chinese poetry has also been used as a textbook and model for teaching Chinese literature in a number of American universities, further cementing the classic status of the CMPs.

In 1996, *An Anthology of Chinese Literature: Beginning to 1911*, translated and edited by Stephen Owen, was published by W. W. Norton & Company. The anthology devotes a subsection of *High Tang Poetry* to Han-shan: The Master of Cold Mountain, and includes five CMPs translated by Stephen Owen himself. He argues, "The closest thing to true 'religious poetry' in the Tang Dynasty was a corpus of poems attributed to one Han-shan ('Cold Mountain'), and a smaller group of poems attributed to his companion, Shi-de."[120] Barrett claims that Han-shan in Stephen Owen's anthology "finds his place in the overall history of Chinese literature".[121] It is clear that the translations and commentaries of leading sinologists and scholars have largely continued the interlingual literary travel of the CMPs, while their inclusion in literary anthologies edited by leading literary figures has undoubtedly given Han-shan and his poems the dazzling aura of a literary classic and placed them among the canon.

Among the literary anthologies of the new century, the first was *The Columbia History of Chinese Literature* (2001), edited by the eminent American sinologist Victor Mair, which referenced Han-shan and his poems in several places (pp. 20; 431; 980, etc.). In 2003, *The New Directions Anthology of Classics Chinese Poetry*, edited by American translator Eliot Weinberger and published by veteran publisher New Directions, included fifteen Han-shan poems translated by Snyder. In 2005, *The Anchor Book of Chinese Poetry: From Ancient to Contemporary, The Full 3000-year Tradition*, translated and compiled by Tony Barnstone and Chou Ping (周平) and published by Anchor Books (a division of the prestigious Random House), devoted a section to Han-shan and his poems, which also selected and translated 23 of the CMPs.

In 2006, another anthology of Chinese poetry, *The Shambhala Anthology of Chinese Poetry*, was published by Shambhala Press in Boston, edited and translated by Jerome Seaton, Professor of Chinese at the University of Northern California. It begins with the poetry of the Zhou Dynasty in the 12th century BCE and continues with the poetry of Su Manshu (苏曼殊) and others from the late Qing Dynasty. In the third chapter, entitled "Out of Place and Time: Six Zen Masters Poets of the Tang", the translator includes poems by Wang Fanzhi (王梵志), Han-shan, Shi-de, Chiao-jan (皎然), Jia Dao (贾岛) and Guan Xiu (贯休). Through these authoritative anthologies, the classic nature of the CMPs is further extended and consolidated in the new century.

In summary, the commentary, interpretation, translation and inclusion of the CMPs in these literary histories and anthologies have greatly expanded the interlingual travel routes of Han-shan poems. The CMPs have not only won the recognition of professional readers, but also brought themselves closer to the general public and, as a result, into the literary lecture halls of many American universities. The canonical status of the CMPs has been substantially disseminated and accepted through literature anthologies and classroom teachings, and has thus been established and secured formally and institutionally.

### 4.4.3 CMPs and the American Public

In addition to the appreciation of academics, novelists, poets, travel writers, filmmakers and the general public, Han-shan and his poems have also begun to appear frequently in novels, poetry collections, travelogues, multimedia, "Poetry Path" and other platforms, with its influence beginning from the 1950s and 1960s "Beat movement" and the "San Francisco Renaissance", and continuing to this day.

In 1958, Jack Kerouac (1922–1969), a pioneering figure and spokesman for the "Beat Generation" published his novel *The Dharma Bums*. The author refers to his ideal hero, Han-shan, and the rather Zen-like poems under his name in it. It is noteworthy that the title page is inscribed with the words "Dedicated to Han-shan". This is the first time that Han-shan and his poems have entered the literary production of an American novelist. As a result of the author's influential reputation in America, the circulation and dissemination of the CMPs has taken a new step.

In 1997, *Cold Mountain*, a full-length novel by the American novelist Charles Frazier, was published. On the title page, the author quoted the first two lines of the sixth poem translated by Snyder, which are "Men ask the way to Cold Mountain/Cold Mountain: there's no through trail". The novel tells the story of Inman, a wounded soldier at the end of the American Civil War, who, after being burnt out from the war, is yearning for his home and his lover, he sets out on a long and arduous odyssey back home. The author's description of Inman's resilience has led some scholars to believe that "The American author Frazier read from the Chinese poet Han-shan the essential nature and mood of Zen Buddhism—perseverance, self-confidence, self-reliance, clarity of mind, and accordance to nature."[122] The novel, which has enjoyed phenomenal sales and won the 1997 National Book Award, was adapted for the big screen by acclaimed Hollywood director Anthony Minghella in 2003.[123] In 2017, a 20th-anniversary edition of the novel was published. The appeal of Han-shan and his poems to American novelists and the American public is thus evident.

In 2006, *Cold Mountain: Han-shan*, a nearly 29-minute biographical documentary, was released in the United States. Co-directed by Mike Hazard and Deb Wallwork, the documentary was shot on location in China, Japan and the United States. In this documentary, Snyder, Watson, Red Pine and American poet James Lenfestey all appear to tell the audience about the life of Han-shan in their minds and recite a number of translated CMPs. The film poster is a Chinese ink painting, which shows the Chinese poet Han-shan in monk's clothing, disheveled, with his arms crossed and scripture on his head, grinning broadly, living the image of a happy poet-monk. The documentary comes almost half a century after Snyder published his translated CMPs. What is even more inspiring is that the four translators share the same stage to remember and interpret Han-shan and his CMPs, which is a testament to the classic status of the CMPs in American translated literature.

In 2007, *A Cartload of Scrolls: 100 Poems in the Manner of Tang Dynasty Poet Han-shan*, a collection of imitation poems by the American poet Lenfestey was published. The author dedicated his book of poems to Watson: "To Burton Watson, who gave me the gift of Cold Mountain's songs". In 1974, after reading Watson's *Cold Mountain: 100 poems by the Tang poet Han-shan*, The author's skin warts were supposedly cured.[124] In 2014, in his book *Seeking the Cave: A Pilgrimage to Cold Mountain*, the poet recounted his travels to Japan and China in the autumn of 2006 in search of Han Yan, Han-shan's place of abode. In the book, the author stated "Han-shan, Cold Mountain, a recluse whose poems I have loved for more than thirty years, who took his final name from the place where he lived". The poet traced his reading of Watson's translation:

His commonplace language, brusque truths, satiric jabs at bureaucracy, and longing for quiet mind entered me unmediated by any teacher, seeming to salve wounds I didn't know I had. I fell in love with that voice, like that of an older brother I never knew.[125]

The poet's writing is interspersed from time to time with poems by the author and Han-shan. Thus, the poet's journey in search of Han-shan is, in fact, a pilgrimage of poetry, religion, language and landscape that will appeal to lovers of the CMPs and travel writing alike. Out of homage and affection, Lenfestey also dedicated this book to Cold Mountain, Burton Watson, Red Pine and his pilgrimage companions Margaret, Mike and Ed.

More intriguingly, Tao Jie (陶洁) wrote in her article that in the Berkeley area of the United States, there is an "American poetry heritage building" called "Poetry Path", where Witter Bynner's translated poems of Li Bai and Snyder's translated poems of Han-shan are both included. It is a clear indication that the CMPs have reached out to the American public community and the general public. So far, the canonization of the CMPs in the United States has been a most legendary journey, beginning with Snyder's translation, continuing with the publication of complete translations, and followed by the inclusion of varied literary anthologies by Cyril Birch et al., as well as the inscription on the "Poetry Path".

If Hu Shi (胡适), Zheng Zhenduo (郑振铎) and Yu Jiaxi (余嘉锡) are believed to bring Han-shan and his poems into the focus of Chinese literary discourse and Chinese literary history, then Waley, Wu Chi-yu and Snyder undoubtedly brought Han-shan into another, more brilliant, literary world. There, this "marginal poet" and his "marginal poems" in Chinese literature stepped into the "central" and "canonical" halls of Western literature with aplomb. Since then, the "Han-shan fever" has been a lively phenomenon in Europe and America. CMPs have even entered the major American literary anthologies and the university lecture halls of East Asian literature. The fever has even returned to Han-shan's homeland, creating a "second wave" of Han-shan studies.

Looking at the interlingual travel and canon construction of the CMPs in the United States, we can see not only the lasting influence that Han-shan poetry has had on literature and the general public since the "San Francisco Renaissance", but also the recognition and acceptance of the views of nature, world and life reflected in the CMPs in the United States today. The Buddhist teachings, Zen mood, wilderness sentiment and ecological consciousness in the CMPs have been explored, interpreted, translated and studied in greater depth since the 1990s. This is evidenced by Eastman's *The Ways of Religion*, *A Drifting Boat: An Anthology of Chinese Zen Poetry*, co-edited by Maloney and Jerome Seaton, Hinton's *Mountain Home: The Wilderness Poetry of Ancient China*, Egan's *Clouds Thick, Whereabouts Unknown: Poems by Zen Monks of China*, and Rouzer's *On Cold Mountain: A Buddhist Reading of the Han-shan Poems* and so on. In an American society that is highly developed in terms of material civilization but is suffering from an environmental crisis, the way of life represented by Han-shan and the ecological vision embodied in the CMPs of pursuing a harmonious coexistence of nature, society and spirituality will continue to have great appeal and vitality, and this will further contribute to the interlingual travel of the CMPs in the cultural polysystem of the United States, and consolidate the canonical status of the CMPs in American translated literature.

**Notes**

1 Translated by Red Pine.
2 Wang Dongfeng. The Literary Status of Translated Literature and the Cultural Attitude of Translators. *Chinese Translators Journal*, 2000 (4): 3.
3 I. Even-Zohar. Polysystem Theory. *Poetics Today*, 1990, 11(1) (Spring): 14.
4 I. Even-Zohar. The Position of Translated Literature within the Literary Polysystem. // J. Holmes, J. Lambert & R. V. D. Broeck (eds.), *Literature and Translation*. Leuven: Academic Publishing Company, 1978: 121.
5 I. Even-Zohar. The Position of Translated Literature within the Literary Polysystem. // J. Holmes, J. Lambert & R. V. D. Broeck (eds.), *Literature and Translation*. Leuven: Academic Publishing Company, 1978: 120.
6 I. Even-Zohar. The Position of Translated Literature within the Literary Polysystem. // J. Holmes, J. Lambert & R. V. D. Broeck (eds.), *Literature and Translation*. Leuven: Academic Publishing Company, 1978: 122–123.
7 However, it seems that the translation behavior in the late Qing Dynasty cannot be summarized so simply. As a matter of fact, with the weakening of the cultural polysystem at that time, translated literature moved from the periphery to the center. Translation did become an important driving force for introducing new ideas and new poetics. The integration of the roles of writer and translator was an important signal of translation activities. However, we find that the actual translation behavior at that time is different from what the theory of polysystems posited: translators tend to convey the "adequacy" of the source text, and the translated text will try its best to be faithful and accurate to the content and structure of the source text. In fact, "Liang Qichao's type of import" ("no organization, no selection, no source, unclear genre, and quantity is the most-valued criterion"; 无组织、无选择、本末不具、派别不明、惟以多为贵) became the main characteristics of the translated text import then. When choosing "what to translate", the new novelists of that time generally believed that "those foreign novels which are not suitable for the Chinese people should not be translated" (Zhongyuanliangzi中原浪子). In their opinion, "it is not that foreign books are not good enough, but that their nature does not suit us Chinese" (Wu Jianren 吴趼人). Therefore, all translation activities are conducted in accordance with the reading style and taste of the

Chinese people at that time. Under such a guiding principle, "heroic translations" of the late Qing Dynasty were everywhere, and it was common to add, delete and tamper with them at will. A large number of translations were seriously added, deleted and modified in terms of the plot and narrative structures of the original work, which seriously marginalized the writing intention of the original author. See Hu Anjiang, Compromise and Distortion: Theoretical Defects of Traditional Translation Criticism from the Perspective of "Mistranslation". *Journal of Sichuan International Studies University*, 2005 (3): 121–122. During the May Fourth Movement, the selection and the "adequacy" of the source texts were much more cautious. However, in terms of the language expression form of the translated text, classical Chinese and vernacular were still attracting readers belonging to each other, and the new language expression form had not been really established then.

8  Ō no Yasumaro. *Records of Ancient Matters* (trans. Zhou Youheng et al.). Beijing: People's Literature Publishing House, 1979: 128.
9  Yue-him Tam's exploration of Japanese translation cause can also illustrate this point:

> Japanese translation of Chinese also started very early. . . . However, the translation of Chinese books in ancient Japan was not that developed, because the education of Japanese intellectuals at that time was dominated by Chinese culture. Most of them could read Chinese classics directly and express their thoughts in the form of Chinese poetry and Chinese essays. Even their private letters and official documents were mainly written in Chinese.
>
> Yue-him Tam. Exploration of Sino-Japanese Cultural Exchange.
> *Study on Sino-Japanese Cultural Relations in Modern Times*.
> Hong Kong: Hong Kong Institute of Japanese Studies, 1988: 106.

10  Yue-him Tam. Exploration of Sino-Japanese Cultural Exchange. // *Study on Sino-Japanese Cultural Relations in Modern Times*. Hong Kong: Hong Kong Institute of Japanese Studies, 1988: 13.
11  Kūkai, also known posthumously as Kōbō Daishi (The Grand Master Who Propagated the Dharma), was a Japanese Buddhist monk, calligrapher and poet who founded the esoteric Shingon school of Buddhism. He travelled to China, where he studied Tangmi (Chinese Vajrayana Buddhism) under the monk Huiguo.
12  Saichō was a Japanese Buddhist monk credited with founding the Tendai school of Buddhism based on the Chinese Tiantai school he was exposed to during his trip to Tang China beginning in 804. He founded the temple and headquarters of Tendai at Enryaku-ji on Mount Hiei near Kyoto. He is also said to have been the first to bring tea to Japan.
13  *Wen Xuan or Selections of Refined Literature* has been much valued by Japanese since the Nara period (710–794). But in the Heian period (794–1192), those literary works of the early Tang Dynasty have become more popular such as those by Chen Zi'ang 陈子昂 (661–701), Li Bai 李白 (701–762) and Bai Juyi 白居易 (772–846).
14  Ye Weiqu. *A Cultural History of Japan*. Guilin: Guangxi Normal University Press, 2004: 115.
15  Yan Shaodang. An Examination on Ancient Chinese Texts from the East to Japan". *Collation and Research of Ancient Books*. Beijing: Zhonghua Book Company, 1991: 260.
16  There are different opinions in terms of the time when Bai Juyi's poems were introduced to Japan. According to 入唐求法巡礼行记 (*A Journey to Tang China for Learning Buddhism*), Egaku went to Tang China to study in the ninth century for three times. In 846 or 847, Egaku brought his hand-copied manuscript of *Baishichangqingj* 白氏长庆集 (*Bai Juyi's Poetry*) to Japan. However, Ye Weiqu 叶渭渠 argued in his 日本文化史 (*Japanese Cultural History*) that Bai Juyi's works were introduced into Japan in 838 when Fujiwara no Okamori brought 元白诗笔 (*The Works of Yuan Chen and Bai Juyi*) to Emperor Ninmyō from some Tang Chinese merchants. The latter's view is more reasonable in that Bai's poems had been introduced to Japan when Bai was still alive. Since Bai Juyi

died in 846, the view that his poems was introduced to Japan in 847 would not hold water.
17 Views differ in terms of the reasons for the popularity of Bai's poems, and they can be generalized as follows. (1) The language is easy and fluent; (2) the poems are rich in Zen spirit; (3) the appreciation of nature is much in tune with that of the ancient Japanese; (4) the world reflected by these poems is similar to Japan in the Heian period; (5) the status of Bai Juyi is similar to those Japanese scholars in the Heian period; (6) Bai Juyi's character is much typical of Japanese then; (7) *Baishichangqingj* 白氏长庆集 (*Bai Juyi's poetry*) is of high cultural value and can serve as a dictionary for Japanese men of letters.
18 Ogata Yosei. *Japanese History of Chinese Literature* (trans. Ding Ce). Taipei: Zheng Zhong Bookstore, 1976: 66.
19 It is revealed that in April 840, "ken-toh-shi" 遣唐使 ("Ambassadors sent to Tang") came back to China, which was the 17th time and marked the end of official exchange between China and Japan. Then the introduction of ancient Chinese works was mainly dependent on trade and communications between the two peoples.
20 Quoted from 日本汉文学史 (*A Japanese History of Chinese Literature*) by Koreyoshi Ogata.
21 According to Osamu Ōba, Fujiwara no Michinaga recorded in his 御堂关白记 (*Journal of Fujiwara*) that a merchant from Song China had presented Japanese monk Nian Jiu念救 *Baishichangqingj* 白氏长庆集 (*Bai Juyi's poetry*) and Wuchen Zhuwenxuan 五臣注文选 (*The Collected Works Annotated by Five Scholars*) in 1006. Then, Nian Jiu 念救 gave them to Fujiwara no Michinaga after he came back to Japan in 1013. It is thus safe to conclude that ancient works of Song China were introduced into Japan in 1013.
22 Ye Zhuhon. *Critical Studies of Materials about Han-shan*. Taipei: Showwe Information Co. Ltd., 2005: 172.
23 According to Osamu Ōba, many printers in the late Yuan Dynasty went to Japan to avoid the incessant wars, and those Chinese works brought by them were reprinted in Japan. Osamu Ōba believed that the Gozan edition published by Zongze Channi was the oldest one of reprinted Chinese works.
24 Ota Tizo. An Explanation of Cold Mountain Poems (trans. Cao Qian). *Southeast Culture*, 1990 (6): 126.
25 Translated by Red Pine.
26 Translated by Red Pine.
27 Quoted in Xiang Chu. Appendix II. // *Annotation of Cold Mountain Poems: Shi-de's Poems Included*. Beijing: Zhonghua Book Company, 2000: 953.
28 Zhang Mantao. Japanese Scholars' Evaluation and Interpretation of Han-shan. // *The Death of the Japanese* (Vol. 65). Taipei: Lai Ming Cultural Enterprise Co., Ltd., 1976: 97–98.
29 F. Kunisu. Solution. *Han-shan and Shi-te* (Vol. 1). Tokyo: Kodansha Corporation, 1985: 26.
30 *The Newly Revised Anthology of Chinese Poets* consists of 17 volumes in which Tao Yuanming and Han-shan are in volume I, Li Bai in volume VII, and Du Fu in volume IX. The editors are Yoshikawa Kōjirō (1904–1980) and Ogawa Tamaki (1910–1993).
31 Sun Changwu once remarked the contributions of Iriya Yoshitaka on Han-shan Studies, "Opinions differ in terms of Han-shan and His Poems. The studies of Iriya Yoshitaka on Han-shan and His Poems are of great value and are quite enlightening." See Sun Changwu's *My Study Tours*) published by the Nankai University Press.
32 Supervised by Keisu Maito, edited by Yue-him Tam 谭汝谦 and Hiroshi Ogawa. 日本译中国书综合目录 (*A Comprehensive Catalogue of Japanese Translations of Chinese Books*). Hong Kong, China: The Chinese University of Hong Kong Press, 1981: 297.
33 Kazuaki Tanahashi & Peter Levitt (trans.). *The Complete Cold Mountain: Poems of the Legendary Hermit Han-shan*. Colorado: Shambhala Publications, Inc., 2018: 1.

34 Kazuaki Tanahashi & Peter Levitt (trans.). *The Complete Cold Mountain: Poems of the Legendary Hermit Han-shan*. Colorado: Shambhala Publications, Inc., 2018: 4.
35 Y. Iriya. A Glimpse into Cold Mountain Poems // Wang Shunhong (trans.), *Collation and Research of Ancient Books* (Issue 4). Beijing: Zhonghua Book Company, 1989: 234.
36 Quoted in Zhang Mantao. *Japanese Scholars' Evaluation and Interpretation of Han-shan* (Vol. 65). Taipei: Lai Ming Cultural Enterprise Co., Ltd., 1976: 100, 108.
37 Ota Tizo. An Explanation of Cold Mountain Poems (trans. Cao Qian). *Southeast Culture*, 1990 (6): 125.
38 Hasegawa Tōhaku was a Japanese painter and founder of the Hasegawa school, who is considered one of the great painters of the Azuchi–Momoyama period (1573–1603), and he is best known for his byōbu folding screens, such as Pine Trees and Pine Tree and Flowering Plants (both registered National Treasures), or the paintings in walls and sliding doors at Chishaku-in, attributed to him and his son (also National Treasures). Kao was a famous Japanese painter in the middle 14th century, and his Ink Wash paintings were considered of the highest level at that time. According to Liu Xiaolu (1953–), a leading expert on the history of Japanese art, this painting should be the work of Kao instead of Hasegawa Tōhaku.
39 Wang Xiaojia. Japan's Han-shan Stamp Issue. *People's Daily* (*Overseas Edition*), 2002: 7.
40 Similar to Han-shan's situation, Liang Kai (梁楷) was neglected in China, and his stick figure paintings were even criticized by the literati of the Yuan Dynasty as "crude, evil and boneless". But in Japan, Liang Kai was greatly admired. From the Kamakura Period (1185–1333) on, a large number of paintings by Liang Kai and other artists of the Southern Song dynasty had been introduced to Japan, while the landscape paintings of the Northern Song Dynasty and the later literati paintings, which are highly valued in China, were rarely introduced to Japan. Liang Kai's exquisite ink painting techniques were favored by the Japanese and had a great influence on Japanese painters after the Muromachi Period (1338–1573).
41 Luo Shijin argues that Han-shan is one of the religious figures that artists have paid the most attention to since the Kamakura period (1185–1333). Luo Shijin. Japanese Painting Creation of Han-shan and Its Origin. *Literature & Art Studies*, 2005 (3): 104. See this article for the "Han-shan fever" in Japanese painting circles.
42 Ogai Mori revealed that he wrote this book according to Lü Qiuyin's preface, and he also mentioned the reason of writing was because his children were curious about Han-shan and Shi-de but they knew nothing about Chinese characters. Regarding Lü Qiuyin, his novel says that

> the story opens on the third day after Lii's arrival at his post in T'ai Chou. He had been covered with the dust of north China at the capital Ch'ang-an.... In preparing for his official examinations some years before, Lü had read the Confucian Classics and had devoted a great deal of time learning to write fivecharacter verse, but he had not read any of the Buddhist scriptures or studied Lao-tzu. For some reason or other, he still had a great sense of respect for Buddhist monks and Taoist priest.
> Ogai M. Kanzan Jittoku (Han Shan and Shih-te. trans. by D. A. Dilworth & J. T. Rimer. *Monumenta Nipponica*, 1971, XXVI(I–2): 160

43 Han-shan Temple is located in Fengqiao Town, about 5 kilometers west of Soochow, Jiangsu Province, China. It was built nearly 1,500 years ago during the Tianjian era (502–519) of the reign of Emperor Wu of the Liang Dynasty in the Six Dynasties. It was formerly known as "Miaolipuming Pagoda Monastery". Legend has it that Han-shan and Shi-de once came from Tiantai Mountain to abbot here, so it was renamed Han-shan Temple. But after meticulous research, scholars tend to think that Han-shan Temple is not named because Han-shan came to live here, and it has nothing to do with the poet Han-shan who lived in seclusion at Tiantai areas. Zhou Qi is among those who hold this view; he believes that the "Han-shan temple" in Zhang Ji's poem

is actually a general reference to the mountain temples outside Soochow. He also believes that the word "Han" (寒, Cold) mentioned in the well-known poem written by Zhang Ji and *To Heng Can* written by Wei Yingwu (737–792?) as well as *Sending a Monk Back to the Mountain* written by Liu Yanshi's (742–813) refers to a solar term in late autumn and late winter because all of the three poems were written at that due time. Zhou Qi thus suggests that before the end of the Yuan Dynasty (1271–1368), the local Chronicles of Soochow called it Fengqiao Temple or Puming Monastery, instead of Han-shan Temple. See Zhou Qi. *Han-shan: Poetry and History*. Hefei: Huangshan Press, 1994: 13.

44 Yu Yue. Newly Restored Chronicle of Han-shan Temple. // Ye Changchi (ed.), *Chronicle of Han-shan Temple*. Nanjing: Jiangsu Ancient Books Publishing House, 1986: 11.
45 Pulleyblank once remarked that Emperor Dezong (780–805), despite his despotic, stingy, unusual and tough personality, was one of the great protectors of Chinese literature at his time. Pulleyblank holds that it was under his reign that the spiritual life was most thriving and vigorous. . . . This is a remarkable period in the history of Chinese culture. Pulleyblank thus calls the Zhenyuan era of his reign the greatest and most important period of intellectual activity. (E. Pulleyblank. Neo-Confucianism, Neo-Legalism and the Life of Intellectuals in the Tang Dynasty. // William Nienhauser (ed.), *American Scholars on Tang Literature*. Shanghai: Shanghai Ancient Books Publishing House, 1994: 237–238.
46 Sun Changwu. Zen as Words. // *My Study Tours*. Tianjin: Nankai University Press, 2004: 91.
47 Chung Ling. *Essays on Literary Criticism*. Taipei: Times Cultural Publishing Co., 1984: 7.
48 R. Benedict. *The Chrysanthemum and the Sword* (trans. Lü Wanhe et al.). Beijing: The Commercial Press, 2005: 167.
49 D. T. Suzuki. *Love of Nature. Zen and Japanese Culture* (3rd Printing). New York: Princeton University Press, 1973: 345.
50 Quoted in D. T. Suzuki. *Love of Nature. Zen and Japanese Culture* (3rd Printing). New York: Princeton University Press, 1973: 342.
51 Quoted in D. T. Suzuki. *Love of Nature. Zen and Japanese Culture* (3rd Printing). New York: Princeton University Press, 1973: 331.
52 Xiang Chu. The Vernacular Poetry School in the Tang Dynasty. *Jiangxi Social Science*, 2004 (2): 40.
53 Wang Gaoxin & Cheng Rentao. *History of Ancient Relations Among the Three East Asian Countries*. Beijing: Beijing University of Technology Press, 2006: 6–7.
54 K. T. Jeo. The Infulences of Chinese Literature on Korean Literature. *Tamkang Review*, No. 1. October 1971–April 1972 (Vol II, No. 2 & Vol III): 107.
55 H. Se-Wook. A Study on Chinese Poetry and Poetry Talks in Korea. *Tamkang Review*, 1971 (2): 99.
56 Li Dechun. A Brief Description of Korean Translations from Chinese to Korean Through the Ages. *Journal of the PLA University of Foreign Languages*, 2005 (4): 77.
57 K. Young-jin. The Influence of Cold Mountain Poems on Korean Zen Masters and Scholars. *Religious Studies*, 2002 (4): 44.
58 K. Young-jin. The Influence of Cold Mountain Poems on Korean Zen Masters and Scholars. *Religious Studies*, 2002 (4): 44.
59 P. Young-hwan. A Survey and Prospect of Contemporary CMPs Studies. // *Proceedings of the International Symposium on Han-shan Zi and the Culture of Harmony*. Hangzhou: Zhejiang University Press, 2009: 228.
60 According to Park Young-hwan, "A study on Chinese and Japanese Paintings of Han-shan and Shi-te" is divided into three main parts. The first part explores the characteristics of these paintings from three perspectives, including the documentary records, the legacies of the Southern Song (1127–1279) painters, and the evaluations of the Zen monks of the Southern Song and Yuan dynasties (1271–1368). The second part explores the changes of paintings of Han-shan and Shi-te. The third part explores the exchanges between China and Japan, and the prevalence of paintings of Han-shan and Shi-te in

Japan. For more details, see Park Yong-hwan. "A Survey and Prospect of Contemporary CMPs Studies". // *Proceedings of the International Symposium on Han-shan and Hehe Culture.* Hangzhou: Zhejiang University Press, 2009: 223–225.

61 P. Young-hwan. A Survey and Prospect of Contemporary CMPs Studies. // *Proceedings of the International Symposium on Han-shan-zi and the Culture of Harmony.* Hangzhou: Zhejiang University Press, 2009: 226.

62 P. Young-hwan. A Survey and Prospect of Contemporary CMPs Studies. // *Proceedings of the International Symposium on Han-shan-zi and the Culture of Harmony.* Hangzhou: Zhejiang University Press, 2009: 226.

63 P. Young-hwan. A Survey and Prospect of Contemporary CMPs Studies. // *Proceedings of the International Symposium on Han-shan-zi and the Culture of Harmony.* Hangzhou: Zhejiang University Press, 2009: 226–227.

64 The title of the book, *Madly Singing in the Mountains*, is taken from Bai Juyi's (772–846) poem "Singing Alone in the Mountains", translated by Arthur Waley. The original poem reads as follows: "There is no one among men that has not a special failing: And my failing consists in writing verses. I have broken away from the thousand ties of life: But this infirmity still remains behind. Each time that I look at a fine landscape, Each time that I meet a loved friend, I raise my voice and recite a stanza of poetry And I am glad as though a God had crossed my path. Ever since the day I was banished to Hsün-yang, Half my time I have lived among the hills. And often, when I have finished a new poem, Alone I climb the road to the Eastern Rock. I lean my body on the banks of white stone, I pull down with my hands a green cassia branch. My mad singing startles the valleys and hills: The apes and birds all come to peep. Fearing to become a laughing-stock to the world, I choose a place that is unfrequented by men. This poem was written by Bai Juyi in the twelfth year of Yuanhe (817), when he was the Secretary of Jiangzhou State. The title of the book is a testament to Waley's personal nature and his love for Bai's poetry.

65 Chung Ling. *Essays on Literary Criticism.* Taipei: Times Cultural Publishing Co., 1984: 10.

66 It is worth mentioning that Japan, as a close neighbor of China, acted as the "travel intermediary" in the text travel of CMPs for many times. Actually, even Snyder's translation, Waston's translation and several other later translations of the CMPs also connect with the "travel intermediary" Japan.

67 This simple and unadorned poem is actually one of the CMPs that starts with the line "old Chung north of town", belongs to the vernacular poems of the CMPs. See more information in J. Turner. Preface. *A Golden Treasury of Chinese Poetry: 121 Classical Poems.* Hong Kong: The Chinese University of Hong Kong, 1976: 17–18.

68 Ryōkan, original name Yamamoto Eizō, (born 1758, Izumozaki, Japan—died Feb. 18, 1831, Echigo province), Zen Buddhist priest of the late Tokugawa period (1603–1867) who was renowned as a poet and calligrapher. The eldest son of a village headman, he became a Buddhist priest at about the age of 17 under the religious name of Taigu Ryōkan. When he was 21 he met an itinerant monk, Kokusen, and followed him to his temple, Entsū-ji, at Tamashima, Bitchū province. He followed a life of monastic discipline there for 12 years. After Kokusen's death he traveled to various parts of Japan as a mendicant priest. In old age he returned to his native Echigo province, where he studied the *Man'yōshū* and ancient calligraphy. http://wordpedia.eb.com/tbol/article?i=110341&db=big5. [2006–12–25].

69 P. Harris. Foreword. // *Zen Poems.* New York: Alfred A. Knopf, 1999: 18–19.

70 A. S. Kline. *Twenty-Seven Poems by Han-shan.* 2006. www.tonykline.co.the United Kingdom/PITBR/Chinese/Han-shan.htm. [2007–3–19].

71 D. Hawkes. Book Review: *Cold Mountain: 100 Poems by the T'ang Poet Han-shan.* Translated and with an Introduction by Burton Watson. pp. 122. New York: Grove Press, Inc., 1962. *Journal of the American Oriental Society,* 1962, 82 (4): 596.

72 T. H. Barrett. Han-shan's Place in History. // Peter Hobson (ed.), *Poems of Han-shan.* Walnut Creek: Altamira Press, 2003: 115.

174  *Cultural Polysystem of Arrivals*

73 T. H. Barrett. Han-shan's Place in History. // Peter Hobson (ed.), *Poems of Han-shan*. Walnut Creek: Altamira Press, 2003: 123.
74 T. H. Barrett. Han-shan's Place in History. // Peter Hobson (ed.), *Poems of Han-shan*. Walnut Creek: Altamira Press, 2003: 124.
75 T. H. Barrett. Han-shan's Place in History. // Peter Hobson (ed.), *Poems of Han-shan*. Walnut Creek: Altamira Press, 2003: 128.
76 T. H. Barrett. Han-shan's Place in History. // Peter Hobson (ed.), *Poems of Han-shan*. Walnut Creek: Altamira Press, 2003: 136–137.
77 T. H. Barrett. Han-shan's Place in History. // Peter Hobson (ed.), *Poems of Han-shan*. Walnut Creek: Altamira Press, 2003: 151.
78 Z. Wesołowski. An Overview of Chinese Studies in the the United Kingdom. *Newsletter for International China Studies* (106 in total), 2008, 27(2) (May): 52.
79 Qian Linsen. *Chinese Literature in France*. Guangzhou: Huacheng Press, 1990: 5.
80 Jacques Pimpaneau is a professor of Université Sorbonne Nouvelle-Paris 3 and Institut national des Langues et Civilisations orientales. His research fields include Chinese poetry and verse, Chinese drama, Piying (Shadow Puppets), and the history of civilization, etc. He studied at Peking University between 1958 and 1960, and also worked at Chinese Foreign Languages Press. He has translated poems, verse and prose written by Qu Yuan, Song Yu, Han-shan, Su Shi, Liu Zongyuan, Wen Yiduo and others. He finished the translation of voluminous 列传 "Lie Zhuan" of Shiji史记 (*Records of the Grand History*) after Chavannes.
81 Biyanlu 碧岩录 *The Blue Cliff*, also known as Foguo Yuanwuchanshi Biyanji 佛果圆悟禅师碧岩录 Records in the Blue Cliff by Zen Master Huanwu, was written by the famous Zen master 圆悟克勤 Huanwu Keqin in Song Dynasty, and consists of ten volumes. The book includes 100 Songgu 颂古 (odes to the past) by Zen master 重显 Chongxian and Pingchang 评唱 (praises and chants) by master Huanwu. The book's name *The Blue Cliff* comes from Zen master Huanwu Keqin's life experience. He was living on Jia Mountain of Yizhou (present-day Hunan Province) at the time; there is a stone called Blue Cliff, and his adobe was named after it. In summer, he gave Zen Buddhism lectures to the students to encourage them to be hardworking and aspirant. Students recorded his words and compiled them into *The Blue Cliff*. After the book was completed, it enjoyed popularity and was known as the "First Book of Zen". Zen master 雪窦 Xuedou's hundred ode to the past has always been considered a masterpiece of Zen literature, and master Huanwu's praises and chants is a perfect match with the ode, thus making the book a classic in the history of Zen literature.
82 This monograph was published as offprints by E.J. Brill Press in 1957.
83 For example, in the *Chuanxin Fayao* 传心法要 (*Transmission of the Dharma Mind*), there is such an expression "恐汝诸人不了, 权立道名, 不可守名而生解" ("I am afraid that you will not be able to understand it, so you have the right to establish the name of the Way.")— author's note.
84 W. Chi-yu. A Study on Han-shan. *T'oung Pao*, 1957, XLV: 397–399.
85 W. Chi-yu. A Study on Han-shan. *T'oung Pao*, 1957, XLV: 400.
86 P. Kahn. Han-shan in English. *Renditions*, 1986 (Spring): 145.
87 J. Pimpaneau. *Le Clodo du Dharma: 25 poèmes de Han-shan*. Paris: Centre de publication Asie orientale, 1975: 7.
88 The original text of this quotation is in French, and it is translated into English for the convenience of the reader. See Wing Fan, C & Collet, H. *Han Shan: Merveilleux le Chemin de Han Shan*. Millemont: Moundarren, 1985 & 1992: 3–4.
89 Qian Linsen. *Chinese Literature in France*. Guangzhou: Huacheng Press, 1990: 44–45.
90 Kunikida Doppo (1871–1908), a Japanese novelist and poet, is the pioneer of Japanese naturalism. His representative work is *Selected Stories of Doppo Kunikida*, which was published in 1904.
91 Sengai Gibon (1750–1837), Japanese Zen monk. His dharna name is Gibon, so he is also called Gibon monk. He was born in Gifu-ken, and lived in 博多圣福寺 Hakata

Shofthe United Kingdomuji. He is good at calligraphy, painting and tea ceremony, and once wrote *The Tea Ceremony*.

92 The poems cited by the author below are listed with the first line of the original poem (translated from French into English by the translators of this book), with the titles added to the French translation by Masumi Shibata in parentheses. Under "To the Reader," the translator has this introduction to Han-shan, "This and the following poems are from Han-shan (Japanese name Kanzan; date of birth and death unknown, but some evidence suggests that the poet may have lived in the ninth century A.D.). 'Han' means cold, cool, icy and piercing, calm and collected. And 'Shan' refers to mountains. When Chinese or Japanese people see or hear the word 'Han', they will feel the chill and calmness. Therefore, instead of the phonetic Han-chan, we use 'Montagne froide' so that the reader can go deeper into these poems. Today, there is absolutely no possibility to confirm his real existence. It can only be inferred that he was a monk in the Tiantai Mountains during the Tang Dynasty who is said to have disappeared one day, leaving behind only 300 poems written on trees or walls".(Shibata Maryse & Shibata Masumi. *Le Recueil de la Falaise Verte: Kôans et Poésies du Zen*. Paris: Éditions Albin Michel, 2000: 73–74.)

93 With the financial support of the French Academy of Sciences, the French Sinology community has set up four research groups, which have recruited almost all relevant Sinologists. The four groups are the Dunhuang group convened by Michel Soymie (1924–2002), the literature group convened by Donald Holzman (1926–), the language group convened by Alexis Rygaloff (1922–), and the Taoist group convened by Kristofer M. Schipper (1934–2021). The Dunhuang Group was established in 1973, and Wu Chi-yu is one of its members.

94 The term "free verse" in English is translated from French term "vers libres". The free verse movement appeared in France around the year of 1880 (also the time of "modern movement" in English literature). This movement popularized quickly in the 20th century. Gao Dongshan 高东山 mentioned that, "this was closely related to the political and economic development of capitalist society, the people's demand for greater spiritual and individual liberation, and the view of all norms as a restraint on freedom." See Gao Dongshan. *The Metre and Appreciation of English Poetry*. Beijing: The Commercial Press, 1990: 281. The New Poetry Movement in China was an essential part of the development of Chinese poetry and Chinese language and literature, and it was also a product under the influence of the Western free verse movement. Therefore, Chinese new poetry tended to be new, but retained some traditions of classical poetry at the same time.

95 Sun Qi. *Han-shan and Hippies*. Taizhong: Putian Press, 1974: 32.

96 Wilt L. Idema, professor of Chinese Literature in the Department of East Asian Languages and Civilizations at Harvard University. He received his Ph.D. from Leiden University in 1974 for his doctoral dissertation on early Chinese vernacular fictions. His research interests include early Chinese vernacular literature, Chinese drama, Chinese modern and contemporary women literature, and Chinese popular narrative balladry. He has published extensively in English, as well as in Chinese and German, and has published more than 30 works in his native language Dutch. In 2004, he became the director of the Fairbank Center for East Asian Studies. He is also a fellow of Royal Netherlands Academy of Arts and Sciences.

97 W. L. Idema. Dutch Translations of Classical Chinese Literature. // Leo Tak-hung Chan (ed.), *One into Many, Translation and the Dissemination of Classical Chinese Literature*. Amsterdam and New York: Rodopi, 2003: 222.

98 Georgette Jaeger, a Belgian Sinologist who was born in 1920 in Anvers, a large city in northern Belgium. She became interested in the Chinese language at the age of twenty, and later she took classes of Chinese language, literature, and philosophy at the Belgian Institute for Higher Chinese Language Education in Brussels.

99  Evangeline S. P. Almberg. From Apology to a Matter of Course // Leo Tak-hung Chan (ed.), *One into Many, Translation and the Dissemination of Classical Chinese Literature*. Amsterdam and New York: Rodopi, 2003: 206.
100 Oldřich Král, a translator and the leading figure in Czech sinological circle. He has spent his life in sinology study and translation of Chinese literature. He was awarded the Czech Best Book Award for his translation of *Zhuangzi*. Notably, his Czech translation of *The Story of Stone* won the International Translation Prize in Commemoration of the 240th Anniversary of the Death of Cao Xueqin in Beijing. In 2010, he received the Czech Republic's National Special Achievement Award, the Czech Republic's National Special Award for Social Science, and the Czech Republic's National Lifetime Achievement Award for literary translation. In 2017, he received the 11th Special Book Award of China from Chinese government.
101 M. Gálik. Tang Poetry in Translation in Bohemia and Slovakia (1902–1999). // Leo Tak-hung Chan (ed.), *One into Many, Translation and the Dissemination of Classical Chinese Literature*. Amsterdam and New York: Rodopi, 2003: 295.
102 Olga Lomová is a famous Czech signologist and the professor of East Asian Studies at the Faculty of Arts of Charles University in Prague. He has long been devoted to the translation and study of Chinese literature. His research fields include the history of Chinese literature, modern literature and cultural perspective, and the study on historical records.
103 H. Hart. *The Hundred Names: A Short Introduction to the Study on Chinese Poetry with Illustrative Translations*. Berkeley: University of California Press, 1933: 1.
104 Wu Yuanyuan. Chinese Scholar's Migrating to the United States during the 1940s and Their Impact on the American Sinology. *Journal of Overseas Chinese History Studies*, 2010 (2): 31–40.
105 In 1965, Press-22 published an offprint of Snyder's translation: *Cold Mountain Poems: Twenty-four Poems by Han-Shan*. In 1970 and 1972, this offprint was reprinted.
106 Xi Mi. *Poetry and Life*. Guilin: Guangxi Normal University Press, 2004: 2.
107 R. Kern. Seeing the World without Language. // *Orientalism, Modernism and the American Poem*. New York: Cambridge University Press, 1996: 237.
108 American famous scholar Maloney mentioned in August 1982 that

> I first encountered CMPs in a crumpled second-hand book, The Beat Generation Series, edited by Thomas Parkinson. It contained 24 of Gary Snyder's poems in translation, and I was impressed by their directness and luminousness. Since then, CMPs have been infecting me and have brought me pleasure and joy throughout the year.
>
> Maloney D. Foreword. // Arthur Tobias et al (trans.),
> *The View from Cold Mountain, Poems of Han-shan and Shih-de*.
> New York: White Pine Press, 1982, No page number.

109 Wu-chi Liu & Yucheng Irving Lo (eds.). *Sunflower Splendor: Three Thousand Years of Chinese Poetry*. Bloomington and London: Indiana University Press, 1975: 549.
110 D. Maloney. Foreword. // Arthur Tobias et al. (trans.), *The View from Cold Mountain, Poems of Han-shan and Shih-te*. New York: White Pine Press, 1982, no page number.
111 A. Tobias. Han-shan. // *The View from Cold Mountain, Poems of Han-shan and Shih-te*. New York: White Pine Press, 1982, no page number.
112 The original poem is:

> Men are mixing gravel and cement
> At Maple Bridge,
> Down an alley by a tea-stall
> From Cold Mountain Temple;
> Where Zhang Ji heard the bell.

The stone step moorage
Empty, lapping water,
And the bell sound has travelled
Far across the sea.

113 P. Stambler. *Encounters with Cold Mountain*. Beijing: Chinese Literature Press, 1996: 13.
114 N. Foster and J. Shoemaker. *The Roaring Stream: A New Zen Reader*. Hopewell, NJ: Ecco Press, 1996, back cover.
115 A. Schelling. Introduction. // R. Pine & Mike O'Connor (eds.), *The Clouds Should Know Me by Now: Buddhist Poet Monks of China*. Boston: Wisdom Publications, 1999: 3.
116 Yogi Chen. *Selected Han-Shan Poems for Hippie Reading*. See www.yogichen.org/chenian/bk049.html. [2006-10-14]. Chen Jianmin also mentioned in the article that Bill Wyatts had translated around 80 CMPs.
117 S. Hamill & J. Seaton. *The Poetry of Zen*. Boston. MA: Shambhala Publications, Inc., 2004: 13-14.
118 Wandering Poet. Foreword. // *Cold Mountain: Transcendental Poetry by the Tang Zen Poet Han-shan*. 2005. no copyright information and page numbers.
119 B. Waston. *The Columbia Book of Chinese Poetry: From Early Times to the Thirteenth Century*. New York: Columbia University Press, 1984: 260.
120 S. Owen. *An Anthology of Chinese Literature: Beginnings to 1911*. New York: Norton, 1996: 405.
121 T. H. Barrett. Han-shan in Translation. // Peter Hobson. *Poems of Han-shan*. Walnut Creek: Altamira Press, 2003: 149.
122 Zi Gui. China's Han-shan and the Movie Cold Mountain. *Journal of Literature and History*, 2004 (6): 29-30.
123 This novel was translated as *Lengshan* (*Cold Mountain*) in Chinese mainland, as translated by Zhou Yujun and Panyuan and published by Nanning Jieli Press in 2004. The movie based on the novel of the same name was also translated as *Lengshan* (*Cold Mountain*) in Chinese mainland. In Hong Kong, perhaps in pursuit of commercial box office and public attention, *Cold Mountain* was translated as *Luanshi Qingtian* (*The Left Hand of God*). Perhaps Han-shan and his poems would have gained more attention and recognition in China if the movie had been correctly translated as *Cold Mountain*.
124 This kind of experience can be found in the author's 11th imitation poem of Han-shan: "Han-shan Is the Cure for Warts". The poem is:

My job was eating me night and day, my wife
threatening to leave, taking even the stroller and the quilt.
A family of warts blossomed on my thumb so big I introduced themto tellers and
    clerks. Ha ha, they'd say, making quick change.
Then I bumped into Han-shan in the bookstore, one hundred poemsso small I read
    them all. We moved to a new place.
My wife smiles out on sidewalks where children ride.I work in a room so quiet I can
    hear my heartbeat.
My warts are gone, no marks, no scars
   Lenfestey James. *Cartload of Scrolls: 100 Poems in the Manner of T'ang Dynasty Poet Han-shan*. Duluth, Minnesota: Holy Cow Press, 2007: 27

Obviously, this way of imitating consolidates the canonical status of the CMPs in the cultural polysystem of American from another aspect.
125 J. Lenfestey. *Seeking the Cave: A Pilgrimage to Cold Mountain*. Minneapolis: Milkweed Editions, 2014: 30.

# 5 Canon Construction of the CMPs in the Cultural Polysystem of Arrivals

A Case Study on Gary Snyder's Translation of the CMPs

From the 1930s to the 21st century, the CMPs have maintained their strong momentum of interlingual travel throughout Europe, Asia, and America. They have been circulated, disseminated and accepted to the greatest extent through varied media and platforms. The international communication capacity and the tremendous impact of the CMPs can be evidently confirmed in the diversified translations, literature anthologies, fictions and movies, religious books and anthologies of Zen poems, because they all appreciate and attach importance to the CMPs. If "classics" are texts that have withstood the test of time, been widely read by the majority, been officially recognized and been authorized to be a part of university lectures, the CMPs earned a status of "classics" in the English-speaking world as early as the 1950s or 1960s. As mentioned in the previous chapter, the interlingual travel of the CMPs to Europe and America was mediated through Japan. Starting with the first introduction in *Poems of the Hundreds of Names* in 1933 by Henry H. Hart (1886–?), an American sinologist, and 27 translated poems by Arthur Waley, a famous British sinologist, in 1954, the CMPs were spread immediately and highly accepted in the English-speaking world that centers on Britain and America. When Gary Snyder published the translation of 24 CMPs in 1958, the description of Han-shan—"Thin grass does for a mattress, the blue sky makes a good quilt. Happy with a stone under head, let heaven and earth go about their changes"—immediately captured attentions and minds of the "Beat Generation" in post-war America. The CMPs then naturally became a best-selling classic of at that particular time.[1]

## 5.1 The Cultural Polysystem in Post-War America

The American economy entered a highly industrialized stage after World War II, but the repression and alienation, which were caused by modern industry, commerce and machinery, exposed various social problems. Many emerging challenges such as the "baby boom", "cold war" and "McCarthyism" even fueled the civil right movements in this country. Old social standards were questioned widely, but new social standards and models were far from being established, leaving the public in a state of extreme confusion and disorder.

When faced with these social problems, a large number of American youth chose a series of extreme behaviors to express their dissatisfaction with American culture and religious traditions: they started the backpack revolution, slept in the wilderness, became addicted to alcohol and drugs, lived in groups, and supported the promiscuity. They regarded these behaviors as a blatant sign of anti-secularism and anti-realism. They were also fond of Buddhistic bracelets, flowers, bell ornaments, dazzling glare, loud music, bizarre attire, and erotic speech. "They thought they merely wanted to overthrow the Western society in 'a peaceful way' and with the inducing force that came from examples."[2] Xu Yu (徐迂, 1908–1980) thought that the hippies had one common feature.

> They were discontented with the reality, hated the industry civilization, despised power, pursued a "successful" but ordinary life. They contemned the hypocritical life principle of "climbing up", rebelled the self-consciousness but discreetly kept in a range. They also transgressed the natural moral order and freed themselves from the traditional and conservative doctrines of Christianity.
> They advocated human love, worshiped nature, prayed for peace, protested war, and wanted to liberate themselves from all kinds of constraints in order to pursue the pure self. As a result, they advocated taking drugs to dissect, develop, liberate, explore, express, and anesthetize themselves![3]

Someone even said, "Being a hippy has become the chief lifestyle of 40 million American youth between the age of fifteen and twenty-five."[4] In 1967, there were 60,000 people settled in Hashbury, the home base of Hippies in San Francisco. Campuses across America were also a full reflection of this Hippie trend.

> American students in 1960s were so influenced by the Hippie culture in that time that they abused alcohol and smoked marijuana. They usually wore long hair, dressed sloppily, smoked pot, attended a rock concert, and demonstrated with the slogan of "Make Love not War"—all of these were typical manifestations. Hippie culture was born in Berkeley. Compared to the students of West coast campuses, those on the Eastern coast were seemingly less influenced, but Hippie still permeated into the lifestyle of students.[5]

Placation, adjustment, and comfort are what the American public needed at the time to ease the noise in the mind. For some Americans, therefore, "the idea of staying far away from the crowd naturally emerged, and a primitive lifestyle of working at sunrise and resting at sundown without competition was highly praised."[6] Americans and the whole society wished that they could borrow from other counties' culture for reference—especially the ancient and harmonious oriental civilization—to reconstruct their nation's culture and spirit. Gary Snyder noted in *Turtle Island* that

> The root of the problem where our civilization goes wrong is the mistaken belief that nature is something less than authentic, that nature is not as alive as man is, or as intelligent, that in a sense it is dead, and that animals are of

so low an order of intelligence and feeling, we need not take their feelings into account.[7]

This is a kind of morbid psychology and misconception that people have acquired under industrial civilization. Snyder had once lived in mountains for a long time and could take a rational look at human's behaviors of sacrificing nature for the progress of civilization, thus he believes, "We need a harmonious and creative civilization that we can live side by side with the wilderness. We must begin to cultivate our civilization here in the new world."[8] Perhaps it was Han-shan's behavior of withdrawing from the mundanity and going into the wilderness that attracted him. In Snyder's mind, wilderness represents freedom, wilderness means wisdom. In other words, nature with wild beauty is "not the place we visit. It's our home".[9]

It is apparent that American society could not get out of the dilemma with its own culture in the process of industrialization, and the first and only way to save American civilization was to change the inherent and conservative mindset of the society. The force of revolution didn't come from the inner power, but the foreign civilization. Because of the call for foreign culture, translated literature jumped to the center of the cultural polysystem of the target language. The culture of arrivals at this time wanted a new pattern that could change the old-fashioned social institution and improve the traditional literature paradigm. At the crucial turning point of the host culture, the social and cultural functions of translation were emphasized and highlighted, while the aesthetic functions were relatively diluted. In that sense, translators' selections of translation material were largely limited by the sociocultural context and dominant ideology. It is inarguable that only when a translated work makes a breakthrough in stating new thoughts and creating a new literature model, can it be recognized and accepted by society. If the cultural attitude of the translator conforms to this viewpoint, the translator, the text and the dominant ideology of host culture can coexist in harmony. Gary Snyder and the 24 CMPs he selected for translation won a harmonious translational discourse field by conforming to the dominant ideology of the culture of arrivals or the culture of host countries.

After World War II, the American economy entered a golden period of unprecedented development. The rapid economic development stimulated and drove the production and reproduction of literature to a certain extent. Taking it as an opportunity, American native literature creation and translation practice entered a fast lane. Since the 1950s, the American translation industry has experienced an unprecedented boom. Scholars in America during the 1950s regarded translation as a special way of coming to know and understand "the other", translation was seen as an important method for the United States to seek out a different culture. American's desire of a nourishment from "the other" was reflected in the attempt of the learning from European cultural traditions, as well as the activities of introducing and translating Asian and some minority cultures. This action was "an act of defiance against the government that was murdering Asian others abroad and the social realities that were oppressing African-American others at home".[10] At the same time, there was demand for foreign language and literature in the reform of American educational curriculum. Additionally, American major poets, scholars and translators of that time tended to believe that the experiences of East Asian civilizations, especially those of ancient China, could be transplanted into American life of the 20th century.[11] Based on such a perception, foreign cultures, especially the long-lasting oriental cultures, were imported continuously. The input of these heterogeneous cultures became an important part of American counter-cultural movements after the war, and brought Americans a brand-new thinking model, as well as an opportunity to remodel themselves.

Represented by famous Jerome P. Seaton (1941–), Jonathan Chaves (1943–), Burton Watson and David Hinton (1954–), American sinologists began to immerse in the translation and study of classical Chinese poetry. In the field of poetry, prominent American native poets such as William Carlos Williams (1883–1963), Kenneth Rexroth (1905–1982) and Gary Snyder started to introduce and translate oriental poetry, especially classical Chinese poetry. They attempted to find an outlet for nation's emotion in the figure mode of Chinese poets as exiled or self-exiled hermit in the wilderness. This huge campaign of translation reached its heyday in the 1960s. By the early 1970s, as the end of social-cultural movements that aimed at dismantling the center system, like the San Francisco Renaissance, the anti-Vietnam War movement, the civil rights campaign and the liberation of women, poets became alienated from the intellectual and cultural circle for different reasons and almost no one engaged in translation. After that, the fervor of translation gradually faded.

Curiously, "the end of the American poet as translator has coincided with the beginning of the American poet as translated author."[12] As a matter of fact, whether they were translated author or not, those poets in a period of cultural fusion inadvertently opened up a door to classical Chinese poetry and then were so influenced by Chinese poems that they creatively integrated various Chinese elements and styles into their original poems. Snyder admitted,

> I tried writing poems of tough, simple, short words, with the complexity for beneath the surface texture. In part the line was influenced by the five- and seven-character line Chinese poems I'd been reading, which work like sharp blows on the mind.[13]

He also acknowledged that Chinese poetic traditions had a great influence on Western poetry, "From the fourth to the fourteenth centuries, the poetry of China reached far (but selectively) into the world of nature. Contemporary occidental poetry had been influenced by that aspect, too."[14] Snyder's English poems, which were full of Chinese feature and Zen thoughts, were profoundly influenced by Chinese landscape poetry and recluse culture. Snyder further recognized, "I do appreciate Japanese culture and poetry, but I feel closer to Chinese poetry." Snyder also translated other Chinese poets' work, including Meng Haoran, Wang Changling, Wang Wei, Du Fu, Bai Juyi, Du Mu, Su Shi and Chinese Zen master Baizhang Huaihai.

When American native poets borrowed and integrated the classical Chinese poetic traditions into their original English poems, their poems with Chinese flavor inadvertently introduced and spread Chinese poetry and Chinese culture in some implicit or explicit way. Chinese poetry then possesses a possibility of becoming the classical translated literature in American cultural polysystem among the public. Snyder's translation and imitation of the CMPs, as well as Rexroth's translation and imitation of Du Fu's poems, established a great literary fame for classical Chinese poetry in the "San Francisco Renaissance", and the subsequent experiments with indigenous poetry.

At the same time, the demand for East Asian literature in the general education curriculum of American university in the 1960s and 1970s was a perfect opportunity for certain Chinese poets and poems to be introduced into the university's lecture hall, and their classical status was finally established through this form. Zhou Yingxiong (周英雄) has made a more precise description about this period:

> In the 1960s, with declining enrollment and rising awareness of civil rights, the literature departments in both the U.K. and the United States tried to salvage their reputation and respond to the needs of minority groups by reforming their curricula, revising the must-read classics to include women's literature, Black literature, non-Anglo-American English literature, and other theme-based courses. Yet this first wave of curriculum reform was hardly a success. The real effect of the curriculum reform may not come until the 1980s, when the orientation of literary criticism shifted from textualism to oppositional criticism, and a variety of minority discourse came into being, firstly at Duke University and Stanford University.[15]

In this sense, it was those civil rights movements that had contributed to the demand for non-Anglo-American literature in British and American universities. It was in this context that Han-shan, a Chinese poet in the Tang Dynasty, and his poems came into the attention of the academy at that time. In fact, it was in Chen Shih Hsiang (陈世骧)'s graduate class "Tang Poetics" that Snyder learned about Han-shan and began to translate his poems.

After World War II, American mainstream culture had tried to establish a new and stable cultural order, yet there was a potential volatile force in the intellectual community that tried to separate itself from the mainstream cultural norms. As a result, various civil rights movements sprang up constantly. It is self-evident that post-war civil rights movement led to a diversified development of native literary polysystem. At the same time, the emphasis on "minority groups" or "ethnic groups" which was created by the writers of a particular ethnic literary group brought attention and importance to some non-native literary genres of other countries. Many classic poets, writers, and scholars began to join the group of translating and promoting foreign literature and culture and participated in the process of constructing new literary norms and cultural norms. As the result, translation came to the forefront of American literary polysystem. It is not difficult to imagine that the central status and discourse power of translated literature of the time could naturally lead periphery texts from foreign countries to the center of the literary polysystem out of the utilitarian purpose, and thus made those texts become members of canonical literary repertoire. The canon construction of translated CMPs by Snyder, without any doubt, can be and should be studied within the intertextual context of the temporal cultural polysystem.

## 5.2 The Mainstream Ideology and the Canonization of CMPs

As what is mentioned before, the canonization of translated texts, like the construction of native literature classics, is neither an overnight achievement nor accomplishment that can be manipulated or influenced by any individual power. On the contrary, it is a long process of identifying the factual meaning and value norms, so it must be an accumulative process of history. As someone asserted,

> the final confirmation of the classics is the result of a combined operation in a certain literary system. . . . The classics are not just shaped by detached reading interests of some individuals. The production, dissemination and acceptance of literature also attribute to the creation of classics.[16]

The canonization of texts is a sophisticated dynamic process that involves many literary and non-literary factors. In addition to the significant influence of the literary system itself on the construction of literary classics, the manipulative power of sociocultural factors—like political system, economic status, historical events-should not be underestimated. The "dominant ideology" that determines the production of texts and translation norms, as well as the "patronage" that produces the literary classics, play a particularly crucial role in the process of canonization.

### 5.2.1. Ideology and Translation Studies

Admit it or not, in addition to the aesthetic value of the text, the canonization of the text largely depends on the final recognition of its classic status by a certain legitimate organization representing the dominant ideology. Otherwise, "what is classic" will always be subjective and idle discussion. Without any doubt, the canon construction of translated texts inevitably involves the recognition or re-recognition of the canonicity of translated texts by the dominant ideology. Maria del Carmen África Vidal discussed about the influence of ideology in translation when she translated conceptual art works:

> And, thanks to the dehierarchization that came about with postmodernist philosophy and poststructuralist practices, translation and translators have now occupied their rightful place. At the same time, it has finally been understood that translation cannot be a pure act or nor an innocent act and that the translator's ideology, the patron's ideology and the ideology of the medium the translation is to be published in etc., are all very important factors that alter the final product. But one thing is that culture is a fundamental element

of translation and that translation is, in a way inevitably, manipulation, and another is that translation is only an excuse for transmitting the translator's ideology.[17]

Vidal clearly expressed the complicit relationship between translation and ideology in this except. Translation is not only a pretext for translators to transmit ideology, but also an objective carrier of translators' own cultural attitudes and ideology. It's widely accepted that translation is an act of converting language of translator in some sociocultural context. Vidal comments on the relationship between language and translator:

Language is the translator's tool, a dangerous tool, a weapon that he use to cause damage with: it is not innocent but always implies a vision of the world which is related, according to the Frankfurt School, to the legitimacy of certain institution and social practices and the power relations maintaining them.[18]

In other words, language inevitably carries the translator's ideological discourse which closely connects with the patronage (what Vidal named the "institution" or "social practices") and its power relations. That is to say, language and the use of language are destined to be non-neutral from the beginning. It (translation) is an instrument of power; or rather, power works through language; or an effective carrier for the ideology represented by power relations. It can be further inferred that the act of translation which uses language to achieve translation purpose is accountable for ideology.

Translation, therefore, is by no means innocent. In the process of language conversion, translators always take a certain ideology as the guide or reference coordinate of translation with or without consciousness. The content and form of the text to be translated are treated in the same way. Generally speaking, power relations controlled by ideology largely influence the transmission and selection of the text content, which is called "structural norms"; and native poetics traditions influenced by ideology govern the final manifestation of the text, which is called "textual-linguistic norms". Both of them affect the translator's comprehensive consideration of translation norms in the decision-making process. The language description of a text by translation, therefore, cannot distinctly separate from the cultural transmission and ideology. Given the interrelationship among language, translation and ideology, it might be said that ideology is not only a basic category of philosophy, but also a basic category of translation studies.

Translation activities in all periods are, more or less, influenced by ideology, hence it is not much to say that "ideology" is the core concept and research object of translation studies. In China, however, many people always confuse ideology with politics in that they overemphasize the political significance of ideology. In actuality, the influence of ideology exists in every aspect of public life, while politics, philosophy, legislation, language, art, aesthetics, religion, ethics and morality are only its manifestations. The "influential scope" of ideology is so wide that it is reasonable for translation to conspire with ideology and use it to realize translators' aesthetic and moral desires, and sometimes such conspiracy is even not dependent on the translation practice or the translator's intention. Christianne Nord (1943–), a German translation theorist, once commented:

> Ideology is an evaluative concept that is mostly used to characterize or even discredit the *other* side—it may be difficult to find people claiming an ideology to characterize themselves. However, if we understand ideology simply as a set of ideas supported by a group, a school, a society or even an individual author, it is obvious that ideology is at work on both sides.[19]

There are arguments for this from all sides. Translation theorists of German functionalism all tend to believe that

> translators work in specific socio-political contexts, producing target texts for specific purposes as identified by their clients. This social conditioning is reflected in the linguistic structure of the target text. That is, the target text will reveal the impact of social, ideological, discursive, and linguistic conventions, norms and constraints.[20]

Nord explains, "It is the translator's task first to find out what the intended purpose of the translation is and then to produce a text that suit this purpose."[21]

> The choice of a source text and the use to which the subsequent target text is put is determined by the interests, aims, and objectives of social agents. But ideological aspects can also be determined within a text itself, both at the lexical level (reflected, for example, in the deliberate choice or avoidance of a particular word) and the grammatical level (for example, use of passive structures to avoid an expression of agency). Ideological aspects can be more or less obvious in texts, depending on the topic of a text, its genre and communicative purpose.[22]

This interpretation further strengthens translators' subjectivity and finds the best theoretical basis for the construction of translators' subjectivity.

Considering the possibility that translators may abuse their power and subjectivity in translation practice, Nord proposes the translation concept of "Function plus Loyalty". It stipulates that translation should fulfill the target readers' wishes, but at the same time, it should not betray the communication intentions and expectations of both the source-text author and the translated-text readers. "Should not betray their expectation" does not mean complying with them all the time, because

> our skopos may sometimes aim precisely at contravening them. In such a case, loyalty would require that translators lay their guiding principles open and justify them with a view on the translation skopos (e.g. in a preface and/or in notes).[23]

The various forms of paratext in translation practice, such as prefaces, postscripts, introductions, appendices and addenda, are all used by translators to achieve a certain translation intention and to justify their behaviors through these additional remarks.

The skopos theory of German functionalists places the greatest emphasis on the target readers and the translation intentions. Scholars of this school stress the communicative function of translated text in the target culture. The translation is supposed to be "faithful" to the author and readers, so "there is no such a thing as a *neutral* translation. In spite of their apparent neutrality."[24] Someone maintained that "translation involves the communication of two cultures. 'Communication' seemingly implies equality and friendship, but what it really indicates is the confrontation between two ideologies. The specious 'equality and friendship' or 'communication" is often a result of compromise after confrontation."[25]

Martha P.Y. Cheung further pointed out:

> Cultural communication is often not a process guided by the idealized cultural communication concept in which two cultures meet frankly, and get to know each other without biases, but a process in which two (or more) cultures contact with each other in different historical and political situations, different knowledge domains and cognitive models, as well as different power relations and discourse networks, thus resulting in the collisions, confrontations, resistance, control and conflicts.[26]

It goes without saying that if the translation is a decision-making process, ideological considerations will always be an indispensable part in this decision-making process.

### 5.2.2 "Ideology" in Snyder's Translation of CMPs

The ideology of the text, as well as the translator's ideology and cultural attitude, tends to follow the dominant ideology of the culture of arrivals. When the departing text travels to the cultural polysystem of arrivals, the impact of this text on the target audience is not so much determined by the translator or the departing text as by the dominant ideology in the cultural polysystem of arrivals. If the translator, the text and the cultural polysystem of arrivals can coexist in harmony, the departing text has the most sufficient and important prerequisite for the canon construction.

#### 5.2.2.1 The Translator

In terms of the translator, Snyder's attitude to culture was undoubtedly positive and constructive. Faced with problems of American culture at his time, Snyder was worried. "I began to perceive that maybe it was all of the Western culture that was off the track and not just capitalism—that there were certain self-destructive tendencies in our cultural tradition."[27] He further pointed out that "one of the key problems in American society now, it seems to me, is people's lack of commitment to any given place."[28] Hence, he decided to be an active practitioner. He participated in the San Francisco Renaissance, which began on October 13, 1955. In the 1960s, he planned the "Great Human Be-In" together with Irwin Allen Ginsberg (1926–1997), a representative of the Beat Generation.[29] In the 1970s, environmentalism and the Green Beauty rose, Snyder became the poetry spokesman of the movement. In 1972, Snyder attended the United Nations Conference on the Human Environment in Stockholm and gave a speech with his poem *Mother Earth: Her Whales*, appealing for environmental protection. In 1975, his poem *Turtle Island*, which reflects the ecology of the North American continent, won the Pulitzer Prize for Poetry.

Obviously, Snyder has been proactively engaging in the construction of the central rule of literature and society when American literature and culture were weak and peripheral. In all relevant activities, Snyder regarded Eastern civilization as a reference for American culture and attempted to bring it into American society through his translations and compositions, as well as his personal practice, "and to form a unique cross-cultural phenomenon by fusing this civilization with American endemicity and North American Indian culture, so as to rewrite American cultural traditions".[30] One held that Snyder attempted to complement and correct Western civilization through the Eastern model of the inter-validation of Zen Buddhism and "Xuanxue" (玄学, a metaphysical post-classical Chinese philosophy) and the combination of Buddhism and Daoism.[31] At the time of Snyder, the most prevalent Eastern cultural thought was Zen Buddhism-after being strongly promoted by Suzuki Teitaro (1870–1966).[32] Alan Watts (1915–1973) also promoted Zen-Buddhism, and after this Zen became particularly popular.[33]

It was in 1951 when Snyder happened to read Suzuki Teitaro's work that he became interested in and studied Zen.[34] He once recalled:

> Before that, I was studying Japanese and Chinese at Berkeley. I had some interest in Sinology and related studies, so I enjoyed doing some study in that field. But at that time, I was also in a bit of a dilemma because I was fascinated by Suzuki Teitaro's books on Zen. They generally took me away from academia and learning, and from believing in books, words and dogma.[35]

Later, Snyder became an auditor at the American Academy of Asian Studies, where Alan Watts was a teacher there. Encouraged and supported by Watts and other friends, Snyder went to Kyoto, Japan, to study Zen in 1959, beginning his indissoluble relationship with Zen.

Because of such a social and cultural atmosphere, as well as Synder's lingering attachment to Zen, he deliberately selected 24 poems by the Chinese hermit poet Han-shan to translate, which are full of Zen thoughts. It might be questioned why the active constructor would translate a recluse's works. In fact, Snyder hoped to introduce a simple and natural lifestyle into the chaotic and noisy society through the figure of Han-shan and his poems. He chose Zen, not for providing a shelter of faith, but for advocating a healthy, active, natural and ecological lifestyle of Zen. As someone concludes,

> Snyder's early poetic pursuits and his understanding of Zen led him to believe that the admiration for nature, the critique of materialism and the naturalistic way of life expressed in CMPs were exactly what Western civilization lacked and should learn.[36]

In his translation, Snyder not only makes Han-shan a hippie, but also places him in the context of American culture. In the preface, the translator even impatiently invites readers to look for Han-shan in contemporary American society. "They (Han-shan and Shi'de) became Immortals and you sometimes run onto them today in the skidrows, orchards, hobo jungles, and logging camps of America."[37] The romantic and intelligent image of the Chinese poet is vividly represented through his translation, especially the unique way of life of Han-shan, which is alienated from the world and going back to nature, deeply captivate the translator himself and his target audience. The confused and bewildered young generation seems to be able to find a spiritual nest in the image of "Han-shan" for their authentic yearns for the true nature of self, free physicality and spirituality.

Han-shan, as Snyder said, is the unity of human, dwelling and mind. In Snyder's translation, the poet's detachment, contentment, serenity and free state of mind in the cold mountain undoubtedly provided a remedy for the "Beat generation" at that time to "absolute freedom". The Zen spirit of spontaneous wandering and individual meditation in the poems arose their admiration, and Han-shan, the somewhat hippy poet, unsurprisingly captivated them. "Zen", a unity of human spirit and nature, was then widely learned and celebrated. Americans who were disappointed with civilized society seemed to see the dawn of "getting past the tangles of the world" in the hermit, so as to believe that Han-shan was a foreign confidant with whom they live in the same world and shared same ideas.

The application of this hermit model suggests that "such model was exactly what American literature needed in the process of cultural self-renewal".[38] Snyder sought to find a new way for American society and individuals to reshape themselves by transporting Eastern cultural traits into American culture, and expected to achieve the melioration of society and literature through translations. As a matter of fact, the importation of new poetics and literary model represented not only a reformation of literary creation form, but also a means by which poets and writers hoped to discover alternative social forms. "The work of this period reveals a tension between certain extravagant claims of transcendence and lived reality, but that tension was also a measure of postwar America's inability to provide a social validation equal to its extraordinary economic success."[39] Hence intellectuals of the time simultaneously studied translated works for a new development model for American. Robert Kern commented,

> Snyder introduces his T'ang dynasty poet into a contemporary American context in the interest of bringing about a fusion and thus an expansion of

horizons for his reader. . . . Ancient Chinese spirituality thus becomes, in effect, a contemporary American possibility. . . . In the process, the book also becomes an expression of the ethos of the Beat Generation and of the San Francisco Renaissance, drawing upon the West Coast radical and activist traditions that precede and inform these movements in their search for what Michael Davidson calls alternative modes "of communal organization within American mass society."[40] And it is interesting to note, in this connection, that Snyder read some of his Han-shan translations publicly at the Six Gallery in San Francisco on October 13th, 1955. . . . This poetry reading, of course, is often cited as the inaugural event of the San Francisco Renaissance, a much publicized and mythologized manifestation of a new cultural, aesthetic, and political formation in the midst of the Cold War era.[41]

Han-shan and Cold Mountain Poem chosen by Synder merely represents a "peripheral culture" or a "subcultural" spirit in Chinese literature. In the translator's view, however, such culture and spirit contained valuable elements, that was, "counter-cultural" and "anti-traditional" spirit opposed to the mainstream American culture of the 1950s and 1960s. Snyder's translation, to some extent, imported new and needed ideas and cultural spirit into the cultural polysystem of American. As a result, his translation gained a chance of being "canonized" in the social and cultural context of the time. Generally speaking, there is nothing more conducive to text travel and canon construction than active selection and inherent need of the cultural system of arrivals.

*5.2.2.2 The Text*

In terms of texts, being influenced and manipulated by ideologies, texts are usually subject to translation deviation and cultural misreading after traveling to another country. As a result, they will be rewritten and transformed in the translation process. Lefevere once pointed out, "Translation is, of course, a rewriting of an original text. All rewritings, whatever their intention, reflect a certain ideology and a poetics."[42] As a matter of fact, this is what is bound to happen in translation. Due to the translator's cultural structure and native consciousness, original texts are inevitably domesticated in accordance with translators' intentions and dominant ideologies. Lawrence Venuti, an American translation theorist, explains, "Translation is often regarded with suspicion because it inevitably domesticates foreign texts, inscribing them with linguistic and cultural values that are intelligible to specific domestic constituencies."[43] In his essay *The Task of the Translator*, published in 1923, Walter Benjamin (1892–1940), a German philosopher, quoted the words of Rudolf Pannwitz (1881–1969) to make a broad discussion about the influence of language:

Our translators have a far greater reverence for the usage of their own language than for the spirit of the foreign works. . . . The basic error of the translator is that he preserves the state in which his own language happens to be instead of allowing his language to be powerfully affected by the foreign tongue.[44]

Venuti, however, believed that such domestication occurs in all stages of translation, including production, circulation and acceptance:

> It is initiated by the very choice of a foreign text to translate, always an exclusion of other foreign texts and literatures, which answers to particular domestic interests. It continues most forcefully in the development of a translation strategy that rewrites the foreign text in domestic dialects and discourses, always a choice of certain domestic values to the exclusion of others. And it is further complicated by the diverse forms in which the translation is published, reviewed, read, and taught, producing cultural and political effects that vary with different institutional contexts and social positions.[45]

In this way, translators and their ideology are always slightly visible during text travel and canon construction. In actuality, Snyder closely kept integrating his ideology with the dominant ideology in every stage—materials selection, translation production, texts circulation and reception. This tendency is firstly reflected in the selection of foreign texts to be translated. It is known that the choice of texts often suggests translator's intention, which means that texts and literature that are incompatible with specific local interests tend to be rejected. The 24 poems selected by Snyder are all about the Cold Mountain the dwelling place and the mind state of Zen since didactic poems not only ran counter to the dominant ideology, but also by no means stroke a chord with target readers on aesthetics. Secondly, Snyder's ideology is even more evident in the preface to the translation, in which he described Han-shan as "a Chinese hermit in rags" and made an introduction to the CMPs that those poems were written in quaint and fresh proverbial language and full of Taoism, Confucianism and Zen ideas. At the end of preface, he even suggested to the target readers that Han-shan might be among them, or be a "hero of many" hidden among them. This "prelude", undoubtedly, had a strong appeal to the Beat Generation who were seeking Zen, transcendence, reclusion and hero of many. For them, Han-shan's lifestyle, spirituality, and pursuit of Taoism were exactly what they had been searching for.

The translator also kept in line with the linguistic convention of mainstream poetic tradition. Snyder translated the CMPs in free form, ignoring the rhyme of original poems, omitting many sentence-initial conjunctions and predicate verbs, sometimes even using participles in place of predicate verbs. Furthermore, American colloquialisms and abbreviations were frequently used. These features obviously catered to the poetic tradition of open freedom and juxtaposition of images, which had been initiated since the American New Poetry Movement, as well as readers' expectation norms and aesthetic habits inherited from the tradition; they were also the strongest evidences of Snyder being deeply influenced by Chinese classical poetry and Japanese haiku. In actuality, classical Chinese poetry has an incalculable influence on the American New Poetry movement, both American poets of the time and modern American poetry. Kenneth Rexroth (1905–1982) pointed out that "it is difficult for them (American poets) not to think in Chinese or Japanese way."[46] Snyder is among them. He digested and transformed stylistic expressions of Chinese classical poetry, and creatively integrated them into his own poetic thoughts and culture soils, as well as his own free-verse composition and translation.

Snyder translated the CMPs mainly in the way of literal translation and "defamiliarization". Those strategies are always adopted when the cultural polysystem of arrivals is at a critical turning point so that the "adequacy" of heterogeneous culture can get highlighted. That's exactly what happened. The "exotic flavor" became a "refreshing breeze", which was thought to be needed for the downhill American culture. The Zen and philosophical lifestyle in the CMPs were something they were willing to accept and emulate. All of those clearly show the intent of the assiduous translator: to incorporate Eastern culture into American culture and to maintain the influence of Chinese classical poetry on American modern poetry for the advancement of American cultural traditions.

On the "native consciousness" lying behind Snyder's intention, Chung Ling analyzed,

Some American poems seemingly focus on the exotic mode of exposition, but in fact, such mode is merely a strategy by which local expositions or poets themselves were highlighted. There are also American poems in which poets try to externalize and localize exotic modes in English verses. Although these poems contain exotic part elements, what they focus on are still Western expositions.[47]

From another perspective, it can be said that Gary Snyder's choice of Han-shan and his poems is nothing more than a way to make use of Chinese poetry to address American problems and to find a solution to these problems. In essence, it is the American cultural tradition that drives Snyder to choose, rewrite, reconstruct and disseminate the CMPs. Qu Hong (区鉷, 1946–) also remarked,

If we trace the origin of the influence of Chinese culture exerts on Snyder, we will find similar or corresponding elements in American cultural traditions. Snyder himself would never admit that Chinese and Japanese culture made him an American poet. On the contrary, he placed great emphasis on "the sense of nativeness".[48]

Influenced by translators' ideology and strong "sense of nativeness", translations are bound to be transformed, reconstructed, and creatively misread after localization and specification. Snyder's practice of Americanizing and hippificating the CMPs is the best evidence. In that sense, translation becomes no longer a simple conversion between two languages, but a cultural and literary activity in the sociocultural context of arrivals, or even a unique political act sometimes, an act different from "ideal translation" but conforming to dominant ideology and the translators' intentions. Any translation activity, including the selection, production, spread and reception of translated texts, has invariably been influenced by ideology. In the case of Snyder's translation of the CMPs, the translator, the text and the dominant ideology were in great harmony and high unity, so these poems were easily recommended and recognized by patrons, the translators and users of the text.

## 5.3  Patronage and Canonization of the CMPs

While the previous discussion of dominant ideology is for the question of "what kind of a canon are the CMPs?", the following analysis of patrons is to answer "whose canon is it?".

### 5.3.1  Patronage and the Canonization of the Text

Andre Lefevere (1945–1996) regards literature as a subsystem of polysystem in his theoretical hypothesis, and believes that there is a double control factor in literary system. One belongs squarely within the literary system, represented by the "professional" including critics, reviewers, teachers, translators; the other is to be found outside of that system, meaning powers (persons and social institutions) that "can further or hinder the reading, writing, and rewriting of literature". Precisely, in Lefevere's view, the latter can be exerted by persons and also by groups of persons, a religious body, a political party, a social class, a royal court, publishers and media (newspapers, magazines and television corporations). The professionals focus on politics, while patronage is more interested in ideology than poetics. Internal factors manipulates the literary system within the limitations set by an external factor. Patronage usually owns three components: an ideological component, an economic component and an element of status. Patronage can be differentiated or undifferentiated. It is differentiated when the literary system is limited by some patronage, while it is undifferentiated when its three components are all dispensed by one and the same patronage, the absolute ruler, for instance.[49]

There is something worth discussing in the previous probe of "patronage". According to Lefevere's definition of patronage, professionals including critics, reviewers, teachers, translators were included in the "internal factor", but they can also "further or hinder the reading, writing, and rewriting of literature". To a large extent, they can manipulate the direction of mainstream poetics, and are hence important forces that "further or hinder the reading, writing, and rewriting of literature". In that sense, patronage should include both professionals (such as translators, literary critics, reviewers, teachers, authoritative literati) and literary institutions and organizations that further or hinder the textual canonization, such as translation initiators, translation agents, universities, literary societies, literary journals, literary anthologies, seminars, film, television, and publishing houses.

When analyzing how English translations of some Chinese poems established their classic statuses in the American poetry circle in the mid-20th century, Chung Ling came to a conclusion that their canonization is attributed to the following forces, (1) the most important one is American poets and translators. They were adept at English writing and translating Chinese poems into beautiful and touching English; (2) American literary anthologies. Some important anthologies selected these creative English translations, regarding them as classical creations; (3) American sinologists and literary critics. They established the status of these translated poems; (4) American poets. They spoke highly of the achievements and influences of these poems.[50] When discussing how the CMPs translated by Snyder became a classic in American poetry, Chung Ling referred to the famous Six Gallery Reading in San Francisco on October 13, 1955, which is often cited as the inaugural event of the San Francisco Renaissance. Chung Ling claims that it is Snyder's reciting of his translation of the CMPs on such an important occasion that opened the way for these poems to the canon. She also mentioned these translations were anthologized in *Anthology of Chinese Literature* edited by Cyril Birch. This anthology, published by Grove Press, was the most prevalent textbook for East Asian and Chinese literature learners in American universities in the 1960s and 1970s.

> In the book, Snyder's translation of CMPs did not become a classic of American literary, but rather a classic of English translation of foreign literature in English-speaking world, in other words, a classic of literature in translation. In Birch's anthology, the history of Chinese literature was rewritten. Han-shan, a poet outside the hall of fame in China, was elevated to a mainstream poet.[51]

Chung Ling has only talked about translator's and anthologist's functions on the canonization of the CMPs. The important role played by patronage, however, that is, "professionals" as the internal factors and "social institutions and social organizations" as the external factors in the canonization of Han-shan's poetry has not been discussed substantially.

### 5.3.2 The "Patronage" in Snyder's Translation of the CMPs

If both professionals and literary institutions as well as organizations that further or hinder the textual canonization are included in "patronage", then it can be said that during the canonization of Snyder's translation of the CMPs, it is the common efforts of Zen masters, Sinologists, translators, the Six Gallery Reading in San Francisco, *The Evergreen Review*, Grove Press, literature historians and target readers that has resulted in such a splendid canon construction in the history of Chinese and foreign literature.

#### 5.3.2.1 Professionals

When it comes to "professionals" within the literary system who influenced the canon construction of Snyder's translation, two contemporary Zen masters cannot be ignored: Suzuki Teitaro (1870–1966) and Alan Wilson Watts (1915–1973), who laid public opinion foundation for the popularity of the CMPs.

As early as the 1940s, Suzuki Teitaro (1870–1966) began to introduce Zen thoughts to the United States. Three series of his book *Essays in Zen Buddhism* were published and reprinted in 1949, 1950, and 1953, this is evident of a huge response in the USA. In 1956, American philosopher and existentialist William Barrett (1913–1992) edited *Zen Buddhism: Selected Writings of Suzuki Teitaro* pushing the "Zen fever" to a higher level. This anthology presents some of Suzuki's previously published monographs and essays on Zen Buddhism in 10 chapters. It is one of the Anchor Books and was published by the prestigious Doubleday & Company, Inc.

At the same time, Alan Wilson Watts's *The Way of Zen* was published in 1957. This book, with two Chinese characters "禅道" (The Way of Zen) on its title page, was an unusual bestseller in the USA at the time. After the first reprint in September 1959, it was reprinted twice in one year: in January and July 1960, and a fourth in June 1961; his other book *The Spirit of Zen* was published by John Murray Ltd. in 1958. It was reissued by the famous Grove Press and was on the list of the Evergreen Edition series.

It can be said that it was the remarkable work of the two scholars in introducing and promoting Zen that "triggered Americans' lasting interest in Zen".[52] In her article "The Dissemination of Cold Mountain Poems" (寒山诗的流传), Chung Ling mentions that Americans in 1958 were not ignorant of Eastern culture. Instead, at that time, Zen Studies was in full wring, even becoming "more fashionable by the minute".[53] For Americans of that time, Zen Buddhism was "no longer a personal choice, but a necessity to save humanity".[54] Zen Buddhism's advocation for austere and simple life, its emphasis for moral norms and its criticism for material desires had made many Americans full of expectation that it could eliminate the alienation of human nature caused by industrial civilization. Han-shan lead a natural and simple, tranquil and satisfied life, showing his Zen realm, ecological consciousness, and philosophy of life. All of these had a strong appeal to the translator and "lost" Americans at the time.

Another important professional for the canon construction of the CMPs is Chen Shih Hsiang, a professor of Chinese literature at the University of California, Berkeley. Chen Shih Hsiang was the first generation of scholars to study sinology in post-war America. He was the dean of the Department of Oriental Languages and Literature at the University of California and helped to plan the establishment of the Department of Comparative Literature, with classical Chinese literature and comparative Chinese and Western literature as his primary courses. Having a profound insight and in-depth study on popular literature, he was even called "the iconic figure in the studies on Jin Yong (金庸, 1924–2018)".[55] Snyder recalled his first translating of the CMPs. It was in the fall of 1955, he was taking a graduate course on T'ang Poetics of Chen Shih Hsiang. The reason why he chose the course was to make some preparations for his trip to Zen temples in Kyoto, Japan.

There were only two students in this class at the time-a Chinese and I. Mr. Chen asked me what I was interested in. I said I wanted to learn about some Buddhist poetry written in the vernacular. He then said, "no problem. Han-shan is exactly the poet you need."[56]

It was under the guidance of Chen Shih Hsiang that Snyder started his translating of the CMPs almost word for word. In fact, Snyder had great trust in Chen Shih Hsiang. He once recalled passionately,

> Chen was a teacher as well as a friend to me. His knowledge of poetry, deep passion for poetry, and great taste in life were all incomparable. From good memory, he can invoke French poetry and write on the blackboard any of the classic poems of Tang (618–907) and Song (960–1279) Dynasties without error. In Chen Shih Hsiang's translation of Lu Ji's (陆机) *Wenfu* (《文赋》, *The Poetic Exposition on Literature*), there is a proverb that says, "in making an axe handle by cutting wood with an axe, the model is indeed near at hand".[57] In the case of poetry, I think this is true.[58]

In fact, in his own poetry and prose, Snyder used to refer to Chen Shih Hsiang as "Axe", which shows Chen's influence on him. With the careful guidance of Chen Shih Hsiang, a professional who enjoyed authoritative status in the American sinological studies at the time, and the mentoring relationship between the two mentioned by Snyder on various occasions, the popularity and recognition of Snyder's translation of the CMPs in American scholarship is a justifiable consequence.

In addition, at the Six Gallery Reading during the San Francisco Renaissance Movement that began on October 13, 1955, Snyder and four other Beat poets-Allen Ginsberg (1926–1997), Philip Whalen (1923–2002), Philip Lamantia (1927–2005), and Michael McClure (1932–2020). McClure made their public debut at the great night which was frequently referred to by literary historians later, and it was Kenneth Rexroth (1905–1982), the famous pioneer of San Francisco poetry, that hosted the reading of the night. Moreover, Jack Kerouac, the soul of the Beat Generation, witnessed this important moment in literary history for himself. In his book *The Dharma Bums*, the author recalls that exciting night:

> Anyway, I followed the whole gang of howling poets to the reading at Gallery Six that night, which was, among other important things, the night of the birth of the San Francisco Poetry Renaissance. Everyone was there. It was a mad night. And I was the one who got things jumping by going around collecting dimes and quarters from the rather stiff audience standing around in the gallery and coming back with three huge gallon jugs of California Burgundy and getting them all piffed so that by eleven o'clock when Alvah Goldbook[59] was reading, wailing his poem "Wail", drunk with arms outspread, everybody was yelling "Go! Go! Go!" (like a jam session) and old Rheinhold Cacoethes[60] the father of the Frisco poetry scene was wiping his tears in gladness.[61]

Later, Gary Snyder read *The Berry Feast*, a poem based on Amerindian coyote tales. He also read his translations from Han-shan.[62] In such an important occasion, with the participation of the famous poet Kenneth Rexroth and Jack Kerouac, the spiritual leader of the Beat Generation, as well as Ginsberg's sensational poem *Howl which was* frequently exposed by the media and public opinion later on, the impact of this poetry reading was actually far more than just in the sense of literary history.

As Chung Ling said, the fact that Snyder was able to read his English translation of the CMPs on such an important occasion in literary history itself opened an important channel for the CMPs to enter the pantheon of literary canons. Evidently, the Six Gallery poetry reading of the San Francisco Poetry Renaissance as well as the "Beat poets" involved in that cannot be ignored in compiling anthologies, literary history and even cultural history of the Untied States of America.[63] These poets including Snyder were known by American public overnight, which paved the way for the later canon construction of Snyder's translated poems in the sense of literary history.

Actually, before this poetry reading, Snyder had already joined Chen Shih Hsiang's tutelage, though he did not complete his translation of Han-shan's poem at that time. After reading Snyder's translation of the CMPs, Achilles Fang, a Chinese literature professor of Harvard University, offered him many suggestions on revisions, and Snyder took Fang's advice and made four pages of notes and revisions. The four-page manuscript is now in the library of Kent State University in the United States. Interestingly, in the third chapter of Kerouac's book *The Dharma Bums*, Snyder, under the pseudonym Japhy Ryder, discussed with Ray Smith (actually, Kerouac) the skills of translating the CMPs and said, "Well, that's what I mean. But my translation has to be approved by the Chinese scholars at the university here before I can do it, and the English expression must be clear and unambiguous."[64] It could be told that Chen Shih Hsiang, Achilles Fangand others were the Chinese scholars to whom Snyder was referring. Then, in Daitokuji Temple in Japan, Snyder also consulted Iriya Yoshitaka, a famous Japanese expert in "Han-shan studies", for advice on translation of the CMPs.[65]

With the guidance of these scholars, Snyder revised his translation of the CMPs several times.[66] After receiving a short note from the publisher who requested to review the CMPs, Snyder typed up the translation after touching it up again on his way back to the United States on a cargo boat.[67] Snyder's humble attitude of seeking advice actually paved the way for the canon construction of the CMPs in American translated literature in a poetic sense. The translated CMPs published after the guidance of scholars were undoubtedly a literary canon jointly shaped by the most gifted scholars at that time, at least it can be said that they are generally accepted and recognized by the academic community. Even when Snyder's translation of the CMPs was published in *The Evergreen Review*, Arthur Waley, a prominent Sinologist in England, wrote to Grove Press to express his confidence in the accuracy of Snyder's translation.[68] Thus, it is safe to say that the 24 Han-shan poems, which Snyder and his scholars worked on together, were in fact a canon at the time.

### 5.3.2.2 Literary Institutions and Literary Journals

Snyder's CMPs translation was published in the fall issue of *The Evergreen Review*, Volume 2, Number 6, in 1958. This magazine was founded in 1957 as a literary journal by Barney Rosset[69] (1922–2012), the publisher who founded Grove Press in 1951. This magazine aimed to bring together the two writing groups of counterculture and anti-traditional style: the emerging post-war American Beat writers and the avant-garde writers who were at the core of "absurd literature" in Europe. Its inaugural issue was not well received, but the second issue took a major turn. It published the work of the core new Beat writers, including Flinty Geddy, Michael McClure, Allen Ginsberg, Gary Snyder and Philip Whalen. Ginsberg's *Howl* and Snyder's *The Berry Feast* were also published in this issue "which brought Beat Writers and *The Evergreen Review* to the forefront of American literature".[70] Since then, the magazine's circulation has soared, which helped the unknown Beat writers receive attention from the American public through this literary venue.

As Ken Jordan put it, "*The Evergreen Review* became more than a literary journal; it became the voice of a movement that helped change literary attitudes and cultural prejudices through the language of art, and it gained a full victory in the end."[71] Snyder's *CMPs* was published the year after *The Evergreen Review* was First issued. *The Evergreen Review* was owned by Grove Press, which was already well known at the time. Meanwhile, with the popularity of the "Beat Generation Movement", the frequent exposure of "Beat writers", and the bold and edgy "Beat poetry" published in it, *The Evergreen Review* soon gained momentum in the American publishing world. Thus, *The Evergreen Review* was credited with the rapid promotion and distribution of Snyder's translation of the CMPs.

In 1958, when Snyder published his translation of the CMPs, *The Dharma Bums*, by Jack Kerouac, the soul of the "Beat Generation", was published almost simultaneously. The issue of *The Evergreen Review* in which *CMPs* appeared also advertised for "just published" *The Dharma Bums* by Viking Press. On the title page of *The Dharma Bums* is the inscription "Dedicated to Han-shan". An influential American avant-garde writer of his time dedicates his work to an "unknown" Tang poet in Chinese literary history who has been dead for over a thousand years. In doing so, Kerouac rehabilitated Han-shan and his poems that had been buried in Chinese literary history and laid an important foundation for the canonization of the CMPs.

In the third chapter of *The Dharma Bums*, Kerouac (alias Smith) and Snyder (alias Ryde) discussed the outstanding character of Chinese poet Han-shan, the remote artistic conception of his poems, and the skills of translating the CMPs. They particularly discussed in detail the translation skills of three poems, "Who takes the Cold Mountain Road", "Once I reached Cold Mountain" and "In the Mountains

It's Cold."[72] Kerouac advocated the five-character translation method (translating five words with five characters), while Snyder thought it best to seek the consent of Chinese scholars first. At the end of the book, Smith climbed a mountain to find his ideal hero, Han-shan. He said, "And suddenly it seemed I saw that unimaginable little Chinese bum standing there, in the fog, with that expressionless humor on his seamed face."[73] In such a portrayal, Han-shan has been obviously Americanized and hippified, being an American tramp "on the road" described by Kerouac in his 1957 masterpiece *On the Road*. The image of the "tramp" was deeply rooted in America at that time, especially in the younger generation.

Regarding the tremendous social impact of the book, Snyder had this to say:

> When his novel *On the Road* was published in 1957, the word 'beat' became famous and overnight America became aware that it had a generation of writers and intellectuals on its hands that was breaking all the rules. This new generation was educated, but it refused to go into academic careers or business or government. It published its poems in its own little magazines. . . . Its members traveled easily, . . . and made their money at almost any kind of work. . . . Better to live simply, be poor, and have the time to wander and write and dig (meaning to penetrate and absorb and enjoy) what was going on in the world.[74]

Considering Kerouac's great influence at the time, it seems fair to say that *On the Road* published in 1957, and *The Dharma Bums* published in 1958, were the pre-preparation and post-promotion for the text travel and canon construction of Han-shan and his poems in the United States. This wise and open-minded "Chinese tramp" was, in the eyes of the young generation at that time, naturally no different from the American tramps who stopped the car in Kerouac's writing. Therefore, on a psychological and emotional level, they would produce a great deal of affection for this Chinese poet and his poems. Thus, in turn, the CMPs had undoubtedly earned a good reputation and had social effect in the canon construction of the American literary polysystem.

Indeed, for most American readers at the time, the authority of the CMPs rested entirely on such influential figures as Synder (the translator) and Kerouac, not just on the text itself. It is no exaggeration to say that the name "Kerouac" greatly increased the popularity of Han-shan and his poems at that time. With the great influence of Kerouac, Snyder's elaborate rewriting of Han-shan's image, and the recommendation of *The Evergreen Review*, the CMPs have made a great step forward on the road to canonization. Therefore, someone says that Snyder was not the greatest contributor to the dissemination of the CMPs, but Kerouac's *The Dharma Bums*.[75] Sun Qi (孙旗) offers his own view that

> because of Han-shan's ragged dress and insane behavior, and Kerouac's vigorous advocacy, the idolization of Han-shan was smoothly shaped. CMPs were also idolized in Snyder's writing. For instance, in his translation of the short preface, Snyder wrote, 'They have become immortals . . .'. This

Americanized Han-shan is the ancestor of hippies'. . . . Strictly speaking, the ancestor of hippies was not Han-shan, but the figures such as Kerouac and Snyder.[76]

The canonization of a text is often closely related to criticism. In 1962, the British sinologist David Hawkes (1923–2009) published an article in *Journal of the American Oriental Society* which fiercely criticized Snyder's translation of the CMPs:

> Of all the English translations I have seen, I think Snyder's is the most unconscionable. His translation is quite inaccurate, and from time to time descends into an outrageous absurdity and folly. It makes him translate gold and jade as diamonds and ermine.[77]

Hawkes was obviously critical of some of Snyder's localization in the translation process. However, the choice of translation strategy actually depends on the translator's consideration of various translation norms and the prevailing ideology in the cultural polysystem of arrivals at that time. Localization in Snyder's translation is not a kind of cultural narcissism, but a means that the translator hopes to use to provoke a sense of identity and cultural belonging of the target readers. In fact, the use of such a means is where the translator hopes that the Chinese poet Han-shan will influence the aesthetic identity of American readers, and of course, the translator intends to cater to the expectations and norms of target readers. In fact, it is the implicit "Americanized" and "hippie" strategy that has earned the translation the widest readership. Despite his blunt criticism, Hawkes acknowledged that of all the translations, Snyder's reads most like poetry. The criticism and compliments by the renowned sinologist has greatly enhanced the visibility of Snyder's CMPs translation in sinological field and promoted the process of canonization of these translated poems.

### 5.3.3 Snyder's Translation of the CMPs and Anthologies of American Translated Literature

Undoubtedly, being included in anthologies or university textbooks is the most important way and evidence of textual canonization. Some scholars point out that there are two conditions for the formation of literary canon: (1) cultural and educational institutions; and (2) selectionism—cultural and educational institutions including schools (especially universities), publishing institutions (especially those with an official position such as the National Archives), newspapers, journals, libraries, foundations, seminars, lectures, radio and television. Selectionism is the operating principle followed by the literary and educational institutions of the dominant culture. That is to select and edit the texts from the vast array of ancient and modern works that are conducive to normative effectiveness and contemporary thought. Then those selected works will be included in curricula or examination lists or be written into literature anthologies, series and histories, serving as language learning materials.[78] It goes without saying that the educational system has the power to "legitimize the dominant culture".[79]

The American literary anthology is a result of universal higher education. According to literary historian Paul Lauter, the creation of this new cultural history is "part of a larger process of building a 'worldview seen from the margins' and a necessary precondition for 'transforming the margins into centers'".[80] That is to say, if marginal and unofficial texts are to acquire the status of classic literature, they must seek to be included in the anthologies that bear the hallmarks of this new cultural history. Only then is the classic status of a text finally accepted by the classic makers of a given period. Michell Marie Pagni, an American scholar, argues that it is righteous to determine the status of an American literary canon according to literary anthologies, because "anthologies are selections from a much larger number of American literary texts, presenting a kind of canon". She also remarks that

> the fact that anthology and canonical studies have not been combined until recently is partly a result of the evolution of anthologies. It was not until the 1960s and 1970s that scholars were able to use anthologies to explore the topic of canonicity.[81]

This situation is certainly in line with what Zhou Yingxiong (周英雄) mentioned earlier,

> As the number of students enrolled in British and American literature departments continued to decline, and as civil rights awareness was on the rise at the time, the literature departments, in order to save their reputations and respond to the needs of minority groups, reformed their curricula by revising the required classics and adding women's literature, black literature, English literature from non-Anglo-American regions, and other subject-oriented courses.[82]

It was in the midst of this climate of scholarship and educational reform that *The Anthology of Chinese Literature: From Early Times to the Fourteenth Century* was published in 1965, edited by Cyril Birch (1925–2018), a leading American professor of comparative literature and chair of the Department of Oriental Languages at the University of California, Berkeley. The anthology was published by the prestigious Grove Press and the "Evergreen" edition of the anthology was published in 1967. It's worth mentioning that this edition is the 11th printing of the book. In fact, the anthology received an overwhelmingly positive response upon publication. *The Asian Student* viewed it as "the best English translation of Chinese literature anthology in recent years"; the *Library Journal* said,

> The book ... is truly the first English translation of Chinese literature anthology and it is rich and rewarding; it is highly readable for students and general

readers alike. . . . (The selected) poetry, prose, drama, and fiction are all highly representative.

Herbert Franke (1914–2011), the German sinologist, also commented the year after the anthology was published (1966),

> The preparation of a literary anthology is a laborious and unpleasant task. The editors expected to include some lesser-known titles, while the reader usually prefers to see a fully representative anthology that includes many famous texts. This new literary anthology is quite successful in combining these two principles.[83]

The editors also confidently declare that "this anthology is one of the most comprehensive in the English-speaking world." Remarkably, this anthology has also been designated as the Chinese Literature Translations Series by UNESCO. In this way, the authoritative status of the anthology was established, along with its authority and guidance as a textbook in the teaching of world English literature. In fact, in the 1960s and 1970s, the anthology was the most commonly used textbook in East Asian and Chinese literature courses at American universities.

In terms of selection, the editor said, "Our definition of literature, first of all, has been modern, Western rather than traditional Chinese, exclusive rather than comprehensive."[84] Subsequently, he mentioned the major categories recognized by Chinese bibliography: *ching, shih, tzu, chi,* namely the classics, historical writings, philosophical writings and "collections" (of the verse and prose of individuals); and claimed that the anthology was also based on the selected materials collected from this system (Chinese bibliography). However, the editor of the book of "*ching*" (classics) only selected *Shijing* (《诗经》, *Classic of Poetry)*; the editor responsible for the book of "*shih*" (historical writings) selected *Shiji* (《史记》, *Records of the Grand History)* of Sima Qian (司马迁) and the editor of the book of "*tzu*" (philosophical writings and collections) selected almost nothing. Regarding the selections, the editors argued, "We did not intend to deny the literariness of *Mengzi* and *Liezi* and others. And we hoped that readers will not struggle too much with those early Chinese concepts and theories when reading and enjoying the selection."

> Naturally we have hoped to be reasonably representative, but not at the risk of presenting a writer of first rank in drab or ill-fitting garb. In particular, we have tried to disperse the air of anonymity which the anthology piece too often seems to exude. . . . For this reason we have preferred to allow more space to each of a smaller total number of writers, even though as a result many names of high lustre must drop out altogether.[85]

The CMPs selected by Cyril Birch are all 24 CMPs translated by Snyder, as well as the preface by Lü Qiuyin (阎丘胤).[86] In this literary anthology, CMPs occupy enough space. Even for the works of Tao Yuanming (陶渊明), the "master of idyllic poetry", the anthology only includes his famous "*Taohuayuan Ji*" (《桃花源记》), "Peach Blossom Garden") and seven idyllic poems; as for the works of Li Bai (李白), the "Poet Saint", only 10 poems and 1 lyric of him were included; for the "Poet-sage", works of Du Fu (杜甫), only 5 poems of him were included. In Birch's literary anthology, "the history of Chinese literature was rewritten, and Han-shan, a marginal poet in China, was elevated to a mainstream poet."[87] The influence of the dissemination of the CMPs in the United States in the 1950s and 1960s is thus evident. Although the compilation of literary history and anthology was, to some extent, influenced by personal preferences, it is undeniable that this anthology represents and reflects, to the greatest extent possible, the dominant ideology of the time and the common will of the various patrons. Thus, it also embodies, to the greatest extent, the identification and interpretation of literary standards and literary values by the cultural polysystem of the United States at the time. It is through this authoritative anthology that the classic status of the CMPs in the English-speaking world was finally established in form.

Like a mirror, Han-shan reflects various literary, cultural and social problems of the United States at the time. After traveling to the United States, this wise Chinese poet prescribed highly relevant Chinese remedies for post-war American literature, culture and society as a whole. Han-shan's love of nature and his philosophical way of thinking as a hermit brought a strange and exotic cultural experience to the "Beat Generation" in the post-war American context. Standing on such a cultural turning point, this Eastern wisdom offered American society a new possibility for spiritual redemption and literary reformation. Specifically speaking, in the face of the social problems, literary vacuum and cultural identity crisis in post–World War II America, Snyder carefully selected and successfully portrayed Han-shan, a Chinese Zen poet, who worshiped nature and lived a tranquil and causal life, for post-war America.

Against this background, the translator creatively adapted and reconstructed the Chinese elements of self-expression, self-identity and self-realization thoughts in the CMPs. At the same time, he took the dominant ideology of the American cultural polysystem as a reference, deeply explored the significance of the Zen aesthetics and philosophical thoughts in the CMPs for American society, and found a remedy for spiritual redemption and literary enlightenment for the "Beat Generation", American society as well as the literary reform of that time, "return to nature". Snyder himself is known as the "Back to Nature Poet" or "Poet Laureate of Deep Ecology". As a popular artist and cultural figure, Snyder has played an important role in the movement to protect wilderness, particularly on the West Coast of America. It is no exaggeration to say that he made a significant contribution to the flourishing of American ecological literature and the growth of the American environmental movement.

Undeniably, Snyder was deeply influenced by Chinese classical poetry, especially by Han-shan and his poems. Meanwhile, his interest in Han-shan and his poems, the various discursive variables and forces involved at the time, made it possible for Han-shan and his poems which were not valued in Chinese literary history to achieve the status of a literary classic in a foreign country. On the one hand, it can be said that the interlingual travel and canon construction of Han-shan and His Poems echo the American cultural polysystem. On the other hand, the polysystem has inadvertently selected and achieved the canonical status of Han-shan and his poems. In fact, the coincidental literary encounters, the efforts of sinologists and Zen masters, the symbolic Six Gallery poetry readings in literary history, the promotion of *The Evergreen Review*, Jack Kerouac, and Grove Press, Snyder's localized reconstructions, the institutionalized selection of literary historians, and the homogeneity of the target audience, all of these elements undoubtedly constitute the most vivid literary pictures and cultural memories of American cultural polysystem of that time.

## Notes

1 Translated by Gary Snyder.
2 Sun Qi. *Han-shan and Hippies*. Taizhong: Putian Press, 1974: 45.
3 Sun Qi. *Han-shan and Hippies*. Taizhong: Putian Press, 1974: 48.
4 Sun Qi. *Han-shan and Hippies*. Taizhong: Putian Press, 1974: 51.
5 Leo Ou-fan Lee. *My Harvard University Years*. Nanjing: Jiangsu Education Publishing House, 2005: 99.
6 Sun Qi. *Han-shan and Hippies*. Taizhong: Putian Press, 1974: 49–50.
7 G. Snyder. *Turtle Island*. New York: New Directions, 1974: 107.
8 G. Snyder. The Etiquette of Freedom. // *The Practice of the Wild*. Berkeley: North Point Press, 1990: 6.
9 G. Snyder. The Etiquette of Freedom. // *The Practice of the Wild*. Berkeley: North Point Press, 1990: 7.
10 E. Weinberger. The Role of the Author in Translation. // S. Allen (ed.), *Translation of Poetry and Poetic Prose: Proceedings of Nobel Symposium 110*. Singapore, NJ, London and Hong Kong: World Scientific Publishing Co. Pte. Ltd., 1999: 245.
11 Chung Ling. *American Poetry and Chinese Dream*. Guilin: Guangxi Normal University Press, 2003: 143.
12 E. Weinberger. The Role of the Author in Translation. // S. Allen (ed.), *Translation of Poetry and Poetic Prose: Proceedings of Nobel Symposium 110*. Singapore, NJ, London and Hong Kong: World Scientific Publishing Co. Pte. Ltd., 1999: 245.
13 D. Allen. *The New American Poetry*. New York: Grove Press, 1960: 420–421.
14 G. Snyder. *A Place in Space: Ethics, Aesthetics, and Watersheds*. Washington, DC: Counterpoint, 1995: 92.
15 Zhou Yingxiong. Canon, Subjectivity, Comparative Literature. // Chen Dongrong & Chen Zhangfang (eds.), *Canon and Literature Teaching*. Taipei: Comparative Literature Association and Department of English at National Central University, 1995: 5.
16 Nan Fan. History of Literature and Classics. Theoretical Studies In Literature and Art, 1998 (5): 11.
17 M. Vidal. (Mis)Translating Degree Zero: Ideology and Conceptual Art. // Pérez María Calzada (ed.), *Apropos of Ideology: Translation Studies on Ideology-Ideologies in Translation Studies*. Manchester: St. Jerome Publishing, 2003: 85.
18 M. Vidal. (Mis)Translating Degree Zero: Ideology and Conceptual Art. // Pérez María Calzada (ed.), *Apropos of Ideology: Translation Studies on Ideology-Ideologies in Translation Studies*. Manchester: St. Jerome Publishing, 2003: 72.
19 C. Nord. Function and Loyalty in Bible Translation. // Pérez María Calzada (ed.), *Apropos of Ideology: Translation Studies on Ideology-Ideologies in Translation Studies*. Manchester: St. Jerome Publishing, 2003: 90.

20 C. Schäffner. Third Ways and New Centres: Ideological Unity Or Difference? // Pérez María Calzada (ed.), *Apropos of Ideology: Translation Studies on Ideology-Ideologies in Translation Studies*. Manchester: St. Jerome Publishing, 2003: 24.

21 C. Nord. Function and Loyalty in Bible Translation. // Pérez María Calzada (ed.), *Apropos of Ideology: Translation Studies on Ideology-Ideologies in Translation Studies*. Manchester: St. Jerome Publishing, 2003: 90.

22 C. Schäffner. Third Ways and New Centres: Ideological Unity Or Difference? // Pérez María Calzada (ed.), *Apropos of Ideology: Translation Studies on Ideology-Ideologies in Translation Studies*. Manchester: St. Jerome Publishing, 2003: 23.

23 C. Nord. Function and Loyalty in Bible Translation. // Pérez María Calzada (ed.), *Apropos of Ideology: Translation Studies on Ideology-Ideologies in Translation Studies*. Manchester: St. Jerome Publishing, 2003: 94.

24 C. Nord. Function and Loyalty in Bible Translation. // Pérez María Calzada (ed.), *Apropos of Ideology: Translation Studies on Ideology-Ideologies in Translation Studies*. Manchester: St. Jerome Publishing, 2003: 109.

25 Wang Dongfeng. An Invisible Hand: Ideological Manipulation in the Practice of Translation. *Chinese Translators Journal*, 2003 (5): 17.

26 Martha P. Y. Cheung. Translation as Discourse: A Re-reading of Wei Yi and Lin Shu's Chinese Translation of *Uncle Tom's Cabin*. *Chinese Translators Journal*, 2003 (2): 19.

27 G. Snyder. *The Real Work: Interviews & Talks 1964–1979*. New York: New Directions Publishing Corporation, 1980: 94.

28 G. Snyder. *The Real Work: Interviews & Talks 1964–1979*. New York: New Directions Publishing Corporation, 1980: 117.

29 P. Gabriel. Gary Snyder: The Postmodern Poet (trans Jian Yulong. //Special Issue of The Poet Snyder: From Beat to Postmodernist. *Contemporary* (Taipei), 1990 (53): 21.

30 Cai Zhenxing. Breakthrough and Proposition: On Snyder's Imagination of *Mountains and Rivers Without End*. *Chung-Wai Literary Monthly*, 2004 (5): 106.

31 Liu Sheng. The Implication of Traditional Chinese Culture in Gary Snyder's Poms. *Foreign Language Education*, 2001 (4): 78.

32 Suzuki Teitaro, professor of Buddhist philosophy at Otani University, is a leading expert in the field of Buddhist philosophy. He was also the first person to introduce Zen to the English-speaking world. His major Buddhist works consist of more than 10 books published in English and about 20 written in Japanese, including *Essays in Zen Buddhism* and *Zen and Japanese Culture*.

33 Alan Watts was one of the most famous theological experts with a Ph.D. in the United States in the last century. He made his mark in Zen philosophy, Indian philosophy and Chinese philosophy. He published more than 20 philosophical and religious psychology works, among which the most representative works are *The Way of Zen* and *The Spirit of Zen*.

34 In 1951, Snyder also read *Laozi* 老子 (*Laozi*) translated by Paul Carus (1852–1919) and *Zhuangzi* 庄子 (*Zhuangzi*) translated by Lin Yutang 林语堂 (1895–1976). Later, he read Confucius, Japanese haiku (He received a four-volume haiku in 1951) and some Buddhist scriptures. By studying Chinese and landscape paintings, he learned about Zen thoughts. See D. Meltzer. *San Francisco Beat: Talking with the Poets*. San Francisco, CA: City Lights Books, 2001: 280.) It can be seen that Chinese and Japanese cultures have an influence on Snyder's poetic thoughts, writing and translation of that time and later.

35 Quoted from P. Murphy. *A Place for Wayfaring: The Poetry and Prose of Gary Snyder*. Corvallis: Oregon State University Press, 2000: 8.

36 Jia Ruifang. Spokesman, Mirror, and Utopia: Comments on Gary Snyder's translation of Cold Mountain Poems. // Chang Yaoxin (ed.), *Multiple Perspectives: Essays on Comparative Studies of Culture and Literature*. Tianjin: Nankai University Press, 1995: 61.

37 G. Snyder. *Riprap & Cold Mountain Poems*. San Francisco: Grey Fox Press, 1965: 33.

38 Chung Ling. *American Poetry and Chinese Dream*. Guilin: Guangxi Normal University Press, 2003: 143.
39 M. Davidson. Preface. // *The San Francisco Renaissance: Poetics and Community at Mid-century*. Cambridge: Cambridge University Press, 1989: xi.
40 Lu Wenhua 陆文华 wrote in his essay 美国西皮大迁移 ("The Great Migration of Hippies in the United States") that a large number of hippies in the US moved to the southwestern state of New Mexico, organizing the so-called "people's commune", "youth commune", "new society" and "Utopia", with at least 1,000,000 members and at least 1,000 communes. Quoted from Sun Qi. *Han-shan and Hippies*. Taizhong: Putian Press, 1974: 51.
41 R. Kern. Seeing the World Without Language. // *Orientalism, Modernism and the American Poem*. New York: Cambridge University Press, 1996: 236–237.
42 A. Lefevere. *Translation, Rewriting and Manipulation of Literary Fame*. London and New York: Routledge, 1992: vii.
43 L. Venulti. *The Scandal of Translation, Towards an Ethics of Difference*. London and New York: Routledge, 1998: 67.
44 W. Benjamin. The Task of the Translator. // R. Schutle & J. Biguenet (eds.), *Theories of Translation: An Anthology of Essays from Dryden to Derrida*. Chicago: The University of Chicago Press, 1992: 81.
45 L. Venuti. *The Scandal of Translation, Towards an Ethics of Difference*. London and New York: Routledge, 1998: 67.
46 Quoted from Zhao Yiheng. *The Muse from Cathay*. Chengdu: Sichuan People's Publishing House, 1985: 2.
47 Chung Lin. *American Poetry and Chinese Dream*. Guilin: Guangxi Normal University Press, 2003: 140.
48 Qu Hong. Perspectives on Gary Snyder. *Foreign Literature Review*, 1994 (1): 33–34.
49 A. Lefevere. *Translation, Rewriting and Manipulation of Literary Fame*. London and New York: Routledge, 1992: 14–17.
50 Chung Ling. *American Poetry and Chinese Dream*. Guilin: Guangxi Normal University Press, 2003: 44.
51 Chung Ling. *American Poetry and Chinese Dream*. Guilin: Guangxi Normal University Press, 2003: 38.
52 Zhao Yiheng. *The Muse from Cathay*. Shanghai: Shanghai Translation Press, 2003: 326.
53 Chung Ling. *The Circulation of Cold Mountain Poems. Essays on Literary Criticism*. Taipei: Times Cultural Publishing Co. 1984: 9.
54 Zhao Yiheng. *Confucian, Buddhist, and Taoist socialists*. //Special Issue of The Poet Snyder: From Beat to Postmodernist. *Contemporary* (Taipei), 1990 (53): 27.
55 Jin Yong 金庸 regarded him as his literary confidant. In the "After Word" in Tianlong Babu天龙八部, Jin Yong wrote passionately, "This book is dedicated to a friend I love, Mr. Chen Shih Hsiang."
56 P. Kahn. Han-shan in English. *Renditions*, 1986 (Spring): 145.
57 It is worth noting that Chen Shih Hsiang's translation of "Wenfu" 文赋 ("The Poetic Exposition on Literature") was also included in the 1965 edition of Birch's *Anthology of Chinese Literature: From Early Times to the Fourteenth Century*.
58 G. Snyder. After Word. // *Riprap & Cold Mountain Poems*. Washington, DC: Shoemaker & Hoard, 2004: 66.
59 That is, Ginsberg.
60 That is, Kenneth Rexroth.
61 J. Kerouac. *The Dharma Bums*. Frogmore: Panther Books Ltd., 1974: 14.
62 M. Davidson. Introduction: Enabling Fictions. // *The San Francisco Renaissance: Poetics and Community at Mid-century*. Cambridge: Cambridge University Press, 1989: 4.
63 Literary historians generally identify the Sixth Gallery poetry reading as October 13 of that year. Snyder's own account, however, is that "at the end of October, we had a poetry

reading. Lamantia, MacCollum, Whalen, Ginsberg, and I read." See also G. Snyder. *A Place in Space: Ethics, Aesthetics, and Watersheds: New and Selected Prose*. Washington, DC: Counterpoint, 1995: 8.
64 J. Kerouac. *The Dharma Bums*. Frogmore: Panther Books Ltd., 1974: 19.
65 Kodama nari Hide儿玉实英. 美国诗歌与日本文化 (*American Poetry and Japanese Culture*). Translated by Yang Zhanwu 杨占武. Xi'an: Shaanxi People's Education Press, 1993: 348.
66 The first, second and final drafts of Snyder's translation of CMPs are in the library of Kent State University, USA.
67 Kodama nari Hide儿玉实英. 美国诗歌与日本文化(*American Poetry and Japanese Culture*). Translated by Yang Zhanwu 杨占武. Xi'an: Shaanxi People's Education Press, 1993: 280.
68 Snyder mentioned this in a letter to the American scholar Fackler. See Leed J. Gary Snyder: An Unpublished Preface. *Journal of Modern Literature*, Mar. 1986, 13 (1): 178.
69 Barney Rosset, the famous American publisher, founded Grove Press at the age of 29. During his publishing career, he brought under his umbrella many post-war star writers including Henry Miller, Borges, Duras, Eugene Ionesco and many others. He has published such banned books as *Lady Chatterley's Lover*, *Lolita*, and *Tropic of Cancer* that other American publishers dare not involve. In 2008, Bassett received the National Book Award for Outstanding Contribution to the United States.
70 K. Jordan. *A Brief History of the Evergreen Review* [OL]. www.evergreenreview.com/100/history.html. [2005-11-11].
71 K. Jordan. *A Brief History of the Evergreen Review* [OL]. www.evergreenreview.com/100/history.html. [2005-11-11].
72 Poems translated by Red Pine.
73 J. Kerouac. *The Dharma Bums*. Frogmore: Panther Books Ltd., 1974: 174.
74 G. Snyder. *A Place in Space: Ethics, Aesthetics, and Watersheds: New and Selected Prose*. Washington, DC: Counterpoint, 1995: 9.
75 G. Snyder. *A Place in Space: Ethics, Aesthetics, and Watersheds: New and Selected Prose*. Washington, DC: Counterpoint, 1995: 9.
76 Sun Qi 孙旗. 寒山与西皮 (*Han-shan and Hippies*). Taizhong: Putian Press, 1974: 63.
77 D. Hawkes. Book Review: *Cold Mountain: 100 Poems by the T'ang poet Han-shan*. Translated and with an Introduction by Burton Watson. *Journal of the American Oriental Society*, 1962 (4): 596.
78 Zhang Jinzhong. The Canon of the Other: The Discussion of Canonicality and African American Women. // Chen Dongrong & Chen Zhangfang (eds.), *Canon and Literature Teaching*. Taipei: Society for Comparative Literature/Department of English and American Languages and Literatures, National Central University, 1995: 153–154.
79 Tao Dongfeng. Literary Classics and Cultural Power. *Chinese Comparative Literature*, 2004 (3): 68.
80 Quoted in Shan Dexing. Creating Tradition: Literary Anthologies and Chinese-American Literature. // *Inscriptions and Representations: Chinese American and Cultural Studies*. Taipei: Maitian Press, 2000: 242.
81 Quoted in Shan Dexing 单德兴. 创造传统：文学选集与华裔美国文学. (Creating Tradition: Literary Anthologies and Chinese-American Literature). // 铭刻与再现——华裔美国文学与文化论集 (*Inscriptions and Representations: Chinese American Literary and Cultural Studies*). Taipei: Maitian Press, 2000: 242.
82 Zhou Yingxiong 周英雄. 必读经典、主体性、比较文学 ("Canon, Subjectivity, Comparative Literature"). // Chen Dongrong 陈东荣, Chen Zhangfang 陈长房. 典律与文学教学 (*Canon and Literature Teaching*). Taibei, China: Comparative Literature Association/Department of English at "National" Central University, 1995: 2.
83 H. Franke. Book Review: *Anthology of Chinese Literature: From Early Times to the Fourteenth Century*. C. Birch. *Journal of the American Oriental Society*, 1966, 86 (2): 254.

84 C. Birch. *Anthology of Chinese Literature: From Early Times to the Fourteenth Century*. New York: Grove Press, 1965/1967: xxiv.
85 C. Birch. *Anthology of Chinese Literature: From Early Times to the Fourteenth Century*. New York: Grove Press, 1965/1967: xxv.
86 According to Herbert Franke, Birch chose Snyder's translation of CMPs over Burton Watson's for reasons of copyright. See H. Franke. Book Review: *Anthology of Chinese Literature: From Early Times to the Fourteenth Century*. C. Birch. *Journal of the American Oriental Society*, 1966, 86(2): 255. But this claim is not really valid. Snyder's *CMPs* was published by *The Evergreen Review* under, and Watson's *100 CMPs* 寒山诗100首 were first published by Grove Press in 1962. The author believes that Snyder's translation was chosen because of the enormous social impact of his translation at the time and the high reputation of its various patrons.
87 Chung Ling 钟玲. 美国诗与中国梦 *(American Poetry and the Chinese Dream)*. Guilin: Guangxi Normal University Press, 2003: 38.

# 6 Return Journey of the CMPs and Their Canon Reconstruction in Chinese Literature

The previous chapter explores how manifold discourse variables jointly contributed to the canonization of Snyder's English translation of the CMPs in the American polysystem of the 1950s and 1960s. Indeed, thanks to the enormous social impact and literary reputation at that time, the CMPs began to be adored in its departure land China because of its legendary literary journey abroad. The CMPs, which had "wandered a million miles", finally ushered in the return journey of "on their way home to Cold Mountain" around the 1960s.

## 6.1 Travel and Return

In terms of the distinction between "travel", "diaspora", "exile" and "migration", Clifford (1945–) once points out, "Diasporas usually presuppose longer distances and a separation more like exile."[1] What makes "diaspora" different from "travel" is that "it is not temporary. It involves dwelling, maintaining communities, having collective homes away from home (and in this, it is different from exile, with its frequently individualist focus."[2] That is to say, for Clifford "diaspora" refers to a long-term state, "travel" to a transitory one, and "exile" to a personal choice. Such an interpretation is in fact rather general and crude.

The dictionary definition of the word "diaspora" refers to the body of Jews (or Jewish communities) outside Palestine or modern Israel, as well as to the dispersion or spreading of something that was originally localized (as a people or language or culture) or to people away from their own country to live and work in other countries. The term "exile" can carry a multitude of different meanings such as, the act of being voluntarily absent from home or country, the state of being sent to live in another country for punishment or political reasons, or a person who willfully chooses to live outside their country. While "migration" refers to the movement of persons from one country or locality to another or to a group of people migrating together (especially in some given time period), it can also refer to the periodic passage of groups of animals (especially birds or fishes) from one region to another for feeding or breeding.

In essence, what distinguishes "travel" from some particular forms of displacement such as "diaspora", "exile" or "migration" is the cyclical mode of going back and forth. "Travel", from the very beginning, presupposes an important "return

DOI: 10.4324/9781003415749-7

journey". After all, the traveler will eventually return to the place of origin, the "home" from which he or she originally sets out. The existence of "home" and the return of the traveler are significant prerequisites for the establishment of "travel", "traveler" and other concepts concerning "travel". With regard to returning, someone states that

> bringing it all back home is nevertheless a dialectical movement. The home we return to is never the home we left, and the baggage we bring back with us will—eventually—alter it forever. The assemblage of memories, images, tastes, and objects that clings to our return will mark the place of that return.[3]

It should be clear that when examining the process of text travel, besides the departure, spatial passage and arrivals, we should also consider the return journey. It is fair to say that after a trip, the text always returns home with more or less different "luggage". Some are depressed by a failed travel experience; Some of them nonetheless have gained a new look and re-examination from their "family members" because of their fruitful travels, and may even usher in the opportunity of canon reconstruction.

From the perspective of Traveling Theory, the dominant ideology and mainstream poetics among other institutional contexts in the polysystem of the departure constitute the initial environment, which is called by Edward Said a place where "the idea came to birth or entered discourse". The confusing life and unorthodox literary origin of Han-shan, the unrestrained form, and the colloquial content of his poems are both hard to be recognized by the dominant ideology and dominant poetics that are primarily characterized by orthodoxy and elegance in Han-shan's home country. Coupled with the conservative literary standpoint of various patrons and the long-standing inferior literary status of popular and religious literature, All of this consigns Han-shan and his poems to a bumpy literary fate within the Chinese polysystem from the very beginning and on their intralinguistic travel. However, after breaking free from the constraints of this realistic policy, social and literary tradition and beginning their interlingual journey, Han-shan and his poems "accidentally" gained a prominent literary reputation and classical status, and even entered the grand narratives of the history of Eastern and Western literature and literary anthologies for a time, creating a fierce "Han-shan fever" in Japan and the United States. It was due to this historical opportunity and under such literary context that Han-shan and his poems began their belated but undoubtedly deserved journey back home.

When Han-shan returned as an "overseas traveler" to the polysystem of its departure where he had once been refused, the long-lost interest and enthusiasm for Han-shan and his poems was miraculously and instantly ignited, and he became a hot topic and object of concern, with all sectors of society reviving the earlier sporadic "Han-shan Studies". As a result, all walks of life, from the civil to the official, from the general public to the intellectual elite, from translation to publishing, from academic research to cultural tourism products, began to explore the connection of Han-shan and his poems with themselves, and "Han-shan Studies" has seen a flourishing scene rarely seen in a thousand years in the Chinese polysystem. In an unprecedented move, Han-shan and his poems achieved their canon reconstruction in the history of their homeland literature, gaining a long-overdue and coveted place in literary history. Compared to the almost dead-end of intralingual literature before the 1960s, and the coincidental interlingual literary journey, such a return journey is a well-deserved glory for Han-shan and his poems.

In her article "The Circulation of Cold Mountain Poems" (寒山诗的流传), Chung Ling remarked on the return journey after the CMPs gained the canonical status of the translated literature in the English-speaking world, and she said, "The fact that CMPs became popular in the United States and Japan must have inspired the whole country, thus leading to a well-deserved and glorious return journey of Han-shan." While it is true when these words are used to describe the reasons for the initial return of the CMPs to Chinese literary history, it would be somewhat absolute to summarize the canon reconstruction of it in the writing of the literary history. In addition to the "external influences" mentioned here, manifold factors such as the transmutation of literary norms within the Chinese polysystem, the transformation of academic research paradigms, and the historical changes in the subject's cultural norms cannot be ignored. Indeed, it is all of these factors that played some role in shaping the conditions for Han-Shan and his poems to win them a canonical status in the history of Chinese literature.

## 6.2 Return Journey of the CMPs and Their Canon Reconstruction

Due to the outbreak of the Cultural Revolution (1966–1976), the CMPs were withdrawn from mainland literary history and academic researches, while in Hong Kong and Taiwan, they had sparked another wave of "Han-shan fever" because of their special significance in comparative literature and comparative cultural studies. This was, of course, more due to the influence of the "Han-shan fever" that was in full swing overseas, especially in the United States. This influence was first felt in Hong Kong in the late 1950s, with enthusiastic response.

### *6.2.1 CMPs in 1960s Hong Kong*

In 1959 (the year of 2503 in terms of the Buddhist calendar, which takes the year of Sakyamuni nirvana as the first year), the-first-of-its-kind *Poems of Han-shan and Appendix of Poems of Shi-de* (《寒山子诗：拾得诗附》), a photocopy of an edition of the Song Dynasty (960–1279), was published and distributed by Hong Kong Yongjiu Fangsheng Fund (香港永久放生基金会). The most influential article of that time, however, was "The Resurrection of the Poet Monk Han-shan" (诗僧寒山的复活), published in *Ming Pao Monthly*, Vol. 1, No. 11, in November 1966 by Hu Juren (胡菊人). The article was published at the time when the mainland was hit by the Cultural Revolution (1966–1976). In a bid to preserve Chinese culture outside the mainland, *Ming Pao Monthly*, a literary publication was founded in Hong Kong in 1966 by the famous Hong Kong writer, Louis Cha Leung-yung (1924–2018). At that time, Louis Cha Leung-yung and his martial arts (historical) novels, as well as *Ming Pao*, which was founded by him in 1959, had already enjoyed a high reputation in the Hong Kong newspaper industry. The article published in *Ming Pao Monthly*, therefore attracted a wide readership in Hong Kong at that time, thus spearheading a new wave of "Han-shan fever" in Hong Kong, which significantly contributed to the continuation and the future prosperity of "Han-shan Studies".

Hu's essay quoted Philip Mairet (1886–1975), a renowned American scholar and translator, as the prologue: "Ideas often pass beyond geographical boundaries and periods of time, germinate and regenerate as soon as they meet people with the right temperament and emotions for them to grow," which implicitly presented the relationship between the CMPs and Snyder.[4] In the first part, the author introduces it by saying that,

> In recent years, a lot has been written about the Beat Generation, so there is no need to talk about it again. However, reading their work has aroused my interest in finding out more about them, and I have discovered something interesting. Although the Beat Generation was produced in the United States, the person they admire, whom they regard as their teacher and spiritual leader, is a Chinese, a poet of the Tang dynasty, a poet-monk. It is Han-shan, who was not included in the *300 Tang Poems*.[5]

Hu Juren (胡菊人) points out that the American "Beat Generation" having access to Han-shan and his CMPs was attributed to the efforts of a poet—Gary Snyder. It is clear that Hu admired this poet, Gary Snyder, as in the following words:

> Snyder is the most highly regarded beat poet in American scholarship, a man and a writer who has not been subjected to any attack from the society. I am afraid that many university professors and sinologists have not been able to catch up with him in his knowledge of Chinese and Japanese literature. His translations of Chinese poems (especially CMPs) have shocked the whole sinological world.[6]

After describing Snyder's personal experience, Hu concludes that

> he is the modern Han-shan of the 1960s in the United States.... His translation of CMPs is to inspire and provide some reference to his fellow writers (he was one of the leading figures of the Beat Generation).[7]

From the reader's point of view, there is no doubt that such a description had greatly enhanced the legendary complexion of the Tang Dynasty poet Han-shan and the modern American poet Snyder among their target readers. This subject matter, for Hong Kong people, not only enriched their literary history cultivation, but also an excellent conversation topic after dinner. At the same time, the debate between elegance and vulgarity really gained little attention in highly commercialized Hong

Kong. On the contrary, popular books "maintain an overwhelming dominance in the Hong Kong reading market."[8] Thus, the legend of Han-shan and his poems, which are popular and simple, found the best entrance into the public and academic world in Hong Kong.

From the theoretical perspective of "patron", it was the influence of Louis Cha Leung-yung in the newspaper industry and the good reputation of *Ming Pao* Publications at that time that created an opportunity for Hu's article to be well-known, thus contributing to the literary fame of Han-shan and his poems in Hong Kong. In gaining attention from all quarters, this article also naturally elevated the literary status of the poet Han-shan and his long-dismissed CMPs. The article explores in detail the sociocultural factors that led to the resurgence of Han-shan in the United States, starting with the tripartite relationship between the Beat Generation, Snyder and Han-shan. On the surface, it is an analysis of the cross-cultural integration of the CMPs, but in fact, it must have made considerable waves among the "trendy youth" of Hong Kong who was also "attracted to the Beat Generation's practices and experiences" at that time. In addition, because of the academic orientation of *Ming Pao Monthly*, the academic community was also intrigued by Han-shan and his poems through this article. The CMPs, which had been "hidden" by the academic community in Chinese mainland during 1966–1976, were "resurrected" in Hong Kong, where the political environment was relatively liberal, and became one of the hottest topics in the media and academic circles at the time. This was also the starting point for a second wave of "Han-shan fever" in Hong Kong and Taiwan.

It is worth noting that the real heat source of "Han-shan fever" in both Taiwan and Hong Kong did not originate in Hong Kong. It could be suggested that because of the commercial nature of its society people were less interested in Han-shan's ideas, which were not utilitarian-oriented, preached seclusion, and a return to nature. Ergo, the readership of the CMPs were mostly limited to the academic community. In the eyes of the general public, it was at best a guidepost for spiritual life and a topic of conversation amongst friends. Of course, it must be admitted that when the Manic frenzy of the Cultural Revolution (1966–1976) receded, the research interest in Han-shan and his poems was quickly revived in Chinese mainland, thanks in large part to the research findings of Hong Kong and Taiwan during this period. In 2001, 35 years after Hu Juren (胡菊人) published his article "The Resurrection of the Poet Monk Han-shan" (诗僧寒山的复活), the first academic research paper on the CMPs appeared in Hong Kong. The thesis was entitled "The Poetry of Han-shan in English: a Cultural Approach" (寒山诗的英译：一种文化取向). This is a 140-page dissertation for the Master of Philosophy in Comparative Literature at the University of Hong Kong by Shin-kei Sydney Fung Chan.

### 6.2.2 CMPs in 1960s and 1970s Taiwan

Following the landmark article by Hu Juren (胡菊人), Han-shan and his poems received far more research attention in Taiwan than in Hong Kong. This is, of course, partly due to the orientation of art and literature in Taiwan areas in the 1960s and 1970s, where more freedom was granted in comparison to the conservative and blockaded literary atmosphere of the 1950s in the mainland. Especially after the highly oppressive policy of art and literature, people's desire for freedom and democracy was self-evident. Thus, the image of Han-shan and the spiritual freedom and uninhibited style projected by his poems resonated to a considerable extent among the Taiwanese readership. The second reason was, of course, the return of overseas Han-shan fever and the fact that Taiwan areas was not hit by the Cultural Revolution. For a while, Taiwan became a major research center for Han-shan and his poems.

In 1967, Commercial Press in Taipei published *Poems of Han-shan-zi and Appendix of Poems of Shi-de* (《寒山子诗：附拾得诗》), based on the 1936 Shanghai Commercial Press microprint of a photocopy which was made by the Zhou family in 1924 according to an edition of the Song Dynasty (960–1279). After it's publication, Hu Juren's "The Resurrection of the Poet Monk Han-shan" (诗僧寒山的复活) had a profound impact on Hong Kong and Taiwan readership at that time. It "greatly interested" Chung Ling, who was still in Taiwan areas at the time. She published "The Status of Han-shan in Eastern and Western Literature" (寒山在东方和西方文学界的地位) in March 1970 in the supplement to *Central Daily News*. Chung Ling explained the unusual "Han-shan phenomenon" in the international literary arena from three aspects: "The Reception of Han-shan in Three Traditions" (寒山在三个传统里所受的接纳), "Why CMPs Causes Different Responses in Three Traditions" (何以寒山诗在三个传统里有不同的反应) and "Han-shan and Modern Literature" (寒山与现代文学), which centers on the wider sociocultural context, such as poetic tradition and religious culture. It begins by exclaiming that "the Chinese poet Han-shan of the Tang dynasty is an outstanding exception in the international literary arena."[9] The author then gives a brief overview of the dissemination and reception of Han-shan in both Eastern and Western literary circles. At the end of the essay, the author states,

> The poet Han-shan, in the symbol of "Han-shan", was united with his own self; and Han-shan believed that people could also be united with their own true self through "Han-shan". In the actual life of the twentieth century, Westerners became more or less acquainted with an Eastern poet and learned a little more about the Eastern world through the symbol of "Han-shan".[10]

Chung Ling's article triggered tremendous response and reaction in Taiwan areas. Just as Chung Ling herself had said, "The response to this article was unexpected. And many articles on Han-shan by different literary figures were published in the supplement to *Central Daily News*."[11]

In July of the same year (1970), a book published by Taipei's Wenfeng Publishing House, *The Anthology of Poems by Han-shan, Feng-gan, Chu-shi, Shi-de and Shi-shu* (《寒山诗集：附丰干、楚石、拾得、石树原诗》), included this essay by Chung Ling in its entirety. The book also included an essay "The Zen Realm and Poetic Sentiment of Han-shan-zi" (寒山子的禅境与诗情) by Chen Dinghuan

(陈鼎环, 1934–2007), which analyzes Han-shan's Zen realm and the artistic achievements of his poems as well as their reception in the international literary arena from the following perspectives, including "Han-shan: A Sage-like typed Philosopher" (仙风道骨一哲人), "Lyric Poems of Manifold styles" (迥异百家的抒情诗), "The Reasons for the Different Responses to Han-shan in China and Japan" (寒山在中日之不同反应原因) and "The Inner and Outer Layer of the Hippie Movement" (嬉皮运动之内层外层).[12] Chen writes with deep emotion in the introductory part,

> I have always loved some of CMPs, and I particularly admire his metaphysical self-cultivation, and the poetic styles that originate from it—the greatest combination of metaphysics and poetry in the history of Chinese culture. Han-shan, a recluse secluded himself from the outside world, had left so many intriguing poems to the secular world and his name "Han-shan" has long been respected by the international literary world. In contrast, many of those who have tried so hard to remain famous for thousands of years have long since washed away with their names and works into the gutters of history.[13]

Both essays undoubtedly signaled to the public the international prominence of the CMPs and its unjust and unequal domestic treatment. The latter's elevation of Han-shan's status to that of a "great poetic philosopher" was a clear attempt to build momentum for the canonization of Han-shan in Taiwanese scholarship. In fact, their essays and *The Collected Poems of Han-shan: Original Poems by Fenggan, Chushi, Shi-de and Shih Shu Attached*, together with a number of monographs on Han-shan studies by Zhao Zifan (赵滋蕃) in 1970 and *Notes and Commentary on Cold Mountain Poems* (《寒山诗笺注》) by Huang Shanxuan (黄山轩), heralded the Han-shan Studies in Taiwan areas.

A series of monographs on Han-shan and his poems published by Zhao Zifan (赵滋蕃) in 1970 carried considerable weight in the field of Han-shan studies at the time. According to Chen Dinghuan (陈鼎环), he was also inspired by the articles of Chung Ling and Zhao Zifan (赵滋蕃). Zhao Zifan's serial studies on Han-shan, among which the author has found, consists of one edited volume and three monographs: *The Zeitgeist of Han-shan* (《寒山的时代精神》, 1970), *Han-shan and His Poems* (《寒山子其人其诗》, 1970), *The Origin of Photocopying the Collected Works of Han-shan* (《影印〈寒山子集〉缘起》, 1970) and *Assessment of Cold Mountain Poems* (《寒山诗评估》, 1970). These articles explained in some detail the poetic characteristics of the CMPs from different perspectives, and have had a great influence on subsequent studies of the CMPs in Taiwan areas. Many articles and monographs that followed after Zhao Zifan's publications saw inspiration and taken a large influence from his work. Some of these articles and publications used Zhao's ideas to either support their own or to disagree with others. Zhao's influence no doubt profoundly affected the Taiwanese academic circle and their studies of the CMPs.

In his article "Han-shan-zi and His Poems", Zhao Zifan (赵滋蕃) said,

> I will take an objective and analytical approach, carefully organizing the material available in various references and making extensive use of the biographical material in CMPs, in order to gain a first insight into the mystery of Han-shan's life. I will also use modern psychoanalysis to look at his personality, attitude to life, living environment and friendships, in order to regenerate the true nature and spirit of Han-shan and to dispel the misconceptions of the American hippies about him.[14]

Zhao lamented that "To read his poems and to see his person, as well as the background and spiritual climate of his time, is not only a matter for literary historians, but also for literary critics."[15] After examining the CMPs as a whole, he "diagnosed" that "Han-shan has a mild hysteria, but is not a big deal."[16] His conclusion is based mainly on his examination of what he calls Han-shan's self-referential poems. The author argued that

> his (Han-shan's) attitude to life was always in conflict with the circumstances of his life, and his psychological loss had a long latent period. . . . It is perfectly understandable that under such a sharp contrast to produce hysteria.[17]

However, Sun Qi (孙旗) was not convinced by Zhao's psychoanalytic approach. He argued that Zhao's use of a so-called "first-person poetry" and a story from the *Jingde Chuandeng Lu* (《景德传灯录》, *The Records of the Transmission of the Lamp*) to prove that Han-shan had "hysteria" is entirely out of ignorance. The reason is that "creative works are fictional and can be written in the third person, not necessarily in the real person or in the real event."[18] Sun Qi, therefore, believed that Zhao's conclusions were purely conjectural. This respectful back-and-forth between the two scholars is evidence of the vibrant and deepening academic debate within Taiwanese scholarship and is an extension of the canonization of the CMPs.

In his essay "Assessment of CMPs", Zhao Zifan (赵滋蕃) commented on the CMPs as follows:

> His poems, through individuality, move towards the self and the inner world, so that the dream world mingles with the Zen world; rather than through poetic metre, towards tradition and vulgarity. He is overflowing with a spirit of defiance in his art. The poems he writes are living, breathing poems of wild power; freshness and lucidity are their excellences. Their weaknesses are openness and lack of artistic sophistication.[19]

This is probably a favorable assessment, but it would be a misinterpretation to regard "openness and lack of artistic sophistication" as a shortcoming of the CMPs, which is in fact a powerful expression of Han-shan's rebellious personality and his resistance to the secular world. Moreover, Zhao Zifan (赵滋蕃) commented positively on Han-shan's practice of not setting poetic titles for his poems, and believed that this had given him the opportunity to be completely free in his poetic thinking. Chao even drew an analogy between this and the style of the Persian poet Omar Khayyam's *The Rubaiyat*. This style, according to Zhao,

> on one hand, destroys the laws laid down by metrical poetry; on the other hand, it regenerates the life of some poems beyond such poetic tricks as "Fengyao" 蜂腰 (Wasp's waist), "Hexi" 鹤膝 (Crane's knees), "Pingze" 平仄 (Level tone and oblique tone) and prosody,[20] which fully highlights the poet's rebellious personality.[21]

As for those poems which are heavily narrative, Zhao pointed out that "the fact that such pure story poems appeared in our literary history thirteen centuries ago is not only meaningful for our literary history, but also presents its true significance and value in the history of world literature." This statement broadly follows the understanding of the value of the CMPs during the May Fourth period. Zhao also stated that the CMPs also vary considerably in quality: "Some poems are excellent, while others are rather poor. As a whole, his poems are distributed in a dumbbell shape."[22] Zhao especially mentioned that the persuasive poems in the CMPs were not considered to be particularly all that convincing. Such an assessment is clearly inconsistent with the important value of the story poems mentioned earlier. It is this early understanding of the CMPs that gives rise to a series of later insights into it in Taiwanese scholarship.

In addition to the reprint of *The Collected Poems of Han-shan: Original Poems by Feng-gan, Chu-shi, Shi-de and Shi-shu Attached* (《寒山诗集：附丰干、楚石、拾得、石树原诗》), other important achievements of Han-shan Studies in Taiwan areas in the 1970s include *Notes and Commentary on Cold Mountain Poems* (《寒山诗笺注》) by Huang Shanxuan 黄山轩 in 1970 and *Interpretation of Cold Mountain Poems* (《寒山诗解》) by Zeng Puxin (曾普信, 1902–1977) in 1971. In these two commentaries, the CMPs were comprehensively combed through and annotated in the form of a monograph. In addition, from 1972 to 1973, *Chinese Poetry Quarterly* (《中国诗季刊》), edited by Hu Dunyu (胡钝俞, 1901–), published four consecutive issues on the CMPs. The series of articles and poems published in these four issues pushed the enthusiasm for the study of Han-shan and his poems to new heights.

In 1974, *A Study on Han-shan* (《寒山子研究》) by Chen Huijian (陈慧剑, 1925–2001), was first published by Huaxin Publishing House in Taiwan areas. The book is a masterpiece of Han-shan studies in Taiwan areas, and it is characterized by detailed and well-researched content. In addition to the examination of Han-shan's life, Chen also provided an in-depth and detailed exposition and classification of the thoughts and contents of the CMPs. Therefore, this book has been extremely influential in the field of CMPs studies. The book was reprinted in 1978 by Heavenly Lotus Publishing Co., Ltd in Taipei and by Dongda Book Company in Taiwan areas in 1984 and 1989. Moreover, influential monographs on Han-shan in Taiwan areas in the 1970s also include *Han-shan and Hippies* (《寒山与西皮》, Taizhong: Putian Press, 1974) by Sun Qi and *Han-shan and His Poems: The Story of Han-shanfrom His Poems* (《寒山子与寒山诗：从寒山子诗中看寒山子之身世》, Taipei: Tailin Press, 1976) and *Han-shan and His Poems* (寒山子与寒山诗, Taipei: Dalin Press, 1977/1984) by Cheng Zhaoxiong (程兆熊，1907–2001).

It is worth noting that, in addition to the interest in the CMPs in the publishing and academic world, Han-shan studies in the 1970s also became an important research topic for postgraduate students in Taiwanese universities. For example, "Notes and Revisions on Han-shan and His Poems" (寒山子其人及其诗之笺注校订) by Zhuo An-qi (卓安其) (Master's thesis, Chinese Culture University, 1971), was the first college thesis all of China to focus on Han-shan and his poems. It marked the beginning of "Han-shan Studies" in the more traditional academic school. Moreover, in 1977 a second master's thesis on Han-shan titled "A Study of Cold Mountain Poems" (寒山诗研究) by Shen Meiyu (沈美玉) (Master's thesis, Chinese Culture University, 1977) appeared. The attention and research of postgraduates in universities across China made the canonization of the CMPs in Taiwan areas an undeniable fact.

### 6.2.3 CMPs in Taiwan Areas After the 1980s

It would certainly not be an exaggeration to say that "Han-shan Studies" in 1970s Taiwan was productive. However, the scholarship in Taiwan did not decline after the 1970s, there was still more publications and new insight into the CMPs to be discussed in the Taiwan academic community. In 1980, the Xin Wenfeng Publishing Company in Taipei published *Han-shan and His Poems* (《寒山及其诗》) by Huang Boren (黄博仁). The unique perspective and novel insights of this book once again gave rise to a large number of excellent achievements of Han-shan Studies in ship. Subsequently, monographs such as *A Study on Han-shan and His Poems* (《寒山及其诗研究》, 1982) by Li Chung-qing, *The Eternal Mountain: A Study of Han-shan* (《永恒之山──寒山子之研究》, 1982) and *Studies on Han-shan and His Poems* (1985) by Yang Ziming were published. In addition, in 1985, Commercial Press in Taipei published a photocopy of *The Collection of CMPs, with Poems by Feng-gan and Shi-de Attached* (《寒山诗集附丰干拾得诗》), a photocopy of *Siku Quanshu* (《四库全书》, *The Imperial Four Libraries*) in the Palace Museum of Taiwan.

Most notably, in 1982, Tianyi Publishing House published the academic results of the "Han-shan fever" from 1966 to 1980 outside of Chinese mainland in seven volumes, titled *Han-shan Biographical Materials* (《寒山子传记资料》). The articles were organized into several major themes, including "Han-shan Studies" (寒山研究), "The Philosophy of Cold Mountain Poems" (寒山诗之哲理), "Assessment of Cold Mountain Poems" (寒山诗评估), and "Essays and Collections on Han-shan Studies" (有关寒山研究之论著及馆藏). These seven volumes of biographical information were the first and only collection of such a large amount of information on Han-shan in Taiwan areas, and its release was undoubtedly a collective display and summary of the previous results of Han-shan fever research. As for its academic achievements, some commentators argued that "the researches on Han-shan of Chung Ling and Chen Huijian are the most striking achievements in the biographical materials with more than three million words outside the mainland."[23] It goes without saying, of course, that the publication of such a large number of issues demonstrates the canonical power and poetic charm of the CMPs, as well as the preservation value of the unanimously recognized research results of "Han-shan Studies".

In addition, "Han-shan Studies" in this period also appeared in the research projects of graduate students in Taiwan areas. For example, *A Study of the Grammar of Cold Mountain Poems* (《寒山子诗语法研究》) by Zhao Fangyi (赵芳艺) (Master's thesis, Tunghai University, 1989). Published in the same year as this master's thesis was a photocopy of *Anthology of Cold Mountain Poems* (《寒山子诗集》), based on *Zeshiju congshu* (《擇是居叢書》, *Zeshiju Series*) (1989). By this time, "Han-shan Studies" in Taiwan areas had entered an unprecedented height, and the enthusiasm for such research further presented a momentum in the research.

At the end of the 20th century and the outset of the 21st century, "Han-shan Studies" in Taiwan areas continued to march forward. However, compared to the frenzy of the earlier period, the research in this period was comparatively more lukewarm. Major research results were limited to the summary and deepening understanding of the earlier "Han-shan Studies", mainly in the form of annotations of the CMPs and the collation of research materials concerning Han-shan. For example, *Annotations on the Poems of the Zen Master Han-shan: Poems of Shi-de Attached* (《禅家寒山诗注：附拾得诗》) (1992) by Li Yi (李谊, 1935–) and a master's dissertation by Ye Zhuhong (叶珠红) "Critical Studies of Materials about Han-shan" (寒山子资料考辨) (National Chung Hsing University, master's thesis, 1992), followed by the 1997 publication, *A Collection of Essays of Patriarchs of Successive Generations and Liao-Fan's Four Lessons* (《了凡四训等历代祖师推介要文合刊》). The collection includes four parts: "Cold Mountain Poems" (寒山诗), "Lao Tzu" (老子), "Purifying Cultivation of Avatamsaka Sutra" (华严经净行品) and "Collected Essays on the Recommendation of Patriarchs of Successive Generations" (集录历代祖师推介要文). It is noteworthy that for the first time, Han-shan was categorized as an important figure in the master's category, which was undoubted of great significance in continuing to establish Han-shan and his poems as a canon in the religious and literary fields.

Moreover, as a result of the influence of academic "Han-shan Studies", there was also a great affection for Han-shan in Taiwan's popular fiction scene. In the 1990s, two new fictional editions of Han-shan appeared in Taiwan areas: *A Biography of Master Han-shan* (《隐逸寒岩性自真：寒山大师传》, 1995) by Xue Jiazhu 薛家柱 (1937–2021) and *Three Holy Monks: Han-shan, Shi-de and Feng-gan* (《风狂三圣僧：寒山拾得丰干》, 1997) by Sui-wen Lin (林淑玟, 1956–). The former is part of *A Collection of Biographies of Eminent Monks in Chinese Buddhism* (《中国佛教高僧全集》) and *Fo Guang Biographical Canon Series* (《佛光史传丛书系列》), while the latter is included into *Eminent Monks Novels Series* (高僧小说系列). These two novels are quite scholarly in their standpoint, in addition to being entertaining.

In the introduction to the volume, Xue Jiazhu (薛家柱) provided a more detailed overview of Han-shan's life and the dissemination and reception of the CMPs. The author pointed out that, "Han-shan, also known as Han-shan-zi, was a famous vernacular poet of the Tang dynasty and an eminent Zen master, who was not only known in China but also enjoyed a high reputation in Japan and the United States."[24] At the end of the preface, the author stated that the references for his book included *Han-shan, Shi-de and Their Poems* (《寒山拾得和他们的诗》) by Xu Guangda (徐光大), "The Status of Han-shan in Eastern and Western Literature" (寒山在东方和西方文学界的地位) by Chung Ling, and "The Zen Realm and Poetic Sentiments of Han-shan-zi" (寒山子的禅境与诗情) by Chen Dinghuan (陈鼎环). In the "Afterword" to the book, he referred to his motivation for writing by saying that,

> In the autumn of 1988, I was asked by the Beijing Movie Institute Audio & Video Publishing House to write an eight-episode television series: "Cold Mountain".... I then learned that a wave of "Han-shan fever" had started on American campuses from 1958.... Foreigners were so enthusiastic about Han-shan, but in modern China, he was treated with indifference, which was so unfair to this senior monk of his generation. At this time, Taiwan's Fo Guang Publishing House proposed to publish a set of 中国佛教高僧全集 *A Collection of Biographies of Eminent Monks in Chinese Buddhism*.... Coincidentally, Master Han-shan was included in the list of 100 monks to be written.[25]

In the General Preface to another eminent monk novel, *Three Holy Monks: Han-shan, Shi-de and Feng-gan* (《风狂三圣僧：寒山拾得丰干》), the preface's author, Sheng-Yen (1931–2009), when referring to the motivation for the publication of the series, elaborated that as follows:

> In order to make the original texts easily accessible to modern readers, especially to young people, and to share their wisdom and compassion through the biographies of the senior monks, our company, Dharma Drum Culture Co. has launched 高僧小说系列 *Eminent Monks Novel Series*, in which the biographies of forty monks are selected, after more than two years of planning and operation. A group of contemporary children's literature writers from the old, middle and young generations are invited to present to the readers vividly in the form of modern novels based on historical and biographical information, using their brilliant writing, rich emotions and keen imagination, together with the editing techniques of film montage.... This series is mainly aimed at young people, but it belongs to all people, and is a Buddhist book that transcends the age level.[26]

As the novel is intended for younger readers, it is also illustrated with a large number of pictures. The use of illustrations is undoubtedly intended to bring young readers closer to the novel, and also to increase the authenticity and credibility of the novel's characters and events, thus making Han-shan a real and palpable presence to young readers. Obviously, the use of the novel form makes the image of Han-shan and the essence of the CMPs more accessible, especially for young readers to begin to recognize and understand Han-shan and his poems. This will undoubtedly be of greater importance to the canonization of the CMPs, which will be extended and inherited to the greatest extent possible.

The monographs published in Taiwan areas in the 21st century on the "Han-shan Studies" include three books by Ye Zhuhong: *The Pearls of Life: The Interpretation of CMPs* (《人生的珠玑:寒山诗解》, Taipei: Fubon Teng Books, 2004), *Investigation into Anthology of Cold Mountain Poems* (《寒山诗集校考》, Taipei: The Liberal Arts Press, 2005), 《寒山资料考辨》 (*Critical Studies of Materials about Han-Shan*), Taipei: Showwe Information Co. Ltd., 2005), *Compilation of Materials about Han-shan* (《寒山资料类编》, Taipei: Showwe Information Technology Co., Ltd., 2005) and *Papers on Cold Mountain Poems* (《寒山诗集论丛》, Taipei: Showwe Information Co. Ltd., 2005).

Objectively speaking, the previously mentioned four works by Ye Zhuhong (叶珠红) are by far the most remarkable monographs on "Han-shan Studies" in Taiwan areas, both in terms of depth and breadth. *Investigation into Anthology of Cold Mountain Poems* (《寒山诗集校考》) is a revision of her master's thesis, "Critical Studies of Materials about Han-shan" (寒山子资料考辨). The first half of this book is proof of different editions of the CMPs, containing the best-arranged editions as well as the examination of the dissimilarities and misprints in various editions. The second half of the book is a postscript that contains descriptions of the editions, comparisons of discrepancies in texts, and comparisons of dissimilar texts between various editions of the same system. The editions covered are as follows—the "Tianlu Song" edition, the "Song" edition, the "Goryeo" edition, the "Joseon" edition, the "Yongle DaDian" edition, the "Ming published white mouth eight-line" edition, the "Guoqing temple" edition, the "Siku Quanshu" edition, the "Japanese Imperial Palace" edition, and the "Quantangshi" edition. Thus it is an impressive work on "Han-shan Studies", with its detailed and thorough contents which display the author's ability to conduct the examination.

The book *Critical Studies of Materials about Han-Shan* (《寒山资料考辨》) is based on Ye's master's thesis which was edited three times in two years, and two appendices were added: "A Comparison Between 'One Volume of CMPs and One Volume of Poems by Shi-de and Feng-gan Respectively Attached' from the Continuation of '*Imperial Collections of Books*' and '*Poems by Han-shan and Shi-de*' in the Yongledadian Edition" (天禄琳琅〉续编〈寒山子诗一卷附丰干拾得诗一卷〉校以〈永乐大典〉本〈寒山拾得〉之异文) and "The Copy of Different Editions of Cold Mountain Poems" (寒山诗版本影). Her book is divided into six chapters along with an introduction and conclusion, "An Exploration into Han-shan's life" (寒山子生年浅探), "Identification of Legends about Han-shan" (寒山传说考辨), "Critical Studies of Cold Mountain Poems from the *Yongledadian* Edition" (《永乐大典》本《寒山诗集》考辨), "A Comparison of Cold Mountain Poems from '*Yongledadian* Edition' and 'Tianlu Linlang' Edition" (大典本与《天禄》宋本《寒山子诗集》之比较). The book, characterized by thorough examination and detailed content, is of great insight and with many unprecedented statements, thus obtaining good academic and historical value.

Ye's *Compilation of Materials about Han-shan* (《寒山资料类编》), as its name suggests, is a compilation of literature on Han-shan. It consists of four major topics, namely, "Materials on Texts" (文本资料), "Materials on Deeds" (事迹资料), "Materials on Imitations" (拟和资料) and "Materials on Poetry" (诗话资料). This book, exhaustive and comprehensive, is a rare reference for "Han-shan Studies". Moreover, *Papers on Cold Mountain Poems* (《寒山诗集论丛》) contains 11 papers on the "Han-shan Studies" written by Ye, including an investigation of the editions of the CMPs, an examination of the different names of Han-shan, a survey of Han-shan Studies outside Chinese mainland from 1962 to 1980, the misinterpretation and misunderstanding of the CMPs by contemporaries, and a discussion of the "Fengrenti" 风人体 (Pun Poems), the legend of the "Three Sages of Tiantai" and the "Sleeping in Harmony" painting, etc. At the end of the collection, there are 11 portraits of Han-shan, Shi-de and Feng-gan painted by Chinese and Japanese painters. Li Jiankun (李建崑, 1950–) from department of Chinese Language and Literature, Chung Hsing University, said that "this book is one of the few important works on Han-shan studies in Taiwan areas, and it will certainly spark attention and dialogue among Han-shan researchers at home and abroad."[27]

Throughout the 40 years of "Han-shan Studies" in Hong Kong and Taiwan areas, we have seen the active and extensive participation of publishers, academia, the fiction industry and the reading public in the canon construction of the CMPs and the remarkable achievements of Han-shan Studies in all major academic fields. With regard to the canon construction of literary classics, many scholars have mentioned that a text can become a canon because it can satisfy the demands and desires of those in cultural power. Academics and publishers are undoubtedly among those who have cultural power and hold sway in mainstream poetics. In this sense, we can safely say that it is the academia and the press that contribute to the canonization of the CMPs in Hong Kong and Taiwan areas. In fact, the sustained and in-depth examination and discussion by the academic, the publication and reprinting by the publishing sector, the brilliant interpretation by the popular fiction, and the unprecedented enthusiasm of the target readership, have together constructed a harmonious discourse field that has made Han-shan Studies in Hong Kong and Taiwan areas, especially in Taiwan areas, unparalleled success and achievement.

### 6.2.4 CMPs in the Chinese Mainland After the 1980s

As mentioned earlier, the frenzy for Han-shan in Japan and the United States led to the marvelous return of the CMPs to China, Han-shan's homeland, after an overseas journey. The first station in the return of the CMPs is the academic circles of Hong Kong and Taiwan areas. Since the 1960s, Han-shan and his CMPs have gained great literary fame and prominent literary status in these two regions both in academic research and in the teaching of literary history. During the same period in Chinese mainland, however, despite occasional articles and treatises on the Han-shan Studies on the eve of the 1960s, the dominant ideology then, such as so-called "literature and art should serve politics" and "literature and art should serve the workers, peasants and soldiers" prevailed. Thus, much attention was paid to the literary works of Zhao Shuli (赵树理, 1906–1970) and Liuqing (柳青, 1916–1978), whose works could reflect the realities of the times, and naturally, the research on Han-shan and his poems was put a sudden stop. However, the feverish Han-shan Studies in Hong Kong and Taiwan areas renewed the Han-shan Studies in Chinese mainland, which displayed its immeasurably pivotal role. In addition to the abundant research achievements in Hong Kong and Taiwan areas, the significance of preservation and continuation of the lifeblood of Han-shan Studies can never be overestimated.

*6.2.4.1 Han-shan Studies in Chinese Mainland in the 1980s*

In the late '70s, with the end of political chaos, a relatively relaxed and active academic environment is reignited. In 1980, Wang Yunxi (王运熙) and Yang Ming (杨明) published the article "The Dating of Cold Mountain Poems" (寒山子诗歌的创作年代) in the fourth issue of *Journal of Chinese Literature and History*, which was included in 1981 in the book *Collection of Literary Essays of the Han, Wei and Six Dynasties and Tang Dynasty* (《汉魏六朝唐代文学论丛》) by Wang Yunxi (王运熙). As Luo Shijin (罗时进) remarked, "This is another in-depth and solid examination after Yu Jiaxi' *Sikutiyaobianzheng* (四库提要辩證, *Discussions on the Summary of the Four Treasuries*)".[28] The article divides the CMPs into two major categories in terms of poetic style, and finds that they do not bear the poetic characteristics of those poems during the "Reign of Zhenguan" (627–649) and even during the early days of the reign of Emperor Gaozong of Tang (649–683), or even the entire early Tang period,

> for he could never have written many five-character-regular-verse poems at a time when the form-obsessed court poets had not yet formally established the rhyme system. . . . His poems must have been produced after the rhythmic poetic system had become quite popular,

Luo continued.[29] This article is a powerful complement to Yu Jiaxi's findings that the well-known Lü Qiuyin's preface is a pseudo-work, and it is in favor of the so-called "the Dali Hypothesis" (argument for Han-shan's lifetime during the Dali Reign) regarding Han-shan's life. In fact, this article, based on the existing studies of Yu Jiaxi in 1958, adds to and enriches Yu's studies. Therefore, it acts as a transitional role in Han-shan Studies at that time.

In 1980, another paper on Han-shan Studies was "Han-shan-zi and his poems" (寒山子和他的诗) by Li Jingyi (李敬一, 1946–). The author analyzed the ideological content and artistic characteristics of the CMPs and considered them to be meaningful for inheriting the classical poetic heritage, exploring the path of development of new poetry in China, and even for cultural exchanges between China and abroad.[30] In 1982, Qian Xuelie's master's thesis "A Study of the Language of Cold Mountain Poems" (寒山诗语言研究, Beijing: Renmin University of China), also belongs to the type of linguistic analysis. Qian Xuelie further published "A Preliminary Study of the Grammar of Cold Mountain Poems" (寒山诗语法初探) in *Language Teaching and Linguistic Studies* in 1983 and "A Study of the Rhymes of Cold Mountain Poems" (寒山诗韵部研究) in *Linguistic Researches* in 1984, which continued his exploration into the linguistic and formal features of the CMPs in depth.

In 1983, Li Zhenjie (李振杰) published an article entitled "Hanshan and His Poems" (寒山和他的诗), in which the author, based on the contents of the Preface to CMPs and the surviving poems, speculated and examined Han-shan's life. Then he pointed out that "people used to regard Han-shan as a poetic monk, but in fact, he was a hermit who believed in Buddhism. His thoughts were complex, and in addition to Buddhist thought, he also had Taoist and Confucian ideas."[31] In 1984, Wang Jinsan (王进珊) in her article "Han-shan-zi: Eleven Poems" (寒山子：诗十一首) (*Journal of Chinese Literature and History*, No. 1, 1984) adopted a similar approach, starting from the content of the CMPs and analyzing and summarizing Han-shan's life. Shi Zhecun (施蛰存), a famous Chinese scholar, also wrote an article about Han-shan, "Han-shan-zi: Eleven Poems" (寒山子：诗十一首) in October 1984 (collected in his book *On Tang Poetry* (《唐诗白话》), published by Shanghai Chinese Classics Publishing House in 1987). After briefly sorting out Han-shan's life and the versions of the CMPs, he analyzed the content of Han-shan's eleven poems and pointed out the influence and ideals of Confucianism, Buddhism and Taoism in his poems, as well as the pun-using approach and Han-shan's ideas about poems, and he deemed that the CMPs should be composed by a hermit scholar in the Middle Tang period. In 1985, Zhong Wen (钟文) "On the Life and Works of Han-shan-zi" (关于寒山子的生平及其作品) (Journal of Shantou University, 1985) also followed the same approach of content analysis.

In 1986, the third issue of the prestigious religious journal *The Voice of Dharma* carried a short introduction to Han-shan and his poems:

> Han-shan has been known in China and Japan for 1,300 years. However, it is for the first time in the Western world that the complete poems of our Tang Dynasty monk poet Han-shan have been translated and published. In his book *Le Mangeur de Brumes:L'oeuvre de Han-shan, Poèt et Vagabond*, Patrick Carré has translated into French all of Han-shan's three hundred and eleven short poems, with a preface and commentary. Han-shan was a wise man who traveled widely and cared nothing about worldly wealth and sensual temptations. In the 1950s, the young post-war wanderers in America especially revered him as their ideal role-model. The American writer Jack Kerouac even dedicated his novel *The Dharma Bums* to Han-shan in 1958. The American poet Gary Snyder translated nearly twenty CMPs into English in 1956, and another French translation of twenty-five short poems was published in 1975.[32]

Although what is described in this message is not very accurate, it has, to a certain extent, stimulated and driven the interest of domestic researchers in Soochow Han-shan Temple.

The book *Chronicle of Han-shan Temple* (《寒山寺志》), compiled by the famous bibliographer Ye Changchi (叶昌炽, 1849–1917), was published first by Mingwen Book Company in Taipei in 1980, and then by the Jiangsu Ancient Books Publishing House in 1986. The latter in January 1990 also published an edition of *Chronicle of Han-shan Temple* (《寒山寺志》), revised by Zhang Weiming (张维明), editor-in-chief of Guwuxuan Publishing House in Soochow, Jiangsu. These two books are important reference materials for the Han-shan Studies. This period also witnessed several articles and couplets being published on the big bell, the planning, design, and construction of the Han-shan Temple as a scenic spot.

Thus, it takes a little stretch of the imagination to conclude that the Han-shan Studies in the 1980s basically followed the research path from the form of language to the content of poetry, and then to the study and planning of Han-shan Temple. In a sense, the attention and examination of Han-shan Temple as a tourist attraction in turn favorably promoted and reinforced academic research on Han-shan and his poems. In May 1989, Tiantai County of Zhejiang Province, where the legendary poet Han-shan resided, saw the establishment of the Tiantai Mountain Cultural Research Association, which is unanimously dedicated to the Han-shan Studies.

*6.2.4.2 Han-shan Studies in the Chinese Mainland in the 1990s*

In 1990, *Southeast Culture*, sponsored by the Nanjing Museum and openly distributed at home and abroad, published a special issue of the Tiantai Mountain Culture Research Association for its research results (No. 6, 1990, No. 82 in total). Many famous scholars, such as Ren Jiyu (任继愈, 1916–2009), Luo Yuanzhen (罗元贞, 1906–1993) and Xu Jie (许杰), inscribed the special issue for celebration. The seven monographs and one short paper published in this special issue have been crucial players in promoting the Han-shan Studies in Chinese mainland at that time, and they are as follows: "On the Thought and Poetic Style of Han-shan-zi" (论寒山子思想和诗风) by Xu Guangda (徐光大), "The Circulation and Influence of Cold Mountain Poems" (寒山子诗歌的流传与影响) by Xu Sanjian, "On the Poems of Shi-de" (谈拾得的诗) by Xu Guangda, "Remarks on Han-shan-zi" (寒山子解说) by Ota Tizo, translated by Cao Qian (曹潜), "An Analysis of the Poetic Rhymes of Cold Mountain Poems" (寒山子诗韵试析) by Zhu Rulüe (朱汝略), and "A New Inquiry into the Life of Han-shan-zi" (寒山子生平新探) by Lian Xiaoming (连晓鸣) and Zhou Qi (周琦), and "Han-shan Fever at Soochow University" (苏州大学喜逢"寒山热") by Ding Xixian (丁锡贤).

With the help of scholars and the government of Tiantai County, the "First Chinese Tiantai Mountain Cultural Symposium" was held in Tiantai County from June 3rd to the 6th, 1993, with the theme "The Communication of Tiantai Mountain Culture and Its Impact at Home and Abroad", and this symposium was jointly sponsored by Cultural Bureau of Taizhou, Zhejiang Province, Government of Tiantai, Tiantai Mountain Cultural Research Association, Institute of World Religions of the Chinese Academy of Social Sciences, Institute of Asia and Pacific Studies, and the Research Institute of Buddhist Culture of China. Nearly 80 scholars attended the conference, and 53 papers were received. At this conference, scholars once again launched a lively discussion on Han-shan and his poems which was also one of the core themes of the conference. In 1994, the second issue of *Southeastern Culture* published five conference papers from this symposium, three of which discussed the life of Han-shan: "A Tentative Research on the Life of Han-shan-zi" (试论寒山子的生活年代) by Lian Xiaoming and Zhou Qi (连晓鸣 & 周琦), "An Examination of the Life of Han-shan-zi" (寒山子身世考) by Yan Zhenfei (严振非) and "On Han-shan: A Concurrent Discussion of Dali Hypothesis" (泛论寒山——兼与寒山"大历说"者商榷) by Yu Chaoqing (俞朝卿). In addition to these three, another paper titled "On the Tomb Tower of Han-shan" (关于寒山子墓塔的探讨) by Chen Xi and Chen Bingxiang (陈熙&陈兵香) dealt with the tomb of Han-shan, and the fifth paper "An Overview of Research on Han-shan-zi" (寒山子研究概述) by Ding Miao (丁苗) made a literature review of Han-shan Studies since 1989, all of which comprehensively introduced the latest achievements in Han-shan Studies at that time.

From September 16th to the 18th, 1997, the "Second Chinese Tiantai Mountain Cultural Symposium", organized by the Institute of World Religions of the Chinese Academy of Social Sciences, the Tiantai County People's Government and the Tiantai Mountain Cultural Research Association, was held again in Tiantai County, with more than 80 experts and scholars present, and the theme of the conference was "Tiantai and East Asian Culture". At this symposium, 51 papers were collected and the study of Han-shan and his poems still remained one of the major topics. Some scholars, after analyzing the rhyme of the CMPs, argued that all the poems were rhymed and that Han-shan-zi was a man of letters; others deemed that Han-shan-zi, neither a Taoist nor a monk, should be regarded as a hermit poet; others gave an introduction to the Han-shan fever in the United States and other situations. The proceedings of the conference were published in the 1997 supplement of *Southeast Culture*.

These two conferences, organized by academics, local governments and private academic groups, have largely contributed to the further deepening of the Han-shan Studies, and marked the fast internationalization of domestic Han-shan Studies. As Luo Shijin said, despite many questions still troubling domestic scholars, the Han-shan Studies has been launched and has been getting somewhere, and many complicated, complex and indistinct questions will spark people's interest in research, thus pushing forward and further deepening the research of Han-shan Studies.[33]

In 1990, the articles that explored the influence of Han-shan and his poems in the East and West were "The Circulation and Influence of CMPs" (寒山子诗歌的流传与影响) by Xu Sanjian and "On CMPs and Its Influence in the East and West" (论寒山诗及其在东西方的影响) by Wang Qingyun (王庆云), and these two articles are actually based on the essays of Hu Juren (胡菊人) and Chung Ling. Their introduction is actually intended to draw the attention of the academic community in Chinese mainland to the comparison of Han-shan Studies home and abroad because "while the Han-shan Studies in Chinese mainland gains popularity, the Han-shan fever overseas, however, is gradually cooling down. Therefore, the mainland academic community mostly did not know that there was such a fever overseas."[34] Wang Qingyun also remarked that

> there are always complex reasons behind an international cultural phenomenon. At the same time, Han-shan and his poems have a deeper cultural connotation and strong artistic charm that aren't familiar to us yet, so we are expected to re-examine and further grasp them.[35]

Though Wang's article has underestimated the overseas influence of the CMPs, however, it serves to draw the attention of Chinese scholars to the Han-shan Studies abroad.

The Han-shan Studies in the 1990s showed a "pluralistic" and "inclusive" research pattern, and there are seven research paths in summary.

(1) Language studies. For example, "Functionalization of the Auxiliary Words "liao", "zhe" and "de" as Seen in Poems by Wang Fanzhi and Han-shan" (从王梵志诗和寒山诗看助词"了"、"着"、"得"的虚化) by Qian Xuelie in *Journal of Shenzhen University*, 1993; "A Fresh Textual Research on Han-shan's lifetime" (寒山子年代的再考证) in *Journal of Shenzhen University*, 1998.

(2) Influence studies. For example, "On the quotation and imitation of CMPs: A Study of the Influence of CMPs in the Zen and the Literary Field and Their Editions" (寒山诗之被"引"、"拟"、"和"——寒山诗在禅林、文坛中的影响及其版本研究) by Chen Yaodong 陈耀东 in *Journal of Jishou University* (Social Science), 1994.

(3) An addendum to lost poems. For example, "A collection of Lost Poems by Han-shan and Shi-de" (寒山、拾得佚诗拾遗) by Chen Yaodong in *Literary Heritage*, 1995.

(4) Studies of editions. For example, "A Study on the Japanese Editions of Cold Mountain Poems Collections" (日本国庋藏《寒山诗集》闻知录——《寒山诗集》版本研究之四) by Chen Yaodong in *Journal of Zhejiang Normal University*, 1995; "A Study of the Edition of *Cold Mountain Poems Collection*" (《寒山子诗集》版本研究匡补) by Duan Xiaochun (段晓春) in *Library Tribune*, 1996; "A New Exploration of Collections of Cold Mountain Poems " (寒山子诗结集新探——《寒山诗集》版本研究之一) by Chen Yaodong in *Journal of Zhejiang Normal University*, 1997; "On the Edition of Anthology of Cold Mountain Poems in *Yong Le Da Dian*" (永乐大典本〈寒山诗集〉论考) by Zhong Shilun (钟仕伦) in *Journal of Sichuan University* (Philosophy and Social Science), 2000.

(5) Comparative studies. For example, "A Comparative Study of Wang Fanzhi's Poems and Cold Mountain Poems" (王梵志诗、寒山诗比较研究) by Lu Yongfeng 陆永峰 in *Journal of Sichuan University* (philosophy and Social Science), 1999; "Cold Mountain and Han-shan" (《寒山》与寒山) by Hu Ying (胡缨) in *Dushu*, 1999; "A Tentative Discussion of the Similarities and Differences between Wang Fanzhi's Poems and Han-shan's Poems" (试论王梵志诗与寒山诗之异同) by Kim Tal-chin in *Religious Studies*, 2000.

(6) Studies on religious thoughts. Such as, "An Exploration of Han-shan's Buddhist Thought" (寒山子佛学思想探析) by Cai Haijiang (蔡海江) in *Journal of Taizhou Teachers College*, 1996; "A Brief Discussion of the Taoist Thought in Han-shan-zi's Poems" (浅谈寒山子诗的道家思想) by Zhang Lidao (张立道) in *Journal of Taizhou Teachers College*, 1997; "An Elementary Analysis of Han-shan-zi's Poems of Chan Yue" (寒山子禅悦诗浅析) by Qian Xuelie in *Journal of Renmin University of China*, 1998; "A Tentative Discussion of Confucianism and Taoism in Han-shan's Poems" (试论寒山诗中的儒家与道家思想) by Qian Xuelie in *Chinese Culture Research*, 1998.

(7) Studies on Annotation of the CMPs. For instance, *Annotations of the Poems of Han-shan-zi* (《寒山子诗校注》) by Xu Guangda in 1991; *Annotations of Cold Mountain Poems* (《寒山诗校注》) by Qian Xuelie in 1991; *Commentary on the Poems of Han-shan* (《寒山诗注释》) by Guo Peng (郭鹏) in 1995; *Commentary on the Poems of Han-shan and Shi-de* (《寒山拾得诗校评》) by Qian Xuelie in 1998; *Commentary on the Poems of Han-shan: with Notes on the Poems of Shi-de* (《寒山诗注（附拾得诗注）》) by Xiang Chu (项楚) in 2000.

It is self-evident that the Han-shan Studies in the 1990s was still mainly based on language, edition, content and supplements, and the existing comparative studies and impact studies were mostly limited to the Chinese polysystem; relatively speaking, the study of editions of poems, religious thoughts, proofreading, commentaries and annotation were the most important topics for researchers in this period. In terms of the geographical distribution of researchers, they are mainly concentrated in a few universities in Jiangsu and Zhejiang, Sichuan and Shenzhen, and most of the researchers have Chinese academic background.

*6.2.4.3 Han-shan Studies in the Chinese Mainland in the 21st Century*

Since the beginning of the 21st century, Han-shan Studies has received great attention from Chinese government, the academic community and the publishing industry, thereby contributing to the blooming academic discussions. The "Third Chinese Tiantai Mountain Cultural Symposium", held in Tiantai County from May 15th to the 18th, 2002, was co-organized by Tiantai Mountain Literature Research Association and Institute of World Religions of Chinese Academy of Social Sciences, with more than 100 participants, and Han-shan Studies was still one of the important topics. Some scholars pointed out that the ideological and artistic achievements of the CMPs were incomparable to those of unknown vernacular poets; some scholars even claimed that it was possible that more than 300 CMPs were composed by one single person since the phenomenon of Confucianism, Buddhism and Taoism appearing in parallel in the work of a single individual is not uncommon in the Middle and Late Tang Dynasty; other scholars also argued that Snyder's poetic writing was greatly influenced by Han-shan after introducing and analyzing Snyder's *Riprap and Cold Mountain Poems*.

On November 26, 2007, the First Han-shan Temple Cultural Forum, hosted by Han-shan Temple in Soochow, Jiangsu Province, was held at Han-shan Temple. The forum was attended by local people, experts and scholars from Soochow, and received a total of 30 academic papers and research articles. Of the papers received, 15 are on "the connotation, characteristics and research significance of Han-shan Temple culture", 6 on "Hehe culture and its contemporary values", 4 papers on "Han-shan and His Poems", and other 5 on other studies. After that, more than 20 papers were selected and compiled into *Han-shan Temple Cultural Forum Proceedings 2007*, which was published by China Literature and History Press in February 2008. The collected papers include Luo Shijin's "Han-shan's Identity and the Changing Role of His Vernacular Poetry Narrative" (寒山的身份与通俗诗叙述角色转换), Ren Ping's "Han-shan Spirit: The Hehe Culture is Going Global" (寒山精神：走向全球的"和合"文化), and Wen Bo's "Han-shan Temple Culture and Its Modern Significance" (寒山寺文化及其现代意义). Luo reviewed and analyzed studies on Han-shan's identity in domestic and foreign academia, and pointed out that

> if we just treat this complex and special thing in a simple way rather than immerse ourselves into the text and social background to think and discover, Han-shan's real and vivid life will be obscured, and the charming poetic texts with different emotional tones created by constantly changing identity and narrative roles will also fade.[36]

From May 10th to the 13th, 2008, the International Symposium on Han-shan and Hehe Culture, jointly sponsored by the Institute of World Religions of the Chinese Academy of Social Sciences, Zhejiang Federation of Humanities and Social Sciences Circles, the Propaganda Department of the CPC Taizhou Municipal Committee and the Tiantai County Government, was held in Tiantai, Zhejiang Province. Approximately 100 or so experts and scholars from the United States, Korea, Japan and China attended the conference. Quite impressively, the most famous research scholars in Han-shan Studies were present, such as the American translator of *The Collected Songs of Cold Mountain*, Chung Ling, Ye Zhuhong (叶珠红), Lee Jongmee (李钟美) from Lingnan University in Korea, and scholars from Chinese mainland such as Qian Xuelie (钱学烈), Chen Yaodong (陈耀东), Zhou Qi (周琦) and so on.

This symposium received more than 60 papers, and 39 of them were selected by Zhejiang Federation of Humanities and Social Sciences Circles selected and compiled into *Proceedings of the International Symposium on Han-shan and Hehe Culture* (《寒山子暨和合文化国际学术研讨会论文集》), which was published by Zhejiang University Press in June 2009. The first part of the proceedings is "Han-shan and His Poems", which contains 24 articles, including Me and Cold Mountain by Red Pine, "Han-shan and American Poetry" (寒山与美国诗歌作品) by Chung Ling, "Is the Poem 'I've seen Seng-yu, by nature rare and unique' from Yong Le Da Dian is Incomplete?—Based on the Verse 'Their dragons flew, their goblins ran'" (由"龙行鬼走"试证 "永乐大典本"《寒山诗集·余见僧繇性希奇》一诗为缺漏) by Ye Zhuhong, "Ancient Printed Versions of Cold Mountain Poems: A Systematic

Examination" (古印本寒山诗版本系统考) by Lee Jongmee, "A Survey and Prospect of Contemporary Studies on Cold Mountain Poems" (当代寒山子研究的现状和展望) by Park Young-hwan and "Exploring Doubts about Han-shan and His Poems" (寒山子与寒山诗研究探疑) by Qian Xuelie. In addition, there are also some papers from the perspective of the "horizontal influence" of the CMPs, some discussed the canonization of the CMPs in American translated literature and the shaping of Han-shan's image by Western culture. The second part is "Two Saints of Hehe and the Harmony Culture of Tiantai Mountain", which contains 15 articles, including Zhou Qi's "An Introduction to the Harmony Culture of Tiantai Mountains" (天台山文化"和合学"概论) and Cui Xiaojing's "Han-shan and Shi-de: Two Saints of Hehe" (寒山拾得与"和合二仙").

This is the first international academic symposium named after "Han-shan" in China, the holding of which marked three trends in Han-shan Studies: the studies on Han-shan and his poems are increasingly internationalized and diversified; the Han-shan Studies tend to separate from "popular literature studies" and "religious studies" and become more independent; the academic community has started to explore the folk images and folk legends of Han-shan, which are associated with the social discourse of constructing a "harmonious society" and "Hehe culture" in Chinese mainland. Considering all of the previous issues, this conference can be seen as a crucial player in the historical process of Han-shan Studies, the classic status of Han-shan and his CMPs will be consolidated as never before by the current research fruits and the emerging "Hehe culture" studies.

From the 28th to the 31st of December, 2008, Han-shan Temple Cultural Symposium, hosted by Han-shan Temple in Soochow and organized by Han-shan Temple Cultural Research Institute, was held at the Soochow Central Hotel. The theme of the forum was "Hehe World—Harmonious Society". The conference received a total of 117 papers, and 95 papers of them (about 700,000 words) were included in the compilation of the conference papers. Among them, 31 were on "Hehe culture", 30 on Han-shan and his poems, 29 on Han-shan Temple Culture and 5 on Buddhist Culture. Thus it can be seen that the study of Han-shan and his poems is still a major topic. These papers include Luo Shijin's "The Connotation and Formation of Han-shan-style Poems in Tang Dynasty" (唐代寒山体的内涵与形成原因), Ye Zhuhong's "The Reasons for Emperor Yongzheng's Conferring of 'the Harmony Saints' on Han-shan and Shi-de" (寒山雍正敕封"和合二圣"原因析探), Yan Zhenfei's "An Analysis of Different Studies on the Life Time of Han-shan" (寒山子生活时间诸说考析), He Shanmeng's "The Legend of Han-shan and its Cultural Significance" (寒山传说及其文化意义), Hu Anjiang's "The Return Journey of CMPs and its Dissemination and Reception in Hong Kong and Taiwan" (寒山诗的返程之旅及其在港台地区的传布与接受), etc. Scholars in Han-shan Studies such as Luo Shijin, Ye Zhuhong, Chen Yaodong, Zhou Qi, Yan Zhenfei, Xu Lixin attended the symposium. The proceedings of the symposium, which included a total of 94 selected papers, were officially published and distributed by Shanghai Ancient Books Publishing House in June 2009. As of 2020, Han-shan Temple Cultural Forum has been held for 13 consecutive sessions, which has delivered a huge impact on all sectors of society, and academia (both domestic and abroad).

Meanwhile, Han-shan and CMPs received unprecedented attention in the publishing world. In 2001, *Anthology of Cold Mountain Poems* (The First Series of Photocopies of Chinese Books from the Song and Yuan Dynasties, Collected in Suling Department of Imperial Household Agency of Japan, The Imperial Library of Japan) (《寒山诗集》(日本宫内厅书陵部藏宋元版汉籍影印丛书第一辑)), edited by the National Committee for Ancient Writings Collations in Higher Education Institutions, was printed and published by the Thread-Binding Books Publishing House. In 2002, the Key Cultural Project, co-sponsored by Ministry of Finance and Ministry of Culture and undertaken by National Library of China, included the *CMPs Collection* as one of "China Rare Book Reprinted Collection", which is a testament to its literary and documentary value. The purpose of this project is to "protect, develop, and utilize rare ancient books in a reasonable manner through large-scale and systematic reproduction and publication so that they can be used by the academic community and shared by the public".

In January 2004, China Social Science Press published *Illustrated Appreciation and Analysis of poems by Han-shan and Shi-de* (《寒山拾得诗赏析：图文本》), edited by Shi Yuanpeng (史原朋). The book contains a total of 367 poems of Han-shan and Shi-de, and each of them is divided into three major sections: commentary, modern translation, and appreciation. The commentary section is more than detailed, the present-day translation section is plain and clear, and the appreciation section is simple and informative. Meanwhile, each poem is equipped with ancient illustrations, displaying the editor's hope to expose the readers to the wonderful Zen world so that they can derive the same joy, unworldliness and leisure as Han-shan did. In October 2004, Beijing Publishing Group published a 26-volume set of "Chinese Buddhist Classics", in which *Poems by Han-shan and Shi-de* (《寒山拾得诗》) was included. In the Preface, the editors' words read like this:

> Cold Mountain Poems bear the stamp of music folk songs, and they are content-rich, sometimes describing a kaleidoscope of human beings, sometimes ridiculing the ills of the time, and sometimes expounding Buddhist doctrine. ... The language is straightforward and shallow, smooth and natural, while the Zen interest is abundant, profound and thought-provoking, which is the distinctive feature of Cold Mountain Poems.[37]

In addition, 6 poems by Han-shan are also included in *Selected Zen Poems (Senior Monks Volume)* (《禅诗精选》(高僧卷)) of this collection. The editors point out that "the achievements of Zen poetry are generally on poetry or on theory. In terms of poetry, a large number of Zen poetry masters and superb works have emerged. High monks such as Han-shan, shi-de."[38] In January 2005, Beijing Publishing Group once again included *Poems by Han-shan and Shi-de* (《寒山拾得诗》) (*245 poems by Han-shan*) in the series "Chinese Traditional Culture Classics: compiler's Edition: Two-color Classics", edited by Jiang Zifu 姜子夫.

In September 2005, *Modern Chinese Reader* (《近代汉语读本》) (Shanghai: Shanghai Century Publishing Co., Ltd), edited by Liu Jian (刘坚, 1934–2002), also included 14 poems of Han-shan and 3 poems of Shi-de. All of the CMPs selected for the reading book are vernacular poems. In the table of contents, the editor has such a passage:

> Han-shan, also known as Han-shan-zi, is said to have been a senior monk during the Zhenguan Reign (some also say he lived during the Dali Reign). His lifetime is nearly unknown, and he lived in seclusion at Han Yan in Tang Xing County, Tiantai. Foreign researchers generally believe that there are two "Han-shans". One was a man in the Sui dynasty, born in the 7th century, and most of the CMPs are written by him; the other was a man in Tang dynasty, born in the 9th century. Shi-de, a monk of the Guoqing Temple, a friend of Han-shans'. They both recited poems and composed Buddhist gathas, which, for the public, appeared to be maniac and crazy. They, influenced by Wang Fanzhi, used vernacular in their poetry. There is a collection of poems by Han-shan, with an appendix of poems by Shi-de, which is now transcribed from *Sibu Congkan* (《四部丛刊》, *Collectanea of the Four Categories*).

It is evident that the idea of "two Han-shans" by "Foreign researchers" in the quotation is derived from what Pulleyblank called "Han-shan I" and "Han-shan II". In the previous passage, the editors also explain the relationship between the poems of Han-shan and Shi-de and those of Wang Fanzhi. It is worth mentioning that this book is part of the series of new textbooks for the 21st-century liberal arts of Chinese higher education. After listing the selected titles, the editors give detailed and professional post-textual notes. In fact, this method has positive and far-reaching significance for contemporary university students to understand the popular nature of the CMPs and the colloquial character of the society at that time.

In the field of academic research, the Han-shan Studies in Chinese mainland have been put on the fast track to development. What strikes people most is that the research has begun to take on a new tendency of academic production. The number of doctoral and master's papers on Han-shan and his poems is increasing, which is undoubtedly a welcome change and marks the beginning of the popularization of Han-shan Studies from scholarly research to student research. In the past ten years, nearly 70 theses have been written on "Han-shan" or "CMPs", which is an academic spectacle that no one would have dared to imagine before.

*Table 6.1* Doctoral Dissertations on Han-shan Studies in China

| Author | Doctoral Dissertation Title | Major | Graduation Institution | Graduation Time |
| --- | --- | --- | --- | --- |
| Cui Xiaojing 崔小敬 | A study of Han-shan and His Poems 寒山及其诗研究 | Ancient Chinese Literature | Fudan University | 2004 |
| Hu Anjiang 胡安江 | CMPs: Text Travels and Canon Constructions 寒山诗：文本旅行与经典建构 | English Language and Literature | Sun Yat-sen University | 2007 |

Table 6.2 Master's Dissertations on Han-shan Studies in China

| Authors | Masters Dissertation Title | Major | Graduation Institution | Graduation Time |
|---|---|---|---|---|
| Miao Yu 苗昱 | A Comparative Study on the Rhythms of Wang Fanzhi's and Han-shan's (including Shide's) Poems 王梵志诗、寒山诗（附拾得诗）用韵比较研究 | Chinese Philology | Soochow University | 2002 |
| Cao Shuying 曹疏影 | From Han-shan to "Cold Mountain": A Study of Snyder's Translation 从寒山到"寒山"：斯奈德译诗研究 | Comparative Literature and World Literature | Peking University | 2005 |
| Zhang Guanglong 张广龙 | The Reception of CMPs in the United States 寒山诗在美国 | General and Applied Linguistics | Capital Normal University | 2005 |
| Zhou Haiyan 周海燕 | A Study of Han-shan's Zen Poems 诗僧寒山禅诗研究 | Ancient Chinese Literature | Northeast Normal University | 2006 |
| Qi Hua 齐画 | A Study of Several Groups of Pronouns in CMPs 寒山诗几组代词研究 | Chinese Philology | Sichuan Normal University | 2006 |
| Rui Yimin 芮逸敏 | American Poet Snyder's Reception and Imagination of Chinese Culture 美国诗人史耐德对中国文化的接受与想象 | Comparative Literature and World Literature | East China Normal University | 2007 |
| Liu Yajie 刘亚杰 | On the Reception and Influence of CMPs in America: A Case Study of Cultural Misreading 论寒山诗在美国的接受与影响 | General and Applied Linguistics | Henan University | 2007 |
| Li Yan 李砚 | Study on Han-shan's Philosophical Thought 寒山哲学思想研究 | Chinese Philosophy | Hebei University | 2007 |
| Yang Fengbing 杨锋兵 | The Acceptance and the Bringing Understanding of CMPs in United States of America 寒山诗在美国的被接受与被误读 | Ancient Chinese Literature | Shaanxi Normal University | 2007 |
| Ouyang Huijuan 欧阳慧娟 | A Study on CMPs 寒山诗歌研究 | Ancient Chinese Literature | Hunan University | 2007 |
| Wang Xi 王玺 | A Study on the Translation of Han-shan Poetry by Snyder: From the Perspective of Lefevere's Theory of Rewriting 从 Lefevere 的改写理论看斯奈德的寒山诗英译 | English Languages and Literatures | Central China Normal University | 2008 |

Return Journey of the CMPs and Their Canon Reconstruction 233

| Author | Title | Field | University | Year |
|---|---|---|---|---|
| Li Zhiling 李志凌 | On the Generation and Realization of Poetic Care in English Translation 论中西译者汉诗英译中诗艺关怀的生成与实现——以寒山诗学西渐为缘起 | Chinese Historical Philology | Shandong University | 2008 |
| Yang Fuhao 杨富皓 | Study on CMPs 寒山诗歌研究 | Ancient Chinese Literature | Zhejiang University | 2008 |
| Chen Jiajia 陈佳佳 | Three Topic on the Research of Han-shan's Poems 寒山诗歌研究三题 | Ancient Chinese Literature | Zhejiang University | 2009 |
| Lai Shaomei 赖绍梅 | Study on the Semantic Construction of Modifying Compound Words in CMPs 寒山诗歌偏正式复合词的语义构词研究 | Chinese Philology | Sichuan Normal University | 2009 |
| Zhou Chuanchao 周传超 | The Research of Han-shan and His Poetry 寒山及其诗歌研究 | Studies of Chinese Classical Text | Sichuan Normal University | 2009 |
| Han Xiaojing 韩小静 | A Comparative Study of the English Translation of Han-shan's Poems 寒山诗英译对比研究 | Comparative Literature and World Literature | Capital Normal University | 2009 |
| Li Qianqian 李倩倩 | A Manipulated Manipulator on Snyder's Translation of CMPs 被操纵的操纵者——斯奈德对寒山诗的译介 | Foreign Linguistics and Applied Linguistics | Central South University | 2009 |
| Yuan Henglei 袁恒雷 | Han-shan Harmony Ethics Thought 寒山和合伦理思想探析 | Ethics | Soochow University of Science and Technology | 2010 |
| Wang Haiyan 王海燕 | A Study on Gary Snyder's Translation of CMPs 论加里.史耐德翻译的寒山诗 | English Languages and Literatures | Shandong University | 2010 |
| Chen Lan 陈岚 | Han-shan Ecological Ethics Research 寒山生态伦理思想研究 | Ethics | Soochow University of Science and Technology | 2011 |
| Liao Zhihua 廖洽华 | Reconstruction of the Writer's Cultural Identity in the Process of Translation from Postcolonial Perspective: A Study on Snyder's *Riprap and Cold Mountain Poems* 后殖民视阈下寒山诗英译过程中原作者文化身份重构——基于史耐德《乱石坝与寒山诗集》译本的研究 | English Languages and Literatures | Northwest Normal University | 2011 |

(Continued)

Table 6.2 (Continued)

| Authors | Masters Dissertation Title | Major | Graduation Institution | Graduation Time |
|---|---|---|---|---|
| Han Dandan 韩丹丹 | On Deviation of Poem Translation in Translating Process: A Case Study of Gary Snyder's Translation of CMPs 诗歌英译过程中偏离现象研究—以Gary Snyder所译《寒山诗》为例 | Foreign Linguistics and Applied Linguistics | Central South University | 2011 |
| Zhang Honglei 张红蕾 | A Deconstructive Study of Han-shan Fever and His Translated Poems in English 寒山热与英译寒山诗的解构主义解读 | English Languages and Literatures | Northwest University | 2011 |
| Tian Hui 田慧 | On the Canonization of Han-shan Poems Translated by Snyder from the Perspective of Memetics 模因视角下的史耐德寒山译诗的经典构建 | Foreign Linguistics and Applied Linguistics | Wuhan University of Science and Technology | 2011 |
| Zhu Bin 朱斌 | A Study of CMPs Translated by Snyder: From the Perspective of Translation Norm Theory 翻译规范观照下的史奈德《寒山诗》英译本研究 | English Languages and Literatures | Sichuan International Studies University | 2012 |
| Cai Yazhou 蔡亚洲 | On Snyder's Translation of Cold Mountain Poetry from Perspective of Intertextuality 从互文性理论析加里·斯奈德英译寒山诗 | Foreign Linguistics and Applied Linguistics | Southwest University of Finance and Economics | 2012 |
| Liu Kun 刘昆 | A Comparative Study of the Translating Strategies of Han-shan's Zen Poems 寒山禅意诗歌翻译策略对比研究 | Foreign Linguistics and Applied Linguistics | Southwest University for Nationalities | 2012 |
| Liu Lunan 刘鲁南 | A Study on the Consciousness of Nature in Han-shan's Poems 寒山诗中的自然意识研究 | Aesthetic | Shandong Normal University | 2012 |
| Zhang Ge 张格 | Reconstruction of Polysystem Theory based on Translator's Subjectivity: A Case Study on Canonization of English Translation of Han-shan 基于译者主体性的多元系统理论重构—以寒山诗英译经典化为例 | English Languages and Literatures | Hangzhou Dianzi University | 2012 |

Return Journey of the CMPs and Their Canon Reconstruction 235

| | | | | |
|---|---|---|---|---|
| Huang Jiayan 黄佳燕 | On Snyder's Creative Treason in the Translation of CMPs from the Perspective of Reception Theory 从接受美学视角看斯奈德寒山英译本中的创造性叛逆 | English Languages and Literatures | Hangzhou Dianzi University | 2012 |
| Ma Jiajia 马佳佳 | On Creative Treason from the Perspective of Rewriting Theory: A Case Study of CMPs 改写理论角度下创造性叛逆研究——以寒山英译为例 | English Languages and Literatures | Jiangsu University | 2012 |
| Jin Minfang 金敏芳 | A Comparative Study on the Translation of Han-shan's Poems by Gary Snyder and Arthur Waley: Translating as a Form of Textual Traveling 从文本旅行角度研究比较斯奈德和韦利的两个寒山诗翻译版本 | English Languages and Literatures | Zhejiang University | 2013 |
| Tang Juan 汤涓 | The Research of Content Words in the Poetry of Han-shan 寒山诗歌实词研究 | Chinese Philology | Sichuan Normal University | 2013 |
| Xu Ying 徐莹 | The Han-shan Complex of Philip Whalen 菲利普·惠伦的"寒山情结" | English Languages and Literatures | Hunan University | 2013 |
| Mao Xiaoxu 毛晓旭 | A Study on Snyder's Translation of CMPs from the Perspective of Chesterman's Translation Norms 从切斯特曼翻译规范论看斯奈德的寒山诗英译 | English Languages and Literatures | Zhengzhou University | 2013 |
| Chen Caicai 陈彩采 | On Creative Treason in Translation of Tang Poetry from the Perspective of Steiner's Hermeneutics: A Case Study of Translation of CMPs 斯坦纳阐释学翻译观视角下唐诗英译中的创造性叛逆——以寒山诗歌英译为例 | English Languages and Literatures | Xi'an University of Technology | 2013 |
| Guo Shihong 郭世红 | Translator's Subjectivity in Snyder's Translated Cold Mountain Poetry from the Perspective of Steiner's Hermeneutics 从斯坦纳的翻译阐释观看译者主体性在斯奈德寒山诗英译本中的体现 | English Languages and Literatures | Hangzhou Dianzi University | 2013 |
| Peng Jing 彭井 | A Study on Gary Snyder's English Translation of CMPs from the Perspective of Eco-translatology 生态翻译学视角下的斯奈德寒山诗英译本研究 | English Languages and Literatures | Hangzhou Dianzi University | 2013 |
| Qin Aijuan 秦爱娟 | A Comparative Study of the Cao Tang Poems and Han-shan Poems: Centering on the View of Impermanence 《草堂诗集》与《寒山诗集》的比较研究——以无常观为中心 | Japanese Languages and Literatures | Capital Normal University | 2014 |

(Continued)

Table 6.2 (Continued)

| Authors | Masters Dissertation Title | Major | Graduation Institution | Graduation Time |
| --- | --- | --- | --- | --- |
| Ji Jun 鞠俊 | A Study on Han-shan and His Poetry 寒山及其诗歌研究 | Ancient Chinese Literature | Nanjing Normal University | 2014 |
| Zhou Yangguang 周阳光 | A Comparative Study of the Two English Translations of CMPs Form the Perspective of Reception Theory 接受美学视阈下寒山诗两个英译本的对比研究 | English Languages and Literatures | Central China Normal University | 2015 |
| Guo Xiaochun 郭小春 | On the Reception and Deviation of Han-shan's Poems in America: A Case Study of Snyder's Translation of Han-shan's Poems 寒山诗在美国的接受和变异研究——以斯奈德寒山诗译本为例 | Foreign Languages and Literatures | Southwest Jiaotong University | 2015 |
| Zhang Beibei 张贝贝 | A Study on Han-shan Imagery in the Paintings of the Song Dynasty 宋代绘画中的寒山形象研究 | Art | Yangzhou University | 2015 |
| Wang Zhuoya 王倬雅 | Study on the Translator's Style from the Perspective of Translation Norms: A Case Study of Arthur Waley's 27 Poems by Han-shan 翻译规范视阈下的译者风格研究——以阿瑟·韦利的寒山诗27英译本为例 | English Languages and Literatures | Guizhou University | 2015 |
| Wang Mengnan 王梦楠 | Resonance and Intimate beyond Time and Space: The Influence of Cold Mountain's Poetry on Snyder 隔世共鸣，异域知音——寒山诗对斯奈德的创作影响 | Chinese Language and Literature | Zhejiang University of Technology | 2015 |
| Zhao Yanhua 赵彦华 | A Study on Snyder's Translation of the CMPs from an Ecological Perspective 生态视角下的斯奈德寒山诗英译研究 | Foreign Linguistics and Applied Linguistics | Xi'an International Studies University | 2015 |
| Cao Yuling 曹裕玲 | The Effects of Han-shan on the Buddhist's Monastery of Ming Dynasty 寒山在明代丛林中的影响 | Chinese Classical Literature | Jaingxi Normal University | 2016 |
| Chen Mengyu 陈梦宇 | The Impermanence in the Works of Ryūnosuke Akutagaw: Centering on Han-shan and Shi-de 芥川龙之介作品中的无常观——以"寒山拾得"为中心 | Japanese Languages and Literatures | Dalian University of Technology | 2016 |

| Author | Title | | Field | University | Year |
|---|---|---|---|---|---|
| Zhou Meng 周蒙 | A Study on the Translation of CMPs from the Perspective of Reception Aesthetic: A Case Study of Snyder's Translation 接受美学视角下寒山诗英译研究——以斯奈德英译为例 | | Foreign Linguistics and Applied Linguistics | Hangzhou Normal University | 2016 |
| Yang Shumiao 杨舒淼 | A Study of Buddhist Words of Han-shan's Poems 寒山诗佛教词研究 | | Chinese Philology | Yunnan University | 2016 |
| Qiao Fang 乔芳 | A Study on Cultural Default Insynder's Rendering of CMPs from the Perspective of Relevance Theory 关联理论视阈下斯奈德译《寒山诗》中的文化缺省研究 | | Foreign Linguistics and Applied Linguistics | Xi'an International Studies University | 2017 |
| Yue Lanxiang 岳兰香 | A Study on the Han-shan's Poetry and Evolution of the Legendary Story of Han-shan and Shi De 寒山及相关问题研究 | | Chinese Philology | South University of Science and Technology | 2017 |
| Wang Nana 王娜娜 | A Sociological Study on Gary Snyder's Translation of CMPs: A Bourdieusian View 布迪厄社会学视角下加里·史耐德英译寒山诗研究 | | Translation Studies | Xi'an International Studies University | 2018 |
| Li Jiao 李娇 | On Foreignization and Domestication in the German Translation of Han-shan's Poems 论寒山诗德译本中的异化与归化 | | Translation Studies | Sichuan International Studies University | 2019 |
| Wang Zhixin 王至新 | A Corpus-based Stylistic Study on the Translation of Han-shan Poems by Arthur Waley and Gary Snyder 英译寒山诗语料库文体学研究·以斯奈德和韦利译本为例 | | Foreign Linguistics and Applied Linguistics | Anhui University | 2019 |
| Zhang Ge 张格 | The Three Main Topics in the Study of Han-shan Poems 寒山诗研究中的三个主要问题 | | Theory of Literature and Art | Zhejiang Normal University | 2019 |
| Wang Xiaohui 王晓惠 | A Study of Creative Treason in Gary Snyder's Translation of Han-shan Poetry from the Perspective Medio-Translatology 译介学视角下加里·斯奈德英译寒山诗的创造性叛逆研究 | | Translation Studies | Xihua University | 2019 |
| Xiao Ying 肖英 | Translator's Subjectivity in the Image Translation on CMPs from a Cognitive Translation Perspective 认知翻译观视阈下寒山诗中意象翻译的译者主体性研究 | | Foreign Languages and Literatures | Hunan University of Science and Technology | 2019 |
| Xie Shifa 谢石发 | A Contrastive Study on Translator's Subjectivity in English Translations of Han-shan Poems from the Perspective of Eco-translatology 生态翻译学视域下寒山诗英译本的译者主体性对比研究 | | English Languages and Literatures | Gannan Normal University | 2019 |

(Continued)

Table 6.2 (Continued)

| Authors | Masters Dissertation Title | Major | Graduation Institution | Graduation Time |
|---|---|---|---|---|
| Chen Minying 陈敏颖 | The Use of the Formal Language of Painting in Chinese Poetry Translation: A Comparative Study on Translation of CMPs 绘画形式语言在汉诗英译中的运用—《寒山诗》译本的对比研究 | Translation Studies | Guangdong University of Foreign Studies | 2020 |
| Wang Xing 汪星 | Research on the Style and Its Changes of Han Shan Shi De's Theme Paintings 寒山拾得题材绘画的风格及流变研究 | Fine Arts | Jiangxi Normal University | 2021 |
| Yuan Fuhuan 袁富欢 | A Study of Translation on Hanshan Poems in America (1930–2020) 寒山诗在美国的译介研究（1930–2020） | Translation Studies | Sichuan International Studies University | 2022 |
| Zheng Hao 郑好 | Performance Analysis of Cello Solo *Four Pieces for Cello*: "*Han Shan*" 大提琴独奏作品《寒山子于寒岩隐逸》的演奏分析 | Music and Dance | Wuhan Conservatory of Music | 2022 |

As can be seen from the previous tables, by 2022, a total of 67 doctoral and masters' dissertations have taken Han-shan and his poems as their research target with an average of about four theses per year. The year 2013 and 2019 were the most productive years with seven and six dissertations respectively. Most notably, among the 67 dissertations, 38 were addressed from the perspective of translation studies, accounting for almost 55 percent. Of these 38 dissertations, 29 directly explore the English translation of Snyder's CMPs, taking up nearly 78 percent of the total. To sum up, Chinese academic dissertations are mainly focused on Snyder's English translation of the CMPs from the perspective of translation, which, from another aspect, also reflects the notable academic and social response and lasting impact of Synder's translation. The table also reveals that researchers in traditional research fields such as Ancient Chinese Literature, Studies of Chinese Classical Text, and Chinese Philology show strong interest in Han-shan and his poems. Since 2011, "Han-shan Studies" have also attracted much attention in other fields, like Comparative Literature and World Literature, English Languages and Literatures, Foreign Linguistics and Applied Linguistics, Ethics, Theory of Literature and Art, Arts, Music, and Chinese Historical Philology—so much so that 35% of the dissertations in the field of foreign language and literature study CMPs, followed by Foreign Linguistics and Applied Linguistics with 16 percent, and Ancient Chinese Literature with 13 percent. In regard to the language distribution of the disciplines, except for the dominant English language and literature, German Language and Literature as well as Japanese Language and Literature have also shown interest in Han-shan and his poems. It is interesting to note that the geographical composition of researchers in Chinese mainland has also changed significantly. Historically the academic community was previously only based in the provinces of Jiangsu, Zhejiang, Guangdong, and Sichuan. Further provinces now contribute to the academic study of Han-shan and his poems, these provinces are Beijing, Shanghai, Shandong, Heilongjiang, Liaoning, Shaaxi, Hunan and Hubei. A reason for this could be the impressive development and easier access to education across the country.

As a matter of fact, the few dissertations before 2004 were still "longitudinal" studies and studies within the Chinese literary system, while from 2004 to 2022, the 34 dissertations exploring the translation, reception and influence of the CMPs in the United States were actually "horizontal" studies. For example, taking the 24 CMPs translated by Snyder around 1955 as the main object of her study, Cao Shuying (曹疏影) examines Snyder's translation strategy, identification and transformation of the image, and linguistic characteristics of Han-shan and his poems in a specific cultural context, then studies the motivation and significance of this translation in conjunction with Snyder's creative thoughts and ideology. Zhang Guanglong (张广龙) also studies the translation of the CMPs in the United States and points out that "culture constrains the production and survival of translated works; the transiting American literature stimulated the translation and acceptance of the Cold Mountain Poems."[39] In order to prove the inevitability and rationality of cultural misinterpretation, Liu Yajie (刘亚杰) tries to analyze the "Han-shan Phenomenon" from the perspectives of hermeneutics and reception aesthetics. Yang Fengbin (杨锋兵)

explores the reasons why the CMPs were misread from the perspective of social and cultural factors of that time in the United States. Using rewriting theory as the theoretical base, Wang Xi (王玺) develops a comprehensive study of Synder's translation of the CMPs from the perspectives of ideology, poetics and patrons. Wang states that it was the social ideology of the United States at that time, the rebellion of the Beat Generation against the society, Snyder's Zen thought and understanding of nature, and the poetic pursuit of the United States at that time that contributed to Synder's rewriting of the CMPs and their popularity in American society. Li Zhiling (李志凌) discusses both internal and external factors of the "westward traveling" of the CMPs. He remarks that the glamor of Han-shan's personal image, the unique charm of his poetry, together with the multiple factors of geographical distribution, time and intermediary, contributed to the spread of the CMPs in the Western world. Han Xiaojing's dissertation presents a comparative study of the English translations of the CMPs by Monk Chisong and Robert Henricks from three aspects: (1) comparison of translation techniques, (2) comparison of translation purposes and strategies, and (3) misinterpretation in their English translations. The appendix section of Cui Xiaojing's doctoral dissertation "A Study on Han-shan and His Poems" (寒山及其诗研究), investigated the acceptance of Han-shan and his poems in China, Japan, South Korea and the United States from the perspective of acceptance, and pointed out that the excellence of the CMPs and the social and historical circumstances are important factors contributing to the dissemination of the CMPs to the world. These research dissertations have enriched the study of the "horizontal" influence of the CMPs to a certain extent.

Recent years witnessed some new explorations and breakthroughs in terms of research methods of "Han-shan Studies". Using a corpus research approach, Wang Zixin (王至新) presents a more systematic quantitative analysis of the corpus stylistic features of Snyder and Waley's translations of the CMPs, and explores the causes in their canon construction process as well as translation styles of the two Sinologists. Chen Minying's (陈敏颖) study, on the other hand, conducts a comparative study of Snyder and Monk Chisong's translations of the CMPs from the perspective of the painting-style language. By explaining how the translator's drawing experience affects his/her artistic cognitive mechanism in the translation process, Chen's study reveals the role drawing experience played in enhancing the aesthetic effect of the translated poems and also highlights the significance of cross-art studies in poetry translation. Researchers have also interpreted and studied Han-shan and his poems from perspectives of Eco-translatology, Postcolonial Studies, Receptive Aesthetics, Intertextuality Theory, Sociological Theory and Relevance Theory; however, innovative contributions are rare, and repeated research is relatively common. Besides, researchers' attention has mainly focused on the translation and dissemination of the CMPs in the United States; little is paid to other countries and regions. By now, only one dissertation discusses the translation strategy of the German translation of the CMPs. This shows that the comparative study, influence study and translation study of the CMPs in Europe, Asia and other regions still need to be expanded.

Of course, the previously given statistics only include the dissertations with "Han-shan" and "CMPs" in their titles, while some doctoral and masters' dissertations that study them within chapters are not covered. For example, in the third chapter of Zhang Junmei's (张君梅) (Fudan University, 2013) doctoral dissertation on ancient Chinese literature, "From Metaphysical Interpretation to Evidence: On the Development and Evolution of Buddhist Poetry in China" (从玄解到证据—论中土佛理诗之发展演变), she discussed the early Zen verses as well as the Buddhist poetry of Wang Fanzhi and Han-shan. In the second chapter of another doctoral dissertation on ancient Chinese Literature, "A Study on the Buddhist Monks' Poets in the Medieval Tang Dynasty" (中唐诗僧研究), Yang Fenxia (杨芬霞) (Shaanxi Normal University, 2006) discussed the life of Han-shan and Shi-de, the vulgar and elegant forms of the CMPs as well as their meditating poems in the Tang and Song dynasties. Wang Dan's (王丹) (Zhejiang University of Technology, 2012) master dissertation, "A Study of the Poet Monk Shi-de in the Tang Dynasty" (唐代诗僧拾得研究) included several chapters on Han-shan and his poems. From the perspective of metaphor studies, Hou Fei's (侯菲) (Ocean University of China, 2013) master dissertation "Metaphors in Chinese Zen Poetry: A Cognitive Case Study" (中国禅诗隐喻：认知个案研究) explored the conceptual metaphors in Han-shan's Zen poems.

In May 2007, Chen Yaodong's "A Study on the Edition of CMPs" (寒山诗集版本研究) (a project funded by the National Science Foundation and the Jiangnan Culture Research Center of Zhejiang Normal University) was published by World Knowledge Press. The book has comprehensively and systematically sorted out the edition of the CMPs into three major parts: research, edition, and data. It is a conclusive achievement with high academic value.

To sum up, in this period, "Han-shan Studies" in the Chinese mainland has maintained a "horizontal" study on the influence of Han-shan and his poems from a comparative literary perspective, based on the traditional research directions. Except for dissertations, researchers managed to write academic monographs on the cross-regional influence of the CMPs. For instance, some researchers put Han-shan along with American writers of nature literature in the 20th century, noting that "what they have in common is shifting the focus of literary description from man to wilderness."[40] Kim Young-jin examines Han-shan's influence in Korea in terms of the Korean Zen community's records and the poetry written by Korean Zen masters and literati. He argues that "when Han-shan and his poems travels to Korea, they dominated the literary stage and became one of the constituent elements of Korean Buddhist literature."[41] Zi Gui (子规) explores the references and significance of Han-shan in China in relation to the book Cold Mountain written by American best-selling writer Fraser (1950–), and Zi Gui firmly believes that

> there is no doubt that from the Chinese poet Han-shan, Fraser learned some basic dispositions and conceptions of Zen Buddhism: perseverance, self-confidence and self-reliance, clarity of mind, and pure believe in nature . . . and he introduced them quietly into his own novel Cold Mountain. That is

why he respectfully quotes Cold Mountain's poem in the frontispiece because he is to reveal this secret to the readers.⁴²

From the perspectives of travelling theory and translation studies, Hu Anjiang (胡安江) has explored the "creative misreading" and "canonization" of the CMPs in the United States. He believes that

> when a text travels to an unfamiliar place, the local translator takes the dominant ideology and poetic tradition as the starting point and reference item for translating and interpreting the foreign culture. Owing to the specificity of the translator's cultural identity and the complexity of the objective environment, the translation activities always carry certain *skopos* and local cultural awareness, and thus the translated text will always deviate from the original text to a greater or lesser extent in nature. The intentional intervention, transformation and selective acceptance of the foreign culture, or the "creative misreading", further strengthen the cultural identity represented by the translator.⁴³

The author even goes so far as to suggest that the canonical status the CMPs maintained in America is actually the result of the translator Gary Snyder's "creative misreading" of Han-shan and his poems based on his own cultural patterns and poetic traditions.⁴⁴

Since the 1970s, Chinese academic research on the "horizontal" influence of Han-shan and his poems has been mostly limited to the combing and analysis of their translations in the United States and Japan. These monographs on "Han-shan Studies" published in the new century have, to a large extent, enriched the existing achievements on the Chinese mainland. Of course, to achieve more fruitful results and establish an influential specialized field for the study of Han-shan and Cold Mountain poetry, researchers in Chinese literature, foreign literature, religion, comparative literature and cross-cultural studies, as well as translation studies, are expected to work together. Unfortunately, few interdisciplinary projects in this area have been found yet.

Outside the academic world, Han-shan and his poems gained much attention from the public community. This will undoubtedly contribute to the flourishing and prosperity of "Han-shan Studies". In 1984, Han-shan Literary Society was established, and the journal *Han-shan* (mimeo) was launched by Tiantai County at the foot of Tiantai Mountain, where Han-shan lived in seclusion. Moreover, a 1.6-meter-tall wooden statue of Han-shan was carved; a tomb tower for Han-shan was rebuilt. The Tiantai area also developed cultural products named after Han-shan, such as "Han-shan tea", "Han-shan bamboo mat", "Han-shan shirt" and "Han-shan handicraft". Moreover, communities such as "Han-shan Poetry Club", "Han-shan Academy", "Han-shan Painting and Calligraphy Club", "Han-shan Martial Arts Center", "Han-shan Yueju Opera Troupe" and "Han-shan Craft Factory" also came out successively, and even a street was renamed to "Han-shan Road' after the poet. Online magazines such as *Han-shan Forum* (《寒山论坛》), *Han-shan*

*Poetry Society Forum* (《寒山诗社论坛》), *Han-shan Temple Forum* and *Han-shan Temple Buddhism* (《寒山寺佛学》) have also appeared. It was reported on Xinhua. net on November 25, 2005 that after more than eight months of fine carving, on November 14, 2005, Pan Yuguo (潘裕果), a Soochow micro carver, finished carving 388 poems in *A Collection of Han-shan-zi's Poems* (《寒山子诗集》) into 216 seals of agalmatolite in the form of poems with paintings. In December of the same year, the micro-carved stone seals were displayed at the Han-shan Ancient Bell Museum in Han-shan Temple, Soochow. The CMPs have been so well received by Chinese folk communities; it is apparently rather unusual in the classical Chinese poetry world.

It is worth mentioning that in September 2003, the Han-shan Academy named after Han-shan, was also established in Soochow. The first president of the academy was the venerable Ming Xue (明学), former vice president of the Buddhist Association of China (BAC), former chairman of the Advisory Committee of BAC, former abbot of Soochow Lingyan Mountain (灵岩山) Temple, and former president of the Lingyan Mountain Branch and the Qixia Mountain Branch of the Buddhist Academy of China. In 2017, approved by the National Religious Affairs Administration, Han-shan Academy was upgraded to Han-shan Institute of Jiangsu Buddhist College. The institute adheres to the teaching philosophy of "equal emphasis on learning and cultivation", upholds the mode of "integrating learning and cultivating, embracing the nature", and fosters modern monks who can promote Buddhism, serve living beings, read Buddhist scriptures, learn Buddhist morality and doctrines, and are qualified with both ability and integrity.

"Han-shan Studies" in China after the 1960s has roughly gone through such a research process: from traditional "vertical" studies within the literature to interdisciplinary and cross-regional "horizontal" influence studies, from Chinese literature to religion, foreign literature, comparative literature, and translation, from academia to folk society, from research monographs to Han-shan cultural products, from the periphery of literary history to the center of academic research, from overseas to the homeland. Han-shan and his poems have thus embarked on the most remarkable journey of text travel and canon construction in Chinese literary history.

## 6.3 CMPs and the History of Chinese Literature

Throughout "Han-shan Studies" in China, scholars have worked diligently on traditional studies such as language, editions, annotations and addenda, and have made considerable achievements. Yet it should be noted that the approaches and perspectives domestic researchers adopted are still relatively homogeneous, with few studies on the folkloristic and cultural-historical significance of the CMPs, as Sun Changwu (孙昌武) suggests. Moreover, the "horizontal" research on the influence of the CMPs is also relatively weak, and the existing studies in this area only focus on the introduction and overview. At the same time, we note that most of the research in China, has been concentrated on particular scholars or majors (e.g., Chinese Language and Literature, English Language and Literature, Religion) in certain universities, instead of forming a large scale of research and cooperation. The current poor research situation has resulted in a general lack of awareness of Han-shan, the CMPs, and the "Han-shan phenomenon" among mainland publishers and literary historians. Thus, artificially setting barriers to the dissemination and popularity of the CMPs in the new era, and imitating the style of creation of the CMPs.

### 6.3.1  Canon and Literary History

In literary history, there is always a dynamic migration between the "canon" and the marginalized "non-canon". Some "non-canonical" texts, which are relatively unknown in the cultural polysystem of their origins, are "rediscovered" and "canonized" after traveling to the cultural context of their arrivals or host countries, gaining a much greater literary reputation than that of their origins. This was, in fact, the fate of William Shakespeare (1564–1616), a classic writer at the center of the English literary canon. Tolstoy once joked that Shakespeare was primarily German, because

> until the end of the 18th century Shakespeare not only failed to gain any special fame in England but was valued less than his contemporary dramatists: Ben Jonson (1572–1637), John Fletcher (1886–1950), Francis Beaumont (1584–1616) and others. His fame originated in Germany, and hence was transferred to England.[45]

Through text travel and "localization" in the cultural polysystem of arrivals, Shakespeare first achieved his canonical status in German translated literary, and was thus recognized by the British cultural polysystem. Harold Bloom (1930–2019) even asserted that "at once no one and everyone, nothing and everything, Shakespeare is the Western canon."[46] Stephen Owen, an American sinologist, even pointed out that "we can no longer judge Shakespeare because Shakespeare is already part of the standard by which good literature is measured."[47] In other words, his canonical status is no longer affected by changes of aesthetic taste, and the literary quality of his works has become the standard of literary value by which people judge later literary works.

In analyzing the existence of canons and the canonical status of Li Bai (李白) and Du Fu (杜甫), Stephen Owen addresses the previous point. He argues that the canon exists, of course, but only as a historical phenomenon. Li and Du's persistent canonical status, in his view, reflects some profound problems in the Chinese tradition. He remarks that by the Northern Song Dynasty, it was difficult to judge Li and Du independently because the quality of their works had become part of the standard of the literary value. He also points out that this might be a kind of historical inertia. Taking Du Fu as an example, he indicates that

> between the ninth and eleventh centuries, Du Fu's "greatness" was no longer available for judgment—his poems were recognized as great literary works,

and since the standard of conformity was provided by Du, Du's poems were certainly recognized as canons. He shaped in person the values by which people would comment on him.[48]

It can be seen that "canon" and "literary history" are in fact interdependent. Whether a literary work or a literary genre can be defined as a "canon" and added to the reading list and examination reference for general readers and school students, depends actually on whether it can be included in mainstream literary history and be taught in the classroom. Conversely, writers whose works were previously ignored by literary history but later listed by authorities in literary history can instantly gain "canonical" status. The eminent modern and contemporary Chinese writers Shen Congwen (沈从文, 1902–1988), Qian Zhongshu (钱钟书, 1910–1998) and Eileen Chang's (张爱玲, 1920–1995) works, along with Chih-Tsing Hsia's (夏志清, 1921–2013) *A History of Modern Chinese Fiction* (《中国现代小说史》, Yale University Press, 1961) is a representative case of this. As is stated next:

> Judgments on the value of individual works, their suitability for preservation, are thus always made in the institutional context of the school and its needs, its social function. Moreover, the school did not emerge merely as an institution for the preservation of works. On the contrary, the school was assigned the general social function of distributing various kinds of knowledge, including the knowledge of how to read and write as well as *what* to read and write. . . . The problem of the canon is a problem of syllabus and curriculum, the institutional forms by which works are preserved as *great* works.[49]

Therefore, despite the attention and influence, if the text does not enter the literary or literary history textbooks of the school, if it is not "selected", "preserved" and "protected" by literary historians and literary anthologies, and if it is not "disseminated" by school education or "read and written" by students, then it does not seem to be a literary canon in the real sense. Because the most direct definition and sign of literary canon is undoubtedly being selected into the school literature textbook or literary anthology or literary history. The profound and practical literary, moral, social and other influences that the authority and canonicity of the literary canons played, are expressed and consolidated through the use of such literary materials for literary education in schools. Therefore, a literary history written by authoritative literary figures, published by authoritative publishers, complies with the dominant ideology and is suitable for literature teaching, is actually a synonym for a collection of literary canons.

Generally speaking,

> literary history first made its debut in secondary schools and universities, gained a foothold in the disciplinary establishment, and then became a compulsory course in professional universities and gradually realized its institutionalization. Through this institutionalization, Chinese literary history has finally become a consensus and a collective memory.[50]

Texts that enter this "consensus and collective memory" have undoubtedly acquired temporary "canonical" vestments. The final appearance of this "consensus and collective memory", however, actually depends on the selection standard as defined by canonizers. While in terms of the compilation of literary history, the selection of canonical texts is generally in line with dominant ideology and teaching patterns in the school.

As should be apparent by now, owing to the long-term rejection of institutionalized contexts, Han-shan and his poems have long been absent from Chinese literary history and literary anthologies, not to mention entering the "syllabus" and "curriculum" of schools. This old-fashioned and customary force of literary history writing style has enables the "slapdash" or "invisible" situation of Han-shan and his poems. "How such an important literary phenomenon could be and has been ignored is a shame. It really is a great pity that such a long-term deficiency existed in the study on literary history."[51] It is even puzzling that despite the significance of the "Han-shan Phenomenon", it is almost absent in the history of Chinese translated literature.

### 6.3.2 *CMPs in Chinese Literary History*

Although the CMPs had been included in *Quan Tangshi* (《全唐诗》, *Complete Tang Poems*) and *Siku Quanshu* (《四库全书》, *Complete Library of the Four Treasures of Knowledge*）, they were not suitable for literature teaching, so it seems that no teachers or schools used them as literature textbooks. In the early years of the Republic of China, the CMPs were included into *History of Vernacular Literature and The History of Chinese Popular Literature* (《中国俗文学史》). They were used as literary textbooks, but as the earlier-mentioned says, Hu Shi (胡适) and Zheng Zhenduo's (郑振铎) attempts to bring "vernacular literature" and "folk literature" to the "center of Chinese literary history" were merely utilitarian and short-term acts. After the wave of "promoting vernacular" and "remoulding ideology" passed, the two books, *Complete Tang Poems* and *Complete Library of the Four Treasures of Knowledge*, only functioned as quoted materials for research.

### 6.3.2.1 *CMPs in The Development History of Chinese Literature*

A literary history published in the 1940s, however, changed the awkward situation of the CMPs. This literary history is compiled by famous scholars, published by authoritative publishing houses, and were widely recognized by college literature teachers throughout China. Therefore, when Han-shan and his poems appeared in such a literary history, they gained their "long-lost" central position. It is *The Development History of Chinese Literature* (《中国文学发展史》), written by the prominent literary historian Liu Daji (刘大杰, 1904–1977) and first published by Shanghai Zhonghua Book Company. This literary history volume was completed in 1939 and published in 1941 (the first volume was reprinted in 1947). The second volume was completed in 1943 and published in 1949. When the second volume was published in 1949, its cover impressively stated its purpose: "For Universities only".[52]

This literary history has been highly praised in three places on both sides of the Taiwan Straits, and the publishing house is particularly fond of it. After its first publication in Shanghai Zhonghua Book Company in 1940s, Shanghai Classical Literature Publishing House revised and published it in the form of three volumes in 1957 and 1958 respectively. In 1962, the Beijing Zhonghua Book Company also published three volumes. In 1963, the Shanghai Zhonghua Book Company published *The Development of Chinese Literature History* (《中国文学发展史》) in a two-volume edition, issued by Xinhua Bookstore Shanghai Publishing press. In 1973 and 1976, *The Development of Chinese Literature History* (《中国文学发展史》) (revised edition) was republished by the Shanghai People's Publishing press. It is worth mentioning that due to the influence of extreme leftist thoughts at that time, the content about Wang Fanzhi, Han-shan and Shi-de was completely deleted in the 1976 edition.[53] It was not until 1982 that Shanghai Chinese Classics Publishing House and Xinhua Bookstore issued a reprinted new edition revised from 1962, which resumed its original appearance and related discussions and content were once again used as a literature history teaching material for liberal arts students in domestic colleges and universities. In 1990, Shanghai Bookstore reprinted a two-volume copy of Zhonghua Bookstore's 1949 edition. In 1997 and 1999, the three-volume was published by Shanghai Chinese Classics Publishing House and Tianjin Baihua Literature and Art Publishing Press respectively. The latter more clearly defines it as "canonical academic history of the 20th century"; and the former solemnly introduces this literary history to readers in "Publishing Notes":

> *The Development History of Chinese Literature* by Liu Dajie is a masterpiece on the history of literature from the Shang Dynasty to the Qing Dynasty. It focuses on the literary masterpieces of each period and gives other literary varieties into consideration as well. Literati creations and folk works are given equal attention. While explaining various historical stages and literary genres, it also attaches great importance to showing the context of literary development and evolution. It is an academic work completed independently by the author on the basis of long-term teaching and research. The unified style, the consistency in viewpoints and standard of materials selection, the fluency of the literary style, and prominent personal style are hard to achieve for other collective compiling. Therefore, it is unique and enjoys a long-lasting reputation.[54]

Its unique writing perspective and detailed literature materials truly and comprehensively reflect the development process of Chinese literature, which makes it one of the most important works in the general history of Chinese literature in modern times, and has a pivotal position in the study of Chinese literature history. Due to its great influence domestically, this literary history has long become a classic in the history of literature. Therefore, it naturally became the first choice for teaching Chinese literary history at that time and even today.

In Taiwan, this book was published by the Taipei Zhonghua Book Company in 1956. In the years, 1960, 1962, 1966 and 1968, the Taipei Zhonghua Book Company republished the book in Chinese mainland under the name *The Developed History of Chinese Literature* (《中国文学发达史》). Another book named *Poetry of the Early Tang Dynasty* (《初唐的诗坛》) published by the same company in March 1966 has a section titled "Wang Ji and Wang Fanzhi" (王绩与王梵志), Liu Dajie's discussion of Han-Shan is more detailed in this. The author believes that "Han-shan is the direct successor of Wang Fanzhi's poetry school." He also believes that

> the indistinction between poetry and gatha is the common feature of Fanzhi and Han-shan. However, because he writes in a wide range and expresses natural artistic conception from time to time, his poems are not as dry as those of Wang Fanzhi, but have a kind of charm and taste.[55]

Later, 9 of Han-shan poems were quoted to introduce to readers the "lofty and ethereal taste" in Han-shan's excellent works, the vernacular reasoning poems "opposing the style of poetry of the day" and the Han-shan's theory that expresses his opinions. The detailed and comprehensive introduction once again introduced Han-shan and the CMPs into the readers' view. Because of the extensive quotation in literary history teaching, the classical status of the CMPs in *The History of Chinese Literature* (《中国文学史》) is gradually established.

In 1976 and 1980, China's Hua Zheng Book Company published a revised edition of *The Development History of Chinese Literature*, including "Revised Preface to *The Development History of Chinese Literature*" (December 24, 1976) and "Preface to the revised and enlarged edition of *The Development History of Chinese Literature*" (July 19, 1975), written by Mao Zishui (毛子水, 1893–1988), a reputed Chinese scholar. Mao commented on *The Developed History of Chinese Literature* (《中国文学发达史》) which had been revised several times that " there are two reasons for this book's popularity in Chinese mainland academia for over 30 years—one is that it contains a detailed narration; the other is the fair discussion." Mao believes, "I think the new edition is really the most useful and reliable for everyone who focuses on the history of Chinese literature."[56] Reprinted many times by the press and highly recommended by authoritative scholars, this *History of Literature* has achieved what the predecessors have never gained, and its canonic status has been gradually promoted. In 1980, Taipei Zhonghua Book Company republished a two-volume edition of *Development History of Chinese Literature*. In 1990, the revised version (one volume) was republished by Taiwan Huazheng Book Company.

In Hong Kong, in 1964, two years before Hu Juren (胡菊人) published *The Resurrection of the Poet Monk Han-shan* (《诗僧寒山的复活》), China Ancient Book Press published for the first time a three-volume of *History of the Flourishing of Chinese Literature* (《中国文学发达史》) and then reprinted it in 1972 and 1973. In 1978, *Development History of Chinese Literature* was published by Hong Kong Xuelin Limited Company and reprinted by the same company in Kowloon in 1981.

This book was published in 1990 and 1992 by Hong Kong Hongguang Bookstore and Hong Kong Sanlian Bookstore. The latter was actually published by Shanghai Zhonghua Book Company in 1962.

It can be seen from the publishing pomp of this book that Han-shan and his poems have no longer been unfamiliar with the study of literary history and the teaching of literary history in China's universities. Moreover, with the acceptance of this book as canon and authority of literary history, Han-shan and his poems have gradually been recognized and affirmed by the academic circle.

#### 6.3.2.2  Writing of the CMPs in Literary History from the 1940s to the 1960s

As a matter of fact, *The Development of Chinese Literature History* (《中国文学发展史》), published in the 1940s, is not the only literary history book that records Han-shan and his poems. In 1944, Shanghai Writers' Book Company published Chen Zizhan's (陈子展, 1898–1990) *History of Literature in Tang Dynasty* (《唐代文学史》). This dynamic literary history of Han-shan and the CMPs is quite detailed at that time and even today. The author believes that "Han-shan was probably born in the early to the interim Tang Dynasty and he was still alive even in the middle of Dali period."[57] Then, the author quotes several of the CMPs to introduce his poetics and poetic ideals to readers. The author made a comment after selecting "several good poems":

> These poems are sort of Zen saying, which is undoubtedly influenced by the Zen thought of the time. The language is humorous but the meaning is serious. it seems plain and easy, but sharp and wisdom in essence, that is the charm of this sort of poem. . . . The time Hui Neng lived is between Wang Fanzhi and Han-shan. Naturally, it is not an accidental miracle that Wang Fanzhi and Han-shan made this kind of poem, which is neither the Buddhist verse nor poetry.[58]

This practice that compares Han-shan with the presumed years of his life can undoubtedly restore what Han-shan really was and what his poems really transfer. In addition, showing the popularity, literariness and religiousness of the CMPs one by one enables readers a more comprehensive and objective understanding of the CMPs. Therefore, this book was very important in academic research and literary history.

First published by Hong Kong Commercial Press in 1938, republished by Shanghai Commercial Press and Hong Kong Commercial Press in 1950 and 1954, *Outline of the History of Chinese Literature* (《中国文学史大纲》), by Yang Yinshen (杨荫深, 1908–1989), gave a brief introduction to Han-shan and the CMPs in the section of "Early Tang Writers" (初唐作家) in Chapter 11, "The Golden Age of Poetry" (诗的黄金时代). The author reminds readers in this section, "Before the Four Great Poets of Early Tang Dynasty, we should not forget several vernacular poets, Wang Fanzhi, Han-shan and Wang Ji."[59] In the introduction to Han-shan, the author first quoted the statement in Volume 55 of *Taiping Guangji* (《太平广记》,

*The Extensive Records of Taiping Era*), which briefly introduced his life experience the author pointed out, "This strange monk has always been regarded as a mythical figure. Up to now, he is still worshiped in Tiantai Guoqing Temple." As for the CMPs, the author mentioned *Works of Han-shan*, and cited two Han-shan Poems "Wang Xiucai" and "A Wife of the Owner", as examples. The author concluded that

> the former refers to his attitude towards poetry. It can be inferred that he didn't approve of the aesthetic appreciation like "Fengyao" (蜂腰, Wasp's waist) and "Hexi" (鹤膝, Crane's knees) at all. The latter is easy to understand in terms of vernacular, but the words carry a much deeper insight and carry a heavy weight.[60]

The introduction of Han-shan in this literary history includes not only literary-historical materials, but also folklore and poetry as evidence. Therefore, short as it is, it is objective and beneficial to enrich readers' knowledge of Han-shan.

Han-shan was also mentioned as a "vernacular poet" by Liu Cunren (柳存仁), a famous scholar in China, in his book *The History of Chinese Literature* (《中国文学史》) in 1956. In the preface, Liu stated that the purpose of his compilation is to supplement "novelty" in addition to the "parallel prose", which is the largest part of ordinary textbooks. However, the author also pointed out,

> I'm not to prove the superiority of the "new difference" over the proposition of the predecessors. I merely made some adjustments, focusing on the top priority. Colloquial articles are for the convenience of scholars' browsing so as to avoid what Lin Shu (林纾, 1852–1924) mentioned as the fatigue of scholars. Meanwhile, it does not contradict the achievements in solving the new problems over the past 50 years.[61]

In Chapter 10, "Poems in the Early and Interim Tang Dynasty" (初唐和盛唐的诗), the author mentions:

> There are also many poets who, at this time, specialize in a kind of vulgar and humorous vernacular poetry, which, in our view, can be regarded as a reactionary practice to the popular style at that time. The source of this kind of poetry is probably mostly from works that mock the society or works used for argument when Zen Buddhism was popular. Therefore, although this kind of poetry is relatively popular, it lacks literary embellishment and implication. To view it aesthetically, there is not much to praise apart from its sociality. The most famous vernacular poets who sprang from such a social atmosphere were Wang Fanzhi, as well as other eminent monks such as Han-shan, Feng-gan and Shi-de.[62]

The editor held a dim view to poems like Han-shan's and Wang Fanzhi's. His evaluation of this genre of poetry is slightly unwarranted. However, it could be suggest that it is in contrast with the "praise" of the previous literary history to a certain extent. The writing of literary history with a little "derogatory" has deepened the understanding of Han-shan and the CMPs by ordinary readers and academic researchers. As we mentioned in the last chapter, the construction of canons is indispensable from the criticism and opposition, which at least show a deep concern. This "anti-tone" will effectively enhance the study of Han-shan and his poems significantly.

*6.3.2.3 Writing of the CMPs in the Literary History from the 1960s to the 1980s*

From the 1960s to the 1980s, the tendency of the writing of the Chinese literary history "focuses on social reality, acceptance of historical materialism, and great interest in grand narration."⁶³ Therefore, the writing of Han-shan and the CMPs are only included in *Development of Chinese Literature History* (all relevant discussions were deleted in the 1976 version) by Liu Dajie (刘大杰), *The History of Chinese Literature* (《中国文学史》) by Naoaki Maeno (1920–1998), co-authored by scholars from the University of Tokyo in Japan; *The History of Chinese Literature: A Complete Introduction to the Appreciation of Chinese Literature* (《中国文学史：中国文学欣赏导读全集》) by Liu Ts'un-ren (柳存仁, 1917–2009) and *The History of Chinese Literature* (《中国文学史》) (Volume 1) by Ye Qingbing (叶庆炳, 1927–).

Naobin Maeno mentioned in *The History of Chinese Literature* (《中国文学史》):

> One of the characteristics of the middle and late Tang Dynasty is the emergence of a group of monk poets and female poets such as Xue Tao (薛涛, 768–832) and Yu Xuanji (鱼玄机, 860–874). Among the monk poets, Wang Fanzhi and Han-shan are unique characters. In fact, there are also saying that both of them lived in the early Tang Dynasty. But the detailed experience of them has been unclear. . . . Generally speaking, Wang Fanzhi has the vulgarity of educating the masses, while Han-shan is strong in Zen, both used colloquialisms of the time and stiff and strange words to write unique poems.⁶⁴

Because Japan has a profound tradition of "Han-shan Studies", the definition of Han-shan and the CMPs in this volume of literary history is relatively objective, and the conclusion is basically consistent with the mainstream views of modern academic circles. Liu Ts'un-ren (柳存仁) mentioned in his book that poems of the two are vulgar and humorously vernacular, reactionary to the prevailing style of poems at that time. "The most famous ones are Wang Fanzhi, and some eminent monks like Han-shan, Feng-gan, Shi-de and etc."⁶⁵ The introduction of the CMPs in this literary history is relatively simple, only mentioning the characteristics and achievements of Han-shan's vernacular poems. Ye Qingbing (叶庆炳) mentioned in preface that the book he compiled was originally the lecture notes of his courses on the history of Chinese literature in universities. The first volume was published as a textbook in 1965 and then reprinted in 1980 due to the demand from readership. In the 15th lecture/chapter "Poetry of the Early Tang Dynasty" (初唐诗), he introduced to readers the life experience of Han-shan and two types of the CMPs: vernacular poems and poems describing the scenery and life interests in the mountains. He recorded two CMPs as examples. The characteristics featuring this literary history are historical materials, analysis, and examples and application to the teaching of literary history in universities.

In all these books of this period, despite the words of Han-shan's deeds and the analysis of the CMPs, the descriptions are extremely perfunctory and singular, and the comments are not comprehensive. Moreover, the four books were mainly circulated in academia and universities in China at that time. Therefore, their influence was extremely limited and did not have a big impact on those outside of the academic circles at this time.

It is worth mentioning that *The History of Chinese Literature* (《中国文学史》) compiled by Xiong Lihui (熊礼汇, 1944–) in the late 1980s (edited by Wang Wensheng. Beijing: Higher Education Press, 1989) came out in the context of the advent of self-taught examination system in China in the early 1980s, when a large number of specialized talents were needed by the society. With the acceleration of China's economic construction, the masses had a strong desire to learn, and the existing higher education infrastructure proved hard to meet the needs of the society. Therefore, the Ministry of Education set about research and established a self-study examination system for higher education. On March 3, 1988, the former State Education Commission, after summarizing the experience of various localities, submitted to The State Council for approval and promulgated *The Interim Regulations on Self-study Examination for Higher Education* (《高等教育自学考试暂行条例》), which clearly stipulated the nature, tasks, status, institutions, specialties, examination methods and use of graduates of the self-taught examination system in the form of national administrative legislation. This volume of literary history published by Higher Education Press was used as an examination book for Chinese language majors in the Higher Education Self-taught Examination. Han-shan was officially included in the first chapter of "The Poetry of Sui, and Early Tang Dynasties" (隋代和初唐的诗歌). The author believes that Han-shan was born in the Yonghui period (680–681) of Emperor Gaozong of the Tang Dynasty, and mainly introduces the characteristics of Han-shan's exhortation poems and others that use allegorical sayings for reasoning and tend to express the true meaning of the end of the article. The author also points out: "Han-shan learns from Wang Fanzhi to write vernacular poems, but CMPs are more beautiful in terms of words, images and artistic conception than Wang Fanzhi's poems."[66] Except for the account of Han-shan's life experience, other existing comments are quite accurate with several of the CMPs as supplementary evidence. Therefore, this book, which is used for self-taught examination of higher education, is quite objective and fair to the writing of Han-shan and his poems.

*6.3.2.4 Writing of the CMPs in Literary History since the 1990s*

Since the 1990s, due to the prosperity of "Han-shan studies" research in the Chinese mainland, Han-shan and his poems have also been written into a variety of Chinese literary history. As far as we can see, there are roughly ten kinds as follows:

(1) In 1992, Ma Jigao (马积高, 1925–2001) and Huang Jun (黄均) edited *Zhongguo Gudai Wenxue Shi* (《中国古代文学史》, *History of Ancient Chinese Literature)* (Volume 2) (Changsha: Hunan Literature and Art Publishing House) has a brief introduction to Han-shan.

(2) *Zhongguo Wenxue Tongshi Jianbian* (《中国文学通史简编》, *Compendium of the General History of Chinese Literature*) (Volume 1) (Beijing: Popular Literature Publishing House), written by Chen Yugang (陈玉刚) in 1992, also gave a brief introduction to Han-shan. According to the author, Han-shan's vernacular poetry is "the best vernacular poetry in ancient China",[67] however, what the author states is vague and ambiguous in details. There is a lack of evidence to support his lofty claims.

(3) The 12th chapter of *Zhongguo Gudai Wenxueshi Changbian* (《中国古代文学史长编》, *Chinese Ancient Literary History) (Sui, Tang and Five Dynasties Volume)*(Beijing: Beijing Normal University Press) quoted the introduction to Han-shan's life in the preface of Lü Qiuyin (闾丘胤) and the 55th volume of *Taiping Guangji* (《太平广记》, *The Extensive Records of Taiping Era*). In addition, it also analyzed the content and characteristics of the CMPs in detail and quoted many CMPs (Pages 508–511). The book's introduction and analysis of Han-shan and his poems are objective and detailed. The book also indicates that it is used as a liberal arts textbook for colleges and universities, which has a positive effect on the promotion of Han-shan and his poems among young students.

(4) Luo Zongqiang (罗宗强) and Hao Shifeng (郝世峰) edited *Suitangwudai Wenxueshi* (《隋唐五代文学史》, *Literature History of Sui, Tang and Five Dynasties)* (Volume 2) (Beijing: Higher Education Publishing House) in 1994, which included an article titled "Han-shan and His Poems"[68] by Xiang Chu (项楚). This article was also included by Xiang Chu in his book *Han-shan Shizhu (Fu Shi-de Shizhu)* (《寒山诗注(附拾得诗注)》, *Notations of Han-shan Poems (with that of Shi-de))* (Beijing: Zhonghua Book Company, 2000). Xiang Chu (项楚), professor of religion and expert in philology, studied and introduced Han-shan and his poems, which is the most comprehensive and valuable monograph on "Han-shan Studies" in the history of literature. This set of books was published and distributed by a higher education publishing house and was used as a designated coursebook in the history of liberal arts literature in many universities. It is of great significance to the popularization and re-understanding of Han-shan and his poems. Therefore, its target readers have an access to a comprehensive understanding of Han-shan and his poems, as well as its literary value, literary status, social influence and the reason why it becomes cannon.

(5) In 1996, the contents (including page numbers) about Han-shan in *Zhongguo Wenxue Tongshi* (《中国文学通史》, *General History of Chinese Literature*) (Volume 1) (Beijing: Xiyuan Publishing House) by Chen Yugang (陈玉刚) is exactly the same as the *Zhongguo Wenxue Tongshi Jianbian* (《中国文学通史简编》, *Compendium of General History of Chinese Literature*) (Volume 1) compiled in 1992.

(6) There is a section entitled "Hermit and Monk Han-shan and Shi-de"[69] in *Zhongguo Wenxue Shihua* (《中国文学史话》, *History of Chinese Literature)* (Volume of Sui, Tang and Five Dynasties) edited by Wang Xiang (王祥) (chief editors: Guo Jie (郭杰) and Qiu Fu (秋芙). Changchun: Jilin People's Publishing House) in 1998 specifically introduces Han-shan and his poems.

(7) The section of "Sui, Tang and Five Dynasties" in *Zhongguo Gudai Wenxueshi* (《中国古代文学史》, *History of Ancient Chinese Literature*)(Volume 2) (Taipei: Wanjuanlou Book Limited Company.), edited by Ma Jigao (马积高, 1925–2001) and Huang Jun (黄均) in 1998, gives a brief introduction to Han-shan and quotes "Han-shan Duoyouqi" (《寒山多幽奇》, "Han-shan is More Secluded and Strange") and "Jinri Yanqianzuo" (《今日岩前坐》, "Sitting in Front of the Rock Today").

(8) Compilation of *Zhongguo Gudai Wenxueshi Changbian* (《中国古代文学史长编》, *Ancient Chinese Literature History*) (Volume of the Sui, Tang, and Five Dynasties Volume, Liberal Arts Textbook for Colleges and Universities), published in 2000 by Guo Yuheng (郭预衡, 1920–), is reprinted on the basis of the 1993 edition. Therefore, the style and discussion on Han-shan are still the same as in the 1993 edition. In the Preface, the editor says,

This literary history works is compiled to meet the following needs—First, for the convenience of the teachers' lecturing in Chinese literary history. Second, for the convenience of Chinese majors in colleges and universities. Third, for the reference of self-study readers in Chinese literature history. If this book can be better used, it will be of great significance to the inheritance of CMPs.[70]

(9) In 2000, Cai Zhenchu (蔡镇楚, 1941–) said in his *Zhongguo Gudai Wenxue Pipingshi* (《中国古代文学批评史》, *History of Ancient Chinese Literary Criticism*) (Changsha: Yuelu Book Press) that the prosperity of Buddhism gave birth to the emergence of a special group of poets. Poet monks represented by Wang Fanzhi and Han-shan, from poetry creation to poetry criticism, added a sense of magical and spectacular Buddhist halo to the poetry of the Tang and the Five Dynasties.[71]

(10) *Zhongguo Wenxueshi* (《中国文学史》, *History of Chinese Literature*) (Second Edition, Volume 2), edited by Yuan Xingpei (袁行霈) and Luo Zongqiang (罗宗强) in 2005, was listed as "Curriculum Textbook for the 21st Century" for students of Chinese Department of Colleges and Universities. In the third section of the "Introduction" part of "Literature of Sui, Tang and

Five Dynasties", "The Influence of Buddhism and Taoism on Tang Literature", the editor said,

The more direct influence of Buddhism on Tang literature was the emergence of a large number of poet monks in the Tang Dynasty. *Quantangshi* (《全唐诗》, *Complete Tang Poems*), compiled in the Qing Dynasty, collected 2,783 poems by 113 monks. The poems of these monks include Buddhist moral poetry, exhortation poetry, and gathong. But there are more general pieces, such as traveling, communicating with scholars, giving farewell and so on. Among the monk poems, the more important ones are created by Wang Fanzhi and Han-shan.[72]

As to the characteristics of Han-shan's poems, the editor said, "Cold Mountain Poems include the description of secular life, the study on immortals and Buddhism. Among them, poems that show Zen's interest have a wide and far-reaching influence."[73] As far as the traditional writing of literary history is concerned, many poetry monks have a literary reputation far greater than that of Wang Fanzhi (王梵志) and Han-shan. However, in this literary history, the artistic achievements of the CMPs have been promoted to a new level. Its status in the history of Chinese literature has also been redefined by the two Tang poetry experts. As a result, an important poet has been added to the history of Chinese literature, who has been neglected for a long time. However, it is a missed opportunity that this book does not include any example of the CMPs themselves, only comments on them. Therefore, for readers who are not familiar with Han-shan and his poems before, such descriptions still seem somewhat specious.

(11) In 2009, the CMPs were included for the second time in the section of "Literature of Early Tang Dynasty" of "Suitangwudai Wenxueshi" (隋唐五代文学史, "literary history of Sui, Tang and Five Dynasties") in *Zhongguo Wenxueshi* (《中国文学史》, *History of Chinese Literature*)(Wuhan: Wuhan University Press) by Xiong Lihui (熊礼汇, 1944–). This section is entitled "vernacular poems Found by Wang Fanzhi (王梵志) and Han-shan". According to the editor, Han-shan and the other poets come from the lower class. Quoting two of the CMPs and one Shi-de's poem, the editor discusses the reasons for the rise of vernacular poetry, and he deduced that Han-shan lived during Yonghui years (680–681) of Emperor Gaozong of the Tang Dynasty (618–907), and the major purpose of his poems is to advocate good deeds and punish evil as well as promote Buddhism.[74]

(12) *Zhongguo Wenxueshi* (《中国文学史》, *History of Chinese Literature*) (Shanghai: Fudan University Press), by Maeno Zhibin (1920–1998) in 2009, introduced Han-shan and Wang Fanzhi (王梵志) as representatives of poetry monks in this period in the section of "Wantangshi" (晚唐诗, Late Tang Poetry). According to the editor, their life experience is still unknown. Both of them wrote poems in common sayings and stiff and strange languages at that time, most of which feature reasoning poems. The CMPs are strong in

Zen characteristics. The author discusses poetry monks like Han-shan and female poets like Xue Tao (薛涛) together in this section. He thinks that this is the expansion of the poet group and the expansion of the poetry world. At the same time, he points out that this is a sign of the gradual prosperity of decadence literature.[75]

(13) In 2015, in *The History of Chinese Literature* written by Huang Ren and proofread by Yang Xuhui (Suzhou: Soochow University Press), there is an introduction to Han-shan titled "Representatives of litterateurs in the Middle and Late Tang Dynasties" in the chapter of "Tangdai Wenxue" (唐代文学, "Literature of the Tang Dynasty"):

No one knows Han-shan's life experience. Living in Hanyan, Tangxing County, Tiantai, he returned to Guo Qing Temple from time to time. With birch skin as the crown, cloth fur, and shoes, he sometimes sings in corridors or villages. No one knows him. Lü Qiuyin (闾丘胤) was appointed to the officer in Danqiu, When he was about to leave, he met Feng-gan who came from Tiantai. Lü asked Feng-gan who could be his teacher. Feng-gan said, "Han-shan is like Manjusri Buddisattva and Shi-de is like Samanta Bhadra, they are helping in the kitchen of the Kuo Qing Temple." Three days after the arrival of Lü Qiuyin (闾丘胤), he paid a formal visit to the temple, and saw Han-shan and Shi-de, and greeted them. The two men laughed and said, "The Buddha didn't know who we are." Then went out of the temple, and returned to the cold rock. Han-shan entered the cave, and the cave closed itself. He had written poems on bamboo and left more than 300 poems on the walls of villas and houses.[76]

The introduction here is obviously taken from the relevant records in the foregoing preface of Lü Qiuyin (闾丘胤). It is worth noting that the history of literature in this section also includes the introduction of poet monks such as Wu Ke (无可), Jiao Ran (皎然), Wu Jun (吴筠) and Lü Yan (吕岩). The selection of Han-shan among them in the middle and late Tang Dynasty (618–907) shows Han-shan and his poems are highly recognized and praised by the editor.

Like the previously mentioned, the introduction of Han-shan and his poems in literary history or literary anthologies will greatly promote readers' cognition and understanding of the two, and even attract the attention of the potential readers' research on them. There is no doubt that the collection, introduction, translation and research of Han-shan and his poems by later generations have given them new life and laid the foundation for their circulation, dissemination and canonization.

### 6.3.3 Han-shan Poems in Dictionaries

In addition to literary history, Chinese academia has always been in the habit of compiling dictionaries. Han-shan and his poems are also listed as important items in several literary and religious dictionaries in the 1990s, such as:

(1) *Zhongguo Gudai Wenxue Cidian* (《中国古代文学词典》, *Dictionary of Chinese Classical Literature*) by Liao Zhongan (廖仲安), Liu Guoying (刘国盈)

and Li Jingjie (李景结) (Beijing: Beijing Publishing House, 1989). The dictionary has an entry for "Han-shan", according to which Han-shan is a poet monk living in the Zhenguan period (627–649) of the Tang Dynasty (618–907). His poems advocate good deeds and punish the evil, satirize the common world, his poet style is similar to that of Tao Yuanming (陶渊明) and Xie Lingyun (谢灵运), but more colloquial.[77]

(2) *Tangshi Baike Dacidian* (《唐诗百科大辞典》, *Encyclopedia of Tang Poetry*), edited by Wang Hong&Tian Jun (Beijing: Guangming Daily Press, 1990). In the section of "Overseas Research: The Tang Poetry Overseas", there are "CMPs in Japan" written by Song Hong (pp. 872–874) and "Han-shan Across the Ocean" by Kang Won (pp. 874–875). The former introduces the circulation, annotation, adaptation, translation and research of CMPs in Japan. The latter mentioned the translation of the CMPs by Waley, Snyder, Watson and other translators since 1950s, the imitations of *The Dharma Bums* by Kerouac, "Cold Mountain Fever" in the United States, two doctoral dissertations on Cold Mountain poems and Pulleyblank's monograph on Han-shan studies. In the section of "Selected Works on the Study of Tang Poetry in Hong Kong and Taiwan", the editor mentions 17 kinds of works on Han-shan studies by Sun Qi, Huang Boren and some other scholars from 1971 to 1986 (page 956); In "A Selection of Foreign Works on the Study of Tang Poetry", the editor briefly introduced the previously mentioned two doctoral dissertations and Watson's English translation, as well as nine Japanese works of scholars such as Tsuya Yotaka, Ota Tizo, Tsuda Yoyoyoshi, Kusha Toshio and so on (pp. 986–987). In "Tang Dynasty Poets", there is a special entry for "Cold Mountain". The editor positioned him as a "vernacular poet of the Tang Dynasty" and introduced him by quoting Han-shan-zi, Volume 55 of *Taiping Guangji* (太平广记, *The Extensive Records of Taiping Era*). The editor said, "This is the earliest written record of Han-shan, whose poetic language is popular, vivid, simple and elegant, just like spoken language; His scenery description is graphic and inclusive."[78] At the end of the entry, the editor also mentioned the popularity of Cold Mountain poems abroad and their inclusion in *The Complete Tang Poems*.

This is the most detailed description of Han-shan and the CMPs in China; it objectively presents the historical origin and literary influence of Han-shan and his poems. It is particularly worth mentioning that experts and scholars from varied disciplines including literature, linguistics, religion, history, Sinology, music and dance, fine arts, folklore and drama participated in the compilation process of this encyclopedia, which fully embodied the characteristics of interdisciplinary, trans-temporal and trans-genre compilation. It also fully reflects the latest achievements of "Han-shan studies". Therefore, the dictionary's introduction of Han-shan and his poems is remarkable for its objectivity, timeliness and authority. The chief editor Wang Hong said in the preface:

It is the time to make a comprehensive summary of Chinese literature, especially classical Chinese literature. It is the time for scholars of various disciplines to cooperate closely and cooperate with each other. In fact, compiling such a multi-angle, interdisciplinary and all-round reference book for the learners of Chinese literature and representing the fruits of the studies of Chinese literature at home and abroad in all aspects, therefore, have become our purpose and ideal for compiling this series of encyclopedias of Chinese literature.[79]

Objectively speaking, the compilation ideas of this dictionary in the 1990s should have certain reference value for the current monotonous writing of Chinese literary history, especially for the writing of such an all-encompassing literary phenomenon as Han-shan and his poems. If there is no interdisciplinary, trans-space, trans-genre writing ideas, the writing of literary histories will become a cursory, superficial and parroting behavior.

(3) *Fojiao Wenhua Cidian* (《佛教文化词典》, *Dictionary of Buddhist Culture*) (Hangzhou: Zhejiang Ancient Books Publishing House, 1991), by Ren Daobin (任道斌), has entries of "Han-shan" and "Shi-de" The dictionary calls Han-shan "a poet monk in Tang Dynasty" and supports the "Dali Hypothesis" (766–779) of Han-shan's life experience. As for the characteristics of the CMPs, the editor says:

The language of the poems is easy, natural and fluent. Some words are solemn, some are witticism. Most of which describe natural scenery, but there are some advocate Buddhist thoughts, or satirize politics of the time, representing the vernacular poets in Tang Dynasty (618–907).[80]

This brief but accurate introduction objectively presents the characteristics of Han-shan and his poems.

(4) In *Zhongguo Wenxueshi Tonglan* (《中国文学史通览》, *Chinese General Literature History*) (1994), the editor mentioned in the section of "Chutangshi" (初唐诗, Poetry of the Early Tang Dynasty):

Wang Ji (王绩) has far-reaching horizon and is the precursor of Wang Bo (王勃, 650–676) and Meng Haoran (孟浩然). Popular and unique poems by Wang Fanzhi (王梵志) could be called the predecessor of Han-shan and Shi-de and have influenced poets in Song Dynasty (960–1279) such as Huang Tingjian (黄庭坚, 1045–1105) and so on. However, some created scant poems are of humble status, therefore, it's hard to make some differences.[81]

Like the *Fojiao Wenhua Cidian* (《佛教文化词典》, *Dictionary of Buddhist Culture*), the introduction of the CMPs here is still objective and fair, and highlights the fact that Han-shan is on the periphery of literary history writing.

(5) *Zongjiao Dacidian* (《宗教大辞典》, *Dictionary of Religious Terms)*, edited by Ren Jiyu (任继愈, 1916–2009), takes an alphabetical order, and the introduction to Han-shan is quite brief:

It referred to "Han-shan" as "Han-shan-zi" (寒山子, Han-shan master) or "Pin Zi" (贫子, poorness master), a monk of the Tang Dynasty (618–907). According to "Feng-gan Zhuan" (风干传, Biography of Feng-gan) in *Song Gaoseng Zhuan* (《宋高僧传》, *Biography of Eminent Monks in the Song Dynasty*), Han-shan lived in Hanyan (Cold Mountain), from the end of the 7th century to the early 8th century and made friends with Shi-de in Guoqing Temple. He was good at reciting Buddhist poems. There were inscriptions of his poems in the temple of woods, and later generations collected them in volumes called *The Poem of Han-shan-zi* and collected more than 300 poems.[82]

Since it is a Dictionary of Religious Terms, Han-shan in this dictionary is addressed as a monk, but there is no explanation of the characteristics of his poems. However, the records of these authoritative dictionaries enrich readers' recognition and understanding of Han-shan and his poems, thus consolidating the CMPs as a canon and its literary status.

From *Quantangshi* (《全唐诗》, *Complete Tang Poems*), *History of Vernacular Literature* to various literary histories and dictionaries in the new era, the journey of the canonic construction of the CMPs was obviously not smooth. However, with the exploration of the literary value of his poetry, attention to popular literature in the field of cultural research and the driving of the worldwide Zen fever, the CMPs finally found their place in the history of Chinese literature after completing the worldwide interlingual travel and returning home.

To conclude, this is certainly caused by the overseas "Hanshan fever". Secondly, it is also related to the open and diversified academic research atmosphere and the transformation of academic research paradigm. However, it needs to be pointed out that, as a literary phenomenon which has been neglected for a long time in the Tang literature, but has had great historical and current influences, "Han-shan Studies" has not received due and sufficient attention in Chinese academic circles. Sun Changwu (孙昌武) once pointed out,

> As complicated as it is, the current work can only be regarded as the beginning. Apart from a large number of materials and textual research work to be carried out in-depth, there are still a large number of complex issues involving religious history, linguistic history, folk history, general spiritual history, cultural history, and other fields that need further investigation. Therefore, it will take time to understand and evaluate the CMPs more deeply and correctly so as to interpret the "Han-shan phenomenon".[83]

Seen from another perspective, we might say that there should be a broader space and prospect for "Han-shan Studies" in the years to come.

## Notes

1. J. Clifford. *Routes: Travel and Translation in the Late Twentieth Century*. Cambridge, MA and London: Harvard University Press, 1999: 246.
2. J. Clifford. *Routes: Travel and Translation in the Late Twentieth Century*. Cambridge, MA and London: Harvard University Press, 1999: 251.
3. G. Robertson et al. (eds.). *Travelers'tales: Narratives of Home and Displacement*. London: Routledge, 1994: 4–5.
4. Hu Juren. The Resurrection of the Poet Monk Han-shan. *Ming Pao Monthly* (Hong Kong), 1966, 1(11): 2.
5. Hu Juren. The Resurrection of the Poet Monk Han-shan. *Ming Pao Monthly* (Hong Kong), 1966, 1(11): 2.
6. Hu Juren. The Resurrection of the Poet Monk Han-shan. *Ming Pao Monthly* (Hong Kong), 1966, 1(11): 2.
7. Hu Juren. The Resurrection of the Poet Monk Han-shan. *Ming Pao Monthly* (Hong Kong), 1966, 1(11): 2.
8. Chen Shuo. *Canon-making: The Cultural Politics of Jin YongStudies*. Guilin: Guangxi Normal University Press, 2004: 70–71.
9. Chung Ling. The Status of Han-shan in Eastern and Western Literature. // Han-shan et al. (eds.), *The Anthology of Poems by Han-shan, Feng-gan, Chu-shi, Shi-de and Shih Shu*. Taipei: Wenfeng Press, 1970: 1.
10. Chung Ling. The Status of Han-shan in Eastern and Western Literature. // Han-shan et al. (eds.), *The Anthology of Poems by Han-shan, Feng-gan, Chu-shi, Shi-de and Shih Shu*. Taipei: Wenfeng Press, 1970: 19–20.
11. Chung Ling. *The Circulation of Cold Mountain Poems. Essays on Literary Criticism*. Taipei: Times Culture Publishing Co. 1984: 15.
12. Chen Dinghuan's argument that Han-shan's poem embodies Zen meaning in every word was refuted by Sun Qi. The latter argues that, according to Han-shan's nature, this is not Zen either! But we should not judge Han-shan's cultivation of Zen on this basis. Sun Qi even refuted Hu Shi's statement that "Han-shan and Shi-de have become Zen masters who can talk about Zen subtleties and investigate a Meditation topic," saying that it was only a kind of verbal Zen. See Sun Qi. *Han-shan and Hippies*. Taizhong: Putian Press, 1974: 17.
13. Chen Dinghuan. The Zen Realm and Poetic Sentiment of Han-shan-zi. // Han-shan et al. (eds.), *The Anthology of Poems by Han-shan, Feng-gan, Chu-shi, Shi-de and Shih Shu*. Taipei: Wenfeng Press, 1970: 21.
14. Zhao Zifan. Han-shan-zi and His Poems. // Sun Qi (ed.), *Han-shan and Hippies*. Taizhong: Putian Press, 1974: 112.
15. Zhao Zifan. Han-shan-zi and His Poems. // Sun Qi (ed.), *Han-shan and Hippies*. Taizhong: Putian Press, 1974: 112.
16. Zhao Zifan. Han-shan-zi and His Poems. // Sun Qi (ed.), *Han-shan and Hippies*. Taizhong: Putian Press, 1974: 124.
17. Zhao Zifan. Han-shan-zi and His Poems. // Sun Qi (ed.), *Han-shan and Hippies*. Taizhong: Putian Press, 1974: 133.
18. Sun Qi. *Han-shan and Hippies*. Taizhong: Putian Press, 1974: 3.
19. Zhao Zifan. Han-shan-zi and His Poems. // Sun Qi (ed.), *Han-shan and Hippies*. Taizhong: Putian Press, 1974: 139–140.
20. Shen Yue 沈約 (441–513) is widely believed to have created the poetic metrical theory of si sheng ba bing 四聲八病 (four tones and eight defects) and divided the four tones into ping 平 (level tone) and ze 仄 (oblique tone) categories. "Fengyao" 蜂腰 ("wasp's waist") and Hexi" 鶴膝 ("crane's knees") are two of the eight defects, and the former means that within a single line of a pentasyllabic poem, the second and fifth syllables in the same tone; the latter means that in a pentasyllabic poem, the second and fifth syllables in the same tone.

21 Zhao Zifan. Han-shan-zi and His Poems. // Sun Qi (ed.), *Han-shan and Hippies*. Taizhong: Putian Press, 1974: 144.
22 Zhao Zifan. Han-shan-zi and His Poems. // Sun Qi (ed.), *Han-shan and Hippies*. Taizhong: Putian Press, 1974: 157.
23 Ye Zhuhong. An Overview of Han-shan Studies Outside the Chinese Mainland from 1962–1980. // *Papers on Cold Mountain Poems*. Taipei: Showwe Information Technology Co. Ltd., 2006: 95.
24 Xue Jiazhu. *A Biography of Master Han-shan*. Kaohsiung: Buddha's Light Press, 1995: 1.
25 Xue Jiazhu. *A Biography of Master Han-shan*. Kaohsiung: Buddha's Light Press, 1995: 268–269.
26 Sheng-Yen. General Preface of Eminent Monks Novel Series. // Lin Shu-wen (ed.), *Three Holy Monks: Han-shan, Shi-de and Feng-gan*. Taipei: Fagu Culture Co. 1997.
27 Li Jianyong. Preface. // Ye Zhuhong (ed.), *Papers on Cold Mountain Poems*. Taipei: Showwe Information Technology Co., 2006: iv.
28 Luo Shijin. *The Evolution of Tang Poetry*. Nanjing: Jiangsu Education Press, 2001: 111.
29 Wang Yunxi. The Dating of CMPs. // *Essays on Literature of the Han, Wei, Six Dynasties and Tang Dynasty)*. Shanghai: Shanghai Ancient Books Press, 1981: 217.
30 Li Jingyi. Han-shan-zi and His Poems. *Jianghan Forum*, 1980 (1): 97–103.
31 Li Zhenjie. Han-shan and His Poems. *Literary Review*, 1983 (6): 96.
32 The complete collection of CMPs translated into foreign languages has been published in Paris. *The Voice of Dharma*, 1986 (3): 54.
33 Luo Shijin. *The Evolution of Tang Poetry*. Nanjing: Jiangsu Education Press, 2001: 99.
34 Wang Qingyun. On CMPs and Its Influence in the East and West. *Yantai Teachers University Journal (Philosophy and Social Sciences Edition)*, 1990 (1): 56.
35 Wang Qingyun. On Han-shan's Poetry and Its Influence in the East and West. *Journal of Yantai Normal College (Philosophical and Social Edition)*, 1990 (1): 57.
36 Luo Shijin. Han-shan's Identity and the Changing Role of His Vernacular Poetry Narrative. // Qiu Shuang & Yao Yanxiang (eds.), *Proceedings of Han-shan Temple Cultural Forum* (2007). Beijing: China Literature and History Press, 2008: 107.
37 Song Xianwei. Preface. // *Poems by Han-shan and Shi-de*. Beijing: Beijing Dazhong Press, 2004: 1.
38 Song Xianwei. Preface. // *Selected Zen Poems of Eminent Monks*. Beijing: Beijing Dazhong Press, 2004: 1.
39 G. L. Zhang. Abstract. // *The Reception of CMPs in the United States*. Thesis for Master of Arts, Capital Normal University, May 2005: vi.
40 Cheng Hong. Communication Across Time and Space: Contemporary American Writers on Nature Literature and the Chinese Poet Han-shan of the Tang Dynasty. *Foreign Literature*, 2001 (6): 71.
41 Jin Yingzhen. Influence of Han-shan's Poems to Chan Masters and Literatis in South Korea. *Regious Studies*, 2002 (4): 44.
42 Zi Gui. China's Han-shan and America's *Cold Mountain*. *Journal of Literature and History*, 2004 (6): 29–30.
43 Hu Anjiang. Textual Travel and Translational Deviation—On the Creative Misreading of CMPs by Gary Snyder. *Journal of PLA University of Foreign Languages*, 2005 (6): 64.
44 Zi Gui. China's Han-shan and America's *Cold Mountain*. *Journal of Literature and History*, 2004 (6): 67–68.
45 S. Bassnett. Transplanting the Seed: Poetry and Translation. // S. Bassnett & A. Lefevere (eds.), *Constructing Cultures: Essays on literary Translation*. Clevendon: Multilingual Matters, 1998: 59.
46 B. Harold. *The Western Canon: The books and School of the Ages*. New York: Harcourt Brace & Company, 1994: 75.
47 S. Owen. The Lost Literary History (Trans. Tian Xiaofei). // *Borrowed Stone—Stephen Owen's Selected Essays*. Nanjing: Jiangsu People's Publishing House, 2003: 10.

48　S. Owen. The Lost Literary History (trans. Tian Xiaofei). // *Borrowed Stone—Stephen Owen's Selected Essays*. Nanjing: Jiangsu People's Publishing House, 2003: 10.
49　J. Guillory. Canon (trans. Wen Lisan). // F. Lentricchia & T. McLaughlin (eds.), *Literary Criticism Terminology* (trans. Zhang Jingyuan). Hong Kong: Oxford University Press, 1994: 328–329.
50　Dai Yan. Preface. *The Power of History of Literature*. Beijing: Peking University Press, 2004: 8.
51　Qian Xuelie. *Commentary on the Poems of Han-shan and Shi-de*. Tianjin: Tianjin Ancient Books Publishing House, 1998: 597.
52　The statement of Luo Shijin罗时进 in *The Evolution of Tang Poetry* that *A History of the Development of Chinese Literature* was published in Taiwan in the 1940s and 1950s by the Chung Hwa Book Bureau is probably not true. Liu Dajie's literary history was first published in the 1940s by the Shanghai Chinese Bookstore as A History of the Development of Chinese Literature, and in the 1960s in Taiwan by the Taipei Chinese Bookstore as *A History of the Development of Chinese Literature*.
　　See Luo Shijin. *The Evolution of Tang Poetry*. Nanjing: Jiangsu Ancient Books Press, 2001: 110.
53　The edition of 1976 only mentions Wang Ji (585–644) in its introduction to this school of poets. The introduction to him was also clearly influenced by the dominant ideology of the time. For example, in "In Wang Ji's Thought", there is a contempt for Confucianism and a mockery of Zhou and Confucius. See Liu Dajie 刘大杰. 中国文学发展史：第二册 (*The Development History of Chinese Literature* (Vol. II). Shanghai: Shanghai People's Publishing House, 1976: 39.
54　Shanghai Classics Publishing House. *The Development History of Chinese Literature*—publication notes. // Liu Dajie (ed.), *The Development History of Chinese Literature*. Shanghai: Shanghai Classics Publishing House, 1997.
55　Liu Dajie. *The Developed History of Chinese Literature*. Taipei: Zhonghua Book Company, 1966: 315–316.
56　Mao Zishu. Preface to *The Development History of Chinese Literature* (Updated Version). // Liu Dajie (ed.), *The Development History of Chinese Literature* (Updated Version). Taipei: Huazheng Book Company, 1980: 1–2.
57　Chen Zizhan. History of Literature in Tang Dynasty. // Liu Ts'un-ya & Chen Zizhan (ed.), *A History of Chinese Great Literature* (Vol. 1). Shanghai: Shanghai Bookstore, 2001: 225.
58　Chen Zizhan. History of Literature in Tang Dynasty. // Liu Ts'un-ya & Chen Zizhan (eds.), *A History of Chinese Great Literature* (Vol. 1). Shanghai: Shanghai Bookstore, 2001: 227.
59　Yang Yinshen. *Outline of the History of Chinese Literature*. Hong Kong: Commercial Press, 1954: 152.
60　Yang Yinshen. *Outline of the History of Chinese Literature*. Hong Kong: Commercial Press, 1954: 154.
61　Liu Ts'un-yan. Preface. // *The History of Chinese Literature*. Hong Kong: Da Kung Book Company, 1956: 1.
62　Liu Ts'un-yan. *The History of Chinese Literature* (Vol. 1). Hong Kong: Da Kung Book Company, 1956: 118–119.
63　Chen Pingping. The Establishment of "Literary History" as a Discipline. // *The Formation and Construction of Literary History*. Nanning: Guangxi Education Press, 1999: 12.
64　N. Maeno. *The History of Chinese Literature* (trans. Lian Xihua & He Jipeng). Taipei: Chang'an Press, 1979: 119.
65　Liu Ts'un-yan 柳存仁, 中国文学史：中国文学欣赏导读全集 *(The History of Chinese Literature: A Complete Introduction to the Appreciation of Chinese Literature)*. Taipei: Zhuangyan Publishing House, 1982: 146.
66　Xiong Lihui. *The History of Chinese Literature*. Beijing: Higher Education Press, 1989: 426–427.

67 Chen Yugang. *Chinese Ancient Literary History* (Volume of the Sui, Tang and Five Dynasties). Beijing: Beijing Normal University Press, 398.
68 Luo Zongqiang & Hao Shifeng. *Literature History of Sui, Tang and Five Dynasties* (Vol. 2). Beijing: Higher Education Publishing House, 1994: 336–351.
69 Wang Xiang. *History of Chinese Literature* (Volume of the Sui, Tang and Five Dynasties). Changchun: Jilin People's Publishing House, 1998: 191–195.
70 Guo Yuheng. *Ancient Chinese Literature History* (Volume of the Sui, Tang and Five Dynasties). Beijing: Captial Normal University Press, 2000: 1.
71 Cai Zhenchu. *History of Ancient Chinese Literary Criticism*. Changsha: Yuelu Book Press, 2000: 197.
72 Yuan Xingpei & Luo Zongqiang. *History of Chinese Literature* (2nd edition, Vol. 2). Beijing: Higher Education Press, 2005: 173.
73 2 Yuan Xingpei & Luo Zongqiang. *History of Chinese Literature* (2nd edition, Vol. 2). Beijing: Higher Education Press, 2005: 173.
74 Xiong Lihui. *The History of Chinese Literature*. Wuhan: Wuhan University Press, 2009: 37–40.
75 1 N. Maeno. *History of Chinese Literature*. Shanghai: Fudan University Press, 2012: 98.
76 Huang Ren. *History of Chinese Literature*. Suzhou: Soochow University Press, 2015: 206.
77 Liao Zhongan & Liu Guoying (eds.). *Dictionary of Chinese Classical Literature*. Beijing: Beijing Press, 1989: 88–89.
78 Wang Hong & Tian Jun. *Encyclopedia of Tang Poetry*. Beijing: Guangming Daily Press, 1990: 1400–1401.
79 Wang Hong & Tian Jun. General Preface. // *Encyclopedia of Tang Poetry*. Beijing: Guangming Daily Press, 1990: 2–3.
80 Ren Daobin. *Dictionary of Buddhist Culture*. Hangzhou: Zhejiang Ancient Books Publishing House, 1991: 113.
81 Ren Daobin. *Dictionary of Buddhist Culture*. Hangzhou: Zhejiang Ancient Books Publishing House, 1991: 113.
82 Ren Jiyu. *Great Dictionary of Religion*. Shanghai: Shanghai Dictionary Publishing House, 1998: 301.
83 Sun Changwu. Preface. // Qian Xuelie (ed.), *Commentary on Cold Mountain Poems and Shi-de's Poems*. Tianjin: Tianjin Ancient Books Publishing House, 1998: 12.

# 7 Concluding Remarks

Due to the deep-rooted thinking pattern of conventional academic traditions, researchers and publishers still prefer works of macro narration and those of the mainstream writers in a traditional sense. Therefore, the CMPs are still in an awkward situation of "being kept in boudoir with little knowledge". In the history of Chinese translated literature, what is even more unfortunate is that Han-shan and his poems are almost nowhere to be found. Only the book *Hanji Waiyi Shi* (《汉籍外译史》, *The History of Translating Chinese Classics*) (1997) by Ma Zuyi and Ren Rongzhen has ever introduced poet Han-shan as well as the studies and translation of his poems but in an extremely brief and rough way. There is no greater irony than this. The "Han-shan phenomenon", which has exerted such an important influence in the comparative literature and translation circles of the East and the West, has met such a cold acceptance in all histories of translated literature named after "Chinese history of translated literature". It is advisable that the translation studies triggered by this phenomenon are necessary for further discussion and demonstration in terms of writing space and writing thought of translated literature's history. Until today, the CMPs have only acquired the status of "a peripheral canon", although it has changed its neglected fate in literary history and earned a place in the polysystem of Chinese literature. However, for the comprehension and research of Han-shan, as well as the publication of his poems, "the road is long and hard". The text travel and canon construction of the CMPs are undoubtedly a unique cultural memory in the history of Chinese and Western literary exchange, and they bring us diverse and profound afterthoughts.

## 7.1 Reflections on Travelling Theory

It is beyond doubt that there is no such thing as a universally applicable theory, for there is a theoretical vacuum and incompleteness in the explanatory power of any theory. However, when explaining the text with a theory, if we examine the tension between the text and theory critically, we may be able to constantly promote the construction and perfecting of the theory. Actually, from the perspective of text travel, whether it is "Travelling Theory", written by Edward Said or "Polysystem Theory", written by Even Zohar, there is still space for discussion when explaining the text travel of the CMPs.

In addition to the vague and incomprehensible theoretical statements discussed in the second chapter of the book, there are other theoretical vacuums in Said's "Travelling Theory". First of all, it only presupposes a "one-way" mode of theory and thought travel, which obviously neglects to pay attention to the important travel mode of "return journey", because the latter often either strengthens or weakens the power and influence of source theory or source thought. Paying attention to this process is of great significance for studying the changes of the cultural norms of the subject, the mutual influence between the culture of the place of departure and the culture of arrivals (destination), and the true face of literary communication between the two cultures.

Secondly, from the perspective of the text travel of the CMPs, the text was "introduced or tolerated" by the cultural polysystem of arrivals only after the dominant ideology and subject poetics in the cultural polysystem of arrivals as well as the translator's "localization" to a certain extent, and on this basis promoted the recognition and reception of the CMPs by the home culture. Therefore, the four major stages of theory and thought travel proposed by Said also have theoretical defects in sequence, and the third and fourth stages of his theoretical model need to be readjust in practice.

Similarly, three types of situations mentioned in the "Polysystem Theory" of Zohar describe the conditions contributing to the central position of translated literature in the cultural polysystem of the destination from a macro-perspective. If we observe three situations with the travelling theory, then the shift in status between the "periphery" and the "center" can also be regarded as a kind of travelling or moving of theories and ideas. It is undeniable that if we use the theoretical hypothesis of Zohar to look into the travel and reception of the CMPs in the United States, then the polysystem theory is reasonable to some extent. However, it would be an overstretch if the hypothesis were to be used when discussing the travel and reception of the CMPs in European countries such as Germany, France and the UK. This same problem would arise if we were also to discuss the travel and reception of the poems when looing at Asian countries like Japan and Korea. The theoretical hypothesis of Zohar only discusses three presuppositions for translated literature to take a "center" position on the part of the nature and existing stage of the cultural polysystem of arrivals. Therefore, it only refers to the situation when the cultural polysystem of arrivals has not yet established, or is in the period of weakness and transition, but ignores the situation when the translated literature can also occupy the "central position" in the period of political openness and cultural prosperity. This seems to have something to do with the fact that this theory was born in a relatively not quite as established culture like that of Israel.

Secondly, what the polysystem claimed, "In short, it is a major goal, and a workable possibility for the Polysystem theory, to deal with the particular conditions under which a certain literature may be interfered with by another literature, as a result of which properties are transferred from one polysystem to another." are also flawed for the vagueness in its expression.[1] More specifically, Zohar only mentions three special cases in which destination literature is influenced by translated literature, and further points out that in all three cases, the status and position of translated literature usually shifts and changes, thus occupying a central and primary position of the destination literature system. But Zohar does not seem to be concerned about how the translated literature is canonically reconstructed in the host culture after it has taken the central position in the literary system of arrivals and "returned from its journey". In brief, the theoretical mode of shifting and changing by Zohar is only a "one-way" mode, rather than a normal mode of two-way. There is no doubt that the shift of status between translated literature and home literature, like the dynamic transformation of canon and non-canon, should be a two-way and reversible process. In the case of the CMPs, it has been recognized as the canon by the literary system of arrivals, and seems to have naturally gained the canonical status, which is recognized by the literary orthodoxy of the host culture afterwards. Though it is merely "a peripheral canon" or "periphery in the canon" when compared with other literary canon in the history of Chinese literature. Therefore, the theoretical framework of polysystem theory would be enriched if we had a profound examination on how the translated literary canon reconstructed in the cultural norms of the host culture after its return journey.

## 7.2 Reflections on Writing the History of Literature

The existing popular histories of (translation) literature are either blank or "downplaying" in their accounts of Han-shan and his poems. How to correctly evaluate the literary value and influence of Han-shan and his poems, so as to establish their proper position in literary history is a problem that should be faced and solved seriously in literary history writing. Or at least, we cannot turn a blind eye to the influence they have had or are having in the literary history, cultural history, and spiritual history of East and West. Needless to say, if the study on Han-shan and his poems stagnate then there might never be any substantial progress in recording Han-shan and his poems in the history of literature. Therefore, the essential prerequisite for Han-shan and his poems to leave a mark on Chinese literary history is to develop relevant academic research. More precisely, we should give a comprehensive and unprejudiced evaluation of the linguistic and artistic achievements of the CMPs, rather than emphasize their achievements as "vernacular poems" while ignoring their identity as "religious poems" and "mainstream poems". Otherwise, with the guiding ideology of emphasis on the nature and influence of literature, Han-shan and his poems will never reverse their status as a "peripheral canon".

In addition to such literary perception, another reason for the CMPs' status of "peripheral canon" is that the literary creation mode and linguistic expression mode of the CMPs are far from being models to imitate in the literature and language courses. In other words, its creation mode has not yet become a subject cultural norm and a "worthy-to-follow" literary mode in the cultural polysystem. It should be noted that this book is not intended to push the CMPs to a "core canon" status, but only to draw more attention to the CMPs and their enormous influence on literature and culture worldwide through the statement that the CMPs are a "peripheral canon". After all, "classic" is only a literary phenomenon. Once the power relations represented by the dominant ideology, the dominant poetics and the literary patrons shift, the "classic" is likely to be "de-canonized". Therefore, the "periphery" and the "center", the "peripheral canon" and the "core canon" are just products of the shift of ideology and literary fashion. In other words, to ignore or disregard such peculiar and typical literary phenomenon is nothing else but admitting our closed and old cultural position and literary attitude. Of course, it is not possible for the writing of literary history to be all-inclusive, but we should give more space for Han-shan and his poems in the books on the dynastic history of literature (like the Tang Dynasty history of literature, the Da Li period history of literature), on the history of specialized literature (like the history of monastic literature, the history of religious literature), on the history of genre-specific literature (like the history of popular literature, the history of vernacular poetry), on the history of location-specific literature (the history of Zhejiang literature, the history of Tiantai literature) and other specialized books. After all, the literary landscape and literary influence of Chinese literature through the ages cannot only be assessed by the single criterion of the nature of literature and the definition. The very nature of literature keeps changing. Therefore, it is necessary to innovate the old literary concepts and change the inherent mode when writing literature history. Even if the CMPs could never possess a more natural place in literature and surpass the solid status of classic works written by famous poets like Tao Yuanming (陶渊明), Xie Lingyun (谢灵运), Li Bai (李白) or Du Fu (杜甫). Breakthrough is bound to be made in academic studies on folklore, local history, linguistic history and cultural history reflected in more than 300 poems, which are of various contents and believed to be from the lower class. In-depth and substantive studies on those elements will have great social and academic value since they can provide information about the society, political system, imperial examination system, customs, ethics, dialects of the Tang Dynasty, and even the identity of Han-shan. Therefore, we may explore the cultural significance of Han-shan and his poems from the perspective of intellectual archaeology, so as to outline the spiritual life of literati from the lower class and the societal landscape of Tang Dynasty. This may be a future direction of the study on the CMPs and one of the valuable inspirations we get from the study on the text travel and canon construction of the CMPs. Moreover, present studies on the influence of the CMPs are unsatisfactory, so more efforts need to be made if we want to give them an accurate assessment when writing literary history. In terms of its vertical influence, most of the studies of the CMPs merely focus on the parts of "vernacular poetry" and "religious poetry" and few on the "mainstream poetry". As for its "horizontal" influence, studies are even more scarce. Domestic scholars have studied their impacts on Japan and America while little research has been done on their influences on other Asian and European countries.

While appealing for objective and fair "Han-shan Studies" and comprehensive reassessment of the status and influence of the poet and the poems in Chinese literary history, it seems that the writing of literary history also needs to renew its traditional writing ideas. In the case of *Zhongguo Wenxue Shi* (《中国文学史》, *The History of Chinese Literature*), the compiler should make judgments independently on the basis of the arguments of his predecessors instead of merely following them and neglecting the examination of the time and sociocultural context of their discourses. The epochal character and sociocultural context of discourses are two important factors that need to be taken account of. Stephen Owen emphasizes that

> a literary work should not only be discussed in the context of the history of its genre, but it also belongs to a system that I call "discourse system", which refers to the group that reads, listens, writes, reproduces, changes and disseminates the text at a given time.[2]

This requires compilers to be sensitive to literature and to keep their compiling work abreast of modern academic research. Only in this way can the literary history be composed relatively objective. *Suitangwudai Wenxueshi (Zhongjuan)* (《隋唐五代文学史(中卷)》, *Literature of Sui, Tang and Five Dynasties* (Volume 2) (Beijing: Higher Education Press, 1994), edited by Luo Zongqiang and Hao Shifeng, is an excellent example. This book shows a wise insight into literature of the two compilers. Moreover, it adopted the most authoritative research results of "Han-shan Studies" in its introduction and evaluation of Han-shan and his poems. This writing mode of literary history seems to be a classic model for the editors of *The History of Chinese Literature*.

As a matter of fact, present studies of literary history and the history of literature in literature are mostly introductions of research status and lists of research materials, but evaluation of them is scarce. Even more, even the introduction is vague and ambiguous, so much so that the errors are copied. A possible reason for this is caused by the lack of careful textual research, as well as the insufficient communication and exchanges with related disciplines. If editors of literature history can comprehensively examine the whole "discourse system" of literary works—production, circulation, transmission, translation and reception, then the current situation of literary history writing will certainly be improved fundamentally. Therefore, researchers of Chinese literature, religion, comparative literature, translation and publishing, as well as writers of literary history should strengthen cooperation and communication so as to promote the construction of the "discourse system" of literary history writing.

### 7.3 Reflections on Travel Mode and Canon Construction of the CMPs

As mentioned earlier, the dominant ideology and dominant poetics of cultural norms in the culture of the place of departure greatly impact and restrict the intralingual travel of the departing text. If both the form and the content of a text conform to the ideology and poetics standards recognized by the subject cultural norms, and the author of the text is recognized by the subject cultural norms as orthodoxy, then this text is expected to become a classic in the departure's cultural polysystem during its intralingual travel both diachronically and synchronically. Chances are that this text obtains a "lawful seat" in literary history. But if these requirements are hard to meet, the text is likely to be ignored, marginalized, even erased out of the mainstream literature history. When paradigm shifts happen to the subject cultural norms and the literary concept owing to the changes of ideology, poetic traditions, academic ethos, etc., there may be a chance for the text to be circulated, popularized, interpreted, studied and even canonized. Of course, this is only a simplified description of the canon construction of literary texts in the departure-the original cultural polysystem, but the fate and conditions of the CMPs are far more complex.

Diachronically, as China's East Asian neighbor, Japan has close ties with China in relation to their shared histories, shared language traits, and shared characters. In addition, Japan enjoys a cultural polysystem with compatible ideology and poetic traditions. Therefore, it embraced the CMPs, which had been "marginalized" in their original subject cultural norms. Since their introduction to Japan in the Northern Song Dynasty (960–1127), the CMPs have had a significant and positive impact on the study on language, literature, religion, art and even spiritual history in Japan. Hence, the CMPs integrated into the cultural polysystem of Japan successfully and gained an immortal canonical status. This phenomenon could be called the "Japanese Model" of canon construction of the CMPs, which is caused partly by the kinship between China and Japan in terms of language and cultural background, and partly by the latter's positive and open cultural attitude. In such a cultural polysystem, literature in translation may enjoy a literary status almost equal to that of original literature, and even become its "center" and "mainstream". Therefore, for foreign cultures and texts, especially for the culture and text forms conforming to the dominant ideology and poetics tradition of the host country, they will do their best to import and translate. In such subject cultural norms, even if some culture and text forms are not in line with the dominant ideology and poetic tradition of the host country, they generally import these cultures and texts first and then transformed and domesticated them in some localized ways for their own use. Such examples are not uncommon in the history of translation. It is in such a harmonious discourse field of the destination culture that the CMPs can be "transformed". In addition, due to the openness and inclusiveness of Japan as a cultural subject, many Western countries tend to choose Japan as an intermediary of cultural input. As for the typical case of the CMPs, it is Japan, the "travel intermediary", that sets up multiple communication platforms between the CMPs and European and American cultures, so that the CMPs have the opportunity to start their interlingual literary journey in the cultural polysystem of destinations.

With the facilitation of Japan as an "intermediary", the society, politics, and culture of America which was in a special period (the 1950s–1960s) of transition, the manipulation of patrons and the poet-translator Gary Snyder's fully consideration of target audience's "expectancy norms", the carefully "localized" CMPs appeared frequently in various literary history works and anthologies, as well as the humanities lectures of many universities. In the canon construction of the CMPs, a craze of "Han-shan Studies" among the general public and the academic circles was aroused. This phenomenon proves that when the cultural polysystem of arrivals (the destination) is in a period of infancy, marginality or transition, translated literature can move from "peripheral" to "central" position and thus become an "intrinsic part of a revolutionary force". At this particular point, if the literary text which is traveling into this cultural polysystem goes through "localization", it can easily acquire an identity as "canon of translated literary" in the targeted cultural polysystem. This process can be defined as the "American Model" in the canon construction of the CMPs.

The "localization" mentioned here is a means of translation "rewriting" to cater the dominant ideology and mainstream poetics as well as the "native consciousness" of the target audience. The main purpose behind this "rewriting" and "localized interpreting" is to stimulate a sense of cultural and even national identity and belonging from the aspects of language, characters, aesthetics, as well as emotion among the target audience. In this way, the "localized" texts are more likely to gain the recognition and support of the largest readership and classic makers in the cultural polysystem of arrivals, thus achieving the desired goal of canon construction more smoothly. It should be pointed out that the "localization" attempt is not limited to the linguistic level, but also involves various "localized" efforts in achieving the canon construction of a text, such as seeking to conform to the dominant ideology and to gain recognition and support of various patrons.

Due to the stimulation of great literary influence won by the CMPs in Japan and the United States, as well as the change of literary concept and cultural research, the traditional cognition mode of "classics" and "elegance and vulgarity" in the subject literary norms began to shake. When the CMPs began their return journey, they easily gained the "special respect" of the cultural polysystem where it originated. Except for attention from folk forces, Han-shan and his poems, long ignored by the Chinese literary orthodoxy, also received attention from the academic circles and literary history writing, and finally earned itself a place in Chinese literary history and anthologies. For various reasons, however, the CMPs remain a "peripheral canon" in current studies of Chinese literature history and translated literature. In contrast to the ideological and artistic achievements of the CMPs, and their great influence on comparative literature, media studies and translation studies, their position of "peripheral canon" is an irony. If this "peripheral canon" mode is defined as the "Chinese Model" in the canon construction of the CMPs, then this mode undoubtedly reveals huge space and congenital deficiency in the study on the CMPs.

In fact, both the "Japanese model" and "American model" reflect an open and inclusive attitude of cultural subjects without exception. What they both reveal is the recognition and reference of one culture and literature to another culture and literature, and on this basis, some available elements are organically integrated into the construction of local culture, and then take this as a breakthrough to find a new development model of their own cultural subject. It is hard to say that the concern of nature, ecology, environmental protection and Zen in today's cultural polysystem of Japanese and American culture has not been influenced by Han-shan and his poems.

In a sense, Han-shan and his poems offered a new opportunity for spiritual redemption and literary reformation for the cultural polysystems of Japanese and American cultures. This is truly a very high level of cultural appropriation, the premise of its success is nothing more than to hold no prejudice to foreign culture. The "Chinese Model", on the contrary, reveals a relatively closed and conservative cultural mentality of the source culture. In such a mode, the literary authorities and cultural conservatism set stringent selection criteria and numerous restrictions on text travel and canon construction, neither endeavoring to explore the constructive factors of text nor to promote the integration and innovation of texts with local culture. Therefore, in the face of the established literary and cultural norms, these texts are always in a marginal and exile state in the local cultural polysystem. However, once they have the opportunity to embark on the journey of interlingual travel, they are often favored and recognized by the cultural polysystem of arrivals to which they go, thus performing a literary drama of "blossoming inside the wall and perfuming outside the wall".

In summary, the "Japanese Model" is mainly based on the close tie between the CMPs and the Japanese language and culture. That is, the "intra-textual factors" play a decisive role in this mode. As for the American Model, it is resulted from "extra-textual factors" such as dominant ideology, poetic tradition, patrons, and translators and readers besides the "intra-textual factors". While the "Chinese Model" swings both ways, whether it is "extra-textual factors" or "intra-textual factors", the CMPs are ignored by both. Even though occasional interest in the CMPs is shown, it is merely out of a literary view of utilitarianism. Even returning to his homeland in glory, the CMPs are no more than an ornament in the current repertoire of classic Chinese literature. Consequently, the study on the textual value and literary influence of the CMPs is smattering so much that the current Chinese literary, religious, publishing and other social circles still have almost no knowledge of the CMPs, not to mention any deeper understanding of the significance of "Han-shan Studies". To conclude, our exploration should not be limited to the studies on the poet and his poems, nor to the improvement of theories and literary histories. What Chinese academia should reflect on is the attitudes, the perspectives, as well as the approaches to viewing native culture and foreign cultures.

Undoubtedly, stepping out of the enclosed territory of one's home culture is the greatest enlightenment that the text travel and canon construction of the CMPs have brought to people.

**Notes**

1  I. Even-Zohar. Polysystem Theory. *Poetics Today*, 1990, 11 (1): 25.
2  S. Owen. The Lost Literary History (trans. Tian Xiaofei). // *Borrowed Stone—Stephen Owen's Selected Essays*. Nanjing: Jiangsu People's Publishing House, 2003: 10.

# Afterword

Although it has been difficult for Chinese and foreign academic circles to reach a discourse consensus on the iconic Chinese poet Han-shan discussed in this book and those Cold Mountain poems attributed to him, Chinese and foreign readers can still feel the real existence of this figure and his poems from varieties of literary anthologies, poetry anthologies, literary histories, poetry histories, art histories, histories of folklore and histories of literary exchanges. If we are willing to believe his identity as an enduring poet in the Tang Dynasty (618–907) and all those amazing legendary stories about him, then this Chinese monk hermit who lived more than a thousand years ago has truly pleased and warmed those who love him all over the world. His tramp appearance, ragged clothing, unworldly temperament, as well as the inspiring wit, Buddha nature and harmonious thought in the poems that were not favored by his Chinese compatriots but were extremely popular with target readers outside China, are nowadays remarkably unforgettable and memorable. Regardless of the affection and ravishment of the academic community and literature lovers in the proceeding dynasties, his magical prophecy of "one day I'll meet someone with eyes, then my poems will plague the world", and his poems being highly commended by Emperor Yongzheng in the Qing Dynasty (1636–1912) of "straight words" and "perfect splendor", as well as him and his companion Shi-de being mythologized of "Immortals of Harmony/Two Saints of Hehe" in the Chinese folklore, are enough to make him superior to all his contemporaries and successors throughout the world.

As a matter of fact, Han-shan and his Cold Mountain poems have long been famous all over the world. The muse from Cathay has made a great story in the history of literary exchanges between China and foreign countries through his nearly thousand-year interlingual travel. If his world influence is expressed according to the current discourse system, we might say that he and his poems have expanded the international influence of Chinese literature, and enhanced China's international academic discourse in philosophy and social sciences. In this sense, it is necessary for today's Chinese people and the people who have little knowledge of him overseas to have a novel understanding of this legendary figure who enjoys a high literary prestige worldwide and his Cold Mountain poems which contain variety of universal wisdom.

The book *Cold Mountain Poems: Text Travel and Canon Construction*, which is in front of you dear readers, was recommended to Tsinghua University Press by the prestigious professors Martha Cheung, Xu Jun and Wang Ning. It was then included in the series of "Translation and Interdisciplinary Research" edited by Professor Luo Xuanmin and published by Tsinghua University Press in 2011. Bookstores and websites have already sold it out, thanks to good response from readers and the book market. As early as five years ago, Professor Luo had kindly urged me to produce a hardcover edition, but due to my indolence, I had been putting it off with various excuses. However, owing to the reputation of Han-shan and his Cold Mountain poems, the book I applied for the topics of China Academic Translation Project was fortunately selected into the list in September 2020. My recommendation is that the translation, introduction and dissemination of Cold Mountain Poems is one of the most classic case studies in the history of Chinese literature and the history of Chinese and foreign translated literature, and the ideas of harmony and traditional Chinese culture represented by Han-shan and his poems are superb Chinese cultures with the greatest value of international communication, and also an important window for the international community to better understand Chinese literature, culture and society. In the following application for this national translation project, thanks to the kindness of the academic community, scholars from English, Russian, French, German, Spanish, Japanese and some other languages applied for the translation of this book. In the list announced at the beginning of 2021, Dr. Zhu Jinyu from School of Western Languages and Culture of Sichuan International Studies University has been approved for her Spanish application, which admittedly gives Han-shan and his Cold Mountain poems a chance to visit the fascinating and passionate Spanish-speaking world. I am wondering whether the poet himself is grinning happily in some corner of the world at this time, for it seems that he have never set foot on that vast and wondrous continent ever before.

Presumably because of some sort of recognition and encouragement from the earlier-mentioned project, I guess it is time to revise the previous manuscript now. Therefore, I spent more than half a year to make a thorough and meticulous revision from beginning to end. The work was far more complicated than I had expected, and I even wanted to give up halfway. However, whenever I thought it was a golden opportunity to tell the story of China in academic discourse to the people overseas who love Han-shan and his poems, I was then reinvigorated and continue to move forward.

Here, I would like to thank Ms. Jianhua Hao and Mr. Zhenyu Yang of Tsinghua University Press for their warm encouragement and hard work as well. In particular, I would like to express my heart-felt thanks to Ms. Xizhen Liu for her kind help, which made this English translation possible. Meanwhile, I also want to thank my graduate students Hongyan Peng, Bingxue Jia, Lei Nian, Junyao Li, Wenjing Xie, Qianyun Feng, Jiaojiao Zhang and Kunpeng Zhang for participating in the arduous translating work of this book. I would also like to thank Ms. Jing Xu from Tsinghua University Press and Jack Hay from School of Translation and

Interpreting of Sichuan International Studies University for their professional suggestions in the process of proofreading this English translation manuscript.

I would like to dedicate this book to my wife, Xiaolin Zhou, and my daughter, Kang'en Hu. Thank you for your years of care and companionship. I would also like to thank my deceased mother, Ms. Yixiu Wei (1954–2012), and my late Ph.D supervisor, Professor Martha P. Y. Cheung (1953–2013), for inculcating me in life and in academic research. I also want to say thank-you to all my friends for your help, support and encouragement throughout, which give me the strength to overcome the difficulties and the courage to keep going ahead.

Anjiang Hu

# References

Adams, H. 1994. Canons: Literary Criteria/Power Criteria. Zeng, Z. Z. (trans.). *Chung-Wai Literary Monthly* (2): 6–26.
Allen, D. 1960. *The New American Poetry*. New York: Grove Press.
Allén, S. 1999. *Translation of Poetry and Poetic Prose: Proceedings of Nobel Symposium 110*. Singapore, NJ, London and Hong Kong: World Scientific Publishing Co. Pte. Ltd.
Almberg, E. S. P. 2003. From Apology to a Matter of Course. // Chan, Leo Tak-hung (ed.), *One into Many, Translation and the Dissemination of Classical Chinese Literature*. Amsterdam and New York: Rodopi.
Barrett, T. H. 1993. Book Review: The Poetry of Han-shan (Cold Mountain): A Complete, Annotated Translation, by Robert G. Henricks. *Bulletin of the School of Oriental and African Studies*, 56(3): 647–648.
Barrett, T. H. 2003a. Hanshan in Translation. // Hobson, P. (ed.), *Poems of Hanshan*. Walnut Creek: Altamira Press.
Barrett, T. H. 2003b. Hanshan's Place in History. // Hobson, P. (ed.), *Poems of Hanshan*. Walnut Creek: Altamira Press.
Bartsch, R. 1987. *Norms of Language: Theoretical & Practical Aspects*. London and New York: Longman.
Bassnett, S. 1993. *Comparative Literature: A Critical Introduction*. Oxford and Cambridge: Blackwell.
Bassnett, S. & Lefevere, A. (eds.). 1998. *Constructing Cultures: Essays on Literary Translation*. Clevendon: Multilingual Matters.
Benedict, R. 2005. *The Chrysanthemum and the Sword* (trans. Lü, W. et al.). Beijing: The Commercial Press.
Benjamin, W. 1992. The Task of the Translator. // Schutle, R. & Biguenet, J. (eds.), *Theories of Translation: An Anthology of Essays from Dryden to Derrida*. Chicago: The University of Chicago Press.
Birch, C. 1965/1967. *Anthology of Chinese Literature: From Early Times to the Fourteenth Century*. New York: Grove Press.
Bloom, H. 1994. *The Western Canon: The Books and School of the Ages*. New York: Harcourt Brace.
Bokenkamp, S. R. 1991. Book Review: *The Poetry of Han-shan (Cold Mountain): A Complete, Annotated Translation. Robert G. Henricks*. Albany: State University of New York Press, 1990. p. 486, *Chinese Literature: Essays, Articles, Reviews*, 13.
Borgen, R. 1991. The Legend of Hanshan: A Neglected Source. *Journal of the American Oriental Society*, 111(3).

Cai, Z. X. 2004. Breakthrough and Proposition: On Snyder's Imagination of Mountains and Rivers Without End. *Chung-Wai Literary Monthly* (5): 106–128.

Cao, X. 1997. The Bosom Friend of Cold Mountain Poems in the Song Dynasty—Also on the Circulation and Influence of Cold Mountain Poems in the Song Dynasty. // *Chinese Classics & Culture Essays Collection* (4th edition). Beijing: Zhonghua Book Company, 121–133.

Chen, D. H. 1970. The Zen Realm and Poetic Sentiment of Han-shan-zi. // Han-shan et al. (eds.), *The Anthology of Poems by Han-shan, Feng-gan, Chu-shi, Shi-de and Shih Shu*. Taipei: Wenfeng Press.

Chen, D. R. & Chen, Z. F. 1995. *Canon and Literature Teaching*. Taipei: Society for Comparative Literature/Department of English and American Languages and Literatures, National Central University.

Chen, H. J. 1984. *Studies on Han-shan-zi*. Taipei: The Grand East Book Company.

Chen, P. Y. 1999. Chen Pingping. The establishment of "Literary History" as a Discipline. // *The Formation and Construction of Literary History*. Nanning: Guangxi Education Press.

Chen, S. 2004. *Canon-making: The Cultural Politics of Jin Yong Studies*. Guilin: Guangxi Normal University Press.

Chen, W. P. 1991. A Review of Waston's The Columbia Book of Chinese Poetry: From Early Times to the Thirteenth Century. *Chinese Translators Journal* (1): 44–48.

Chen, Y. *Selected Han-Shan Poems for Hippie Reading* [OL]. www.yogichen.org/chenian/bk049.html. [2006-10-14].

Chen, Y. & Li, H. C. 2003. *Tang Poems in the Context of Confucianism, Buddhism and Taoism*. Beijing: Kunlun Press.

Chen, Y. C. 2001. Chen Yinchi. Two Worlds of Han-shan. // *The Great World: Buddhist Literature*. Kunming: Yunnan People's Publishing House.

Cheng, H. 2001. Communication Across Time and Space: Contemporary American Writers on Nature Literature and the Chinese Poet Han-shan of the Tang Dynasty. *Foreign Literature* (6): 67–71.

Cheng, W. F. & Collet, H. 1985/1992. *Han Shan: Merveilleux le Chemin de Han Shan*. Millemont: Moundarren.

Chesterman, A. 1997. *Memes of Translation: The Spread of Ideas in Translation Theory*. Amsterdam and Philadelphia: John Benjamins Publishing Company.

Cheung, M. 2003. Translation as Discourse: A Re-reading of Wei Yi and Lin Shu's Chinese Translation of Uncle Tom's Cabin. *Chinese Translators Journal* (2): 17–22.

Chi-yu, W. 1957. A Study of Han Shan. *T'oung Pao*, XLV.

Chung, L. 1970. *The Status of Han-shan in Eastern and Western Literature. Han-shan's Poems: With Poems by Feng Gan, Chushi, Goude, and Shi Shu Yuan*. Taipei: Wenfeng Press.

Chung, L. 1984. *The Circulation of Han-shan's Poems. Essays on Literary Criticism*. Taipei: Times Cultural Publishing Co.

Chung, L. 2003. *American Poetry and Chinese Dream*. Guilin: Guangxi Normal University Press.

Chung, L. 2008. Han-Shan and American Poems (1980–2007). *Academic Forum* (7): 61–65.

Chung, L. 2018. *Deep Layers of the Text: Cross-cultural Fusion and Gender Exploration*. Taipei, China: National Taiwan University Press.

Clifford, J. 1992. Traveling Cultures. // Lawrence Grossberg et al. (eds.), *Cultural Studies*. New York and London: Routledge.

Clifford, J. 1999. *Routes: Travel and Translation in the Late Twentieth Century*. Cambridge, MA and London: Harvard University Press.

Dai, Y. 2004. *The Power of History of Literature*. Beijing: Peking University Press.

Davidson, M. 1989. *The San Francisco Renaissance: Poetics and Community at Mid-century*. Cambridge: Cambridge University Press.
Duan, X. C. 1996. A Study of the Edition of CMPs Collection. *Library Tribune* (1): 62–64.
Even-Zohar, I. 1978. The Position of Translated Literature within the Literary Polysystem. // Holmes, J., Lambert, J. & Broeck, Raymond Van Den (eds.), *Literature and Translation*. Leuven: Academic Publishing Company.
Even-Zohar, I. 1990. Polysystem Theory. *Poetics Today*, 11(1), Spring.
Fackler, H. 1971. Three English Versions of Han-Shan's Cold Mountain Poems. *Literature East and West*, XV.
Fang, A. 1953. Some Reflections on the Difficulty of Translation. // Wright, A. (ed.), *Studies in Chinese Thought*. Chicago and London: The University of Chicago Press.
Fokkema, D. and Ibsch, E. 2000. *Knowledge and Commitment, A Problem-oriented Approach to Literary Studies*. Amsterdam and Philadelphia: John Benjamins.
Foster, N. and Shoemaker, J. 1996. *The Roaring Stream: A New Zen Reader*. Hopewell, NJ: Ecco Press.
Franke, H. 1966a. Book Review: *Anthology of Chinese Literature: From Early Times to the Fourteenth Century*. Birch, C. *Journal of the American Oriental Society*, 86(2).
Frankel, H. 1960b. Book Review: *Poems by Wang Wei*, by Chang Yin-nan & Lewis C. Walmsley. Rutland and Tokyo: Charles E. Tuttle Company, 1958. *Journal of the American Oriental Society*, 80(2).
Frankel, H. 1986. Book Review: *The Columbia Book of Chinese Poetry: From Early Times to the Thirteenth Century*. Translated and edited by Burton Waston. *Harvard Journal of Asiatic Studies*, 46(1), June.
Frodsham, J. D. 1973. The Origin of Chinese Nature Poetry. The Translation Committee of Chinese Classics of the Chinese University of Hong Kong. // Deng, S. L. (trans.), *British and American Scholars on Classical Chinese Literature*. Hong Kong: The Chinese University of Hong Kong Press.
Fung, S. K. & Lai, S. T. 1984. *25 T'ang Poets: Index to English Translations*. Hong Kong: Chinese University Press.
Gálik, M. 2003. Tang Poetry in Translation in Bohemia and Slovakia (1902–1999). // Chan, Leo Tak-hung (ed.), *One into Many, Translation and the Dissemination of Classical Chinese Literature*. Amsterdam and New York: Rodopi.
Gao, D. S. 1990. *The Metre and Appreciation of English Poetry*. Beijing: The Commercial Press.
Ge, Z. G. 1998. *Essays on Chinese Religion and Literature*. Beijing: Tsinghua University Press.
Ge, Z. G. 2000. *A History of Chinese Zen Thought: From the 6th to the 9th Century*. Beijing: Peking University Press.
Gong, P. C. 2001. *A Spiritual and Cultural Historiography of Travel*. Shijiazhuang: Hebei Education Press.
Graham, A. C. 1965. *Poems of the Late T'ang*. Middlesex: Penguin Books.
Guo, S. T. 2005. *Travel: Intercultural Imagination*. Beijing: Peking University Press.
Hamill, S. & Seaton, J. *2004. The Poetry of Zen*. Boston, MA: Shambhala Publications, Inc.
Han-shan. 1959. *Cold Mountain Poems (The Song Dynasty Edition)*. Hong Kong: Hong Kong Society for Permanent Release.
Han-shan. 1960. Poems. // Dingqiu, Peng (ed.), *Complete Tang Poems* (Vol. 23). Beijing: Zhonghua Book Company.
Harris, P. 1999. *Zen Poems*. New York: Alfred A. Knopf.

Hawkes, D. 1962. Book Review: *Cold Mountain: 100 Poems by the T'ang Poet Han-shan*, Translated and with an Introduction by Burton Watson. p. 122. New York: Grove Press, Inc., 1962. *Journal of the American Oriental Society*, 82(4): 596–599.

Henricks, R. 1990. *The Poetry of Han-shan: A Complete, Annotated Translation of Cold Mountain*. New York: State University of New Work Press.

Hermans, T. 1996. Norms and the Determination of Translation: A Theoretical Framework. // Alvarez, Román & Vidal Carmen-Africa, M. (eds.), *Translation, Power, Subversion*. Clevedon and Philadelphia: Multilingual Matters Ltd.

Hobson, P. 2003. *Poems of Hanshan*. Walnut Creek: Altamira Press.

Hu, A. J. 2005a. Compromise and Metamorphosis: The Theoretical Limitations of Traditional Translation Criticism. *Foreign Languages and Literature* (3): 121–125.

Hu, A. J. 2005b. Textual Travel and Translational Deviation—On the Creative Misreading of Cold Mountain Poems by Gary Snyder. *Journal of PLA University of Foreign Languages* (6): 63–68.

Hu, A. J. 2007a. The Intention of Translation—a Study of Five Sinologist Translations of Fengqiaoyebo. *Journal of Tianjin Foreign Studies University* (6): 63–68.

Hu, A. J. 2007b. Textual Travel and Translation Studies. *Journal of Sichuan International Studies University* (5): 117–122.

Hu, A. J. 2007c. The Dissemination and Reception of CMPs in France. *Comparative Literature in China* (4): 95–109.

Hu, A. J. 2008a. The Dissemination and Reception of CMPs Outside China. // *Yearbook of Literature Studies of the Tang Dynasty*. Guilin: Guangxi Normal University Press, 268–285.

Hu, A. J. 2008b. Towards the Canon Construction of the Translated Text. *Foreign Languages Research* (5): 93–96.

Hu, A. J. 2009a. A Study on the English Translation of CMPs by American Scholar Burton Watson. *Journal of PLA Foreign Languages Institute* (6): 75–80.

Hu, A. J. 2009b. Encounter with Han-shan—A Study on the Dissemination and Reception of CMPs in Britain. *English Studies* (3): 59–64.

Hu, A. J. 2009c. A Study on Arthur Waley's Translation of CMPs. *Foreign Languages and Their Teaching* (9): 53–57.

Hu, A. J. 2009d. Towards Gary Snyder's Poetics in Translation. *Foreign Language and Literature* (2): 130–134.

Hu, A. J. 2009e. Research on the Complete Translation of CMPs by American Scholar Robert Henricks. // *Proceedings of the second Pearl River International Poetry Association and academic Symposium*. Guangzhou: Sun Yat-sen University Press, 218–224.

Hu, A. J. 2009f. The Return Journey of CMPs and its Dissemination and Reception in Hong Kong and Taiwan. // Qiu, S. & Yao, Y. X. (eds.), *Proceedings of the Second Han-shan Temple Cultural Forum* (2008). Shanghai: Shanghai Ancient Books Publishing House, 207–221.

Hu, A. J. 2010. Travel Writings and Roles of Translation Studies in Ancient China. *Journal of Foreign Languages Research* (1): 113–117.

Hu, A. J. 2011. The Three Worlds of CMPs. // Qiu, S. & Yao, Y. X. (eds.), *Proceedings of the Fourth Hanshan Temple Cultural Forum and International Hehe Culture Conference* (2010). Shanghai: Shanghai Sanlian Bookstore, 596–604.

Hu, A. J. 2014. The Dissemination and Reception of CMPs outside China. // Qiu, S. & Yao, Y. X. (eds.), *Proceedings of the 7th Hanshan Temple Cultural Forum* (2013). Shanghai: Shanghai Sanlian Bookstore, 32–47.

Hu, A. J. 2020. *From Text to Audience: Essays on Translation and Cultural Studies*. Beijing: Science Press.
Hu, A. J. (forthcoming). On Gary Snyder's Tradaptation of Cold Mountain Poems and Its Spiritual Salvation and Literary Enlightenment in Postwar America. *Comparative Literature and Culture*.
Hu, A. J. & Hu, C. F. 2012. The Translator Model and the Translating Strategy Revisited——With the Dissemination of CMPs in the English World as an Example. *Foreign Language Learning Theory and Practice* (4): 55–61.
Hu, A. J. & Zhou, X. L. 2008. The Politics of Language and Translation: Ideology and the Construction of Translator's Subjective Identity. *Journal of Sichuan International Studies University* (5): 103–107.
Hu, A. J. & Zhou, X. L. 2009. Towards Red Pine and His Complete Translation of CMPs. *Journal of Southwest University of Political Science and Law* (3): 131–135.
Hu, A. J. & Zhou, X. L. 2012. A Study of Wu Chi-yu's Translation of CMPs. *Foreign Language and Literature* (5): 108–112.
Hu, J. R. 1966. The Resurrection of Poet Monk Han-shan. *Ming Pao Monthly* (11): 2–12.
Hu, S. 1959. *The History of Vernacular Literature*. Hong Kong: Yingzhong Bookstore.
Huang, B. R. 1981. *Han-shan and His Poems*. Taipei: Xinwenfeng Publishing Company.
Huang, M. J. 2004. Classic in Modern Chinese Literature: Recognition and Lasting. *Social Sciences in China* (3): 149–159+208.
Huang, R. 2015. *History of Chinese Literature*. Suzhou: Suzhou University Press.
Huang, X. Z. 1998. *Collected Writings on Chinese Character Culture*. Changsha: Yuelu Publishing House.
Hung, E. 1999. *Translation Literature Culture*. Beijing: Peking University Press.
Hung, E. 2005. *Rewriting Chinese Translation History*. Hong Kong: The Chinese University of Hong Kong.
Hung, E. & Yang, C. S. 2000. *The Traditions and Modern Trends of Translation in Asia*. Beijing: Peking University Press.
Idema, W. L. 2003. Dutch Translations of Classical Chinese Literature. // Leo Tak-hung Chan (ed.), *One into Many, Translation and the Dissemination of Classical Chinese Literature*. Amsterdam and New York: Rodopi.
Iriya, Y. 1989. A Glimpse into Cold Mountain Poems. // Shunhong, Wang (trans.), *Collation and Research of Ancient Books* (Issue 4). Beijing: Zhonghua Book Company.
Islam, S. M. 2000. *The Ethics of Travel: From Marco Polo to Kafka*. Manchester: Manchester University Press.
Jakobson, R. 2004. On Linguistic Aspects of Translation. // Venuti, L. (ed.), *The Translation Studies Reader* (2nd edition). New York: Routledge.
Jeon, K. T. 1972. The Infulences of Chinese Literature on Korean Literature. *Tamkang Review*, II(2) & III(1), October 1971–April.
Jia, R. F. 1995. Spokesman, Mirror and Utopia: Review on Gary Snyder' translation of Cold Mountain Poems. // Chang, Y. X. (ed.), *Multiple Perspectives: A Collection of Essays in Comparative Cultural and Literary Studies*. Tianjin: Nankai University Press, 56–63.
Jordan, K. *A Brief History of the Evergreen Review*. www.evergreenreview.com/100/history.html. [2005–11–11].
Kahn, P. 1986. Han Shan in English. *Renditions*, (25): 140–175.
Kampf, L. & Paul, L. (eds.). 1972. *The Politics of Literature: Dissenting Essays on the Teaching of English*. New York: Pantheon Books.

Kern, R. 1996. *Orientalism, Modernism and the American Poem.* New York: Cambridge University Press.

Kim, Y. J. 2002. The Influence of Cold Mountain Poems on Korean Zen masters and Scholars. *Religious Studies* (4): 44–47+144.

Kline, A. S. 2006. *Twenty-Seven Poems by Han-shan.* www.tonykline.co.uk/PITBR/Chinese/HanShan.htm. [2007-3-19].

Kodama, N. H. 1993. *American Poetry and Japanese Culture* (trans. Yang, Z. W.). Xi'an: Shaanxi People's Education Press.

Kong, Y. D. 2004. *Annotation of Book of Changes.* Beijing: Jiuzhou Press.

Kusumoto, B. Y. 1985. *Han-shan and Shi-te* (Vol. 1). Tokyo: Kodansha.

Lauter, P., et al. (eds.). 1994. *The Heath Anthology of American Literature.* Lexington, MA: D.C. Heath and Co.

Lee, J. M. 2008. A Systematic Examination on Ancient Printed Editions of Cold Mountain Poems. *Compilation of Papers from the International Symposium on Han-shanzi and Harmony Culture.* Hangzhou: Zhejiang University Press, 149–165.

Leed, E. 1991. *The Mind of the Traveler: From Gilgamesh to Global Tourism.* New York: Basic Books.

Leed, J. 1984. Gary Snyder, Han Shan, and Jack Kerouac. *Journal of Modern Literature,* 11(1).

Leed, J. 1986. Gary Snyder: An Unpublished Preface. *Journal of Modern Literature,* 13(1), March.

Lefevere, A. 1992. *Translation, Rewriting and Manipulation of Literary Fame.* London and New York: Routledge.

Lenfestey, J. 2007. *A Cartload of Scrolls: 100 Poems in the Manner of T'ang Dynasty Poet Han-shan.* Duluth, Minnesota: Holy Cow Press.

Lenfestey, J. 2014. *Seeking the Cave: A Pilgrimage to Cold Mountain.* Minneapolis: Milkweed Editions.

Lentricchia, F. & McLaughlin, T. (eds.). 1995. *Critical Terms for Literary Study* (2nd edition). Chicago and London: The University of Chicago Press.

Lentricchia, F. & McLaughlin, T. 1994. *Critical Terms for Literary Studies* (trans. Zhang, J. Y. et al.). Hong Kong: Oxford University Press.

Levý, J. 1989. Translation as a Decision Process. // Chesterman, A. (ed.), *Readings in Translation Theory.* Helsinki: Finn Lectura Ab.

Li, D. C. 2005. A Historical Review of Chinese-to-Korean Translation in Korea. *Journal of PLA University of Foreign Languages* (4): 73–78.

Li, F. 1961. *A Collection of Ancient Novels in China.* Beijing: Zhonghua Book Company.

Li, J. J. 1989. *Dictionary of Classical Chinese Literature.* Beijing: Beijing Publishing House.

Li, O. F. 2000. *The Pursuit of Modernity.* Beijing: CDX Joint Publishing.

Li, O. F. 2005. *My Harvard University Years.* Nanjing: Jiangsu Education Publishing House.

Lin, G. 1987. *A Comprehensive Study on Tang Poetry.* Beijing: People's Literature Publishing House.

Lin, G. 1988. *A Brief History of Chinese Literature.* Beijing: Peking University Press.

Lin, S. M. & Liu, J. Z. 1997. *Three Holy Monks: Han-shan, Shi-de and Feng-gan.* Taipei: Fagu Culture Co.

Lin, X. 2006. Creative Translation, Translating Creatively: A Case Study on Aesthetic Coherence in Peter Stambler's Han Shan. // Perteghella, M. & Loffredo, E. (eds.), *Translation and Creativity: Perspectives on Creative Writing and Translation Studies.* London and New York: Continuum.

Ling, C. 1977. Whose Mountain Is This?—Gary Snyder's Translation of Han Shan. *Renditions*, (7): 93–102.
Liu, C. R. 1956. *The History of Chinese Literature*. Hong Kong: Dakung Book Company.
Liu, C. R. 1982. *The History of Chinese Literature: A Complete Introduction to the Appreciation of Chinese Literature*. Taipei: Zhuangyan Publishing House.
Liu, C. R. & Chen, Z. Z. 2001. *A History of Chinese Great Literature* (Vol. 1). Shanghai Bookstore.
Liu, D. J. 1966. *The Developed History of Chinese Literature*. Taipei: Zhonghua Book Company.
Liu, D. J. 1976. *The Development History of Chinese Literature* (Vol. 2). Shanghai: Shanghai People's Publishing House.
Liu, D. J. 1980. *The Development History of Chinese Literature* (Revised edition). Taipei: Huazheng Book Company.
Liu, J. 2005. *Poems by Han-shan and Shi-te. Modern Chinese Readers*. Shanghai: Shanghai Educational Publishing House, 21–24.
Liu, L. 1995. Traveling Theory and the Postcolonial Critique. // *Translingual Practice: Literature, National Culture and Translated Modernity——China, 1900–1937*. Stanford, CA: Stanford University Press.
Liu, S. 2001. The Implications of Traditional Chinese Culture in Gary Snyder's Poems. *Foreign Languages Education* (4): 77–81.
Liu, W. C. & Lo, Y. C. (eds.). 1975. *Sunflower Splendor: Three Thousand Years of Chinese Poetry*. Bloomington and London: Indiana University Press.
Liu, X. F. & Chen, S. M. 2003. *The Power of Classics and Interpretations*. Shanghai: Joint Publishing.
Liu, X. L. 2003. *Japanese Art History*. Shanghai: Shanghai Classics Publishing House.
Liu, Y. C. 2002. Photocopied Notes on Anthology of Cold Mountain Poems. // *Anthology of Cold Mountain Poems*. Beijing: Threadbare Books, 2001.
Lu, K. R. & Feng, Y. J. 1996. *History of Chinese Poetry*. Jinan: Shangdong University Press.
Luo, S. J. 2001. *The Evolution of Tang Poetry*. Nanjing: Jiangsu Ancient Books Press, 98–137.
Luo, S. J. 2005. Japanese Paintings Related to Han-shan and Their Origins. *Literature & Art Studies* (3): 104–111+160.
Luo, S. J. 2008. Han-shan's Identity and the Changing Role of His vernacular poetry Narrative. // Qiu, S. & Yao Yanxiang, Y. X. (eds.), *Han-shan Temple Cultural Forum Anthology* (2007). Beijing: China Literature and History Press.
Luo, Z. Q. & Hao, S. F. 1994. *Literature History of Sui, Tang and Five Dynasties* (Vol. 2). Beijing: Higher Education Publishing House.
Maeno, N. 1979. *The History of Chinese Literature* (trans. Lian, X. & He, J.). Taipei: Changan Publishing House.
Maeno, N. 2012. *The History of Chinese Literature*. Shanghai: Fudan University Press.
Mair, V. H. 1992. Script and Word in Medieval Vernacular Sinitic. *Journal of the American Oriental Society*, 112(2).
Meltzer, D. 2001. *San Francisco Beat: Talking with the Poets*. San Francisco, CA: City Lights Books.
Meng, H. 2001. *Imagology*. Beijing: Peking University Press.
Mill, R. & Morrison, A. 1985. *The Tourism System: An Introductory Text*. Englewood Cliffs, NJ: Prentice-Hall.

Miller, H. 1995. *Crossing Borders: Translation Literature Criticism* (trans. Shan, D. X.). Taipei: Shulin Publishing House.
Morris, I. (ed.). 1970. *Madly Singing in the Mountains: An Appreciation and Anthology of Arthur Waley*. New York, Evanston, San Francisco and London: Harper & Row Publishers.
Murphy, P. 2000. *A Place for Wayfaring: The Poetry and Prose of Gary Snyder*. Corvallis: Oregon State University Press.
Nan, F. 1998. History of Literature and Classics. *Theoretical Studies in Literature and Art* (5): 8–15.
Nienhauser, W. 1994. *American Scholars on Tang Dynasty Literature* (trans. Huang, B. et al.). Shanghai: Shanghai Ancient Books Press.
Nord, C. 2003. Function and Loyalty in Bible Translation. // Pérez, María Calzada (ed.), *Apropos of Ideology: Translation Studies on Ideology-Ideologies in Translation Studies*. Manchester: St. Jerome Publishing.
Ogai, Mori. 1971. Kanzan Jittoku (Han Shan and Shih-te). Dilworth, D. A. & Rimer, J. T. (trans.) *Monumenta Nipponica*, XXVI(1–2).
Ogata, Y. 1976. *Japanese History of Chinese Literature* (trans. Ding, C.). Taipei: Zheng Zhong Bookstore.
Onoyasumaro. 1979. *Pulukotopum* (trans. Zou, Y. H. & Lü, Y. M.). Beijing: People's Literature Publishing House.
Osamu, Ō. 1998. *A Study on the Dissemination of Chinese Classics in Japan During the Edo Period* (trans. Qi, Y. P. et al.). Hangzhou: Hangzhou University Press.
Ota, T. 1990. An Explanation of Cold Mountain Poems. (trans. Cao, Q). *Southeast Culture* (Special Column for Mount Tiantai Culture) (6): 125–126.
Ou, H. 1994. Perspectives on Gary Snyder. *Foreign Literature Review* (1): 32–36.
Owen, S. 1996. *An Anthology of Chinese Literature: Beginnings to 1911*. New York: Norton.
Owen, S. 2003. *Borrowed Stone-Stephen Owen's Selected Essays* (trans. Tian, X. F.). Nanjing: Jiangsu People's Publishing House, 1–18.
Park, Y. H. 2009. A Survey and Prospect of Contemporary CMPs Studies. Zhejiang Federation of Humanities and Social Sciences. // *Proceedings of the International Symposium on Han-shan Zi and the Culture of Harmony*. Hangzhou: Zhejiang University Press.
Partridge, E. 1990. *Origins: An Etymological Dictionary of Modern English*. London: Routledge.
Pimpaneau, J. 1975. *Le Clodo du Dharma: 25 poèmes de Han-shan*. Paris: Centre de publication Asie orientale.
Pincombe, M. 2004. *Travels and Translations in the Sixteenth Century: Selected Papers from the second International Conference of the Tudor Symposium (2000)*. Hampshire: Ashgate.
Pine, R. 1983. *The Collected Songs of Cold Mountain*. Port Townsend: Copper Canyon Press.
Pine, R. 1993. *Road to Heaven: Encounters with Chinese Hermits*. San Francisco: Mercury House.
Pine, R. 2000. *The Collected Songs of Cold Mountain*. Port Townsend: Copper Canyon Press.
Pine, R. 2009. Me and Cold Mountain. Zhejiang Federation of Humanities and Social Sciences. *Proceedings of the International Symposium on Han-shan Zi and the Culture of Harmony*. Hangzhou: Zhejiang University Press, 90–98.
Pine, R. & O'Connor, M. (eds.). 1999. *The Clouds Should Know Me by Now: Buddhist Poet Monks of China*. Boston: Wisdom Publications.

Polezzi, L. 1998. Rewriting Tibet: Italian Travellers in English Translation. *The Translator*, 4(2).
Qian, L. S. 1990. *Chinese Literature in France*. Guangzhou: Flower City Publishing House.
Qian, M. 1959. Two Essays on Reading-Reading Cold Mountain Poems. *New Asia College Academic Yearbook* (1): 1–15.
Qian, X. L. 1998a. *Commentary on the Poems of Han-shan and Shi-de*. Tianjin: Tianjin Ancient Books Publishing House.
Qian, X. L. 1998b. The Circulation and Studies of Cold Mountain Poems. *Journal of Graduate School of Chinese Academy of Social Sciences* (3): 57–60.
Qian, Z. S. 2003. *Seven Essays on Literature and Art*. Beijing: Joint Publishing.
Qu, H, Hu an Jiang. 2007. The Dissemination and Reception of Cold Mountain Poems in Japan. *Foreign Literature Studies* (3): 150–158.
Qu, H. Hu an Jiang. 2008. Textual Travel and Construction of Classics: The Classics of Han Shan poetry in American. *Chinese Translators Journal* (3): 20–25.
Ren, D. B. 1991. *Dictionary of Buddhist Culture*. Hangzhou: Zhejiang Ancient Books Publishing House.
Ren, J. Y. 1998. *Dictionary of Religious Terms*. Shanghai: Shanghai Dictionary Press.
Robertson, G., et al. (eds.). 1994. *Travellers' Tales: Narratives of Home and Displacement*. London: Routledge.
Robinson, G. W. 1963. Book Review: Cold Mountain: 100 Poems by the T'ang Poet Han-shan. *Bulletin of the School of Oriental and African Studies*, 26(2): 456–458.
Rojek, C. & Urry, J. (eds.). 1997. *Touring Cultures: Transformations of Travel and Theory*. London: Routledge.
Room, A. 1996. *NTC's Dictionary of Changes in Meanings: A Comprehensive Reference to the Major Changes in Meanings in English Words*. Lincolnwood, IL: National Textbook Co.
Rouzer, P. 2015. *On Cold Mountain: A Buddhist Reading of the Hanshan Poems*. Seattle: University of Washington Press.
Ruo, F. 1963. *Poetic Rhymes of Han-shan-zi (With Poetic Rhymes of Shi-de)*. (ed. Department of Chinese Language and Literature), *Linguistic Series* (Vol. 5). Beijing: The Commercial Press.
Said, E. 1983. Traveling Theory. // *The World, the Text, and the Critic*. Cambridge, MA: Harvard University Press.
Said, E. 2001. Traveling Theory Reconsidered. // *Reflections on Exile and Other Essays*. Cambridge, MA: Harvard University Press.
Santos, S. 2000. A la Recherche de la Poesie Perdue: Poetry and Translation. // *A Poetry of Two Minds*. Athens, Georgia: University of Georgia Press.
Schäffner, C. 2003. Third Ways and New Centres: Ideological Unity Or Difference? // Pérez, María Calzada (ed.), *Apropos of Ideology: Translation Studies on Ideology-Ideologies in Translation Studies*. Manchester: St. Jerome Publishing.
Seaton, J. P. (trans.). 2009. *Cold Mountain Poems: Zen Poems of Han Shan, Shih Te, and Wang Fan-chih*. Boston, MA: Shambhala Publications.
Se-Wook, H. 1971. A Study of Chinese Poetry and Poetry Talks in Korea. *Tamkang Review*, II(1), April.
Shan, D. X. 2000. *Inscriptions and Representations: Chinese American and Cultural Studies*. Taipei: Maitian Press.
Shi, Z. C. 1996. Han-shan-zi: Eleven Poems. // Shi, Z. C. (ed.), *On Tang Poetry*. Shanghai: East China Normal University Press.
Shibata, M. & Masumi, M. 2000. *Le Recueil de la Falaise Verte: Kôans et Poésies du Zen*. Paris: Éditions Albin Michel.

Snyder, G. 1965. *Riprap and Cold Mountain Poems*. San Francisco: Grey Fox Press.
Snyder, G. 1974. *Turtle Island*. New York: New Directions.
Snyder, G. 1980. *The Real Work: Interviews & Talks 1964–1979*. New York: New Directions Publishing Corporation.
Snyder, G. 1990. *The Practice of the Wild*. Berkeley, CA: North Point Press.
Snyder, G. 1995. *A Place in Space: Ethics, Aesthetics, and Watersheds: New and Selected Prose*. Washington, DC: Counterpoint.
Snyder, G. 2000a. *The Gary Snyder Reader: Prose, Poetry and Translations*. Washington, DC: Counterpoint.
Snyder, G. 2000b. Reflections on My Translation of the T'ang Poet Han-shan. // *Manoa* (Vol. 12, No. 1). Honolunu, HI: University of Hawai'i Press.
Snyder, G. 2004. After Word. // *Riprap & Cold Mountain Poems*. Washington, DC: Shoemaker & Hoard.
Snyder, G. 2019. *Riprap and Cold Mountain Poems* (trans. Liu, X. Y.). Beijing: People's Literature Publishing House.
Song, B. N. 1994. *Chinese Classical Literature Abroad*. Beijing: Beijing Language and Culture Institute Press.
Song, X. W. (ed.). 2004a. *Poems by Han-shan and Shi-de*. Beijing: Beijing Dazhong Press.
Song, X. W. (ed.). 2004b. *Selected Zen Poems of Senior Monks*. Beijing: Beijing Dazhong Press.
Stambler, P. 1996. *Encounters with Cold Mountain*. Beijing: Chinese Literature Press.
Stambler, P. 1999. *Encounter with Cold Mountain: Poems by Han Shan*. Beijing: Chinese Literature Press and Foreign Language Teaching and Research Press.
Stambler, P. 2000. *Coming Ashore Far From Home*. Hong Kong: Asia Limited.
Sun, C. W. 1997. Cold Mountain Poems and Zen Buddhism. // Sun, C. W. (ed.), *Zen Mediation and Poetic Sentiment*. Beijing: Zhonghua Book Company.
Sun, C. W. 2001. *Buddhism in Literature*. Beijing: Zhonghua Book Company.
Sun, C. W. 2004. *My Study Tours*. Tianjin: Nankai University Press.
Sun, Q. 1974. *Han-shan and Hippies*. Taizhong: Putian Press.
Suzuki, D. T. 1973. *Zen and Japanese Culture* (3rd Printing). New York: Princeton University Press.
Tam, Y. H. 1981. *A Comprehensive Catalogue of Japanese Translations of Chinese Books*. Hong Kong: Chinese University of Hong Kong Press.
Tam, Y. H. 1988. *Modern Cultural Exchange between China and Japan*. Hong Kong: Department of Japanese Studies of Chinese University of Hong Kong.
Tao, D. F. 2004. Literary Classics and Cultural Power: Literary Classics in the Perspective of Cultural Studies. *Comparative Literature in China* (3): 68.
Tobias, A., et al (trans.). 1982. *The View from Cold Mountain, Poems of Han-shan and Shih-te*. New York: White Pine Press.
Tong, Y. F. 2003. *The English and Chinese Translation of Rubáiyát. Interpretation and Deconstruction* (eds. Luo, X. & Tu, G.). Hefei: Anhui Literature and Art Publishing House.
Toury, G. 1996. *Descriptive Translation Studies and Beyond*. Amsterdam and Philadelphia: John Benjamins Publishing Company.
Turner, J. 1976. *A Golden Treasury of Chinese Poetry: 121 Classical Poems*. Hong Kong: The Chinese University of Hong Kong.
Urry, J. 2002. *The Tourist Gaze* (2nd edition). London: SAGE Publications.
Venuti, L. 1992. *Rethinking Translation: Discourse, Subjectivity, Ideology*. London and New York: Routledge.

Venuti, L. 1998. *The Scandal of Translation, Towards an Ethics of Difference*. London and New York: Routledge.
Venuti, L. 2004. *The Translation Studies Reader* (2nd edition). New York: Routledge.
Vermeer, H. J. 1996. *A Skopos Theory of Translation (Some Arguments For and Against)*. Heidelberg: TextconText Verlag.
Vidal, M. 2003. *Apropos of Ideology: Translation Studies on Ideology-Ideologies in Translation Studies*. Manchester: St. Jerome Publishing.
Waley, A. 1932. *One Hundred and Seventy Chinese Poems*. London: Chiswick Press.
Waley, A. 1982. Poems by Han-Shan. *Chinese Poems*. London: Unwin Paperbacks.
Waley, A. 1996. *One Hundred and Seventy Chinese Poems*. London: Constable and Company Ltd.
Wandering, P. 2005. *Cold Mountain: Transcendental Poetry by the Tang Zen Poet Han-shan*. London: Everyman's Library.
Wang, D. F. 2000. The Literary Status of Translated Literature and the Cultural Attitude of Translators. *Chinese Translators Journal* (4): 3.
Wang, D. F. 2003. An Invisible Hand: Ideological Manipulation in the Practice of Translation. *Chinese Translators Journal* (5): 17.
Wang, G. X. & Cheng, R. T. 2006. *History of Ancient Relations Among the Three East Asian Countries*. Beijing: Beijing University of Technology Press.
Wang, H. &Tian, J. 1990. *Encyclopedia of Tang Poetry*. Beijing: Guangming Daily Press.
Wang, P. Z. 1983. *Elder Dai's Book of Rites*. Beijing: Zhonghua Book Company.
Wang, Q. Y. 1990. On CMPs and Its Influence in East and West. *Journal of Yantai Normal College (Philosophical and Social Edition)* (1): 52.
Wang, Y. X. 1981. *Essays on Literature of the Han, Wei, Six Dynasties and Tang Dynasty*. Shanghai: Shanghai Ancient Books Press, 204–217.
Wang, Y. X. 1986. *On the History of Medieval Literature*. Beijing: Peking University Press.
Waston, B. 1984. *The Columbia Book of Chinese Poetry: From Early Times to the Thirteenth Century*. New York: Columbia University Press.
Waston, B. 2001. *The Pleasures of Translating* [OL]. www.donaldkeenecenter.org/sen/2001_text.html. [2007-04-29].
Watson, B. 1962. *Cold Mountain, 100 Poems by the T'ang Poet Han-shan*. New York: Grove Press.
Watson, B. 1970. *Cold Mountain, 100 Poems by the T'ang Poet Han-shan*. New York: Columbia University Press.
Weinberger, E. 2003. *The New Directions Anthology of Classical Chinese Poetry*. New York: New Directions Publishing Corporation.
Weinberger, E. & Paz, O. 1987. *Nineteen Ways of Looking at Wang Wei*. Kingston, Rhode Island and London: Asphodel Press.
Wen, Y. D. 2004. *Miscellaneous Essays on Tang Poetry*. Shanghai: Shanghai Ancient Books Publishing House.
Wu, Z. L. 2003. The Reproduction of the Canon: A Case Study on the 'Canonization' Process of the Novel in the Ming and Qing Dynasties. *Literary Review* (2): 120–127.
Xiang, C. 1996. Reading Notes of Cold Mountain Poems. *Studies on Ancient Chinese Books* (Vol. 1). Shanghai: Shanghai Ancient Books Publishing House.
Xiang, C. 2000. *Annotation of Cold Mountain Poems: Shi-de's Poems Included*. Beijing: Zhonghua Book Company.
Xiang, C. 2004. The Vernacular Poetry School in the Tang Dynasty. *Jiangxi Social Science* (2): 36–41.

Xie, S. W. 1993. *Zen and Chinese Literature*. Beijing: China Social Sciences Press.
Xie, S. W. 1995. A Study on Tang Vernacular Poetry. *Chinese Social Sciences* (2): 154–166.
Xiong, L. H. 2009. *The History of Chinese Literature*. Wuhan: Wuhan University Publishing House.
Xu, G. D. 1991. *Annotations of the Poems of Han-shan-zi*. Xi'an: Shaanxi People's Publishing House.
Xue, J. Z. 1995. *A Biography of Master Han-shan*. Kaohsiung: Buddha's Light Press.
Yan, S. D. 1991. An Examination on Ancient Chinese Texts from the East to Japan. // *Collation and Research of Ancient Books* (6th edition). Beijing: China Book Bureau, 255–276.
Yan, Z. F. 1994. An Examination of the Life of Han-shan-zi. *Southeast Culture* (2): 212–218.
Yang, Y. S. 1954. *Outline of the History of Chinese Literature*. Hong Kong: Commercial Press.
Yang, Z. J. & Liu, X. Y. 1999. *New Theory of Translation*. Wuhan: Hubei Education Press, 43–56.
Yasumaro, N. 1979. *Records of Ancient Matters* (trans. Youheng, Z. & Yuanming, L.). Beijing: People's Literature Publishing House.
Ye, C. C. 1986. *Chronicle of Han-shan Temple*. Nanjing: Jiangsu Ancient Books Publishing House.
Ye, W. Q. 2004. *A Cultural History of Japan*. Guilin: Guangxi Normal University Press.
Ye, Z. H. 2005a. *Investigation into Anthology of Cold Mountain Poems*. Taipei: The Liberal Arts Press.
Ye, Z. H. 2005b. *Critical Studies of Materials about Han-shan*. Taipei: Showwe Information Co. Ltd.
Ye, Z. H. 2006. *Papers on Cold Mountain Poems*. Taipei: Showwe Information Co. Ltd.
Yeh, M. 1985. Translation of Cold Mountain Poem and the Riprap and Cold Mountain Poems—The Formation of a Literary Classic. // Zheng, S. S. (ed.), *Chinese and American Literary Relationship*. Taipei: Dongda Book Company, 165–193.
Yeh, M. 2004. *Poetry Life*. Guilin: Guangxi Normal University Press.
Yu, J. X. 1974. *Investigation into Abstracts of The Imperial Four Libraries*. Hong Kong: Zhonghua Book Company.
Yuan, X. P. 1998. *A Study on Chinese Poetic Art*. Beijing: Peking University Press.
Yuan, X. P. & Luo, Z. Q. 2005. *History of Chinese Literature* (2nd edition, Vol. II). Beijing: Higher Education Press.
Yunte, H. 1997. *SHI: A Radical Reading of Chinese Poetry*. New York: Roof Books.
Yunte, H. 2002. *Transpacific Displacement: Ethnography, Translation, and Intertextual Travel in Twentieth-Century Literature*. Berkeley, CA and London: University of California Press.
Zan-ning. 1997. *Biographies of Eminent Monks in the Song Dynasty*. Beijing: Zhonghua Book Company.
Zbigniew, W. 2008. An Overview of Chinese Studies in the the United Kingdom. *Newsletter for International China Studies*, 27(2): 45–52.
Zha, M. J. 2004. Cultural Manipulation and Utilization: Ideology and the Construction of Translated Literary Canons: A Study of Chinese Translated Literature in the 1950s and 1960s. *Comparative Literature in China*, 87(2): 89–105.
Zhang, B. W. 1992. Cold Mountain Poems and Zen Buddhism. // *Zen and Poetics*. Hangzhou: Zhejiang People's Publishing House, 224–255.
Zhang, G. L. 2005. *The Reception of Cold Mountain Poems in the United States*. Unpublished Thesis for Master of Arts, Capital Normal University.
Zhang, L. X. 2004. *Beyond Cultures*. Beijing: Sdx Joint Publishing Company.

Zhang, M. T. 1976. Japanese Scholars' Evaluation and Interpretation of Han-shan. // *The Death of the Japanese*. Taipei: Laiming Cultural Enterprise Co., Ltd., 97–118.

Zhang, M. T. 1978. *Studies on Sino-Japanese Buddhist Relations*. Taipei: Mahayana Culture Press.

Zhang, X. H. 1990. *Studies on Wang Fanzhi's Poems*. Shanghai: Shanghai Ancient Books Publishing House.

Zhang, Z. X. 1995. *Classical and Vernacular Chinese*. Harbin: Heilongjiang People's Publishing House.

Zhao, X. F. 2003. *Translation and Discourse Practice in the New Era*. Beijing: China Social Sciences Press.

Zhao, Y. H. 1982. Gary Snyder's Translation of Chinese Culture. *Dushu* (10): 128–133.

Zhao, Y. H. 1985. *The Muse from Cathay*. Chengdu: Sichuan People's Publishing House.

Zhao, Y. H. 1990. Confucian, Buddhist, and Taoist socialists. Special Issue of The Poet Snyder: From Beat to Postmodernist. *Contemporary (Taipei)* (53): 24–27.

Zhao, Y. H. 2003. *The Muse from Cathay*. Shanghai: Shanghai Translation Press.

Zheng, Z. D. 1984. *A History of Chinese Vernacular Literature* (Vol. 1). Shanghai: Shanghai Bookstore.

Zhou, F. X. & Li, X. 1999. *The History of Literary Exchanges Between China and Foreign Countries*. Changsha: Hunan Education Publishing House.

Zhou, Q. 1994. *Cold Mountain Poems and Its History*. Hefei: Huangshan Publishing House.

Zhou, X. L. & Hu, A. J. 2008. The Dissemination and Reception of Cold Mountain Poems in America. *Journal of Southwest University of Political Science and Law* (2): 125–130.

Zhou, Y. 1994. *General History of Chinese Literature*. Shanghai: Encyclopedia of China Publishing House.

Zhu, G. Q. 2001. *On Poetry*. Shanghai: Shanghai Ancient Books Publishing House.

Zhu, H. 2001. *The Encounter Between Chinese and American Poetry*. Chengdu: Sichuan People's Publishing House.

Zi, G. 2004. China's Han-shan and the Movie *Cold Mountain*. *Journal of Literature and History* (6): 29–30.

# Index

Note: Page locators in **bold** indicate a table.

academic research: conceptual shift 104, 115, 134, 139, 209–210
adaptation 4, 27, 37, 113, 115, 159, 166, 202, 257
afterlife 36, 141, 155
An Shi Rebellion 65, 86
analysis: art of 18; linguistic 63, 132, 223, 240, 252
anecdotes 4, 69, 145, 154
annotations 4, 119–120, 121–122, 130, 218, 243
*Anthology of Cold Mountain Poems* 59, 63, 67, 69–70, 90, 93, 129, 160, 218
arrival, the 50, 256
art: of analysis 18, 122, 126, 158, 183, 197, 240, 269; history 1, 26, 30, 132, 136; of poetry 91; of transcendence 87–88

Bai Juyi 74, 76, 85, 101, 118, 124–125, 135–137, 148, 153, 162–164, 181
*Baishi Wenji* (Bai Juyi) 124
Bangeti (semilattice style) 81
Barrett, T.H. 59, 139–142, 147, 162, 165
Barrett, William 194
Bartsch, Renate 55–56
Bassnett, Susan 38–39
Beat Generation 146, 156–157, 178, 187, 190, 195–197, 202, 211–212, 240
beauty 1, 12, 15–16, 48, 73, 75, 89, 180
behavior: as bizarre 63, 180, 198, 258; social 54, 56–57
Benjamin, Walter 36, 141, 155, 189
Birch, Cryil 155, 164, 167, 193, 200–202
Bloom, Harold 48, 244
Borgen, Robert 62, 93

Boudoir Complaint Literature 26
Buddhist: culture 224, 229; poems/poetry 72–73, 87, 94–95, 97, 103, 159, 195, 241, 259; shrines 1; sutra/scripture 17, 20–22, 62, 72, 118, 126, 129, 146, 243

Cai Zhenxing 48
canon: etymology of 43, 45–46; history 4, 20, 43, 47; literary 49–50, 58, 89–90, 196, 200, 244–245, 266
canon construction; *see also* Cold Mountain Poems (CMPs): interaction 104, 151, 155, 168, 198, 221; process 30, 43, 49, 240, 264; translators 193–194, 196; translation 183, 186, 190
canon reconstruction 209–210
canonical: status 46, 49, 57, 127, 134, 165, 210, 244–245, 266; texts 44, 46–49, 99, 113, 244, 246
canonization 46, 183, 192, 242
Cao Cao 10, 13–14, 16
Cao Pi 11, 57, 75
Cao Qian 224
Carré, Patrick 145, 147, 149, 223
*Cathay* 156, 272
Ch'an myth 1, 158, 161, 163
Chen Bingxiang 225
Chen Dinghuan 213–214, 219
Chen Huijian 216, 218
Chen Shih Hsiang 194–196
Chen Yaodong 226, 228–229, 241
Chen Yinchi 13, 69, 72
Chen Yugang 253–254
Chen Zi'ang 79
Cheng Hsuan 4, 72

Cheng Wing 145, 147–149
Cheng, Francois 144
Chesterman, Andrew 51, 55–57
Cheung, Martha 20, 186, 273–274
Chinese: customs, as old fashioned 20, 180, 246; intellectuals 1, 4, 21, 72, 101, 188, 198; literary history 7, 15, 97, 101, 105, 197, 210, 243, 251, 266; mainstream 21, 26, 41; people 5, 16, 19, 44, 123, 272; social culture 16, 20, 48; travel culture 11, 14–16, 20–22, 28
Chinese literature: classical 142–143, 194, 257; history 12–14, 26, 50, 58, 100, 104, 202, 247–248, 255, 266, 273; polysystem 6, 98, 264
Chi-yu, Wu 60–63, 66, 139–140, 144–146, 152, 167
Chung Ling 50, 93, 158, 191–194, 196, 210, 213–214, 218–219, 225, 228
Chushi (out of the world) 12, 14
Clifford, James 23–26, 28, 30, 39–40, 208
Cold Mountain Poems (CMPs): canon construction 7, 155, 168, 194, 221, 264, 269–271; dissemination 92, 155, 158, 166, 198, 202, 240; history 58–59; influence 96, 164, 226, 229, 239–241, 267, 271; journey/travels of 6–7, 42–43, 89, 94, 98–99, 104, 124, 155, 268; marginalization 21, 38, 50, 57, 90, 95, 115, 156, 244, 269; reasoning and commentary poems (27) 94, 141, 149–151, 154, 165, 230, 248, 252, 255, 98, 134; translations 6, 134, 138, 142, 146, 154–161, 196, 239–240; vague rock 3
colloquial language 4, 72–73, 79–80, 124, 138, 157, 163, 209, 231
commentators 19, 67, 105, 122, 124, 143, 218
comparative studies 6, 142, 226–227
Confucianism: advocacy 75–76, 97, 223; culture 86, 116–117, 133; eclipse of 12, 227
Confucius 18–19, 135
conservative 4, 19–20, 142, 179–180, 209, 213, 271
correct, as standard 43, 54–57
creative misreading 242
cultural: mentality 20–21, 271; norms, prevailing 22, 54, 57–58, 89, 98, 104–105; studies 6, 26, 28, 46, 57, 127, 134, 210, 242
cultural polysystem: canonized 244; concept of arrival/departure 28, 41–43, 49, 51; peripheral and weak 99, 103; translated literature 113–115, 138, 157, 180, 182, 186, 191
culture of arrivals 28, 30, 38, 41, 180, 186, 265

Dali, Reign of 59, 69, 86, 222, 249, 258
Darwinism 27
Davidson, Michael 156, 189
decanonization 43, 46
departure, the 6, 28, 38, 42–43, 54, 209, 269
Derrida, Jacques 36
*Dharma Bums, The* (Kerouac) 146–147, 166, 195–198, 223, 257
Dian 43–44
Dianfan (model) 43
diaspora 28, 208
différance 36
discourse: literary 44, 49, 104, 167; power 25–26; selection 34; systems 8, 42
displacement 10, 20, 22, 24, 28–29, 34–35, 208
dissemination: circulation and 42, 51, 92, 133, 138, 146, 154–155, 158–159, 166; of knowledge 19, 22; process of 28, 42–43, 50–51, 90
domestication 28, 38, 190
dominant 4; culture 57–58, 68, 199–200; ideology 4, 19–21, 43, 49–51, 97, 115, 180, 183, 186, 202, 209, 268–271; poetics 4, 43, 49, 51, 91, 103, 209, 266, 268
Du Fu 15, 74, 143, 148–149, 153–154, 163, 181, 202, 244, 267
Du Guangting 58–59, 62–63, 67, 140

ecological consciousness 4, 127, 157, 168, 194
emotion 14, 43, 81, 91, 117, 181, 214, 270
Emperor: Dezong 124; Gaozong 222, 252, 255; Renzong 118; Shenzong 118; Suzong 145; Taizong 118; Wu 84, 128; Yongzheng 95–96, 98, 119, 229, 272
emptiness 12, 84, 87
*Erh-ya/Erya* 10, 44
ethical 54, 56–57

290  *Index*

etymology 9–11, 16, 22, 29, 43, 45
Even-Zohar, Itamar 28, 46
evolution 27, 46, 57–58, 200
exile 19, 28, 37, 41, 208, 271

Fan Chengda 15
Fang, Achilles 196
Fanyi (act of translating) 16–17
Feng Yuanjun 12, 79
Feng-gan: encounter with 63, 93; existence of 58, 61, 122; poet/poems 101, 119–121, 220, 250; portrait of 221; Zen master 66, 94, 256
Fengrenti (pun poems) 81, 221
Fitzgerald, Edward 49
Five Dynasty/Dynasties 58, 73, 91–92, 254–255
flags 11
flow 28, 34, 43, 127
flux 28, 41
folklore 7, 80, 250, 257, 267, 272
Foster, Nelson 161
Franke, Herbert 201
Frankel, Hans 136, 159
freak 1, 158
freedom 4, 24, 81, 89, 148, 180, 188, 190, 213
Frodsham, J.D. 12–13
functionalism 38, 185
Fung Chan, Sydney S.K. 212

gazer culture 25
Ge Zhaoguang 87
Ginsberg, Allen 187, 195, 197
glory 1, 16, 103, 113, 210, 271
God 18, 26, 115
Gong Pengcheng 11, 16
Goryeo Dynasty 129–130
group travel 9, 11
Guan (view or sightsee) 8, 16, 20, 28
Guo Pu 14–15
Guo Shaotang 16, 26
Guo Yuheng 254
Gushi Shijiu Shou (Nineteen Old Poems) 11, 68, 72, 76

Hamil, Sam 162–163
Han Dynasty 9–11, 13–14, 20, 22, 45, 72, 116, 128, 144
Han-shan: fever 2, 50, 134, 142, 167, 209–213, 217–219, 225; genealogy 2–3, 65–66; image of 4, 50, 113, 115, 122, 124, 213, 220; legend of 69, 89, 93, 122–123, 141 212, 229; life experience 2, 4, 6, 63, 68, 89, 103, 250, 252, 256, 258; message of poetry 4, 21, 223; monk-poet 50, 67, 83, 101–102, 223, 251; poems of 83, 86, 93–95, 102, 119–120, 126, 134, 145, 154, 162, 230–231, 250; spiritual pioneer 5; studies 119, 142, 153, 167, 196, 214–217, 221, 257
Han-shan Temple 123, 160, 223–224, 228–229, 243
Harris, Peter 137–138, 142
Hawkes, David 139, 199
Heaven and Earth 12, 82, 87, 178
Hehe (Harmony) Culture 5, 96, 228–229
Henricks, Robert 64–67, 71, 74, 79, 93, 137, 140, 154, 157, 161, 240
Hermans, Theo 55
hermit (Yinshi): admiration 86; image of (Han-shan) 3–4, 15, 58, 86, 99, 103, 190, 202, 223; lifestyle 65, 67, 121, 141, 148; poems of 134, 139, 160, 187, 225
hierarchy 5, 8, 19–20, 30, 114, 183
Hippies 152, 162, 179
Hobson, Peter 139, 162
horizontal influence 6, 229, 240, 242–243, 267
Hu Anjiang 229, **231**, 242, 274
Hu Juren 61, 93, 210–213, 225, 248
Hu Shi 59, 61–62, 99–101, 103, 105, 156, 167, 246
Hu Ying 226
Hu Yinglin 92
Huang Boren 61, 217, 257
Huang Ren 256
Huang Tingjian 92, 97, 258
human: history 40–41; imagination 38; knowledge 19; nature 12, 148, 180, 194; travel 27–28
Hung, Eva 17, 20–21

Idema, Wilt L. 153
image: conceptual 38, 50, 78, 166, 198, 213, 220, 239–240; legendary 1, 3, 96, 99, 113, 115, 122, 124, 141, 158
immigration 11, 22, 28, 127, 133
impact studies 6, 227
inaction 12
Indigenous culture 8, 39, 152, 182
intellectuals 4, 21, 72, 101, 188, 198

interlingual travel 42–43, 113, 115, 134, 142, 157, 168, 178, 259, 271
interpreter 19, 26, 37
intralingual travel 6, 42–43, 94, 98–99, 124, 268
Iriya, Yoshitaka 58, 66–67, 69, 75, 80–81, 83, 121–122, 126, 156, 158, 196
Islam, Said 34, 42

Jakobson, Roman 42
Jeong Ji-yong 130
Ji Kang 15
Jin Dynasty 12–14
Jing 27, 43–44
Jingdian 43–45
Jordan, Ken 197
Joseon Dynasty 129–130
journey: literary 4, 6, 50, 89, 104–105, 208, 210, 269; return 7, 208–210, 265–266, 270
Juyi Lu 72, 83, 98

Kahn, Paul 67, 93, 146, 160
Kang-i Sun Chang 5
Kern, Robert 156, 188
Kerouac, Jack 146, 166, 195–199, 203, 223, 257
Khayyam, Omar 49, 216
Kim Chijiang 129
Kim Gyeongyeop **131**
Kim Hyeonu **131**
Kim Jaihiun 130
Kim Kwan-sik 130
Kim Kwang-rim 132
Kim Tae-Khôn 132
Kim Tal-chin 130, 132–133, 226
Kim Un Hak 132
Kim Yŏng-dal 130
Kim Young-jin 129, **131**, 241
Kinney, Arthur 8, 29
Kline, A.S. 138
knowledge: acquisition 24; human 19, 22; power of 30, 42, 245, 250; wandered 11
Kong Yingda 10

landscape poetry 13, 85, 181
Lauter, Paul 45, 200
Lee Iljae **131**, 133
Lee Jongmee 94, 129, **131**, 133, 228–229
Lee Sun-Hee 132
Lee Ting-jo 133

Lee, Leo Ou-fan 15
Leed, Eric 27–28, 41
Lefevere, Andre 189, 192, **232**
legendary: hermit 3, 58, 99, 121; journey 4, 157, 208
Lenfestey, James 158, 166–167
Lévy, Andre H. 144
Li Bai 15, 74–75, 85, 135, 143, 148–149, 153–154, 163, 167, 202, 244, 267
Li Shanfu 91–92
Liang Dynasty 12
Lin Geng 13
Lin Shu 21, 218, 250
literary: anthology 44, 48, 51, 95, 113, 140, 164, 167, 193, 200–202, 209, 245, 256; attitude 197, 267; canons 4, 45, 49–50, 196, 245; critics 5, 43, 48, 50, 54, 96, 192–193, 215; enlightenment 157, 202; influence 132, 257, 267, 270–271; innovation 5, 101; marriage 135; norms 6, 44, 50–51, 57, 78, 182, 210, 270; orthodoxy 3, 95, 98, 102, 105, 266, 270; patrons 4, 43, 46, 49, 98, 134, 158, 267; phenomenon 73, 246, 258–259, 266–267; reputation 50, 127, 208–209, 244, 255; status 7, 96, 98, 103, 116, 127, 141, 209, 212, 253, 259, 269; system 5, 46, 49, 183, 192, 239, 266; texts 36, 47–48, 57–58, 200, 246, 269–270; tradition 5, 46, 89, 124, 139–140, 142, 209; travel 113, 115, 156, 164–165; value 4, 48, 73, 89, 103, 133, 202, 244, 253, 266; works 45, 48, 57, 130, 135, 222, 244–245, 268
literary history *see* Chinese literature
Liu Cunren 250
Liu Dajie 73, 246–248, 251
Liu E 15
Liu Kezhuang 15, 92
Liu Lydia 36–37, 40
Liu Song Dynasty 11, 13
Liu Ts'un-ren 251
Liu Wu-chi 159
Liu Xiang 9
Liu Xie 57
Liu Yajie **232**, 239
Liu Zongyuan 75, 137
localization 38, 40, 43, 191, 199, 244, 265, 270
loyalty 38–39, 185

Lü (trip or travel) 8–11, 16–18, 28, 44
Lu-ch'iu 61
Lu Ji 57, 75, 195
Lu Kanru 12, 79
Lü Qiuyin 2–3, 59–63, 66, 69, 93–94, 96, 98, 119, 123, 145, 148–149, 154, 162, 164, 201, 222, 253, 256
Lu You 92
Luo Ping 147
Luo Shijin 68, 222, 225, 228–229
Luo Zongqiang 253–254, 268
Lüxing (travel) 9, 11, 16, 20

madman 3, 5, 156
Maeno, Naoaki 251
Maeno, Naobin 251
Maeno, Zhibin 255
mainstream: culture 19–21, 41, 46, 182; ideology 183; literatures 44, 46, 123, 269; poetics 46, 75–76, 96, 103, 136, 190, 192, 209, 221, 270; poetry 72–73, 89, 133, 142, 267; poets 73, 113
Mair, Victor 71, 80, 165
Mani, Lata 37
May Fourth Movement 101, 105
Meng Haoran 15, 85, 153–154, 181, 258
Meng Jiao 69
migration 9, 12, 19, 30, 37, 46, 208, 244
Miller, Hillis 29
Ming Dynasty 73, 90, 94–95, 98, 163
Minghella, Anthony 166
misinterpretations 36
misreadings 36
mobility 28, 36, 41
Modern Tourism 24–25
morality 45, 54, 184, 243
Morris, Ivan 135

Nan Yue 148–149
native consciousness 39, 189, 191, 270
nature poetry 12–14
networks 8, 29, 186
Nord, Christianne 185
novels: modern 219; popular 103; translation 15, 21, 99, 103, 113, 115

obstacles 21, 40
Ogai Mori 123
Orientalism 24
orthodoxy 4, 19, 91, 95, 209, 268; *see also* literary

Ota, Tizo 122, 224, 257
Owen, Stephen 85–86, 164–165, 244, 268

Pageaux, Daniel-Henri 25
Park Gyeong-ryang 93, 129
Park Roo-hyeon **131**, 133
Park Seok **131**
Park Tu-jin 130
Park Young-hwan 229
Parkinson, Thomas 157
patterns 8, 29, 34, 155, 242, 246
peasant 3, 30, 128, 222
pilgrimage 1, 24–25, 28, 123, 167
Pimpaneau, Jacques 145–147, 152
Pine, Red 54, 64, 67, 82, 86, 160–162, 166–167, 228
plunder 24, 28
poetic: aesthetics 6, 54, 75, 77–78, 104, 136; tradition 20–21, 70, 75, 85, 94, 115, 136, 152, 213, 242, 269, 271
poetry: mainstream 72–73, 89, 133, 142, 267; religious 72–73, 83, 85, 87, 89, 124, 133, 139, 165, 267; vernacular 72–73, 75–76, 79–83, 89, 97, 99, 126, 253, 267
poets: female 251, 256; monk 81, 89, 101, 138, 251; vernacular 99–101, 105, 145, 227, 249–250, 258
Polezzi, Loredana 8, 29, 39
Polysystem Theory (Even-Zohar) 28, 113, **234**, 264–265
Porter, Bill *see* Pine, Red
postmodernism 39
power: norms 49–50; perspective of 1, 26, 37, 43, 46, 184; relations 19, 30, 34, 43, 46, 49, 184, 186, 266
practice, in 8, 29, 265
principalities 27
Pulleyblank, Edwin G. 63, 68–69, 102, 140, 231, 257

Qi Dynasty 12
Qian Linsen 147, 149
Qian Mu 64, 102, 104
Qianshu, Kingdom of 58–59
Qian Xuelie 64–66, 71, 102, 119, 222–223, 226–229
Qian Zhongshu 17–18, 245
*Qian Zi Wen* 116
Qin Dynasty 12, 14, 19–20, 45, 128

Qing Dynasty 10, 17, 21, 72, 90, 95–96, 98–99, 103, 143, 154, 165, 247, 255
*Quantanshi* 71, 73, 95, 97, 99, 103–104, 129, 220, 246
Qu Hong 191
Qu Yuan 14, 76, 139

ragged clothing 2–3, 59, 163, 198, 272
rebellion 5, 81, 89, 97, 240
reception 22, 46, 90, 113–114, 190, 192, 213–214, 239, 265
religion 1, 7, 67, 116, 124, 140, 159, 167, 184, 242, 268–269
Ren Daobin 258
*Renditions* (journal) 137, 160
Ren Jiyu 224, 258
restraint 4, 86
return journey 7, 208–210, 265–266, 270
Roesetti, Dante Gabriel 49
Rojek, Chris 25, 28
Rouzer, Paul F. 164, 168
Ruan Ji 15, 144
*Rubáiyát* 49, 216
Ruo Fan 102, 104
Ryokan 138, 161, 163

Said, Edward 28, 35–38, 40, 113, 209, 264–265
Saigyō 124, 163
San Francisco Renaissance 5, 113, 156–157, 164, 166, 168, 181, 187, 189, 193, 195–196
Santos, Sherod 38
Schafer, Edward 1, 67, 137, 158–159
scholars: claims by 45, 166, 227; historical 26, 89, 257
Seaton, Jerome 161–163, 165, 168
self-analysis 68
self-confidence 3, 166, 241
self-consciousness 80, 179
self-expression 38, 202
self-referential 215
self-reliance 166, 241
Shakespeare, William 244
Shang Dynasty 127, 247
Shangbang 20
*Shangshu Dazhuan* 22, 127
Shanshuishi (nature poetry) 12–14
Shen Yue 11, 15
Shi 44–45
Shibata Maryse 145, 149, 151
Shibata Masum 149, 151

Shi-de: existence of 58, 61–63; monk 2; poems 85, 93, 96, 137–138, 231
Shi Zhecun 67, 69, 223
Shoemaker, Jack 161
signifying systems 8, 29
*Siku Quanshu* 71, 96, 98–99, 103–104, 220, 246
Sima Xiangru 144
sinologist: American 1, 62, 71, 138, 161, 165, 178, 181, 193, 244; British 59, 134, 139, 178, 199; Canadian 68, 102; Japanese 90, 93, 121, 124
Sinology 2, 4, 118, 134, 143–144, 156, 187, 257
Six Dynasties 3, 79, 117, 171
*Six Dynasties Poetry* 5, 117
Skopos theory 37–38
Snyder, Gary 61, 67, 101, 135, 155–157, 160–162, 178–181, 191, 196–197, 211, 223, 242, 269
social: behavior 54, 56–57; ideology 20, 240; problems 178, 202; reject 1, 158; standards 178; status 96, 98; values 54, 115
Song Dynasty 15, 60–61, 72–73, 76, 90, 92–95, 100, 118, 129, 210, 213, 258
*Song Gaoseng Zhuan* 61, 70
soul mates 4
source text 29, 38, 185
*Southeast Culture* (journal) 224–225
spiritual: aspiration 1, 158; enlightenment 85; leader 113, 146, 156, 196, 211; product 20, 54, 57
Spring and Autumn Period 9, 18
Stambler, Peter 161
Su Shi 15, 92, 97, 162–163, 181
Sui Dynasty 15
Sun Changwu 59, 66, 69, 76, 87, 124, 243, 259
Sun Chuo 13
*Sunflower Splendor: Three Thousand Years of Chinese Poetry* (Wu-chi Liu) 1, 138, 158–159
Sun Qi 68, 71, 87, 198, 215, 217, 259
Sun Quan 10
Sun Yat-sen University 137, **231**
Sung Myeongs **131**
Sung Myung-sook 133
Suzuki, Teitaro Daisetz 124–125, 152, 187, 193–194
Swineburne, Algernon Charles 49

Tam, Yue-him 121
T'ang-hsing district 59, 62, 145
Tang Dynasty 15, 44; early 61, 69, 72, 79, 99–100, 251; late 66, 69–70, 77, 85, 146, 162, 251, 256; poet 3, 54, 97, 156, 211, 257
Tao (feeling of) 2, 44, 59, 147
Tao-ch'iao 60
Tao Hsuan 61
Tao Jie 167
Tao Qian 13
Tao Yuanming 3, 72, 76, 149, 163, 201, 257, 267
Taoism 12, 14–15, 67, 76, 86, 117, 133, 154, 190, 227, 255
Taoist 13–15, 58, 63, 67, 71, 85, 124–126, 140, 223, 225
target text 29, 38, 185
Ten Kingdoms Period 58, 73
text travel 28–30, 34, 40–43, 104, 115, 155, 186, 189, 198, 242–244, 264, 271
Tiantai Mountain 58, 64, 93, 138, 242
Tiantai Mountain Cultural Research Association 224–225, 227
Tobias, Arthur 159–161
tourism 25, 39, 209
Toury, Gideon 55–57
tradittore/traduttore 30, 40
transformation 22, 29, 34, 36, 41–42, 210, 239, 242, 259, 266
translated literature: American 7, 157, 166, 168, 196, 229; Chinese 246, 264; cultural status 113–115, 180; history of 7, 49; as weak 99, 103
translation: etymology 29; peripheral role 18, 20, 37, 104; as travel metaphor 29–30
translation studies 6–7, 17, 24, 26, 38, 153, 159, 184, 242, 264, 269
translations: Dutch 153; peripheral 20; significance of 37–38, 49–50; variety 4, 113, 115, 121, 144, 149, 153, 160
translators: cultural attitude 20, 50, 116, 184, 186; role of 43, 114, 185; tongue-men 18
travel: components 40–42; culture (Chinese) 11, 14–16, 20–21, 28; history 25, 27; human 27; intralingual/interlingual 42–43; meanings 9, 23; metaphor 22–24, 28; notes 15, 155; theorist 23–24, 37

travel intermediary 115, 269
travel text 17–18, 42
travel writing: ancient Chinese 8–10, 19, 26; etymology 9, 11, 22, 24; post-colonial 24
travelers 8, 12, 16, 20–21, 25–26, 28, 39
travelling theory: concept of 35–37; perspective 40, 209
travelogues 15, 166
Turner, John 137
*Turtle Island* (Snyder) 179, 187

University of California, Berkeley 1, 157–159, 164, 194, 200
Urry, John 24–25, 28

vagueness 35, 37, 40, 265
Van Den Abbeele, George 24–25
Venuti, Lawrence 38, 189–190
Vermeer, Hans 38
Vidal Carmen África, Maria del 183–184

Waley, Arthur 65, 134–138, 142, 147, 159–160, 167, 178, 196, **235–237**, 240, 257
Wandering Poet 163
Wang Anshi 15, 92, 97
Wang Bo 258
Wang Changling 181
Wang Fan-chih 163
Wang Fanzhi 69, 71–73, 80, 99–101, 105, 126, 140, 152, 163, 165, 226, 231, **232**, 241, 247–252, 254–255, 258
Wang Ji 72, 79, 100, 105, 152, 248–249, 258
Wang Ning 273
Wang Qingyun 225–226
Wang Shixing 15
Wang Shizhen 72, 83, 98
Wang Wei 15, 74–75, 85, **131**, 137, 143, 148–149, 153–154, 162–163, 181
Wang Yao 68–69
Wang Yuanlu 126
Wang Yunxi 222
Warring States Period 9, 14, 127, 139
Watson, Burton 69, 85, 137–139, 157–158, 160, 162–164, 166–167, 181, 257
Way, the 12, 18, 83, 87
wealth 1, 125, 130, 223
Wei Dynasty 11, 116
Weinberger, Eliot 165
Wen river 27

Index   295

*Wen Xuan* 13–14, 117–118
*Wenfu* 75–76, 195
*Wenxin Diaolong* 43–44, 76, 117
Western: literature 36, 104, 139–140, 167, 194, 209, 213, 264; scholars 3, 152–153; travel 6, 23, 25, 27, 134
wilderness 1, 12, 14, 26, 87, 179–181, 202, 241
women 26, 86, 181–182, 200
World War II 37, 143, 156, 178, 180, 182, 202
Wu Chi-yu 60–63, 66, 139–140, 144–146, 152, 167

Xiang Chu 59, 67, 69, 71, 73, 82, 89, 227, 253
Xiang (representationist) 17, 19
Xiangxu (interpreting functionaries) 16, 19–20
Xiao Tong 9, 44–45
Xie Lingyun 12–14, 72, 76, 137, 163, 257, 267
Xie Siwei 64, 72, 80–81
Xing (Atmospherical Introduction) 80
Xing (punishment) 44
Xing (travel or walk) 8–11, 16–17, 20, 28
Xiong Lihui 252, 255
Xu Guangda 64, 154, 219, 224, 227
Xu Jie 224
Xu Jun 273
Xu Lingfu 59, 63, 70–71, 140
Xu Lixin 229
Xu Sanjian 224–225
Xu Shen 9–11, 16
Xu Xiake 15
Xu Xun 13

Yang Hsiu 3, 91
Yang Wanli 15, 149
Yang Wen 65; *see also* Han–shan
Yang Yinshen 249
Yan Hui 147–148
Yan Zhenfei 65, 225, 229
Yan Zhitui 15
Yeh, Michelle 156
Yellow Bird 128
Ye Zhuhong 66, 89, 92–93, 218, 220, 224, 228–229, 251

Yi Jeong-ik 130
Yoo Sung-Joon 132
Youxian poetry 14–15
Yu Jiaxi 59–60, 62, 67, 70, 90, 101, 104–105, 156, 222
Yu-kung Kao 13, 15
Yu Yue 98, 123
Yuan Dynasty 60, 90, 93–95, 118, 122, 129
Yuan Mei 78, 135, 163
Yuan Xingpei 13, 254
Yuan Zhen 76

Zan-ning 2, 61
Zbigniew Wesolowsko 142
Zen Buddhist 3, 86, 94
Zen Masters 133, 165
Zen poems 71, 98, 137, 149–150, 162–163, 178, 241
Zhang Binglin 43
Zhang Bowei 64
Zhang Ji 123, 140, 160
Zhang Junheng 100, 119
Zhang Mantao 120
Zhang Ruoxu 143
Zhang Shouyue 95
Zhang Xihou 73
Zhao Shuli 222
Zhao Xifang 35
Zhao Zifan 65, 81, 214–216
Zheng (principality) 27
Zheng Zhenduo 100–103, 105, 167, 246
Zhenguan Hypothesis 60–61
Zhenguan Reign 60–61, 231
Zhi Nan 61–62
Zhou Dynasty 20, 143, 165
Zhou Qi 64, 66, 224–225, 228–229
*Zhou Rites* 9; *see also* Zhouli
Zhou Yingxiong 50, 182, 200
Zhou, duke of 44
*Zhouli* 16, 19, 27
*Zhouyi* 10, 17–18, 21
*Zhouyi Zhengyi* 10
Zhu Jinyu 273
Zhu Rulüe 102, 224
Zhu Xi 15, 92
*Zhuangzi* 11–12, 14, 65, 72

For Product Safety Concerns and Information please contact our EU representative GPSR@taylorandfrancis.com
Taylor & Francis Verlag GmbH, Kaufingerstraße 24, 80331 München, Germany

www.ingramcontent.com/pod-product-compliance
Lightning Source LLC
Chambersburg PA
CBHW050529300426
44113CB00012B/2014